VIET-NAM WITNESS

VIET-NAM
WITNESS
1953–66

BERNARD B. FALL

FREDERICK A. PRAEGER, *Publishers*
New York · Washington · London

FREDERICK A. PRAEGER, PUBLISHERS
111 Fourth Avenue, New York, N.Y. 10003, U.S.A.
77–79 Charlotte Street, London, W.1, England

Published in the United States of America in 1966
by Frederick A. Praeger, Inc., Publishers

Library of Congress Catalog Card Number: 66-18898

PHOTO LAYOUT BY DOROTHY FALL

All photos not otherwise credited
are from the author's private collection.

Printed in the United States of America

To

JOSEPH A. MENDENHALL

and

CHALMERS B. WOOD

Contents

Introduction   3

I. FRANCE LOSES INDOCHINA   13

1. Solution in Indochina (*March, 1954*)   15
2. The French Communists and Indochina (*April, 1955*)   22
3. The Failure of the Navarre Plan (*December, 1956*)   30
4. Representative Government in the State of Viet-Nam, 1949–54 (*August, 1954*)   41
5. The Cease-Fire—An Appraisal (*September, 1954*)   51
6. Settlement at Geneva—Then and Now (*May, 1965*)   69

II. THE NORTH: TWO DECADES OF REVOLUTION   85

7. The Grass-Roots Rebellion (*March, 1954*)   87
8. Crisis in the North (*January, 1957*)   96
9. Inside Hanoi (*November, 1962*)   105
10. A Contemporary Profile (*July, 1965*)   115

III. THE SOUTH: STILLBORN EXPERIMENT?   137

11. Religion in Politics (*July, 1955*)   141
12. Danger Signs (*May, 1958*)   160
13. The Birth of Insurgency (*July, 1958*)   169

14. The Montagnards (*October, 1964*)   190

15. The Agonizing Reappraisal (*February, 1965*)   197

16. The Scars of Division (*July, 1964*)   206

IV. THE UNSEEN ENEMY   223

17. Communist Military Tactics (*October, 1956*)   225

18. The Viet-Cong (*April, 1965*)   234

19. The New Communist Army (*September, 1965*)   244

V. THE WEST AT BAY   255

20. The Stakes in Southeast Asia (*November, 1962*)   257

21. Full Circle, 1954–64 (*May, 1964*)   269

22. The Roots of Conflict (*January, 1965*)   275

VI. THE SECOND INDOCHINA WAR   293

23. The Impersonal War (*October, 1965*)   295

24. The Statistics of War (*July, 1965*)   307

25. The Year of the Hawks (*December, 1965*)   313

26. Old War, New War (*March, 1966*)   331

Epilogue   343

Bibliography   351

Index   357

FIGURES

		Page
1.	Viet-Nam Before Partition	18
2.	Communist Offensives and the Navarre Plan	32
3.	Feudal Sects in South Viet-Nam	143
4.	Communist Complaints and Rebel Activities	172
5.	Minority and Majority Populations in Indochina	192
6.	Areas Taxed by Viet-Cong, 1963	202
7.	Command Structure of the Vietnamese People's Army	226
8.	Typical Convoy Ambush in a Rice Paddy Area	230
9.	Viet-Minh Guerrilla Infiltration Behind French Lines, 1953	280
10.	Communist Rebel Activities, 1959–60	282

ILLUSTRATIONS

(follow p. 134)

Ricefields, buffaloes, and children in Viet-Nam
Ho Chi Minh at the French Socialist Congress, 1920
North Viet-Nam's leaders in 1954
A South Vietnamese Rhade warrior
Communist Party card of a captured guerrilla
Viet-Minh guerrillas plan a raid in 1947
Temporary bridges for coolie convoys
Vice President Lyndon B. Johnson and President Ngo Dinh Diem
Mme. Ngo Dinh Nhu
American and ARVN pilots prepare for a mission
Viet-Cong prisoners
Work pause for a political lesson at Viet-Tri
People's Army militia girls
President Ho and school girls at Minsk
The author and North Vietnamese Premier Pham Van Dong
Wars of national liberation . . .
. . . vs. counterinsurgency and containment

VIET-NAM WITNESS

Introduction

It is one of America's cardinal virtues that, unlike the older nations of Europe, she is not a prisoner of history. This freedom from the dead hand of the past often permits bold new approaches to seemingly insoluble problems, radical departures from well-established— hence, deeply rutted—paths in search of more imaginative solutions. Foreign aid, for example, is as "American" in its own way as the mass-produced automobile; and in both cases, similar developments by other nations are only pale imitations of the American original.

There are, however, cautionary voices on the other side of the ledger which aver that those who fail to heed the lessons of history are bound to repeat past mistakes. Referring precisely to the case of Viet-Nam and writing from the vantage point gained by his intimate association with the office of the Presidency, Arthur Schlesinger stated that "error creates its own reality." There is, in fact, a great deal of evidence to the effect that much of what went wrong with Viet-Nam between 1953 and 1966 owed more to an appreciation of reality based on the misinterpretation of facts or to the deliberate dismissal of certain important facts as being irrelevant to the problem, than it did to deliberate deception or malicious falsification. Yet the options presently available for a solution—either reunification of Viet-Nam under the Hanoi regime without a political *quid pro quo* for the West, or maintenance of the *status quo* at the price of a major war—would have been the same in either case.

This, then, raises a question often encountered in history: Was a given difficulty or setback avoidable altogether, or could its negative effects at least have been minimized by alternate courses of action? The question is a legitimate one in politics, and vastly different from the favorite game of military leaders in which they

3

replay past battles on the basis of later knowledge. In warfare, battle decisions are often made under dire pressure, sometimes with almost immediately disastrous results: Had General Grouchy correctly understood his orders on June 18, 1815, Napoleon would undoubtedly have won the Battle of Waterloo.

It is rare in politics for the decision-making process to reach such heights of life-or-death immediacy. (The 1962 Cuban missile crisis may well be counted as the exception that confirms the rule.)* Political events usually tend to develop more slowly, and the decision-making process is subject to a variety of influences from within the government apparatus itself as well as various outside interest groups. As a result, over-all policy trends take shape only over a long period through many subtle moves, each of which, by itself, is *not* decisive. The impact of these moves upon the total situation is, up to a point, not permanent and can even be totally annulled. In many cases, so-called options exist, and even the exercise of one option or another still does not entirely foreclose the future until very late in the policy-development process.

But somewhere along the line, the decisions do harden into action, the choices become fewer, and their results entail grave consequences. Policy partners become "allies," opponents become "enemies"—and the hitherto inconsequential options become "solemn commitments" whose bond has to be underwritten with the blood of one's citizens and the total resources of one's economy. And there is an understandable tendency, once the conflict has became overt, to validate retroactively all policy decisions that led to this situation. Thus, when mainland China was taken over by the Chinese Communists, an official American statement was made to the effect that "nothing that this country did or could have done within the reasonable limits of its capabilities could have changed that result; nothing that was left undone by this country has contributed to it."†

The present situation in Viet-Nam is not exempt from certain parallels to that view, and it would not be unfair to state that the

---

* On the other hand, the decision not to use U.S. aircraft in the Bay of Pigs invasion was a *military* one, even though it was made by civilians in a political context.

† Department of State, *United States Relations with China* (Washington, D.C.: Government Printing Office, 1949), p. xvi.

official reports on the situation from 1954 to the present depict a well-nigh unbroken series of seemingly "unavoidable" decisions, all made with the best of intentions and for the noblest of purposes—but each gone awry at the last moment because of outside factors beyond one's control. To this day, South Viet-Nam under the late Ngo Dinh Diem's iron rule is depicted in much of the official writing on the subject as having been well on the way to both democracy and economic "take-off" when it was assailed by North Vietnamese aggressors and rapidly reduced to a shambles. A more sophisticated subvariant will go so far as to say that Diem himself was perhaps somewhat at fault—but mainly for giving free reign to his brother Ngo Dinh Nhu and Madame Nhu.

Both interpretations ignore the salient facts that (a) South Viet-Nam had been converted into a full-fledged dictatorship at the village level—where it is most keenly felt in that kind of society—as early as 1956, when Diem abolished elected village government; and (b) that his regime had been nearly toppled twice before the eventually successful coup—and by his own military rather than the left-wing opposition. In fact, it could well be argued that the Communist-led opposition, coalesced in the Viet-Cong since 1960, had a certain stake in the preservation of the negative image as then conveyed by Saigon. After all, it was easier to create an effective propaganda campaign around a permanent *My-Diem* (American-Diemist) relationship than around the rapidly changing groups of generals and civilians who followed Diem in office.

The same error-created "reality" characterized the relationship between the United States and France as regards Indochina in the early postwar years. Why the United States never applied to France in Viet-Nam the same pressures for decolonization she applied to the Netherlands in Indonesia, for instance, has thus far eluded detailed research. From a warm relationship with Ho Chi Minh's Democratic Republic of Viet-Nam in Hanoi in 1945–46 and a rather well-documented refusal to let France use American-donated military equipment in Indochina, there is an almost incomprehensible transition to full-fledged support for France as of early 1950, even before the outbreak of the Korean War would have given it at least the semblance of a *Realpolitik* explanation. What followed then was an equally fulsome official disregard of French political errors and a binational sharing of military illusions that have few parallels in history. A senior American military commander in the Pacific directly informed President Eisenhower a month before the battle of Dien Bien Phu broke out that contrary to fears expressed by the French themselves, they were doing well militarily. And a month *after* the battle had been joined, when it had become grimly obvious that France was in the process of losing not only the battle but the war as well, Secretary of State Dulles still informed a Senate committee that the French expected to "break the back" of the enemy's forces by 1955.

It is just this kind of attitude that the eminent student of American diplomatic history Ambassador George F. Kennan once decribed as "that curious trait of the American political personality which causes it to appear reprehensible to voice anything less than unlimited optimism about the fortunes of another government one has adopted as a friend and protégé."*

This is where the independent scholar comes into his own as a curious sort of barometer or litmus paper. He is—or should be, if he deserves the designation of "independent scholar"—capable of recording the facts in a given situation as they actually are; and, unburdened by considerations of policy or feudal allegiance to the views of a particular bureaucracy or service, he can make certain predictions of future developments. Although one cannot expect the precision of results yielded by experiments in the exact sciences, the social scientist should, under normal circumstances, be able to provide reasonably accurate views of what the future may bring in a particular area, given the range of options available.

If, over a period of time, the scholar does manage to come up with a number of correct forecasts, his success may well be attributed to one of several factors, as with a good weather forecaster: his luck is phenomenal or his instruments of prediction are more accurate than those of his colleagues—or perhaps his rheumatism is more sensitive to changes than other people's. But in the case of such an area as Viet-Nam he will also have to bear the burden of being the unwelcome bearer of ill tidings. That has been the role of this writer for the past thirteen years, as the selection of articles presented here will attest.

These articles cover the entire range of events from the defeat of

---

* *Russia and the West Under Lenin and Stalin* (Boston: Little, Brown, and Co., 1960), p. 26.

the French at Dien Bien Phu in 1954 to President Lyndon B. Johnson's decision at Honolulu in February, 1966, to attempt once more to settle the Viet-Nam problem by a combination of force, reform, and diplomacy. They were culled by this writer and his editor, Arnold Dolin, not merely on the basis of their long-range accuracy (no matter how soul-satisfying that alone would have been), but on the basis of their relevance to an over-all appraisal of the Viet-Nam situation as we now confront it.

As one peruses the contents of this volume, the present-day importance of seemingly obscure or esoteric elements should come clearly to light: France's failure in 1949–53 to create (or allow the creation of) representative government in Viet-Nam; the strength of Communist grass-roots government in 1953; the impact of the Buddhist sects' rebellion in 1955; and, above all, Saigon's loss of control over its own local administration—*not* in 1961 or 1962, but in 1957. As it now turns out, and as this writer was perfectly aware at the time, each of these factors could then have been subject to several options. But, with the inevitability of a classical Greek tragedy, policy-makers in Saigon, Paris, and Washington (Hanoi was to join the list somewhat later) usually picked the course least likely to produce tangible long-range results, but the one closest to the path of least resistance at the time. While it would be idle to speculate on all the "might-have-beens" in Viet-Nam's history, it is nonetheless important at least to consider one of the most important missed options.

In March, 1946, France recognized Ho's Democratic Republic of Viet-Nam as a "Free State with the French Union," with its own foreign policy and military forces. But a combination of weak regimes in Paris and strongly entrenched colonial interests in Saigon wrecked that auspicious treaty and set off a chain reaction of events whose aftereffects may yet bring the world to the threshold of World War III. Back in 1946, though, a moderate amount of American pressure on the French to rein in their "hawks" in Saigon, and an equal amount of pressure on Ho and his Chinese *Nationalist* backers (the Communist Chinese were, it will be recalled, still holed up in northern China) by the American mission in Hanoi, guided by a firm hand in Washington, might have brought about an entirely different situation. Ho might have become a Tito even before Communist China reached the Vietnamese border in December, 1949, or shortly afterward. Or, on the other hand, he would have revealed his aggressive tendencies far earlier, and to an American-French combination backing a non-Communist regime, just as an American-British combination backed such a regime in Greece at precisely that time. In either case, a French-fought colonial war could have been avoided.

Even a superficial reading of the articles presented here—as well as this writer's other works—should make clear that my purpose is always to attempt to explain events and to analyze existing structures—not to plead a case, expound a theory, or dictate a course of action. This has not been easy, because during the past thirteen years Viet-Nam has been the object (and, more than once, the victim) of well-meaning advocates of many nationalities operating in the mainstream of Ambassador Kennan's theory of unlimited optimism about adopted protégés. Ironically, an additional difficulty has been posed by my French nationality—despite the fact that my entire training in Far Eastern affairs dates from graduate work at Syracuse and Johns Hopkins universities; and far from having any pro-French bias, it must have been obvious from my writing that I share the distaste for the colonial adventures of my country that characterizes the writings of every other respectable French author on Indochina: Philippe Devillers, Paul Mus, Jean Lacouture, to name a few.

Although it may be forgotten now, when domestic American opposition to the commitment of U.S. forces in South Viet-Nam occupies the center of the stage, French opposition to the Indochina War (and the later Algerian War, of course) was widespread and by no means limited to left-wing elements or, as in the case thus far here, to a few legislators and an intellectual minority. American criticism of French actions at the time—mainly concerned either with the philosophical argument of anticolonialism or, at the conservative end of the spectrum, with France's apparent lack of military ability and generalship—was never as scathing or well-documented as that presented by French scholars themselves. This was true for the most part because French scholars had, from past experience or direct observation, more extensive knowledge of the problem at hand; now, by virtue of the U.S. presence in Viet-Nam, it is the turn of American scholars to be in that enviable position.

Early articles of this writer clearly reflect both of these factors. As a Frenchman, I was frequently able to see, in 1953, French mistakes in a clearer focus than could other observers. But American training provided me with perspective, with the ability to judge what I saw with some detachment. In the early spring of 1954, when officialdom in Washington—as reflected in such an authoritative source as President Eisenhower's own memoirs—still believed that the French and the Vietnamese regime under their aegis could win the war, I pointed out in writing and without fanfare that this view, in turn based on overoptimistic official French reporting, was ill-founded. It was easy to document, on the basis of field research, that the Saigon government had already failed to make good its promises for representative government; that chances of a French military victory, despite generous American aid, were nil even before the French disaster at Dien Bien Phu; and that the much-vaunted and American-approved Navarre Plan was a failure. It was also already possible then to document the fact that the Communist-led opposition of the Viet-Minh had developed a tremendously efficient local administration. Within months, the situation in the field and at the conference table confirmed the views I had expressed.

Such views were, of course, not novel at the time and had been voiced, in one form or another, by American observers as well. Matters changed radically in 1957, however, as the United States became fully committed to a separate South Vietnamese state and assumed a role of political leadership in Saigon to the total exclusion of any other power. Unlimited optimism not only became a part of official policy with regard to events in Viet-Nam—it *was* policy as such. And scholars who simply continued to examine the new structures abuilding in South Viet-Nam and North Viet-Nam with the same detachment as before and reported the soon very apparent failings of the new structure and the rapidly widening gaps between alternate courses of action soon found their motives impugned and the validity of their conclusions assailed, not on the basis of an alternate set of facts, but because they interfered with what was said to be "policy."*

* In his excellent book on the operations of the U.S. Embassy in Saigon, of which he was a senior member as Public Affairs Officer, John Mecklin cites State Department cable No. 1006, February 21, 1962, and other measures

When social-science research has reasons-of-state limitations placed upon its conclusions, it runs into heavy risks of losing its validity, as can be seen in many examples from the Communist bloc. Worse yet, the outside government dealing with such a situation soon loses the benefit of the "control" function that scholarship normally offers through its very existence. In the case of Viet-Nam, that situation was finally pushed to a tragic extreme in which practically all specialists dealing with the country were operating under contract either with the Saigon government or with one of the American aid programs. As a result, their often excellent work, by virtue of its quasi-official character, could be kept out of public circulation as a matter of administrative procedure and thus might have no effect in bringing about remedial action. I distinctly recall earnest warnings offered by some of my colleagues in Saigon with regard to the explosive relationship between Vietnamese lowlanders and mountain tribes; *ten years* after they were first brought to official attention, even the "beginning of a beginning" of an effective remedy has not yet been undertaken.

Still, despite the handicaps, no trained social scientist—whether anthropologist, economist, or political scientist—could help but be aware of the fact that the Diem regime was riding into the trough of a popularity wave whose crest may well have been the proclamation of the first republican constitution in October, 1956; that a catastrophically slow land reform and a lagging economic tempo were alienating the vast mass of landless peasants and unemployed or underemployed nonagricultural laborers; and that poverty-stricken but militarily powerful North Viet-Nam could not possibly fail to take advantage of these glaring vulnerabilities, so thoughtlessly and generously offered to it.

It is with considerable pride that I lay claim to having been the first person to establish, on the basis of direct field research and undistorted figures from two unrelated sources, the fact of the resurgence of revolutionary war in South Viet-Nam in 1957,* and to furnish detailed descriptions, as early as 1956,† of the guerrilla tactics that the National Liberation Front still employs success-

---

that were designed to curb the flow of "thoughtless criticism" from Viet-Nam. (See *Mission in Torment* [New York: Doubleday, 1965], pp. 110–11.)

* See Chapter 3.
† See Chapter 4.

fully in Viet-Nam in 1966. As the reader delves into the material
offered here, he will find that most of Viet-Nam's present problems are neither new nor the effect of a sudden North Vietnamese
"aggression," but have been in a state of slow maturation for well
over a decade—and that includes North Vietnamese aid to the insurgents.

If any of this information found its way into official channels,
either from the government's own sources or from the scholarly
journals, American actions until the arrival of General Maxwell
D. Taylor's investigation mission in late fall, 1961, certainly failed
to reflect it. And official reactions to warnings about the surely
catastrophic end results of the course upon which the Saigon authorities—both Vietnamese and American—were embarked fell
upon both deaf and resentful ears, as differences of view between
the trained outside observers and officialdom became irreconcilable.
Here, John Mecklin, from his vantage point of the third- and often
second-ranking Embassy official during the crucial 1962–64 period,
provides us with an explanation that seems to me to cover the
whole previous decade (including the period of the French presence) as well:

> The root of the problem was the fact that much of what the news-
> men took to be lies was exactly what the [U.S.] Mission genuinely
> believed, and was reporting to Washington. Events were to prove
> that the Mission itself was unaware of how badly the war was going,
> operating in a world of illusion. Our feud with the newsmen was an
> angry symptom of bureaucratic sickness.*

Both charity and good taste persuade me not to recite here the
long list of erroneous and wildly overoptimistic statements and
timetables with regard to Viet-Nam that various officials have provided the world for the past fifteen years. But it is necessary to
express serious concern at the thought that even graver decisions
relating to the Viet-Nam problem could conceivably be arrived at
today via the same processes that have operated in the past. I, for
one, would certainly feel somewhat reassured if I could say that at
present the role of the independent (or independent-minded)
scholar and serious publicist has been understood for the beneficial

* Mecklin, *op. cit.*, p. 100.

influence it can have—and indeed *must* have—in the public affairs of a democracy.

If anything, this volume is less a plea and an example for the right to dissent—for dissent, too, has its "organization men"—than for the right to *think independently* and to have one's thoughts accepted and seriously weighed. University and foundation reports indicate only too clearly and too often that scholarship has in many cases become a new kind of "big business." In the long run, this may well stifle the yearning for the unexplored paths and for dissent of a higher level and greater import than a medieval theologians' debate around safely established basic verities.

The present study may well confirm the mature reader's worst fears that the Viet-Nam nettle seems no nearer solution now than it was ten, or even twenty, years ago. The young scholar may find in it belated confirmation that in a democracy even somewhat unpopular ideas, provided they were sound in the first place, will find eventual vindication. And to the member of one of the vast bureaucratic empires who may wish to retrace here the tortured path of past missed options in an extremely unimportant corner of the world as a warning example of what could happen in more important places elsewhere, I would like to leave an admonition that at one time had great currency in the U.S. armed forces and could be applied interchangeably to weapons, equipment, or ideas: "If it works, it is obsolete."

Viet-Nam, it appears, has been a meeting place of well-tested ideas for a very long time.

BERNARD B. FALL

Howard University
Washington, D.C.
February, 1966

PART I

France Loses Indochina

The French Indochina War had begun on December 19, 1946, involving at first about 20,000 French troops and fewer than 50,000 Viet-Minh guerrillas. By the time the French decided to transform what had been essentially a colonial war into a *civil war* by setting up a Vietnamese government under their aegis in March, 1949, the war had grown to 150,000 troops on the French side and nearly a quarter-million on the Viet-Minh side. And at the point the war had become a part of the over-all Western policy of containment of Communism in Asia, following the outbreak of the Korean War, almost a million men were locked in battle and the United States had become involved in the war at the side of the French.

In France itself, the war had never been popular. In fact, contrary to the prevailing mythology on the subject, *no* colonial war ever had been: In 1885, Prime Minister Jules Ferry had been turned out of office for having sent French troops to North Viet-Nam which, in the course of a skirmish with Chinese marauders, had lost a few men. The French Communist Party successfully exploited the unpopularity of the war (and its real cost to France until the U.S. began to finance much of it in 1953), as will be seen in Chapter 2—but what most people have ignored is that it began to call the Indochina War a "dirty war" only *after* the CP's chances of controlling France in the late 1940's became nil. This "chauvinism" of the French Communists certainly was not lost on Ho Chi Minh at the time, and it should be remembered today as

North Viet-Nam once more casts abroad for support in her resistance to American pressure.

The French in Indochina, however, were still searching for an alternate solution to the dilemma of having to negotiate with their
principal military opponent, the Viet-Minh. Yet, as is shown below, representative government under a non-Communist regime
was never given a real try—and still has not been almost two decades later. Militarily, the French did not, as is often assumed,
limit themselves to the defense of static positions. In fact, the
Navarre Plan was perhaps at fault for overextending the limited
French resources of manpower and matériel and wedding the
French to a policy of victory that was clearly unrealistic to anyone
who had seen the war from close up, even before the disaster of
Dien Bien Phu exposed to public view how desperate the French
position really was.

It was this that led me to hope for a compromise solution along
the lines of the Korean armistice even before the battle was fought
—for an undefeated French Army, supported by reform-minded
allies, would have left behind something other than the shambles of
a non-Communist Vietnamese rump state. Yet, as the last two articles in this section show, even the amputated state did have a
good chance of survival, and the Geneva agreements did not foreclose its future altogether, had the violation of some of the provisions of the agreements been accompanied by strict application of
others and by an offer of fruitful alternatives to the northern
brother-state.

It was the total absence of such alternatives that raised the
chances of a violent conflict in Viet-Nam from a remote possibility
to an absolute certitude.

1. Solution in Indochina

March, 1954

"What we have here is a sort of *gouvernment crépusculaire*—a twilight government," said the French colonel in charge of the Pacification Bureau in Hanoi. "In our own area we control the cities and major roads from daybreak till nightfall. Thereafter the Viet-Minh has the country to itself to levy taxes, attack our posts, and execute the 'Vietnamese traitors,' that is, the nationalists who still profess to believe in victory for our side." Such, in a nutshell, is the situation in war-torn Indochina, a country about eight times the size of the Republic of Korea, after more than seven years of bitter fighting. France has spent twice as much on the Indochina War as it has received under the Marshall Plan for its own rehabilitation, and America has furnished much more military and economic aid—calculated on a per capita basis—than it ever gave to Chiang Kai-shek's Nationalists. Why, then, has the war become a military stalemate in which the French and Viet-Nam nationalists are unable to hold the countryside and the Viet-Minh, short of massive Red Chinese intervention, cannot hope to breach French defenses around the major urban strongholds?

Politically, the situation looks even more hopeless for the West. France has not succeeded in convincing the Vietnamese that it will make good its promises of full independence, though it has already granted more independence to Bao-Dai than Ho Chi Minh ever asked for. At the same time the Vietnamese nationalist government, by its accumulating psychological mistakes, has been divorced not only from the mass of the farmers but from its most promising military cadres. A young graduate of the Ecole Militaire Inter-Armes at Dalat said to me: "How do you think it feels getting oneself killed in the jungle for that man who comes up here

Reprinted, by permission, from *The Nation*, March 6, 1954. © 1954 by The Nation Associates, Inc.

to swear us in wearing a Riviera suit, a polka-dot tie, and inch-thick crepe soles?" He was referring to His Majesty Bao-Dai, commander in chief of the Vietnamese forces, who has not yet been seen in the uniform of his army.

As long as the military situation had not too seriously deteriorated and as long as the Chinese Communists were committed in Korea, the possibility of a political solution of the Indochina conflict was pushed into the background by everyone concerned. Now, however, the French are obviously eager to stop the fighting in any way possible, and the Big Four, influenced by the problem of German rearmament, have agreed to a broad conference on both Indochina and Korea to be held at Geneva next month.

Repatriation of the troops in the Far East would increase France's field forces in Western Europe and North Africa from about twelve divisions to an army of some twenty-two fully equipped and well-trained divisions and put a stop to the heavy drain of casualties on its elite commissioned and noncommissioned officers. The easing of the strain upon French financial resources would also speed up domestic economic recovery. This line of reasoning has been expounded by the French left for the past seven years—with emphasis upon the fact that an end to the Indochina conflict would mean "liberation from American tutelage." Last fall the debates in the French Parliament made it dramatically clear that the desire to put a halt to the war had cut across all party lines. It was a Gaullist deputy, a former general, who presented the problem in its simplest form: "Having promised independence to the Associated States, we would have to leave Indochina even if we won a total victory. So what are we fighting for, and for whom?"

The vote to continue the war was more a matter of political pork-barreling than an expression of the deputies' feelings. The widespread desire to "get rid of the whole mess" was heightened by Ho's offer of peace talks made through a Swedish non-Communist newspaper and by Mr. Dulles' threat of an "agonizing reappraisal" of United States foreign policy if EDC did not go through. Another discouraging fact was the refusal of the Vietnamese "congress," which had been hand-picked by Bao-Dai, to rubber-stamp his policy of integration into the French Union or even to vote a motion of thanks to the French soldiers who were fighting and dying within gunshot of the building where the congress met. Few nationalist leaders seem convinced of the "usefulness" of the war, not to speak of the possibility of an ultimate victory for France and the nationalists.

That truce talks must and will eventually take place is by now accepted by every responsible French politician. It is merely a question of when, how, and with whom. A face-saving victory that would make negotiation palatable has eluded General Navarre for the past six months, and the military situation, while by no means desperate, was never more humiliating than at this moment.

On the other hand, self-styled experts on both sides of the Atlantic have oversimplified the situation by comparing it to Korea. Both countries have a Communist government supported by the Soviet bloc and a nationalist government supported by the West, but here the similarity ends. Korea, as a peninsula, has well-defined boundaries on three sides, while Indochina's borders are so uncontrollable that their tracing is a matter of doubt and controversy. Korea is a country of bare hills, while Indochina is 85 per cent covered with thick subtropical jungle which makes movement of large units impossible and considerably reduces the effectiveness of modern heavy weapons. It also renders enemy movements practically immune to air observation and bombing. A Western defeat in Korea would not immediately affect its neighbors, separated from it by hundreds of miles of open sea, but a Communist victory in Indochina would immediately outflank Thailand and rip wide open the unruly northern Burmese border. In the latter area Kuomintang guerrillas are not the only foreign troops. The Cominform headquarters for all Southeast Asia are at Muong-Lene, under the command of a Viet-Minh general, Nguyen Van Long, and are protected by a Viet-Minh regiment alternately stationed in Burma and Yunnan.

There can be no doubt that the United States has already considered what course it would take in the event of the loss of Viet-Nam. It is certainly not by sheer coincidence that General Donovan, wartime OSS chief, is now Ambassador to Thailand. However, the separation from Viet-Nam of the ethnically related states of Laos and Cambodia—as was discreetly suggested in a Thai note to those states a few weeks ago—would have dubious results. The present peacefulness of Thailand, though hailed by the Department of State as the success of a "working democracy," is more

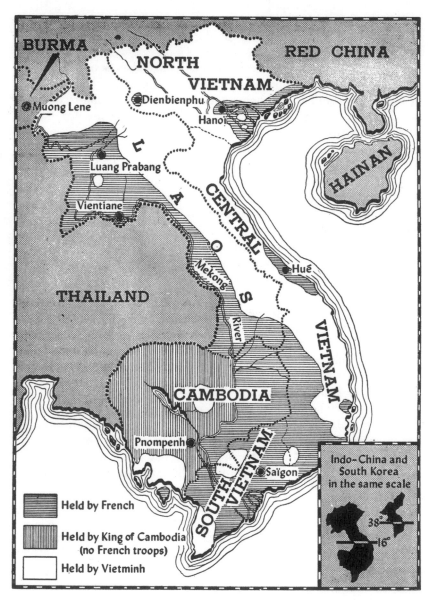

BURMA

NORTH VIETNAM

RED CHINA

Muong Lene

Dienbienphu

Hanoi

L A O S

HAINAN

Luang Prabang

Vientiane

CENTRAL

THAILAND

Mekong

Hué

River

VIETNAM

CAMBODIA

Pnompenh

SOUTH VIETNAM

Saïgon

Indo-China and
South Korea
in the same scale

38°

16°

Held by French

Held by King of Cambodia
(no French troops)

Held by Vietminh

FIGURE 1

probably due to the fact that Thailand is an extremely useful transit base for the Communist regimes around its borders. Arms can be imported through it and such dollar-earning exports as opium, wolfram ore, and rice can be sent out of Viet-Minh–held areas. No one has any immediate interest in disturbing the proverbial goose that lays the golden eggs.

What can be done, by the French alone or by the Big Four at Geneva, to bring about a cease-fire in Indochina? Two alternatives may be ruled out—a "total" French victory and a fighting evacuation à la Dunkirk. A decisive victory would require a war effort which France could not make when the war was still young, and certainly not now, without depleting its European forces to the point of mortal danger. A fighting evacuation is equally senseless, for the army would have to take along 50,000 French civilians living in Indochina, about 300,000 Eurasians who are French nationals, and hundreds of thousands of Vietnamese too compromised to be left behind for mass "people's court" trials. Thus negotiations offer the only solution, and the first step, as Nehru has suggested, must be a cease-fire.

A cease-fire, however, is likely to prove even more difficult to achieve in Indochina than in Korea, where negotiations were held up for eight months, for in Indochina no front and no battle lines exist. The French Army guards the Red River Delta with pillboxes, forts, and bunkers, but French intelligence acknowledges that from 30,000 to 60,000 guerrillas are within the delta, including certain famous regiments. The same infiltration is found along the northern and central Laos fronts, the tiny sliver of French-held Annamite coast, and in sizable areas of southern Viet-Nam. An armistice would stop the French from hitting major enemy units while giving the Viet-Minh a unique chance to enter Franco-nationalist areas in such numbers as to paralyze completely whatever remains of orderly government.

It has been argued that Indochina should be partitioned across its waist, on the 16th parallel, just as Korea was divided. In that case the northern part, which contains the Viet-Minh's strongholds and is contiguous to Red China, would be left in the hands of Ho's regime. This would mean handing over to the Viet-Minh two-thirds of Viet-Nam's population, the bulk of its industry, some of Asia's best anthracite fields, the flourishing port of Haiphong, and the capital city of Hanoi, with its powerful transmitter and the country's only full-fledged university. Most of Indochina's non-ferrous metals, including uranium phosphates, are also located north of the 16th parallel. Moreover, there would be no iron-clad guaranty against further Viet-Minh infiltration into the part of the country left to Bao-Dai. The Franco-nationalist side could hardly win popular support after having sold down the river more than half of the territory and about 14 million of the 23 million inhabitants of Viet-Nam.

If a cease-fire could be arranged, the most promising next step would seem to be the establishment of an intermediary government, after an internationally supervised cooling-off period. The West would still have a number of trump cards in Indochina which the Soviet bloc could hardly match. The southern part of the country is its "iron lung," with its huge rice surplus and dollar-earning exports of rubber, pepper, coffee, and precious woods. It is obvious that, deprived of the south, the Ho Chi Minh regime would face either starvation—as in 1946 when it was deprived of southern imports—or a type of integration into the Red Chinese economy that would be the equivalent of annexation. And any Vietnamese, no matter what his political color, is highly wary of the Chinese "big brother." Therein lies the great opportunity for the West: massive economic aid might swing the balance and substitute for the total loss of Indochina in a creeping war the building-up of a neutral regime. Such a regime would depend upon Western supplies to survive economically, for neither Red China, plagued by its own lack of consumer goods, nor the Soviet Union, already behind in its promised deliveries to North Korea, could possibly fill the immediate requirements of the ravaged country.

Political successes almost entirely due to the intelligent dispensation of economic aid have been won elsewhere—notably in Yugoslavia and Austria. Economic aid to all of Indochina, under either United Nations or neutral auspices, might make possible a solution acceptable to both sides. Ho Chi Minh's interview with the Swedish *Expressen* made specific reference to such aid.

Any solution that accomplishes the effective neutralization of Indochina would be more desirable than this hopeless stalemate in the jungle swamps. In this lies the importance of the Geneva conference. We need have no illusions about Ho's regime; it is of course Communist-dominated. But so are North Korea and Red China, with whom the United States sat at the conference table for two years; and so is the U.S.S.R. and its satellites, with whom the United States, and France, maintain normal diplomatic relations. A farsighted policy in Indochina based on well-administered aid might do more to stem the Communist tide in Southeast Asia than the sending of a few technicians or of a few additional planeloads of napalm.

2. The French Communists and Indochina

April, 1955

The varying positions taken by the French Communist Party (PCF) toward the war in Indochina have provided a striking example of the difficulties and contradictions which a party encounters when it tries to conciliate its local political objectives with the over-all grand design of proletarian revolution woven by the Soviet Union. Its actions, of course, also created a dilemma for the other parties in the French Parliament. As Léon Blum said: "We always find ourselves face to face with the insupportable anomaly represented by the insertion into the French body politic of a foreign nationalist party."[1]

Actually, the French Communist attitude as regards Indochina was far from clear until the abortive Moscow conference of the foreign ministers in April, 1947. Until then, "tripartism" had been the watchword in France. The Communist chieftain, Maurice Thorez, was Vice Premier and Minister of State, another Communist was Minister of Armaments, and other Communists, under one governmental combination or another, held important levers as Ministers of Labor, Reconstruction, Public Health. Indeed, the whole political outlook in 1946 and early 1947 seemed ideally suited to the eventual peaceful and orderly inclusion of France into the ranks of the "people's democracies." Naturally, she would also have brought the French overseas territories into the Soviet orbit, thus permitting them—like more backward Soviet Central Asian areas—to "reach Socialism while bypassing capitalism."

[1] *Débats Parlementaires*, Assemblée Nationale, March 11, 1947, p. 905. (Further quotations given here from parliamentary debates are from the same source.)

This explains the quasi-colonialist enthusiasm of the French Communist parliamentarians when, in the Constituent Assembly of 1946, Edouard Herriot insisted upon tight French control of outlying French imperial bases in Africa and Indochina.[2] The French parliamentary record of Blum's speech of December 23, 1946, asking for strong measures against the Viet-Minh to re-establish order in Indochina, mentions "strong applause . . . to the extreme left" —in which, in fact, the generally colonialist right wing did not share. Better (or worse) yet, a mission to France of the puppet-government of Cochinchina, which was met coolly or noncommittally by most other French political party leaders, had received an enthusiastic welcome by Maurice Thorez at a time (April-May, 1946) when the French Government was still engaged in negotiations with Ho Chi Minh's Democratic Republic. In the words of the head of the mission as he stepped off the plane in Saigon on May 26, 1946:

> But it is Monsieur Thorez, the first [political figure] with whom I could enter into contact, who expressed to me the most remarkable opinion: the Vice Premier has affirmed to me that the Communist Party under no circumstances wished to be considered as the eventual liquidator of the French position in Indochina and that he ardently wished to see the French flag fly over all the corners of the French Union.[3]

A remarkable statement, sounding something like the Churchillian "I have not become Prime Minister to preside over the liquidation of the British Empire." We must remember, however, that for Viet-Nam to break away from French influence would have been a step backward in view of the apparently imminent integration of France herself into the Communist orbit; and this would have been so even if the Ho Chi Minh regime had been 100 per cent Communist. It would have been comparable to what Tito did later in Yugoslavia, for it would have separated the Vietnamese and French Communist parties and set them on divergent paths. The fact that unity actually existed and was considered important by

---

[2] Herriot then stated, to applause from all benches: "In matters such as national defense we must, just as the Soviets did, foresee centralized means; and you know very well that on such matters Russia does not compromise— and she is right."

[3] *Paris-Saigon* (Saigon), No. 19 (May 29, 1946).

the Communists is clearly brought out by Paul Mus, a French expert on Asia:

> I remember how, upon our arrival in Saigon in 1945, General Leclerc met the local group of French Marxists and asked them about the feelings of the French Communists in Indochina toward the "Annamite" Communists. We were answered: "There are no French and Vietnamese Communists. There is *one* Communist Party, and here we [happen to be] in Indochina."[4]

In fact, the French Communist group in Saigon apparently issued a document on September 25, 1945, two days after the entry of French troops into that city, urging the Vietnamese Communists to make sure that their actions met the criteria of what was then Soviet policy.

> It warned that any "premature adventures" in Annamite [e.g., Vietnamese] independence might "not be in line with Soviet perspective." These perspectives might well include France as a firm ally of the U.S.S.R. in Europe, in which case the Annamite independence movement would be an embarrassment. . . . It advised them in particular to wait upon the results of the French elections . . . in October, when additional Communist strength might assure the Annamites a better settlement.[5]

It is still not clear whether Ho Chi Minh's dissolution of the Indonesian Communist Party in November, 1945, was, as has been suggested,[6] a sign of displeasure with such "go slow" orders and whether his subsequent rebellion of December, 1946, was not at first just as much a rebellion against Communist (Soviet) "perspectives" as it was against French imperialism. If so, the approval by the French Communists of a "hard policy" in Indochina was quite in keeping with Soviet political objectives of the time and thus perfectly logical.

The solidarity of the French Communist Party held firm in the French Parliament throughout the first three months of the Indochinese War. The Communist ministers and the Communist

[4] Paul Mus, *Viet-Nam, Sociologie d'une Guerre* (Paris: Editions du Seuil, 1952), p. 342.
[5] Harold Isaacs, *No Peace for Asia* (New York: Macmillan, 1947), p. 173.
[6] Cf. Department of State, OIR Report No. 3708 (declassified), *Political Alignments of Vietnamese Nationalists* (Washington, D.C., 1949), p. 92.

members of the Armed Forces Committee sought in no way to block the reinforcement of the French Expeditionary Corps in Indochina in arms, men, and equipment—a fact which non-Communist members of parliament now are happy to recall. Indeed, the Socialist Premier, M. Ramadier, on March 20, 1947, showered particular praise upon the head of his Vice Premier, M. Thorez, during the discussion of the 1947 war budget for Indochina:

> Permit me to give a share of the credit particularly to Vice Premier Maurice Thorez. He has had the courage to put into words our will, our unanimous will. It was not a partisan idea that inspired us, him and us, but the feeling of France's needs, the will to save France, to safeguard French unity, which is indispensable at the present hour.

Incidentally, this war budget bill, which was fully endorsed by the Communist ministers in the Ramadier government, even included an item of $6,800,000 for purchases of arms and equipment abroad, spent entirely in the United States and Britain.

Nonetheless, the Communist Party (and also, as it turned out, the Socialist Party) was faced with an anticolonial ground swell among its rank and file. They still were somewhat unruly after the years of rather lax party discipline under the German occupation and underground cooperation with Frenchmen of all walks of life, and apparently took little heed of Soviet "perspectives" in the matter.

For a time, then, the French Communists found themselves in a situation which, by all known rules of the book, must have appeared as rank party heresy: on the one hand, Communist ministers approved of a governmental policy which the Communist parliamentary bloc disapproved of on the record and had abstained from voting for; and on the other hand, the Central Executive Committee of the French Communist Party performed the veritable tour de force of approving of both! This rather peculiar situation came about in the middle of March, 1947, at the time of a policy and budget debate.

It is interesting to note that throughout the debate the Communists and members of their satellite group, the Union and Resistance Group, advocated a policy in full accordance with

French national interests. The first speaker, Pierre Cot, developed the point of view as follows:

> First of all, no one among us, and we must affirm it, thinks of a policy of abandonment or renouncement. France has a task to accomplish there and, without wanting to use big words, a mission to fulfill.
>
> Mr. Paul Ramadier, Prime Minister: Very good!
>
> Mr. Pierre Cot: It is necessary to say so in order to discourage both the illusions of certain Vietnamese extremists and the foreign manœuvres which might give rise to such illusions. (*Applause to the extreme left, to the left and in the center.*) . . . France's departure from Viet-Nam would not serve the cause of freedom; quite the contrary. (*Applause to the extreme left and on various benches.*)

It remained for Jacques Duclos, the number-two man of the PCF after Thorez, to formulate Communist policy as regards Indochina in completely unequivocal terms:

> We are for the presence of France in the Far East, but we have the deep-down conviction that the policy which is being pursued will result sooner or later in our being thrown out rather than being able to hold on. (*Applause to the extreme left.*) . . . We are for the presence of France in the Far East, contrary to what is asserted by the newspaper *Le Monde* . . . which pretends that there are groups in the National Assembly that are hostile to the presence of France in the Far East . . . We have understood only too well . . . that our departure from the Far East would result in the arrival of certain other elements of a not-too-democratic character.

The next day, March 19, 1947, the Central Executive Committee of the PCF held a plenary meeting, which decided that it was "impossible" for members of the Communist parliamentary bloc to "vote the military credits for the prosecution of the war against Viet-Nam," but which advised them merely to abstain from voting. And so they did on the following day, despite the fact that even the Communist members of the Armed Forces and Finance committees had favorably reported out the budgetary bill. The bill was passed, 421 to 0, with the Communists and their affiliates abstaining. What had happened?

> Must one look for an explanation of this sudden change in [events] outside France? . . . Or are the motives of an internal nature: pres-

sure of the militants . . . discontented with the too-governmental policy of the Party? Ideological loyalty to an antimilitarist and anticolonialist tradition? Desire to appear abroad as the defender of the colonial peoples? Hope to attract the Socialists and their left-wing followers? All of those factors undoubtedly come into play, but more determining, perhaps, is the will to react against the anti-Communist provocations which they had had to face since the beginning of the Indochina debates.[7]

There is some truth in the latter statement. The Communists in Parliament, who had been "on their best behavior," had indeed been subjected to a concentrated barrage of taunts from right-wing elements. Thus, Communist abstention could well have been designed in part, along with the crippling strikes in French industry, as a public show of force to prove that one could not govern without them.

Two days after that first break in governmental solidarity, the Politburo of the PCF met for a plenary session to hammer out a new party line which would reconcile the irreconcilable:

The Political Bureau, on the proposition of the Secretary-General of the Party [i.e., Maurice Thorez, who had voted *for* the budget], confirms the mandate given the parliamentary group by the Central Committee which "does not believe possible the vote on military credits for the prosecution of the war against Viet-Nam." Nevertheless, considering that the vote taken by the parliamentary group would in no way endanger the other aspects of the general policy of the Government, the Political Bureau decides that there is no reason for the Communist ministers to break ministerial solidarity.[8]

This compromise solution could not be considered a satisfactory long-range policy, the more so as it apparently ran counter to the desires of a large majority of the Party's rank and file. Hence it is likely that such a policy was motivated by events abroad, or, more precisely, in the Soviet Union.

It is clear that the French Communists' conciliatory attitude in March over the Indochina question was due to their desire to remain

---

[7] André Siegfried *et al.*, *L'Année Politique* 1947 (Paris: Editions du Grand Siècle, 1948), p. 41.
[8] Editorial by Jacques Duclos, "Notre Politique," in the publication of the Central Committee of the French Communist Party, *Cahiers du Communisme*, March, 1947, p. 108.

in the government as long as that would enable them to influence French foreign policy in a direction favorable to the Soviet point of view. But at the end of April . . . the Moscow Conference had ended with a break between the U.S.S.R. and France and with an unquestionable *rapprochement* between France and the Anglo-Saxon Powers. As the participation of the Communists in the government had not produced the diplomatic consequences which they regarded as of major importance, they no longer had . . . reasons . . . for preserving at least the appearance of ministerial solidarity.[9]

The time had come for a new twist in the party line. The PCF had to make its exit from the government. There remained only to find a good occasion that would enable the PCF to appear as the victim of a reactionary cabal. Meantime, as one source remarks: "Had the Communist ministers abstained—not even voted against—from voting the military credits, there would have been a governmental crisis and, for all we know, the war might not have continued in Indochina."[10]

From the point of view of party discipline, the PCF performance had been remarkable. However, it had been poor politics.

In the following days, Communist policy was merely to liquidate current problems in preparation for openly entering the opposition —"of going back into the *maquis*," as some politicians said jokingly. The final break occurred on a home issue of great electoral importance: wage-freezing and price control. The government motion supporting such a policy was passed on May 4, 1947, by 346 votes against the 186 of the Communists—including, this time, their ministers. This gave the PCF the desired propaganda headline that the "eviction of the Communist ministers" had taken place "under American pressure."

"Tripartism" and Communist hopes of being able to get control of France and her overseas possession in one swift sweep were ended. The old tactic of "Communism in one country" came again to the fore, and now the country in question was Viet-Nam and not France. By August, 1947, the French Communist Party had set the new course.

[9] François Goguel, *France Under the Fourth Republic* (Ithaca, N.Y.: Cornell University Press, 1951), p. 25.
[10] Mahdi Elmandjra, unpublished manuscript on the PCF, 1946–49 (Cornell University, 1954), p. 20.

Now the Ho Chi Minh government became the "first democracy in Asia,"[11] and the Indochina issue became rapidly involved in the broadening rift between the Soviet Union and the West following the creation of the Marshall Plan and the beginning of American military aid to Greece under the Truman "containment policy." . . .

As the preceeding pages show, the changes of the foreign-policy line of the French Communists on the vital Indochina problem have been far more responsive to actual international conditions than those of any other French party. It must be considered as one of the most serious errors of successive French governments not to have been more aware of the fact that such changes reflected quite accurately concurrent changes in Soviet foreign policy. The French Communist reaction to governmental Indochina policy was substantially more realistic at any given moment than that of most of the other parties. The United States as well as the other allies of France could have put to excellent use the existence of this "direct line to Moscow" to adjust its actions accordingly.

11 For home consumption, the PCF conveniently overlooked the existence of Communist regimes in China and North Korea, unless it did not consider them as "democratic."

3. The Failure of the
Navarre Plan

December, 1956

The problem that faced all the French field commanders in Indochina after the outbreak of hostilities in 1946 was to compel the main battle force of the enemy to make a fight-or-die stand, and to loosen the Communist stranglehold upon the majority of the population. The first of those objectives was strictly military; the second was fraught with political implications, and thus not within the sphere of control of the military commander (except when he, as in the case of Marshal de Lattre de Tassigny and General Paul Ely, simultaneously held the civilian post of French High Commissioner in Indochina).

Until 1953 the French logistical and manpower base was too narrow to permit a full-scale counteroffensive of nearly one-half million men over a terrain *four* times the size of Korea.* However, by 1953, thanks to increasing American aid and French reinforcements, the time now was considered ripe to strike this decisive blow. The man chosen to lead the French Union Forces in this final operation of the war was a newcomer to Indochina, Lieutenant General Henri Navarre.

When General Navarre took over command of the French Union Forces in the Far East on May 28, 1953, he found a situation that was at best stagnant. Surely, the first Viet-Nam People's

---

* *The over-all size of the Korean peninsula is 83,000 square miles, as against 310,000 square miles for all of Indochina. The size of the Republic of Korea (South Korea) alone is 44,000. South Viet-Nam alone covers 65,000 square miles.*

Excerpted, by permission, from "Indochina, The Last Year of the War: The Navarre Plan," which appeared originally in *Military Review*, published by the U.S. Army Command and General Staff College, December, 1956.

Army (VPA) offensive into northern Laos had been stopped short of Luang Prabang, the royal residence of Laos, but at the price of building up another airhead at the Plaine des Jarres, thus again diverting precious troops from the Red River Delta. Navarre brought with him to Indochina the promise of increased American aid and that of additional fresh French troops; seven infantry battalions, the French-reinforced United Nations battalion from Korea (where hostilities had ended in July, 1953), an additional artillery group, and two battalions of combat engineers.

Furthermore, the Vietnamese National Army—which already had more than 100,000 men in the field—fighting as an ally of France was to raise within the year a first group of 19 "light" (that is, 600 men) commando battalions for the purpose of fighting the Communists on their own terrain, to be followed by 35 additional commando battalions within the next fiscal year.[1] Several sub-sectors had been transferred to Vietnamese command in the meantime, in order to create a mobile reserve with the French troops thus withdrawn from duty in the fixed positions in thousands of bunkers of the de Lattre Line.

There had never been an official published program known as the "Navarre Plan." However, according to various public statements made at the time of its inception, the practical meaning and purpose of the plan becomes clear. According to Navarre's own chief of cabinet, Colonel Revol, the Navarre Plan was to endow the French battle corps "with a mobility and an aggressivity which it lacks." According to another authoritative source, Secretary of State John Foster Dulles, the Navarre Plan was designed to break "the organized body of Communist aggression by the end of the 1955 fighting season," leaving the task of mopping up the smaller guerrilla groups to the national armies of Cambodia, Laos, and Viet-Nam.

Whatever the ultimate effect of the Navarre Plan, it cannot be denied that the French Union Forces showed the same offensive ability which they had displayed under the late Marshal de Lattre. In fact, it can even be said that too much activity was displayed too often at too many different places (see Figure 2), thus leaving troops and leaders but little time to prepare for the large-scale

[1] General Henri Marchand, *L'Indochine en Guerre* (Paris: Pouzet, 1955), p. 278.

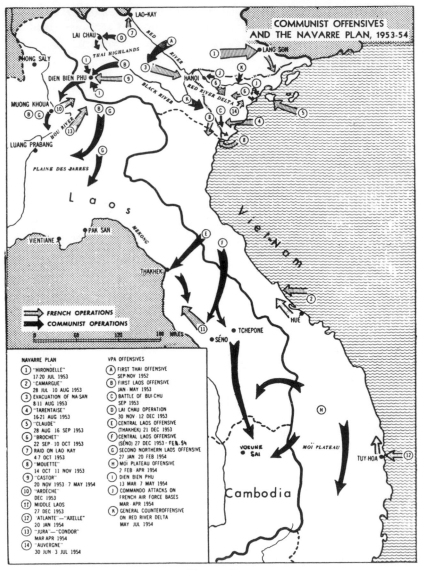

COMMUNIST OFFENSIVES AND THE NAVARRE PLAN, 1953-54

FRENCH OPERATIONS
COMMUNIST OPERATIONS

NAVARRE PLAN	VPA OFFENSIVES
① "HIRONDELLE" 17-20 JUL 1953	Ⓐ FIRST THAI OFFENSIVE SEP-NOV 1952
② "CAMARGUE" 28 JUL-10 AUG 1953	Ⓑ FIRST LAOS OFFENSIVE JAN-MAY 1953
③ EVACUATION OF NA-SAN 8-11 AUG 1953	Ⓒ BATTLE OF BUI-CHU SEP 1953
④ "TARENTAISE" 16-21 AUG 1953	Ⓓ LAI CHAU OPERATION 30 NOV-12 DEC 1953
⑤ "CLAUDE" 28 AUG-16 SEP 1953	Ⓔ CENTRAL LAOS OFFENSIVE (THAKHEK) 21 DEC 1953
⑥ "BROCHET" 22 SEP-10 OCT 1953	Ⓕ CENTRAL LAOS OFFENSIVE (SÉNO) 27 DEC 1953-FEB 54
⑦ RAID ON LAO KAY 4-7 OCT 1953	Ⓖ SECOND NORTHERN LAOS OFFENSIVE 27 JAN-20 FEB 1954
⑧ "MOUETTE" 14 OCT-11 NOV 1953	Ⓗ MOI PLATEAU OFFENSIVE 2 FEB-APR 1954
⑨ "CASTOR" 20 NOV 1953-7 MAY 1954	Ⓘ DIEN BIEN PHU 13 MAR-7 MAY 1954
⑩ "ARDÈCHE" DEC 1953	Ⓙ COMMANDO ATTACKS ON FRENCH AIR FORCE BASES MAR-APR 1954
⑪ MIDDLE LAOS 27 DEC 1953	Ⓚ GENERAL COUNTEROFFENSIVE ON RED RIVER DELTA MAY-JUL 1954
⑫ "ATLANTE"—"AXELLE" 20 JAN 1954	
⑬ "JURA"—"CONDOR" MAR-APR 1954	
⑭ "AUVERGNE" 30 JUN-3 JUL 1954	

FIGURE 2

operations envisaged for the latter phase of the Navarre Plan. (The French still operated with Groupes Mobiles [units the size of a regimental combat team] as their largest tactical unit, while the VPA operated with Chinese-type, 10,000-man divisions.) . . .

In an effort to accentuate pressure upon the enemy's rear communications lines through methods similar to those of the Communists themselves, several Groupes Commandos Mixtes Aéroportés (GCMA), or Mixed Native Commando Groups, made up of French-trained Thai tribesmen and French cadres, began to operate behind enemy lines. They were, however, too weak to influence the outcome of any particular operation but proved useful for long-range reconnaissance. The most significant operation of such a commando group was the parachuting of 40 Meo tribesmen near Lao Kay on October 4, 1953, in an attempt to destroy VPA communications lines at this vital point of entry into Red China. The operation failed, but as late as October, 1955, the Communist authorities in North Viet-Nam complained over their radio about guerrilla tribesmen who refused to surrender.

However, it became clear to the French High Command that the offensives of the Navarre Plan had thus far failed in their two main objectives: destruction of the enemy's organized battle force, and liquidation of the guerrilla threat behind French lines. Under the personal supervision of General Navarre, "Operation Mouette" ("Operation Seagull") was launched on October 14 into enemy territory south of the delta in direction of the important enemy supply center of Phu Nho Quan. More than six Groupes Mobiles, reinforced by tank and amphibious battalions, two French Navy marine units, broke through the Ninh Binh limestone hills in a pincer movement seeking to encircle the VPA's 320th Infantry Division. VPA Regiments 48 and 64 resisted and even counterattacked the vastly superior French forces until all vital supplies and matériel had been removed from Phu Nho Quan.

Contrary to the hopes of the French, Communist General Giap did not let himself be goaded to commit the mass of his elite forces for the sake of saving one division. When Phu Nho Quan had become useless, the VPA forces around it merely melted again into the rice paddies and hills, and the French entered a deserted city. On November 7 they returned to the delta perimeter. The 320th, although severely mauled, was still a fighting unit. The last attempt to force Giap to a decision on a terrain not of his own choosing had failed.

It but remained for General Navarre to seek out the enemy in his own lair, the mountain uplands. Two alternate solutions were open to him: either attack the enemy's main bases in the Thai-Nguyen Tuyen-Quang "redoubt" (with the chance of perhaps capturing a good part of the enemy's central government and supplies), or place his troops astride the traditional invasion routes into Laos. In spite of the entreaties of General René Cogny, the able commander of the Red River Delta, and in all likelihood due to nonmilitary considerations,[2] Navarre chose to defend Laos. At the same time he hoped to make this upland stronghold into a sufficiently attractive bait for Giap to commit his elite divisions against it in the hope of taking it.

The bait chosen turned out to be an oblong valley, about ten miles long and six miles wide, in which the Japanese had built a fairly solid airfield. In pre-French times the little city in the center of the valley had been near the Chinese border and was, therefore, named "Seat of the Border Prefecture," or in Vietnamese, Dien Bien Phu.

Contrary to what has been asserted elsewhere, the attack at Dien Bien Phu was never conceived as a "large-scale airborne raid."[3] Its entire mission from the outset was to become a "meat-grinder" for the bulk of the Communist battle force far from the vital Red River Delta, while the French command would concentrate the remainder of its forces upon mopping up the delta without interference by regular enemy troops. In addition, bomber units stationed in Dien Bien Phu could successfully hamper—if not strangle altogether—the ever-increasing flow of Red Chinese supplies reaching the VPA, and the fortress could become a solid anchor for French raider units operating behind lines, in addition to covering northern Laos.

"Operation Castor"—the code name for the Dien Bien Phu attack—began on November 20, 1953, by the dropping of three

[2] The Kingdom of Laos was the first and thus far the only Indochinese state to sign an association treaty with France. French political circles felt that northern Laos could not be abandoned to the enemy without also endangering political negotiations with Viet-Nam and Cambodia.

[3] Lieutenant Colonel Norman E. Martin, "Dien Bien Phu and the Future of Airborne Operations," *Military Review*, June, 1956, p. 20.

parachute battalions over the valley. While the operation itself was a tactical surprise, a Communist mortar unit and several rifle companies training in the drop zone at the moment of the landing inflicted losses to the parachute force before withdrawing to the nearby ring of hills.

Thus the first objective of destroying enemy forces in the immediate vicinity of Dien Bien Phu was never achieved. Considering the number of troops available for the operation (seven paratroop battalions, three North African battalions, one Vietnamese and two tribal Thai battalions, one combat engineer battalion, one truck company, ten light tanks, two 75- and 105-mm artillery groups, and four 155-mm medium howitzers), the size of the valley prevented the occupation of the high grounds surrounding the fortress and their inclusion in the defense perimeter. Therefore, all French preparations had to be made in presumably full view of Communist reconnaissance parties.

However, the major miscalculation of the Dien Bien Phu operation seems to have been made by French intelligence estimates which initially credited the enemy with an artillery composed of 40 to 60 medium howitzers capable of firing 25,000 rounds. However, they apparently gauged Giap in terms of his attack two years earlier on the Na-San airhead and gave the VPA and its Red Chinese backers, now freed from the drain of the Korean conflict, no credit for improvement. As it turned out, Giap's artillery used an estimated 240 to 350 guns, including Soviet heavy rocket launchers, and fired nearly 350,000 rounds,* while the fortress (initially provided with thirteen days of supplies and less than ten days of ammunition and fuel) had to use its ammunition sparingly in the face of ever-increasing losses of air-dropped tonnage to the enemy as the defense perimeter shrunk to less than a few hundred yards in diameter.

An investigation by a commission of French generals as to the causes of the Dien Bien Phu disaster was held recently. Its results are still classified but as early as June 9, 1954, General Pierre Koenig, then French Minister of Defense, admitted that: "In fact,

---

* *About 120 pieces and 200,000 eventually proved correct. (Editor's Note: In preparing his articles for inclusion in this book, the author has provided annotations in the form of new footnotes. These appear as asterisked, italicized notes.)*

from the outset, the enemy artillery dominated ours. . . . It was the same with the [VPA] anti-aircraft artillery which immediately proved very effective. Under such conditions the drama began with the beginning of the battle."

However, the drama of Dien Bien Phu was only a relatively more spectacular part of a drama that now played throughout Indochina on a far grander scale: General Vo Nguyen Giap's long-promised general counteroffensive.

Ever since his first attack upon northern Laos in the spring of 1953, Giap had retained a corps of about four divisions in the Thai highlands and the northern part of Central Viet-Nam, at almost equal distance between the Red River Delta and Luang Prabang. Throughout the rainy season of 1953 (May to October), Giap successfully avoided engaging his main force while Navarre vainly sought to disrupt the Communist timetable or order of battle. In December Giap was ready. Regiment 101 of the 325th and Regiment 66 of the 304th Infantry Divisions, VPA, drove across the Annamite mountain chain, sweeping ahead of themselves French Groupe Mobile (GM) Number 2 which had been hurriedly sent out of Hué to meet the new threat and whose battered remains now fell back upon the Laotian side of the mountains to the unfortified airfield of Seno.

Once more Navarre had to disperse his already thinly stretched reserves. Along the tried pattern of Na-San, the Plaine des Jarres, and Dien Bien Phu, another fortified airhead was hurriedly created around Seno, and a separate Middle Laos Operational Groupment (GOML) activated on Christmas Day, 1953: three parachute battalions from the general reserve—including two Vietnamese battalions which gave an excellent account of themselves—parts of GM Number 2, all of GM Number 1 and, a few days later, GM Number 51, plus assorted air and supply components, were concentrated 400 miles away from the major battlefronts of the Red River Delta and Dien Bien Phu.

On December 25, 1953, the Communists reached the Thai border at Thakhek on the Mekong—the overland lifeline to northern Laos was severed and Indochina cut in two. In the meantime, Regiment 66 of the VPA directly cut across the mountains (see Figure 2) and one by one crushed the smaller French posts strung out along the road from Viet-Nam to Seno. GM 51, sent to the rescue, fell into a severe ambush of the jungle variety and its lead battalion was practically annihilated on January 24, 1954, losing all its vehicles.

Two of the paratroop battalions of the Seno airhead, by valiant stand at Hine Siu, saved Seno from a direct attack, but Giap's major southern Laos forces bypassed the now well-fortified position and melted into the jungle, only to reappear 20 days later nearly 200 miles farther south, in hitherto quiet northern Cambodia, while another pincer from the Annamese coast suddenly attacked the lightly defended posts of the Moï Plateau.

In northern Laos the situation had also taken a turn for the worse. The entire 316th VPA Division, after having taken the airhead of Lai Chau 55 miles north of Dien Bien Phu, now again marched upon Luang Prabang in four separate columns, liquidating the small garrisons of Muong Nguoi and Muong Khoua, where the year before a small Laotian garrison under a French captain had fought to the death to delay the Communist rush upon Luang Prabang. This time the 2d Laotian Battalion and the 2d Battalion, 3d Regiment, French Foreign Legion, covered the retreat of the small garrisons toward the new defense perimeter around Luang Prabang, being nearly wiped out in the process. On February 13, 1954, Navarre airlifted another five battalions, including a parachute battalion, into Luang Prabang, thus further dispersing his forces and adding another crushing burden to the already heavily taxed air infrastructure. Five additional battalions were diverted to Muong Sai, covering the northern approaches to the city.

Giap thus had fully succeeded in making Navarre progressively throw his painfully gathered mobile reserve into the four corners of Indochina in pursuit of a "single-battle decision" that was definitely not part of the pattern of the war fought in Indochina. Yet, in his New Year's message to his troops, Navarre stated:

> Having lost all hopes of winning a decisive battle in the Red River Delta, the Viet-Minh disperses its forces. . . . However, in that type of warfare, we have the advantage of being able to concentrate our forces rapidly at any essential point. . . . A campaign begun under such conditions can but turn in our favor.

What happened next cannot be readily explained in terms of military strategy and must await careful examination by future students of military history: with Dien Bien Phu threatened, central Laos invaded, northern Laos under attack, and the Red River Delta more infiltrated than ever, Navarre, on January 20, 1954, launched a combined land and amphibian attack against Tuy-Hoa, a stretch of Communist-held coast in southern Central Viet-Nam that had been in Communist hands since 1945 and was of no military usefulness to anyone. "Operation Atlante"—as it was called—diverted another 15,000 troops and, after initial successes in the landing areas, soon bogged down in the jungle-covered hills of the roadless hinterland. The time now was ripe for Giap's last round.

Within a week after the beginning of "Operation Atlante," Giap called off the attack of the 316th Division upon northern Laos and concentrated the bulk of the 304th, 308th, and 312th Infantry Divisions, and all of the 351st "Heavy" Division around Dien Bien Phu. Giap's attack began at 5:30 P.M. on March 13, 1954, by a heavy artillery barrage upon the two major outlying hill positions covering the central redoubt which were overrun forty-eight hours later after several "human sea" attacks.

According to the conservative French weekly Paris-Match, May 12, 1956, the report of the French military investigation commission states that General de Castries had committed "a grave error" in not attempting to hold the two hill positions at all costs.

Attempts were made to constitute a link-up force in northern Laos in order to save the doomed fortress. Under the code names of "Jura" and "Condor," about 5,000 men were assembled under Colonels de Crèvecoeur and Goddard, but the attempt was finally abandoned for the good reason that there were simply not enough reserves left to give the column the necessary strength for at least an even chance of survival against the 40,000 Communist troops concentrated around Dien Bien Phu.

Furthermore, the logistical problem of supplying by air a mobile 12,000-man force over several weeks in addition to supplying Dien Bien Phu with the daily 200 tons it needed was simply insuperable under the then prevailing conditions, the more so as the monsoon weather considerably curtailed air activities throughout the area.

The ensuing disaster, although it deprived the French only of about 4 per cent of their total military manpower in Indochina, proved a crippling blow. Navarre's order of the day of May 9, 1954, that Dien Bien Phu's "sacrifice had not been in vain, for . . . it saved Upper Laos from invasion and preserved the [Red River] Delta," is not too convincing, for the Red River Delta, already thoroughly undermined by Communist guerrillas and infiltrated VPA regulars, already had begun to crack even before the arrival of the victorious VPA divisions from Dien Bien Phu. General Paul Ely, the new French commander who had replaced Navarre, now had to face in the delta area nearly 100,000 Communist regulars and an equal number of guerrillas with less than 80,000 troops of his own. And among the French Union Forces certain Vietnamese units, seeing the signs of the tide, began to disintegrate. . . .

Hostilities ended on July 21, 1954, after a cease-fire had been negotiated at Geneva which gave the Democratic Republic of Viet-Nam control of all of Viet-Nam north of the 17th parallel. The eight years of war had cost the French about $10 billion (in addition to $1.1 billion United States aid delivered before the cease-fire), and 172,000 dead or missing, including three generals and 2,000 other officers.

As General Gavin once said: "Mobility which does not result in concentration for battle is of no use whatever." This is, perhaps, one of the major lessons to be drawn from French tactics in Indochina during the last year of the war. Contrary to the previous years, when a "wall psychology" prevailed, no one can accuse Navarre of immobility. However, the judiciousness of his use of mobility is open to serious question.

As a result, although on the whole the French Union Forces were superior in numbers to the enemy, they were numerically inferior to the enemy at *any* given point of attack. One must add, in all fairness, that the VPA could afford to use hundreds of thousands of slave laborers for logistical and communications support where the French had to use field troops.

The Indochina War had confirmed once more—the Korean conflict being, by and large, another example—the *limited usefulness of air superiority in wars involving underdeveloped areas*. General L. M. Chassin, the former Commanding General of the French Far Eastern Air Force, gave the problem much thought in his book *Aviation Indochine*: "The Communists are well placed to unleash small mass wars in Asia as well as in Africa. They would regain once more all their opportunities for victory if we do not take effective countermeasures."

Chassin asserts that such wars—and Communist operations in Indochina amply bear him out on this—cannot be won by an atomic arsenal. The West at present, by attempting to rely more and more upon unconventional weapons, simply risks finding itself in a position where it will be technologically incapable of effectively dealing with an enemy whose hordes of ground troops advance single file along jungle paths, supplied by swarms of porters from depots and arms factories installed in mountain caves.

The importance of political and social action upon the civilian population, both at home and in the combat area, cannot be stressed enough. At home—and here, the French with regard to Indochina failed to a far greater extent than the Americans with regard to Korea—the objective of such a "limited war" must be made clear in order to obtain the moral and material support necessary to provide the fighting army with all that it needs in terms of manpower and equipment. In the combat area the Western force will always be the "stranger" (sometimes welcome, sometimes not) while the adversary will be on his own home ground. A thoroughgoing psychological warfare program coupled with effective improvements (good local government, public health, and agricultural reform programs) must provide the local population with a reason to commit itself effectively to the Western side without feeling that it betrays its own national interests. In Viet-Nam many of the anti-Communist nationalists felt that a French victory would merely mean a continuation of French colonial influence, while a Communist victory, no matter at what cost to their personal liberties, would bring some type of national "independence."

4. Representative Government in the State of Viet-Nam, 1949–54

August, 1954

In view of the recent Geneva settlement on Indochina, providing for general elections in July, 1956, it may be useful to assess the results achieved by the Vietnamese nationalist administration under its Chief of State, Bao-Dai, since its inception in March, 1949, in building up democratic representative units of government at local and regional levels. While both Cambodia and Laos established constitutional governments of their own[1] as early as 1947 and while the "Democratic Republic of Viet-Nam (the Viet-Minh) had established a semblance of representative government as early as 1946,[2] the State of Viet-Nam hesitated for more than five years before even beginnings of local democratic government were implemented. Even those hesitant beginnings were often enough considered as "premature, considering that our [Viet-Nam's] experience was too short to try ourselves at the game of democracy,"[3] so that by now, the Vietnamese legislative system is still strictly limited to the local level, with some incomplete beginnings at the provincial level. National representative government is entirely nonexistent.

However, even the municipal councils of the most important cities are regulated by governmental decrees as to their composition (number of Vietnamese, French, or Chinese members, etc.), and only very recently have those councils been able to elect a mayor

---

[1] *Documentation Française, Notes et Etudes Documentaires*, No. 633: *Constitution du Royaume du Cambodge*; and No. 725: *Constitution du Royaume du Laos* (Paris, 1947).

[2] See Chapter 7.

[3] Yvonne Pagniez, *Choses vues au Vietnam* (Paris: La Palatine, 1954), p. 163.

Reprinted, by permission, from *Far Eastern Survey*, August, 1954.

from among their members. Until now, the mayors of such cities as Saigon-Cholon, Hanoi, and Haiphong have been also appointed by governmental decree.

There have been, nonetheless, attempts at effective municipal government. The Governor of North Viet-Nam created on July 13, 1950, a special Study Commission for Communal Reorganization, which on September 27 of the same year submitted a confidential report (No. 1032) on such reform measures. Finally, on March 16, 1953, the North Viet-Nam Governor promulgated a municipal reform decree which lessened the influence of the French members of the municipal council and gave greater scope for electoral procedures in the selection of city officials.

That such greater freedom could eventually bring about a regime of limited representative government was proved during the two municipal elections of January and June, 1953. Since this was the first real attempt of the Viet-Nam Government at nationwide elections, they merit closer analysis.

The elections for municipal councilmen were organized throughout all the controlled areas of Viet-Nam by a series of decrees emanating from the central government.[4] A special decree regulated the elections of municipal councils of Hanoi and Haiphong.[5]

The importance of those local elections should not be underestimated. At the time they were held, they were thought to be the first step in a three-stage operation towards the creation of a restricted national assembly: the municipal councilors would elect provincial councils, and both bodies would then elect among themselves those of their members who would represent them at the Viet-Nam National Assembly. Politically, the moment was more than ripe for such a move, since Bao-Dai had promised such elections at the time of his assumption of power in 1949 and the then premier, Nguyen Van Tam, again had promised the creation of a National Assembly for the middle of 1953.

Available documentation shows without doubt that the Viet-Minh feared the eventual success of such elections, and took sev-

[4] State of Viet-Nam, Decision (Arrêté) No. 790/Cab/MI of December 16, 1952; Decree by the Chief of State No. 106/NV of December 27, 1952; Decision No. 804/Cab/MI of the President of the Government, December 27, 1952.
[5] Decision No. 804.

eral measures to sabotage them. A general anti-election plan was elaborated by Viet-Minh Vice President Pham Van Dong, on December 20, 1952. This outlined the various acts of terrorism (including the kidnaping of several candidates) and propaganda designed to make the elections a tremendous loss of "face" for the Viet-Nam national government. The plan was partially successful. Thus, in Hai-Duong (North Viet-Nam) eight out of thirty-three candidates were Viet-Minh members who had infiltrated the city.[6]

Nevertheless, the Bao-Dai regime managed to lose much of the existing genuine goodwill, which by the very fact that the elections took place at all, had begun to build up in its favor. The apparently complete "detachment" of Bao-Dai from the elections—best shown in the fact that Tam's decree implementing the elections was promulgated fifteen days *before* Bao-Dai signed the decree which instituted the elections[7]—and also the fact that the elections were first mentioned three days after Tam's return from France (which made them appear, rightly or wrongly, as "French-ordered"), caused a certain amount of skepticism among not only Vietnamese but also French observers.[8] Electoral and candidacy requirements were in conformity with generally accepted standards (i.e., one year's residence; male suffrage only, however; a minimum age limit of twenty-five and a literacy test were required for eligibility). There was, however, one major limitation which—even in the eyes of the French officials on the spot[9]—was subject to severe criticism: civil servants and close relatives of present members of the government could not present themselves in the elections. While this move was designed to eliminate nepotism and rule by cliques, it also deprived the future National Assembly (if such an assembly was eventually to emerge from the municipal electees) of most of Viet-Nam's most intelligent and experienced administrators.

On the other hand, soldiers on active duty were authorized to

[6] It is, however, hard to tell whether such alleged "Viet-Minh" candidates were not merely antigovernment candidates conveniently dubbed Viet-Minh to be eliminated without contest.

[7] Decision No. 790/Cab/MI and Decree No. 106/NV.

[8] Unpublished communication, Office of the Political Adviser, North Viet-Nam, Office of the Regional Delegate of the Commissioner of the French Republic, Hanoi, January 17, 1953.

[9] The writer saw incontrovertible evidence that there was no French interference in the municipal election process.

vote (but not to be elected), but were not given an absentee ballot. Outside interference was small and, on the whole, inconspicuous. Some foreign observers, such as the U.S. Consul General in Hanoi, objected to the fact that French nationals were maintained on the Hanoi municipal council—and were much surprised to find out that Nguyen Huu Tri, the certainly not-too-francophile northern governor, was in favor of their temporary retention.

A certain amount of pressure was, however, exercised by what one could truly call "political machines," such as the "Doc-lap" ("Independence") group of the Dai-Viet[10] in Haiphong, headed by the appointed mayor, which ran on a platform of: (a) exclusion of the French from membership on the municipal council; (b) creation of an all-Vietnamese chamber of commerce (in opposition to the French and Chinese chambers of commerce).[11]

In Hanoi, an antigovernment (but also anti-Viet-Minh) faction, headed by an ebullient French-trained dentist with American sympathies, Hoang Co Binh, and also by a former companion of Ho Chi Minh, Nguyen The Truyen, ran on a more "political" platform demanding: (a) universal suffrage for national elections; (b) replacement of appointed mayors by elected ones; (c) elimination of French council members and creation of strictly French chambers of commerce in Haiphong and Hanoi; and finally (d) an end of the war. Binh won a smashing victory over the government's candidate, Ngo Thuc Dich, and received twenty-three out of twenty-four elective seats on the city council. French political experts rationalized Binh's victory by the fact that his probity was known and because of "his political virginity and good organization." Indeed, Binh's supporters were at most polling stations, watching the ballot boxes and immediately reporting any attempts to meddle with them.

This success is the more remarkable as there were definite indications that the Dai-Viet, backed by the prestige of the governor if not by his actual help, had definitely attempted to exercise undue influence over the votes of the civil servants, the police, and

[10] The "Great Viet-Nam" Party, a group with fascist overtones which recruits its following mostly from the former mandarins. Its most able exponent is Nguyen Huu Tri. (*Died later in 1954.*)

[11] Unpublished communication from French Deputy Commissioner, Coastal Zone, to Political Adviser, Hanoi, January 22, 1953.

militarized gendarmerie (Bao Chinh Doan) and even the coolies working for the Public Works Department; in brief, over all who made their livelihood from jobs under the Governor's jurisdiction.

In fact, in the North (as in the rest of the country) three main factors influenced the elections: (1) the government and the hordes of government jobholders and their families; (2) the largely neutralist bourgeoisie who wished to express their disapproval of the existing state of affairs; and (3) the "neutralists by fear"—that large segment of the population which did not vote for fear of reprisals by the Viet-Minh.

The press was almost totally indifferent, with the exception of the paper *Gian-sang* in Hanoi (supported by the United States Information Service), which backed Binh, and a few other papers in Saigon. The voters, particularly in the smaller cities where a Viet-Minh reaction was likely or at least possible, were quiet, and almost no incidents occurred. Even the candidates were not too eager to have their names on posters or to appear in public, for fear of being branded *Viet-gian* (traitors) by the Viet-Minh.

In most of the smaller cities, the usual notables ran for what was more a re-election than an election. Most of them were elected without opposition.

The elections took place on January 25, 1953, and the participation figures, while not reaching the overoptimistic level of 90 per cent which had been predicted, reached a creditable 60 to 70 per cent. In all cities but Hanoi, the government lists won overwhelming victories. But one may properly ask, how much of a victory was it in reality?

The important fact the press failed to report was that the number of cities and villages *within* the nationalist zones which were *allowed* to vote rarely exceeded 40 per cent of the total in any given province, and in some provinces ran as low as 2 per cent or less of the total number of townships. Indeed, as far as North Viet-Nam is concerned, the Governor established a list on January 15, 1953, which classified 687 out of a then total of 5,861 controlled townships (about 12.5 per cent of the total) as "safe" enough to hold elections. While this officially meant that it was feared that Viet-Minh candidates would find their way onto the election rolls, even French experts on the spot held that "a considerable number of additional villages could have safely participated in the elections."

Some observers suspected, therefore, that the classification of "safe" and "unsafe"—which lay entirely in the hands of the governor and against which the villages under consideration had no recourse—was made more for reasons of internal politics than of external security.

The result of such an arbitrary discrimination was that very often one village—which had had some contacts with the Viet-Minh—was allowed to vote, while, ironically enough, a neighboring village, which had just beaten off a Viet-Minh armed attack (but whose notables' views clashed with those of the majority party in Hanoi), was declared "unsafe." The result was acrimonious recriminations between the villages thus publicly separated into "white and black sheep" (one must not forget the intense attachment of the ordinary Vietnamese to his native village), and a further loss of popularity for the nationalist government. This was the case particularly in Ha-Dong and Son-Tay provinces.

Two other small, but also important points were overlooked by the government. Firstly, having waited for four full years to hold the elections, they were finally decided in desperate haste, thus giving little time to the weak Vietnamese political parties (which, furthermore, had been inactive for several years by then) to rally a sufficient following. Secondly, the government held the elections in the middle of the rice-planting season, when time is a vital commodity and the Vietnamese farmer is less willing than usual to listen to political speeches, no matter how much entertainment they might provide to break the monotony of life in small villages of the Red River Delta. As a village notable told the writer: "Any government that did not transact its business from a health resort in the mountains should have known that. . . ."[12]

The supplementary election of June 28, 1953, which was supposed to include most of the recently cleared areas, failed substantially to modify the general picture. There was almost no electoral propaganda this time; it was asserted that this was to decrease Viet-Minh interference. In fact, however, this "silencer" put upon electioneering seemed mostly directed against the loyal opposition.

What then was the value of the communal elections to the Viet-

[12] Dalat, the habitual residence of Bao-Dai, is a health resort in the mountains of south Central Viet-Nam.

namese Government? Despite their limited character, the communal elections definitely represented a step forward on the road to representative government, and regional conventions of the communal councilmen to elect a certain number of delegates for a national assembly (as, indeed, the governor of North Viet-Nam proposed on June 30, 1953) could have rapidly given the Bao-Dai regime a certain measure of democratic standing which it has, thus far, failed to attain. Contemporary Viet-Minh documents show beyond a doubt that the Viet-Minh did not relish the idea of seeing its opponent take on the appurtenances of parliamentary democracy, for the fact that the Viet-Minh bases its regime upon the "free, democratic elections"[13] of 1946 is one of its most potent arguments for its popularity.

It is especially regrettable that a few months later, in October, 1953, the Bao-Dai regime relied upon a hand-picked "National Congress" to approve its policy of negotiation with France and met a rebuff that was the more humiliating as it came from its "friends," while a similar rebuff—had it come from an elected assembly—would undoubtedly have strengthened Bao-Dai's hand both at home and abroad. Once more in its brief history, the national government just missed a solution to its legislative impasse that could have held great hopes for the survival of the regime.

Together with the then not unfavorable war situation and the improved psychological climate created by the Laniel Declaration[14] of July 3, 1953, Bao-Dai's regime held, for a fleeting moment, as many trump cards as it ever did, before or after, in order to obtain a settlement with both France and the Viet-Minh under optimum conditions. Again, however, internal jockeying and warring among the various factions of Vietnamese cliques maneuvering for the control of power in Saigon completely paralyzed the Nguyen Van Tam government at the last moment. The provincial elections of October 25, 1953, were but a poor palliative for a country that had hoped for (and had been formally promised by its chief of state) representative national government for the middle of 1953.

In contrast to the municipal elections, which undoubtedly en-

13 See Chapter 7.
14 Declaration by French Premier Joseph Laniel, promising Viet-Nam "to perfect [its] independence."

joyed a great amount of popular participation, the elections for the provincial councils,[15] to be elected by restricted ballot of all the municipal councilors, hardly caused a ripple of interest throughout Viet-Nam. Indeed, they came as an anticlimax to the outburst of Vietnamese nationalism of all tendencies, hardly one week before the elections, during the session of the "National Congress" at Saigon.

Originally set for October 18, 1953, those elections were delayed until October 25 in order to permit various members of the "National Congress" to run as candidates in the provincial elections.[16] As a matter of fact, however, no campaigning whatever was carried on, and the whole electoral process took place *in camera* with more the aspect of a party caucus than of regular elections. Nonetheless, there were approximately 1,600 candidates in 44 provinces for a total of 600 council seats to be filled.[17]

Again, however, the importance of these elections should not be underestimated. In fact, many nationalist personalities—particularly those who could not count too heavily on Bao-Dai's personal favor to remain in power—ran in the provincial elections and thus assured themselves of a certain amount of popular support. Among these were Nguyen Huu Tri, Governor of North Viet-Nam; the Reverend Padre Hoang Quynh, representative of Msgr. Le Huu Tu, Bishop of Phat-Diem; Phan Van Hy, Minister for Veterans Affairs; Pham Van Ngoi, Secretary General of the Socialist Party; Nguyen Van Hung, Minister of Economic Affairs; and Phan Van Giao,* Governor of Central Viet-Nam. The role of the provincial councils has been very limited, restricted mainly to a "deliberative and consultative role"[18] which limits their power to "discussing" taxes and economic and social problems concerning their province. They can also express "wishes" concerning economic and administrative problems of their province.

One can readily see that their usefulness per se is dubious. They can only be justified if they serve their ultimate purpose as a

---

[15] Decree No. 58/NV, by the Chief of State, June 22, 1953.

[16] *Journal d'Extrême-Orient* (Saigon), October 16, 1953.

[17] *Viet-Nam* (bi-weekly bulletin of the Office of the High Commissioner of Viet-Nam in Paris; cited henceforth as *VNB*), November 1, 1953. No French nationals could participate in the provincial elections.

[18] *Ibid.*

* *Died in 1965.*

final step towards creating a Vietnamese national assembly. This latter step, however, has not been taken at the time of writing.

A body similar to the provincial councils, with hardly any wider powers, became the State of Viet-Nam's only tangible effort towards the establishment of a nationwide legislature. During a meeting of the full cabinet on July 5, 1952, it was decided that a temporary National Council was to be established, "representing the political, economic, social and religious tendencies of the country."[19]

The new "Provisional National Council" was instituted by an ordinance of Bao-Dai on July 8, 1952.[20] It was composed of twenty-one members and nine alternates, and its powers were strictly limited to an "obligatory advisory capacity" in national budgetary matters—hardly any advance over the old colonial days of the French Grand Conseil des Intérêts Economiques.

In view of the fact that its members do not wield the same amount of economic influence as their French counterparts did in the days of the Grand Conseil, it may be considered that the National Provisional Council represents a rather regressive step on the path towards national representative government in Viet-Nam.

What then, have been the achievements of the Bao-Dai administration in terms of democratic government? They have been poor indeed. Speaking of the work of the nationalist regime in establishing local self-government, a Vietnamese administrative expert, whose book on the subject was given a prize by Bao-Dai, states: "We must recognize that the achievements [of the Bao-Dai regime] in that field have been insignificant."[21]

Certainly, the spreading war has been a serious obstacle to effective democratic government in Viet-Nam, but this fact has also been too often used as an easy pretext for certain nationalist leaders to prolong a state of affairs which permits retaining a type of personal government incompatible with that of a modern state. It remains to be demonstrated whether a timely establishment of even a limited amount of representative government, particularly at national level, would not have helped greatly to give the Bao-

---

[19] *Ibid.*, July 15, 1952.
[20] Ordinance No. 4, by the Chief of State, July 9, 1952.
[21] Vu Quoc Thong, *La Décentralisation Administrative au Viet Nam* (mimeographed; Hanoi: Presses Universitaires du Viet Nam, 1952), p. 357.

Dai regime some stronger basis of popularity in the country. As the situation stands at the present moment, neither large-scale American economic aid nor French military efforts have succeeded in doing this. Needless to say, the disastrous development of the military situation during the past months, particularly after the loss of Dien Bien Phu and the ensuing partition, only decreases the chances of establishing a working nationwide legislature in Viet-Nam. The fact that France has turned over an increasing amount of executive responsibility to the Vietnamese nationalist regime has merely further pointed up the now essentially Vietnamese problem of broadening the base of popular support. This was clearly recognized in January, 1954, by the Vietnamese government of Prince Buu-Loc, when the latter created a "Ministry for Democratization" and (like preceding Vietnamese governments before him) promised early nationwide elections (which have thus far not materialized). The recent replacement of the short-lived Buu-Loc regime by a new Vietnamese government under the anti-French, American-backed Catholic leader Ngo Dinh Diem, in the hope that he may be able to inspire a wider Vietnamese popular participation, cannot be considered an adequate solution so long as the basic problem of eventually creating a solid basis for constitutional government has not been solved to the satisfaction of a sizable section of the Vietnamese population.

If the Vietnamese nationalist regime fails in this objective, it is to be feared that even an increased amount of external economic backing may not enable it to survive the comparison—particularly in a partitioned Viet-Nam, since the negotiations at Geneva—with the more efficient[22] Viet-Minh regime, with its claims (however misleading) of greater "democratic" support.

[22] See Chapter 7.

5. The Cease-Fire—An Appraisal

September, 1954

While it may still be too early to make a full appraisal of political events in Indochina (mainly in Viet-Nam) during the fateful period preceding and following the cease-fire, it is possible to fit the facts now emerging into a more or less coherent picture. On the very eve of the Geneva conference, the capture of the fortress of Dien Bien Phu, which cost the French Union Forces what many consider to have been their best troops, sounded the death knell of any "military solution" of the Indochina problem favorable to the Western powers without immediate intervention on the part of the United States in accordance with its much-discussed principle of "massive retaliation."

In view of the obvious reluctance of the American Government to intervene under such adverse circumstances—namely, the victory of the Viet-Minh at Dien Bien Phu followed almost immediately by a general offensive against the now completely infiltrated Red River Delta—French negotiators found themselves not only in an unfavorable position vis-à-vis their Soviet bloc interlocutors, but also uncertain of the degree of support they might expect from their Western allies. At the same time, the Vietnamese nationalist government under Prince Buu-Loc, who had come to France at the beginning of March, 1954, to initiate finally the long-awaited independence talks with France, found itself practically isolated, with its "general mobilization" at home a failure, and faced with a gradual disintegration of its administration throughout the country.

A feeling of revolt was mounting in Saigon, where representatives of several politico-religious sects and of the tiny but vocal

Excerpted, by permission, from a two-part article, "The Cease-Fire in Indochina—An Appraisal," that appeared in *Far Eastern Survey*, September-October, 1954.

political coteries and parties began to exercise a certain amount of pressure upon Chief of State Bao-Dai, demanding that he finally give way to an elected and truly representative national government.[1] Those demands were presented in the form of an ultimatum by the "Movement of National Union and Peace" under Ngo Dinh Nhu, brother of Ngo Dinh Diem, francophobe nationalist and later premier. They were embodied in a five-point program which emphasized that such reforms—which included the stipulation that all past and future treaties signed by the Vietnamese Government be ratified by a National Assembly still to be elected— were to be instituted before Bao-Dai's departure on April 10 for his mansion on the French Riviera. However, as often before, truly unified effective action by all major Vietnamese nationalist groups was completely frustrated because of personality clashes among the leaders of the various factions. After a hasty trip to North Viet-Nam to assuage the fears of the "neonationalist" (former Viet-Minh) leaders that they were going to be sold out to the southern sects, and after similar promises, in reverse, had been made to the southern groups, Bao-Dai departed from Viet-Nam on April 10, after having addressed the following message to the Vietnamese people:

> I am leaving for a very brief stay in France, where our independence is emerging, and where we are negotiating a treaty that will define our position within the French Union and will guarantee us against international isolation. . . .
> We shall never agree that all or part of our soil shall become a Chinese satellite.
> We want to be a free nation.
> The rally [of nationalists] around my person which just occurred . . . shows that the hour of unanimity has come.[2]

Bao-Dai's arrival in France had an immediate stiffening effect upon the intransigence of the Vietnamese delegation, which was negotiating for independence with the French at the same time that it was preparing the Vietnamese position for the forthcoming Geneva conference. Assured by repeated statements of American leaders in positions of responsibility that Viet-Nam and Indochina

[1] *Le Monde*, March 10, 1954.
[2] *VNB*, April 15, 1954, p. 3.

were "vital" to the defense of Southeast Asia,[3] and indeed to the whole free world—and that, if need be, the United States might dispatch forces[4]—Bao-Dai quite logically refused to have his delegation sit at the Geneva conference table with what the Western nations were calling the "Vietnamese rebels" of the Viet-Minh.

In Paris, as might have been expected, the Franco-Vietnamese negotiations had bogged down over the definition of the crucial words "independence" and "association," especially because the Franco-Laotian treaty of October, 1953, had set a legal precedent giving a member of the French Union (at least on paper) full equality with France within a revitalized High Council of the French Union. Likewise, the sudden outburst of nationalism in Cambodia in the summer and fall of 1953, which had given that little country much more effective independence than it had ever bargained for at a conference table,[5] greatly strengthened Viet-Nam's position in asking from France all the prerogatives of independence. Included in these demands were the abolition of the mixed court system exempting non-Vietnamese from Vietnamese jurisdiction, and the creation of an independent Vietnamese Army General Staff and High Command (something which the King of Cambodia had obtained for himself in the preceding fall without even the formal signature of a treaty), as well as the abolition of most of the quadripartite (Cambodia, France, Laos, and Viet-Nam) organizations which had been created by the Pau economic agreements of 1950. France's Premier, Joseph Laniel, desired a single "union and independence" treaty. The Vietnamese delegation replied with a formula of "independence and association," to be couched in two *separate* treaties, with the former preceding the latter. As a matter of fact, in his inaugural speech at the first session of the Franco-Vietnamese conference, not once did Premier Buu-Loc even refer to the "French Union."[6]

It is likely that the stalemate would have remained unbroken had the French not been hard pressed to present a united Franco-

[3] See President Eisenhower's speech to the Conference of Governors in Seattle, Washington, August, 1953.

[4] See Vice President Nixon's speech to the American Association of Newspaper Editors, April 16, 1954.

[5] See Ellen J. Hammer, *The Struggle for Indochina* (Stanford, Calif.: Stanford University Press, 1954), pp. 294–97 *passim*.

[6] VNB, March 15, 1954, pp. 11–12.

Vietnamese front at the Geneva conference, hoping to offset to some degree the demoralizing effects of the impending military disasters with a show of political success for the Bao-Dai regime. Therefore, two days after the first session of the Geneva conference, on April 28, 1954, Premier Laniel and Nguyen Trung Vinh, the Vietnamese Vice Premier (Premier Buu-Loc had returned to Viet-Nam on March 25 in an attempt to prevent the complete political chaos with which the country was threatened), finally signed a common declaration agreeing to the subsequent signature of two separate treaties. One of these granted total independence to Vien-Nam; the other established "a Franco-Vietnamese association within the French Union founded upon equality" of the signatory powers. The Bao-Dai regime, five years after its creation, had won its first diplomatic victory.

Five weeks later, after the military disasters in North Viet-Nam had in fact sealed the doom of the "Bao-Dai solution" as it had been envisaged by the French planners of 1949, France and the Bao-Dai regime finally initialed the two treaties establishing Viet-Nam as "a fully independent and sovereign State." Both treaties, like the treaty with Laos, were remarkable for their brevity. The independence treaty formally gives to Viet-Nam all prerogatives of sovereignty, within its borders as well as abroad, and abrogates all previous treaties to the contrary, with France surrendering to Viet-Nam whatever governmental services or prerogatives she still retains in that country (Articles 3 and 4).

The association treaty, on the Laotian precedent, transfers to the High Council of the French Union, "on a basis of sovereign equality," the joint policy-making functions hitherto exercised by France alone (Article 3). An arbitration court with an equal number of French and Vietnamese members is to settle differences between the countries, if necessary (in case of ties) with the help of a neutral arbitrating country (Article 6).

The treaties were initialed by Buu-Loc, just returned from Viet-Nam, and French Premier Laniel on June 4, 1954; they were to be signed later by Bao-Dai and President Coty of France. Several executive agreements were to be elaborated by joint Franco-Vietnamese commissions, for signature at a later date.

A chapter of Vietnamese history that had opened in Paris in March, 1949, was thus closed. It had often been said that French stubbornness, or pride, or sheer lack of political foresight, had given negotiations between France and Viet-Nam the imprint of "too little and too late." This was not entirely true on this June morning of 1954. Sapped by seven years of war, with her best armed men fighting for survival 8,000 miles from home, France had not been stubborn or proud, nor had she given too little. But she had given too late.

It is not certain whether the Communist bloc really intended from the outset to delay the beginning of the Geneva conference until the annihilation of Dien Bien Phu had provided it with a powerful opening gambit, or whether the delay occurred through the last-minute stubbornness of Bao-Dai in refusing to have his delegation sit with the "rebels" of the Viet-Minh.[7] Whichever is true, the fact remains that the belated seating of the delegation of the "Democratic Republic of Viet-Nam" delayed by forty-eight hours the request by French Foreign Minister Georges Bidault for a temporary truce at Dien Bien Phu for the evacuation of the 2,000 wounded in that embattled stronghold—and then it was too late. Official negotiations for a general cease-fire were begun on May 8, 1954, when, in the gloom of the shattering war news of the previous day, they assumed rather the air of suing for an armistice after a lost war.

Secretary of State John Foster Dulles, sensing the unfavorable turn of events, had departed from Geneva on May 4, leaving the American delegation in the hands of Under Secretary of State Walter Bedell Smith. The Vietnamese delegation at the conference played a minor role, despite some interventions on the part of Nguyen Quoc Dinh, Viet-Nam's Foreign Minister. Bao-Dai himself made only a brief appearance at Evian spa, across the Lake of Geneva, between May 14 and 18, before returning to Cannes. As for the Vietnamese delegation, its main thesis appeared to have been that "Viet-Nam had become independent and, hence, the war had become useless,"[8] and that the regrouping of Franco-Viet-namese and Viet-Minh forces in certain zones should not result in a division of the country into two separate areas of government. This was also the thesis of the French Foreign Minister, but the latter's position was seriously threatened by the impending political

7 *Le Monde*, April 30, 1954.
8 VNB, June 1, 1954, p. 3.

crisis at home, which was to topple the Laniel government in mid-June and replace it by that of Pierre Mendès-France, an ardent advocate of a cease-fire.

Viet-Nam's bargaining position became hopeless when it became clear that Britain did not wish at that time to become involved in "united action" in Southeast Asia and when, failing to obtain such action, Secretary Dulles stated, a few days after his return to the United States, that the Associated States were "extremely important. . . . But I do not want to give the impression . . . that if events . . . should lead to their being lost, that we would consider the whole situation hopeless. . . ."[9]

From then on, the Vietnamese delegation fought what might be called a diplomatic rear-guard action. In an emotional appeal before the full assembly of the conference on June 9, Nguyen Quoc Dinh merely asked for "viable zones," for "authentic elections under international control," and for a truly "neutral" supervisory commission, as well as possible recourse to the United Nations in case of conflict.[10] However, neither Viet-Nam nor France had any strong trump cards left, and both delegations were weakened by the knowledge that their governments at home were faltering under the weight of internal political crises. Buu-Loc's policy of "enlightened" autocracy, untempered by any of the several reforms he had promised when he took over the premiership, had made his government even more devoid of popular support than many of the preceding administrations. True, he had obtained a treaty of independence from France, but so had practically every other Vietnamese government since 1949! There had been, in fact, no less than seventeen French declarations between 1949 and 1954[11] to the effect that Viet-Nam was sovereign and independent, so that this diplomatic success was not regarded too highly. On the other hand, Geneva had brought about certain informal contacts between the Viet-Minh and representatives of the various "spiritual families" (i.e., the "Big Five" of Vietnamese politics as well as the various other nationalist groups and the Movement for National Union and Peace), and those groups had become more and more

9 *The New York Times*, May 12, 1954.
10 VNB, June 15, 1954, pp. 5–9 *passim.*
11 Assemblée Nationale, *Journal Officiel*, March 9, 1954, p. 767. Statement by François Mitterrand (U.D.S.R.).

convinced that a "deal" could be made with the opposing side not only in the military but also the political field. Such a solution, however, apparently would have entailed the ousting of Bao-Dai himself as a political leader, a step which Nguyen Quoc Dinh and Buu-Loc were unwilling to take.[12]

The Buu-Loc government resigned on June 15, 1953, after having held a cabinet session at Saigon, stating in its message to Bao-Dai that it had "completed its tasks," which consisted in "establishing the international status of the State of Viet-Nam." Ngo Dinh Diem, the *attentiste* Vietnamese nationalist par excellence, a man with an excellent reputation for integrity, particularly well liked in American Catholic circles and also respected by Ho Chi Minh, agreed to form a new government on the following day.

That a man of the stature of Ngo Dinh Diem was willing to accept such a heavy responsibility at that particularly crucial moment in Viet-Nam's history, was hailed as a veritable victory for Viet-Nam's "true nationalists" and as an admission of defeat for Bao-Dai. In fact, it gave rise to rumors that Bao-Dai had decided to abdicate in favor of his son Bao-Long, or to relinquish his powers to a regency council. Such rumors were strengthened by a statement issued by Bao-Dai's cabinet on June 22, declaring: "It is necessary to recall that His Majesty Bao-Dai does not consider himself invested with any dynastic rights of which He could freely dispose, but [is invested] with a charge of national interest giving Him more duties than rights. . . ." Bao-Dai's statement also contained an interesting admission which, coming at this juncture, seems to prepare the way for such a change of regime: "The governments formed under his authority have, until now, received only restricted powers. . . . The responsibility for the present situation cannot, therefore, be imputed to them. . . ."[13]

In Viet-Nam, the news was greeted with enthusiasm. Vietnamese nationalists who, until now, had held aloof from any political activity, came forward asserting that this was a veritable revolution, that for the first time they would have a truly national government, and that finally a change had come.

Diem immediately set about re-establishing the authority of the national government, which had been deteriorating badly during

---

[12] *Le Monde*, June 16, 1954.
[13] *Ibid.*, June 22, 1954.

the past months of the absentee Buu-Loc regime, and also demanded from the new French commander in chief and commissioner general in Indochina (General Paul Ely, who had taken over
his new command on June 10) that an autonomous Vietnamese
Army High Command be set up. Diem's inaugural speech, made in
France before his departure for Indochina on June 24, still reflected his hope of saving Viet-Nam as an independent and unified state, with the help of France, and the official Vietnamese
news agency declared on June 26 that "if, in spite of the firmness
of the State of Viet-Nam, the division [of the country] is accepted
by other delegations, it is evident that the Geneva conference will
end in an impasse."[14]

The inauguration on June 20 of the Mendès-France government
in France, pledged to "peace within a month," left Diem with an
equally short time to accomplish the "revolution" needed to consolidate his position at home and stiffen his bargaining position at
Geneva, where Tran Van Do, one of his close associates, had taken
over the post of Minister of Foreign Affairs and head of the conference delegation. This was made clear, upon Diem's arrival in
Viet-Nam on June 26, by a declaration of one of his aides: "Everything depends upon [the policy of] Mendès-France. If he does not
believe in a possible improvement and negotiates at Geneva a
peace of capitulation, our efforts will have been vain. . . ."

In France, in the meantime, as often in the past, a period of
overoptimism engendered by the Navarre Plan had been followed
by one of black despair, further darkened by the premature dis-
closure of the "Ely Report." This report on the military situation
in Indochina, by General Ely (then Chairman of the French Joint
Chiefs of Staff) and Generals Salan and Pelissier, was made after
the disaster of Dien Bien Phu and advocated a contraction of the
French-Vietnamese battle line around easily defensible beach-
heads, and called for increased allied aid, and eventual withdrawal
of the French Union Forces if draft reinforcements from France
and such increased aid were not forthcoming.[15] While the report
was certainly sound and its conclusions hardly surprising to ob-

14 *Viet-Nam Presse* (Saigon), June 26, 1954.
15 *L'Express* (Paris), May 28, 1954, p. 4.

servers who had been following developments in Indochina, its "leaking"—attributed to Marc Jacquet (Secretary of State for Associated States Affairs), who promptly resigned—at that juncture convinced the French public and the politicians that nothing further could be saved in Indochina and that the time had come, as the French saying goes, to "save the furniture" from the burning house. Therefore, Vietnamese objections to a treaty which entailed the abandoning of the Red River Delta and the dividing of the country were met with a blunt: "What do you expect to do—continue the war alone?"[16]

There was little that Diem could do under the circumstances, as he found out once the euphoria of a "real change" had subsided in nationalist circles. Diem found himself isolated from the majority of the southern sects and their armies. The northern Catholics were facing political annihilation when the French, in the process of the contraction of the delta defenses into a tighter perimeter along the Hanoi-Haiphong road and rail link, decided to abandon 600,000 of them to the advancing Viet-Minh. Many of the "neo-nationalists" in Hanoi and also in Saigon reproached Diem with having allowed himself to be drawn into an arrangement which, instead of bringing about the elimination of Bao-Dai, perpetuated the regime with all its faults. "Where we expected an execution, we find only an exchange of polite formulas," is the way one of Diem's own disgruntled supporters stated the case.[17]

In the midst of such difficulties (for Diem, after two weeks in power, still had not formed a cabinet) came the bombshell of the evacuation of the southern part of the delta, with its strong Catholic militia, which fled to Hanoi with Bishops Le Huu Tu of Phat-Diem and Pham Ngoc Chi of Bui-Chu, while Msgrs. Mazet, the French Bishop of Son-Tay, and Ubernia, the Spanish Apostolic Vicar at Thai-Binh, announced their intention of staying with their flock to await the arrival of the Viet-Minh. Once more the French apparently had acted without consulting the Vietnamese Government, and voices were heard in Diem's entourage speaking of a French "deal" with the Viet-Minh. It has not been proved that

[16] *France-Soir*, June 30, 1954.
[17] *Le Monde*, July 8, 1954.

this allegation is true, and the desperate military situation which
Viet-Minh infiltration had produced in the evacuated area for the
past year certainly justified the move militarily. Politically, however, it broke Diem's back.

The new government, which was finally constituted on July 7,
was comparatively small, with nine ministries (Interior; National
Defense; Foreign Affairs; Economics and Finance; Labor and
Youth; Public Works; Education; Agriculture; and Health) and
eight state secretariats. Diem himself kept the portfolios of National Defense and Interior in addition to the premiership. Tran
Van Chuong, the father-in-law of Ngo Dinh Nu (Diem's brother)
was given the portfolio of Economics and Finance,[18] and Tran
Van Do (Chuong's brother) those of Foreign Affairs and head of
the Vietnamese delegation at Geneva. Another relative, Tran Van
Bac, was given the portfolio of Education. Dr. Pham Huu Chuong,
one of Hanoi's "neonationalists," became Minister of Health, the
same post he had held under Ho Chi Minh until 1951. Ngo Dinh
Luyen (another brother of the Premier) became roving ambassador for the government. In other words, the Diem cabinet was no
worse than its predecessors, but little better. Some observers remarked the predominance of the Ngo and Tran families in the
cabinet and called it a "family affair"; others pointed to the unique
fact that the government had no South Vietnamese members,
despite the fact that it must depend more and more upon southern
support for any sort of popular basis. Publicly, at least, Diem still
reckoned with the "support of our associate, France; and of America, who has helped us so generously," to arrive at a cease-fire without a final dividing line and without abandoning the Catholic
population of the southern part of the Red River Delta, whose loss
Diem refused to consider as "an irremediable *fait accompli.*" In
fact, he asked that the abandoned "zone be placed under the administration of our government."[19] Coming so late, his declarations
had a pathetic air of unreality, for both at Geneva and at Trung-
Gia events had moved far beyond the point of no return. As for
American action in Indochina at that juncture. Diem probably
acted as Dr. Syngman Rhee a few weeks later was said to have

---

[18] Tran Van Chuong was also appointed Ambassador to the United States.
[19] *Le Monde,* July 8, 1954.

done: "He based his policy on Washington's words instead of on Washington's actions. And he believed his mail."[20] . . .

In Geneva, new French Premier Pierre Mendès-France raced against his own deadline of "thirty days till peace." The official conference table became merely a sounding board for some unimportant statements for the record. The actual business of negotiating was conducted in successive conversations between Mendès-France and the top leaders on the opposing side, mainly Chou En-lai, who appeared more and more to be playing the leading role. Both Molotov and Eden appear to have acted as go-betweens to both parties, while most of the other delegations played only secondary roles. This was particularly true for the delegation of the Vietnamese nationalist government, in the face of the contempt of its enemies and the indifference of its allies. The Vietnamese delegation must have been particularly sensitive to the attitude of the French negotiators, whose government, only a few weeks earlier, had been so eager to obtain Viet-Nam's adherence to the French Union, but who now completely bypassed the Vietnamese delegation to deal, directly and alone, with the enemy.

On July 17, Tran Van Do handed an official note to the French delegation, protesting against France's negotiating with the Communist bloc without keeping Viet-Nam informed, and advanced a plan calling for the total disarmament of both belligerents and the placing of the whole country under provisional United Nations administration.[21] However, it became increasingly clear that such statements were intended merely for face-saving at home. In fact, on the following day Tran Van Do told the British Foreign Secretary, that "despite his statement . . . his government would be prepared to consider any solution reached at the conference."[22] The United States, for all practical purposes, had withdrawn from the conference as an active participant. Britain had no desire for additional commitments in an area where she already had her own difficulties. As for France, Indochina had become a liability that was rapidly exhausting her regular army and undermining her pres-

[20] James Reston, "A Visitor Learns Something of Shadow and Substance," The New York Times, August 1, 1954.
[21] The New York Times, July 19, 1954.
[22] Ibid.

tige both in Africa and in Europe. Ngo Dinh Diem and Viet-Nam were quite alone in the last days before the signature of the cease-fire. At Geneva, Diem's Foreign Minister Tran Van Do, except for a few other protests for the record, let events take their course.

July 20, 1954, in Geneva was spent by most delegations in making last-minute changes in the final draft of the cease-fire, originally to have been signed at 9:00 P.M. At the last moment, however, Cambodia's delegate, Tep Phan, refused to sign the terms of the cease-fire neutralizing his country, and refused to budge from his position despite last-minute entreaties by all major parties to the conference. Surprisingly enough, the Soviet bloc gave way and Cambodia obtained for itself and for Laos—whose delegates already had gone to bed and were told about the diplomatic windfall in the morning[23]—concessions in the field of defense and alliances. Viet-Nam's delegation did not resist its fate, although it did not sign the cease-fire agreement. It did not have to, as the agreement was a military one requiring only the signature of the respective delegates of the military high commands. Cambodia already had obtained its autonomous army command, while in Viet-Nam the National Army still was subordinate to the French Union High Command. Thus French Brigadier General Delteil signed for both the French and the Vietnamese forces. On July 21, 1954, at 3:42 A.M., the agreement was signed. . . .

The news came to Viet-Nam at 3:00 A.M. on July 22, in the form of a telegram from Tran Van Do to Ngo Dinh Diem:

> We fought desperately against partition and for a neutral zone in the Catholic area of North Viet-Nam. Absolutely impossible to surmount the hostility of our enemies and the perfidy of false friends. Unusual procedures paralyzed the action of our delegation. . . . All arrangements were signed in privacy. We express our deepest sorrows in this total failure of our mission. We respectfully submit our resignation.

Consternation followed the publication of the results in the severely censored Vietnamese press, and panic broke out in the northern areas which were now sure to come under Viet-Minh domination. The Movement for National Union and Peace strongly condemned the settlement, and Le Van Vien, the head of the Binh Xuyen group and general manager of Indochina's biggest

[23] See *Time*, August 2, 1954, p. 18.

gambling establishment, called the settlement a "deal between Communism and French colonialism."[24] Fears were expressed that France had sought to hold only the rich southern areas where there are large private French economic interests, and now again would reduce the residual part of Viet-Nam to the status of a French dependency, along the lines of the old "Autonomous Republic of Cochinchina." While this is not an impossibility, it is, as far as can be foreseen, unlikely. As a matter of fact, the State of Viet-Nam received full command of its own armed forces on August 11, 1954, and the transfer of all residual French services to Viet-Nam is being carried out in accordance with the directives of Premier Mendès-France.

It is obvious that the crucial problems of Viet-Nam are far from solved, from the point of view of the Western world, particularly of France. In fact, the real struggle now begins—a struggle which the West must win in order to demonstrate the superiority of the "democratic way of life" by developing an efficient and representative governmental system in the southern part of Viet-Nam, truly independent from France and yet strong enough to resist Communist pressures from within as well as from without.

Here we should take stock of what has been surrendered to the Viet-Minh in terms of population, terrain, and means of production. Too often the cease-fire in Indochina has been branded as a "sell-out," a "shameful surrender of 12 million Vietnamese to Communism." The Red River Delta, which under the terms of the cease-fire came entirely under Viet-Minh control, has even been described in the U.S. Senate as exporting yearly 500,000 tons of rice to Japan and as being "the rice bowl which takes care, also, of Burma, Thailand, Cambodia, Laos, Formosa, Indonesia."[25]

Most of the above statements are fiction. According to statistics prepared in November, 1952, by the Vietnamese National Office of Statistics, in the area then controlled by the Bao-Dai regime there were 10.6 million Vietnamese of an approximate total of 25 million in all of Viet-Nam (there are an additional 3.5 million Cambodians and 1.5 million Laotians). Hence, and this is clearly visible on any accurate map of the war situation before the cease-

[24] *The New York Times,* July 23, 1954.
[25] Senator Everett Dirksen, in the *Congressional Record,* April 6, 1954, p. 4408.

fire, the State of Viet-Nam now gains more population than it stands to lose and has a better chance of actually *governing* the people it controls than it ever had before. Even if the evacuation of the non-Communist population from the north—whose numbers seem to vary between 200,000 and 700,000*—is only partly successful, the Vietnamese Government south of the 17th parallel should find itself in theoretical control of at least half of the population. As far as area is concerned, the Viet-Minh controls approximately 62,000 square miles, while Viet-Nam south of the 17th parallel controls slightly more, approximately 65,000 square miles. Free Laos and Cambodia cover an additional 159,000 square miles. The territorial settlement thus cannot be considered simply a "sell-out."

Economically, the southern half of Viet-Nam is not only self-sufficient; it is also—contrary to a popular misconception—the traditional "rice bowl" not only of all Indochina but of other parts of Southeast Asia as well. South Viet-Nam produces a profitable export crop of natural rubber, valuable spices, and corn, as do Cambodia and Laos. Laos also has several rich tin and tungsten mines and valuable hardwoods. Hence South Viet-Nam, comparatively little damaged by war, should have no difficulty re-establishing itself in a satisfactory economic position, particularly with American and French economic aid. The refugees from the North should provide a much-needed labor supply for wide tracts of land on the high plateau of South Annam and for the still underdeveloped rice lands of the Trans-Bassac in South Viet-Nam.

On the other hand, the Viet-Minh's "Democratic Republic of Viet-Nam" now faces the tremendous problems of having to re-build its part of the country practically from the ground up. The Red River Delta, far from being a rice bowl, must import 250,000 tons yearly to meet its own minimum needs. The adjacent smaller rice-surplus areas of the Thanh-Hoa and of Thai-Nguyen can fill only a small part of that deficit. Furthermore, the Viet-Minh must rebuild the communications system (canals, power stations and lines, roads, bridges, and railroads) it has so efficiently sabotaged and destroyed for eight years and must make good on its promises of land reform. This Ho Chi Minh will find difficult to do, for 96 per

* Actually, there were 860,000 refugees, and North Viet-Nam's population remained 3 million larger than that of South Viet-Nam.

cent of the land in the delta is tilled by owners each having less than two acres of rice fields, and more than half a million farmers are landless, while the South not only produces a surplus of rice but also has a comfortable margin of land which can be reapportioned among the now landless farmers and refugees from the North. In other words, with an even moderately intelligent policy, southern Viet-Nam should be able to turn the tables on the Viet-Minh and carry out the promises which the Viet-Minh has made during the past seven years, and will find difficult to fulfill in the now greatly impoverished and war-ravaged North.

This the Viet-Minh has clearly recognized. It realizes too, that neither the Soviet Union nor Red China—the latter beset by floods and by urgent relief requests of its other protégé, North Korea—will be able immediately to furnish it with the huge amount of consumer goods it will require. This partly explains the reassurances privately given by Viet-Minh delegates at Geneva to French business interests in North Viet-Nam, that their rights would be respected. There is even a possibility that, for the time being, the Viet-Minh might wish to remain within the French currency bloc.[26]

Does all this mean that truncated South Viet-Nam faces cheerful prospects of independence and security? Far from it. Unlike South Korea, it has no large battle-tested armies. It does not even have a smoothly working local administration. The notable shortcomings of the Bao-Dai regime, both external and internal, have left the country in a state of political chaos, facing the enormous problem of sheltering the northern refugees who now pour in at a rate of more than 3,000 a day, and of administering the large areas of South Viet-Nam and South Annam, recently evacuated by the Viet-Minh, where nearly 4 million Vietnamese have been bombarded with Communist propaganda for more than seven years.

Thus far, the results obtained by the Diem government have been extremely disappointing to everyone concerned. Even in the areas which before the armistice had been solidly in the hands of the nationalist administration, there are now centers of Viet-Minh agitation; and in certain southern provinces, such as My-Tho, Go-Cong, and Bac-Lieu, which hitherto had been considered "paci-

[26] *L'Express*, June 28, 1954.

fied," Viet-Minh civilian tribunals, instead of those of the nationalist administration,[27] are now administering justice. Most big cities in the South, including Saigon, are the scene of Viet-Minh–sponsored parades clamoring for an early reunification of the country.

As for the government itself, it has lost much of its former prestige as a "revolutionary" government. "General" Le Van Vien was still controlling South Viet-Nam's security police months after Diem's rise to power. Diem's government has also failed in other ways to make a clean break with the past and thus catch the imagination of the populace and renew its faith in an independent Viet-Nam, free from both French colonial and Chinese Communist influence. In the words of one disappointed nationalist: "The administrators of M. Diem are the exact image of his government: they are intellectuals practically covered with diplomas but they are inefficient, and one does not stop the Communist tide with diplomas and good manners but with men who have both physical and moral courage.[28]

As for the reforms, both administrative and legislative, which Diem had requested so urgently so long as he was not in power—representative government, governmental responsibility to a parliament, real land reform, etc.—nothing has been undertaken thus far to differentiate the achievements of the Diem administration from those of its more or less ineffectual predecessors. However, Diem did obtain plenary powers from Bao-Dai. Moreover, he suffers from less French interference than his predecessors. In the field of civil liberties or representative government, progress has come to a standstill since the local elections of 1953,[29] and recent measures undertaken by Diem's new Minister of Information, Phan Xuan Thai, which provide a kind of exile in "special zones" and pillorization of all illiterates who have failed to learn how to read within six months, are reminiscent of the Middle Ages. Likewise, the Diem government, instead of making a new approach towards representative government, again meddles with the idea of establishing a wholly *appointive* "National Assembly" made up of "persons designated by the religious groups, the labor unions, re-

27 *Le Monde* (weekly ed.), August 5–11, 1954.
28 *Ibid.*
29 See Chapter 4.

gional assemblies, business associations and professional groups."[30]

Both the anti-illiteracy measure and the creation of an appointive "National Assembly" merely reiterate decrees passed by previous Vietnamese governments.[31] The recent and still unsettled struggle for power between Diem and the Chief of Staff of the Vietnamese National Army, Major General Nguyen Van Hinh, which brought about a complete reorganization of Diem's cabinet in favor of the southern feudal politico-religious sects, has acutely shown Diem's lack of "grip" on the country and has given Bao-Dai another chance to exercise the balance of power among the various rival groups.

There can be no doubt, of course, that the present weak position of the Vietnamese Government is in good part due to Washington's attitude—defeatist as far as Indochina is concerned—and to the changed French attitude which seems again (as it once was in 1946) in favor of dealing with what appears to be the strongest partner on the Indochina scene—the Viet-Minh. Thus, French policy appears to favor a "national reconciliation in which northern Communism should be forced to come to terms with a revitalized southern nationalism."[32] The beginnings of the implementation of such a policy may perhaps be seen in the recent Franco-American conversations in Washington, in which the French Minister for the Associated States, Guy La Chambre, declared that France was ready to evacuate her military forces from Viet-Nam by March, 1956, three months before the elections which will decide Viet-Nam's fate.[33] Among the Vietnamese nationalists, however, there is still a persistent feeling that the French made a "deal" with the Viet-Minh at Geneva, behind the backs of the powerless Vietnamese nationalist delegation, and the latter are not likely to forget the snub they suffered both at Geneva and later at the military truce talks at Trung-Gia in North Viet-Nam. There is also the not unnatural fear that France might use Viet-Nam's present obvious weakness to discredit the most anti-French nationalists, who are now rallied around Diem, until a succeeding, less ultranationalistic

[30] Tillman Durdin, "Vietnam Outlines Stern New Policy," *The New York Times*, September 28, 1954.

[31] See Chapter 4.

[32] Robert Guillain, *Indochine—La fin des illusions* (Paris: Centre d' Etudes de Politique Etrangère, 1954).

[33] *The New York Times*, September 30, 1954.

government might allow them to attempt a "sort of return in strength of colonialism" and a "thinly disguised reestablishment of a protectorate.[34]

There is, nevertheless, a ray of hope for South Viet-Nam. It can still become a testing ground for democracy in the two years before it enters an electoral contest with its Communist rival to the north. Non-Communist Viet-Nam can still reckon with the active help of its Western allies in the field of rehabilitation and even in that of military training, for while no new outside help may come in under the truce terms, Viet-Nam may retain its French and even its United States Military Aid and Assistance Groups,[35] and it is likely that, if necessary, additional technical aid would be provided by appropriate United Nations agencies. Nonetheless, and this the Vietnamese leaders must not forget, final salvation can come only *through their own efforts.* The fundamental political reforms that will differentiate a democratic Viet-Nam from the northern "Democratic Republic" and from such Communist regimes elsewhere in Asia must be carried out by Viet-Nam and not by the United States or France if they are to be successful in the long run. Viet-Nam's rulers will have to muster the courage to face their own people and to stand the test of popular scrutiny. They must also have the moral courage to step down from the rostrum of power and help those who are chosen to replace them, if a free Viet-Nam is to survive. The time is long past for governments by cliques, feudal sects, "spiritual families," "leading personalities," "technicians," or even "untainted intellectuals."* Viet-Nam must have a working government and administration very soon, or, in the words of its former Foreign Minister, Nguyen Quoc Dinh, at the Geneva conference, "history will tell . . . whether it was necessary, in order to end colonial domination . . . to introduce Communism and . . . to become a satellite of China."

[34] Guillain, *op. cit.*
[35] *The New York Times,* July 31 ,1954.

* *This appraisal, written in 1954, has not lost any of its validity in 1966.*

6. Settlement at Geneva— Then and Now

May, 1965

The war in Viet-Nam continues to escalate. Yet, above the sound of mortar fire and jet bombers, one repeatedly hears the phrase "the essentials of the Geneva agreements of 1954." . . . If there is to be an end to the Vietnamese conflict, it seems, it must be on the basis of the Geneva agreements. But just what were they?

There are many interpretations of what the agreements meant. What exactly was signed by whom? There is even a question whether some nations signed anything at all, though they were physically present and listed as full participants. Lastly, there exists the major question, hotly disputed by both sides, as to who violated the agreements first—and how, therefore, a future similar agreement could produce a more adequate machinery to deal with such violations. In order to understand these problems it will be necessary to return briefly to the background of what brought about the Geneva agreements.

Soon after the cease-fire in Korea, in July, 1953, Communist equipment and advisers began to flow more plentifully to Ho Chi Minh's Viet-Minh forces fighting the French in Indochina. Pressure began to build up in France for a negotiated settlement along Korean lines. At the Bermuda conference of December, 1953, President Eisenhower, Prime Minister Churchill, and Premier Joseph Laniel of France decided to discuss the Indochina problem with the Soviet Union at the foreign-minister level.

The foreign ministers, meeting in Berlin, in February, 1954, agreed to a conference of interested powers to discuss both Korea and Indochina, to be held at Geneva toward the end of April,

1954. That was the signal for General Vo Nguyen Giap, Ho's Commander in Chief, to deliver a stunning blow to the French in Indochina, so as to strengthen his side's negotiating position to the utmost.

When the conference began at Geneva on April 27 the ghastly news of the agony of Dien Bien Phu completely overshadowed the Korean part of the negotiation, which soon quagmired into a stalemate. By the time the delegates turned to Indochina on May 8, 1954, Dien Bien Phu had fallen a few hours earlier, and France's Foreign Minister, Georges Bidault, his voice choked with tears, could do little else but to begin the discussion with a eulogy to his country's fallen heroes.

But in areas other than Dien Bien Phu, the war was not going well for France, either. Indeed, only in South Viet-Nam proper was the situation at all encouraging. Terrorism in Saigon had been brought to an almost total standstill, and the Buddhist Cao-Dai and Hoa-Hao sects and Roman Catholic militia units had cleared extensive sections of the Mekong Delta of Viet-Minh control. But the determining factor was the deteriorating situation in the North: Vietnamese morale fell rapidly as the situation worsened.

The Vietnamese National Army, created by France in 1948, counted about 200,000 regulars and 50,000 village militiamen by February, 1954, while another 30,000 Vietnamese served within the 178,000-man French Expeditionary Force in Indochina and another 50,000 Cambodians and Laotians served in the armies of their own countries in the struggle against the Viet-Minh.

On the Communist side, Ho Chi Minh's forces had come a long way from the badly armed guerrilla bands of the mid-1940's. The Viet-Nam People's Army now comprised seven hard-core divisions abundantly equipped with modern American weapons captured by the Chinese in Korea and passed along. The Communist forces, with fewer than 100,000 regulars, 50,000 regional semiregulars, and about 225,000 local guerrillas, were numerically inferior to the French Union troops, but in a type of war where experts believe that the defending force must hold a 10-to-1 superiority in order to win (in 1965 the South Vietnamese and American forces hold a 5-to-1 lead over the Viet-Cong), the French 1.2-to-1 edge made the military contest—all other factors aside—well-nigh hopeless.

The French felt that the only way to tip the scales in their favor

—or at least to prevent an outright military disaster—would be an open military commitment by the United States on their behalf. An American Military Assistance Advisory Group (MAAG) to the French forces in Indochina had been set up as early as July, 1950, and American financial and matériel aid to Indochina had totaled an actual expenditure of $1 billion by the time the fighting stopped.

But the United States was reluctant, so soon after the Korean War, to become embroiled again in an Asian conflict—and one in support of a colonial power, at that. Britain was eager not to jeopardize the chances of a détente between East and West over what seemed a marginal issue at best, and a lost cause at worst.

Besides the Western "big three," the other participants in the talks were the French-sponsored State of Viet-Nam, Laos, and Cambodia on the one hand and, on the other, the Viet-Minh's Democratic Republic of Viet-Nam, Russia, and Communist China. Britain and Russia, in the persons of Foreign Secretary Anthony Eden and Foreign Minister Vyacheslav Molotov, were co-chairmen.

At first, the Saigon delegation insisted on territorial unity for all of Viet-Nam and national elections under U.N. supervision. Considering the progress of the war, the Western powers felt that partition would be unavoidable. The Viet-Minh delegation, like Saigon, at first opted for nationwide elections, but after a hurried meeting between China's Premier Chou En-lai and Ho, it agreed to accept partition into "temporary regroupment areas."

What followed then was merely a "battle of the parallels"— attempts by both sides to enlarge the zones allotted them and to fill in the details of the armistice supervisory machinery—all punctuated by further bad news for the French and Vietnamese as their military efforts failed and Saigon's administrative machinery slowly disintegrated.

The American delegation, under pressure from home not to give the impression of "approving" a "surrender to Communism," had for all practical purposes ceased to influence events. Secretary Dulles had left Geneva on May 4, even before the Indochina conference began. In President Eisenhower's words, the "American delegation [was] downgraded to an 'observer' mission." This attempt at saving face at home was to have important consequences as the negotiations reached their climax.

It must be remembered that the Geneva agreements were *military cease-fire* agreements, though negotiated at the highest political and diplomatic level. The actual signature of the agreements and their ultimate execution were to be reserved to *military* authorities on both sides.

On July 20, agreement was reached on Viet-Nam when the hitherto intractable Molotov relented and made the Viet-Minh accept the 17th parallel as the cease-fire line (though it meant relinquishing territory they held in the south). Separate agreements on Laos and Cambodia remained to be worked out, but by about 2 o'clock the next morning the package was completed.

Brigadier General Henri Délteil, representing the French Army High Command in Indochina, signed first. Brigadier General Ta Quang Buu, Oxford-educated and a former leader of the French-sponsored Vietnamese Boy Scout Movement, signed for the Viet-Minh and invited Delteil to share a glass of champagne with him. Delteil quietly said: "I am sure that you understand that this is not possible." At 3:43 A.M. of July 21, 1954, the First Indochina War was over.

The document signed by the two generals was officially known as an "Agreement on the Cessation of Hostilities in Viet-Nam," covering forty-seven articles and a brief annex on the geographic delineation of the regroupment areas. Chapter I of the agreement deals with the establishment of a demarcation line and a demilitarized zone on the 17th parallel, and Chapter II with the technicalities of moving troops and equipment through each other's area. In that section, one important article, number 14, has a bearing on present events:

> a—Pending the general elections which will bring about the unification of Viet-Nam, the conduct of civil administration in each regrouping zone shall be in the hands of the party whose forces are to be regrouped there in virtue of the present agreement. . . .
>
> c—Each party undertakes to refrain from any reprisals or discrimination against persons or organizations on account of their activities during the hostilities and to guarantee their democratic liberties.
>
> d—. . . until the movement of troops is completed, any civilians residing in a district controlled by one party who wish to go and live

in the zone assigned to the other party shall be permitted and helped to do so by the authorities in that district.

It is Chapter III, however, which constitutes the heart of the agreement, with its ban on the introduction of new troops and weapons and of new military bases. Article 17 bans "reinforcements" (that is, increases above replacement of equipment already there) "in the form of all types of . . . war matériel, such as combat aircraft, naval craft, jet engines and jet weapons, and armored vehicles." Article 18 prohibits "the establishment of new military bases . . . throughout Viet-Nam territory," and Article 19 makes the following important points:

> . . . no military base under the control of a foreign state may be established in the regrouping zone of either party; the two parties shall ensure that the zones assigned to them do not adhere to any military alliance and are not used for the resumption of hostilities or to further an aggressive policy.

Article 24 contains a potentially potent clause in its quiet reminder that both sides are to respect the "territory under control of the other party and shall not engage in blockade of any kind in Viet-Nam."

The final section of the agreement deals with the establishment of an International Commission for Supervision and Control. The ICSC[1] was to be composed (and still is) of Canadian, Indian, and Polish members, with India presiding, and was to set up fixed and mobile teams to supervise the execution of the cease-fire provisions. Its decisions on procedural matters were to be decided by majority vote, but all decisions dealing with substantive violations must be taken unanimously. And that is, of course, where the system failed.

An important adjunct to the ICSC was to be a system of Joint Commissions (JC) composed of representatives of the two opposing armies and operating in small teams. Their role was particularly important when it came to extricating the various irregular units infiltrated in remote areas and in settling dangerous incidents on the spot. (As will be seen, they were abolished later at South Viet-Nam's request.)

The agreement left the political arrangements for Viet-Nam unresolved. They were settled at Geneva later in the day on July 21,

---

[1] Also known as the ICC.

in the course of the final meeting of the conferees, presided over by Anthony Eden. One by one, he read off the list of documents that were part of the conference record, adding: "Finally, gentlemen, there is a draft declaration by the conference which takes note of all these documents."

In turn, every conference member spoke his approval of the draft declaration: Britain, France, Laos, Red China, the Soviet Union, Cambodia, the Democratic Republic of Viet-Nam—there were no disclaimers so far.

Then it was the turn of Under Secretary of State Walter Bedell Smith of the United States. Smith stated that "my Government is not prepared to join in a declaration by the conference such as is submitted." Instead, he submitted a separate declaration in which the United States affirmed that it would "refrain from the threat or the use of force to disturb" the agreements but would view "any renewal of the aggression in violation of the aforesaid agreements with grave concern and as seriously threatening international peace and security." Smith added that, in the "case of nations divided against their will," the United States supported efforts "to achieve unity through free elections, supervised by the United Nations. . . ."

This left the delegation from the State of Viet-Nam to be heard from. The nominal head of state, former Emperor Bao-Dai, had just named the courageous nationalist Ngo Dinh Diem to be Premier. Diem's Foreign Minister and delegate at Geneva was Dr. Tran Van Do, a former chief of the Vietnamese Army's medical service and a man with a reputation of towering integrity. (He was to break with Diem a few months later over the latter's growing authoritarianism; he was imprisoned by Diem; now he is again South Viet-Nam's Foreign Minister.) Cold-shouldered by everyone, Dr. Do had fought a lonely battle, trying to save his country from partition and what then seemed imminent domination by Ho Chi Minh.

Dr. Do now rose to make a final plea, but the matter was obviously considered settled by everyone else. All that he could obtain was that the other conferees "take note" of the State of Viet-Nam's promise "not to use force to resist the procedures for carrying the cease-fire into effect." A few minutes later, he informed Diem in Saigon by cable of the failure of his mission. . . . But the final Declaration stood.

Articles 6 and 7 of the Final Declaration were to be of deep significance for Viet-Nam:

> The essential purpose of the agreement relating to Viet-Nam is to settle military questions with a view to ending hostilities. . . . The military demarcation line is provisional and should not in any way be considered as constituting a political or territorial boundary. . . .
> So far as Viet-Nam is concerned, the settlement of political problems, effected on the basis of respect for the principles of independence, unity and territorial integrity, shall permit the Vietnamese people to enjoy fundamental freedoms, guaranteed by democratic institutions established as a result of free general elections by secret ballot. . . . General elections shall be held in July, 1956, under the supervision of an international commission composed of the Member States of the International Supervisory Commission. . . .

There is no question as to the language of that declaration: It fully prescribes the mechanism of general elections for all Viet-Nam, to be held two years hence. But there is some question as to the declaration's form—for it was an *unsigned document*.

This fact has not entirely escaped astute observers, and surely was not an oversight on the part of the negotiators in either camp. Two authoritative French writers, Jean Lacouture and Philippe Devillers, in a book on the Geneva negotiations,[2] have noted that this absence of a signature "would permit [the participants] to act as if the organization of elections in Viet-Nam within two years had been a simple project" rather than a formal commitment. They added: "The Geneva conference will thus have invented a new form of peaceful coexistence—that which results from the tacit consent of the negotiators—as well as a new form of legal obligation between states: the unsigned treaty."

The question of why the Communists accepted a document whose legal force was so questionable has never been satisfactorily resolved. Some authorities say that, since South Viet-Nam was expected to collapse anyway, the two-year provision was a mere face-saver for the West (just like the clause in the 1962 transfer of West Irian from the Netherlands to Indonesia, which provides for "free elections" for the hapless Papuans in 1969). Others hold that, on the contrary, Hanoi accepted the final declaration, knowing that it would never be implemented, in preference to a con-

---

[2] *La fin d'une guerre* (Paris: Editions du Seuil, 1960).

tinuation of the war and the always possible chance of American intervention on the French side—even at the late date. In view of the situation then prevailing in Viet-Nam, the first of the two hypotheses seems the more convincing.

In Viet-Nam itself, the state of affairs which resulted from the Geneva settlement was grim: 860,000 refugees—more than 500,000 of them Catholics—began to pour into what was now rapidly becoming "South Viet-Nam"—i.e., Viet-Nam south of the new demarcation line at the 17th parallel. North of the line, stolid-faced Viet-Minh regulars began to occupy the cities and towns left behind by withdrawing French troops.

Some 190,000 Franco-Vietnamese troops moved south of the demarcation line, although many of the Vietnamese whose home villages were in the North preferred to desert in order not to be separated from their families. In the South, it is now admitted (though it was carefully hushed up at the time), perhaps as many as 80,000 local guerrillas and regulars and their dependents, including almost 10,000 mountain tribesmen, went northward.

Perhaps another 5,000 to 6,000 local hard-core guerrillas—probably the elite of the Viet-Minh's military and political operators in the South—simply went underground. They hid their weapons and radio equipment and became anonymous villagers—at least for a while. In the cities, others, such as the Viet-Cong's present leader, Nguyen Huu Tho, created "legal struggle" organizations with the aim of propagating the new catch-phrase of "peace and reunification in two years." They, however, were soon disbanded or arrested by the Saigon police.

In Saigon, the fledgling Diem regime was trying to cope both with the administrative chaos resulting from partition and the influx of refugees, and with the challenges against its survival from various political and religious groups and sects. The government's chances of surviving even as long as the two-year election deadline were rated as poor. President Eisenhower summed up the situation in his memoirs:

> I have never talked or corresponded with a person knowledgeable in Indochinese affairs who did not agree that had elections been held as of the time of the fighting, possibly 80 per cent of the population would have voted for the Communist Ho Chi Minh as their leader rather than Chief of State Bao-Dai.

Since the North controlled a population of more than 15 million and the South fewer than 12 million, and since the North could be trusted to "deliver" its electorate in overwhelming numbers, such an election would beyond a doubt have resulted in a peaceful takeover of all of Viet-Nam by Ho Chi Minh in July, 1956. (It is worth noting that Diem disposed of Bao-Dai by a rigged plebiscite, held in 1955. Diem got 98.8 per cent of the vote. Diem was overthrown and assassinated in a coup in 1963; Bao-Dai is now living in France.)

Little wonder, then, that the Diem government almost immediately took the position that the Geneva agreements, signed by a foreign military command (i.e., the French) "in contempt of Vietnamese national interests," were not binding upon it. It not only refused to consult with its northern counterpart about elections, but it also turned down repeated proposals by North Viet-Nam to normalize economic and postal regulations, arguing that "we cannot entertain any Communist proposal as long as we do not have evidence that they place the interests of the Fatherland above those of Communism."

That attitude amounted in fact to an economic blockade—which hurt, for North Viet-Nam had until then received an average of more than 200,000 tons a year of southern rice to cover its internal food deficit.

The French, already embroiled in the beginnings of a new colonial war in Algeria, offered little argument when the Diem regime requested in February, 1956 (that is, before the July deadline on elections), that they withdraw their troops. The French High Command in Indochina, which had been the formal signer of the 1954 Geneva agreements, was dissolved on April 26, 1956. Some hotheads in Saigon toyed with the idea of declaring the Geneva accords null. Indeed, carefully coached mobs ransacked the Saigon offices and billets of the International Commission for Supervision and Control on the first anniversary of the Geneva cease-fire.

But cooler counsel prevailed (some say, at American behest) and a few days before the July, 1956, deadline for national elections, the South Vietnamese Foreign Secretary, while denouncing the validity of the agreements, established what he called "*de facto* cooperation" with the ICSC. The Joint Commissions, however, were soon abolished; Saigon argued that the North Vietnamese members stationed in Saigon were engaging in subversive activities and obtained their recall in 1957.

As for the elections, the deadline passed without either a ballot or undue incident. Both North Viet-Nam and the Soviet Union made protests against this apparent violation of the Geneva agreements, but both South Viet-Nam and the United States—the latter in a statement by Walter S. Robertson, then Assistant Secretary of State, on June 1, 1956—argued that North Viet-Nam already had violated the cease-fire provisions with regard to increases in troops and equipment, as well as with regard to the freedom-of-movement provisions. Indeed, in a diplomatic note sent in April, 1956, by Britain to the Soviet Government, as co-chairman of the Geneva conference, London pointed out that North Vietnamese regular units had increased from seven to twenty divisions.

In the South, difficulties arose over such matters as the entry and departure of military equipment and American advisers, about whose exact numbers there were disagreements from the start. The ICSC complained, in its January, 1957, report, that "while the commission has experienced difficulties in North Viet-Nam, the major part of its difficulties has arisen in South Viet-Nam."

As for the North Vietnamese, the passage of the July, 1956, election deadline was the signal that South Viet-Nam would not come to terms willingly. As long as there was even a remote chance of peaceful reunification, Hanoi—as well as the guerrilla stay-behinds inside South Viet-Nam—had presented to the outside world a picture of sweet reasonableness: after all, there was hardly any point in risking international goodwill, as well as valuable cadres, to hasten what was assumed to be an orderly takeover.

But within a few months after the deadline had passed in 1956, the killing of village chiefs in South Viet-Nam began—by stay-behind guerrillas, not the "outside aggressors" of 1959–60 cited by the recent State Department white paper. By the time the South Viet-Nam problem had become a military challenge to the United States late in 1961, the Second Indochina War had been under way for almost five years.

In all this turmoil, the ICSC led an increasingly shadowy and ineffectual life. If the North Vietnamese interfered with the freedom-of-movement provisions of the cease-fire, the South Vietnamese interfered with the section dealing with reprisals against former enemy combatants. They finally informed the commission that they would no longer provide it with information in the matter. An order issued by Diem in January, 1956, providing for indefinite detention in concentration camps of all those "who are considered dangerous for national defense and public security," gave an inkling of what was going on, however.

Soon, both sides were openly violating the armament provisions of the cease-fire. Personal observations in both zones have provided me with my own stock of ludicrous stories about nonenforcement, such as that of U.S. warplanes being landed by an aircraft carrier in sight of Saigon's main thoroughfare, while a handsomely turbaned Indian ICSC officer said: "Yes—but *officially* we have not been informed of the presence of the aircraft carrier."

Or there is the response given to the ICSC by the Hanoi government, when the commission wanted to inspect the largest airfield in North Viet-Nam, Haiphong's Cat-Bi airport:

"But you cannot visit that airport."

"Why not?" asked the ICSC representative.

"Because it belongs to a private flying club—and private property is exempted from commission control."

Not that the commission did not try to do its job. In June, 1962, its legal committee, by a two-to-one vote (Poland dissenting), found that "there is evidence to show that the PAVN [People's Army of Viet-Nam] has allowed the zone in the North to be used for inciting, encouraging and supporting hostile activities in the Zone in the South, aimed at the overthrow of the Administration in the South . . . in violation of Articles 19, 24 and 27 of the agreement. . . ." That part of the report, pleasant to Western ears, finds itself widely reported to this day.

What is somewhat less prominently displayed is Paragraph 20 of the same report, in which the commission, by the same majority, concludes that "the Republic of Viet-Nam [i.e., South Viet-Nam] has violated Articles 16 and 17 of the Geneva agreement in receiving increased military aid from the United States," and that the "establishment of a U.S. Military Assistance Command in South Viet-Nam, as well as the introduction of a large number of U.S.

military personnel . . . amounts to a factual military alliance, which is prohibited under Article 19 of the Geneva agreement."

The recent American air raids on North Viet-Nam gave rise to another split report—this time with India and Poland voting in the majority. On February 13, 1965, both nations addressed to the British and Soviet co-chairmen a note pointing to the "seriousness of the situation and indicat[ing] violations of the Geneva agreement," while the Canadian member argued that the American raids could not be taken out of the wider context of being "the direct result of the intensification of the aggressive policy of the Government of North Viet-Nam." The two co-chairmen failed to act on either report.

Within South Viet-Nam, ICSC teams have found it increasingly difficult to move about, the Saigon government arguing that it cannot guarantee their security. In North Viet-Nam, the Hanoi government has demanded their recall—on the grounds that their lives were being endangered by American air raids. There matters stand.

Where did the old agreements fail, and how could new (or renovated) agreements do better?

1) The original 1954 agreements failed politically and economically before they even failed militarily. There can be no doubt but that the Diem regime's total intransigence in the field of trade relations—whose existence (as in the case of the two Germanys) could have eased the situation considerably—contributed to a rapid exacerbation of the conflict. It is a documented fact that until 1958 Hanoi made repeated overtures for low-level agreements with the South, all of which were turned down by Saigon.

2) The constant drumfire of the Saigon government against the 1954 agreements did not enhance respect for the agreements on either side of the demarcation line. The fact that the other Western participants in the 1954 conference did not, at least publicly, reaffirm their support of the "essentials" of the agreements must have given considerable encouragement to the activists in Hanoi who saw in the Geneva cease-fire a mere way station to ultimate domination of all of Viet-Nam—if not all of Indochina.

3) The sudden development of respect for the ICSC by South Viet-Nam and the United States as the situation inside South Viet-

Nam worsened in the early 1960's added ammunition to Hanoi's contention that the ICSC had come down on the side of the West. From a tone of polite solicitousness toward the ICSC, the Ho regime became increasingly vituperative. After the June, 1962, ICSC report, Hanoi (this writer was there at the time) was treated to the spectacle of a "public demonstration" against the commission.

4) On the Western side, the obvious ineffectualness of the ICSC in dealing with guerrilla depredations as distinct from overt invasion (contrast this record with those of truce commissions in Korea, Palestine, the Sinai, or Cyprus) augurs ill for yet another such experiment. In Laos, the commission neither stops the Pathet-Lao and its North Vietnamese sponsors from attacking in the Plaine des Jarres or from using staging areas, nor does it stop American jets from operating all over the country at will.

A new, or "renovated," Geneva conference would have to embody conditions and an enforcement mechanism stronger than now exist. There are some encouraging signs that the West and, perhaps to a lesser degree, Moscow (though probably not yet Hanoi, and certainly not Peking) would be willing to accept a somewhat more realistic attitude toward the problem than prevailed under John Foster Dulles and Diem in 1954.

Relations with the other side, far from being considered a mortal sin, may now include, as President Johnson has indicated, some sort of economic "carrot"—of which direct aid may perhaps be less important to Hanoi than the removal of the *de facto* economic blockade with which it has been surrounded since 1954.

President Johnson's affirmation at Baltimore that South Viet-Nam shall be free to "shape its relationships to all others" constitutes a definite return to the spirit of the Geneva agreements of 1954, just as did the late President Kennedy's statement of March 23, 1961, about Laos: "And if in the past there has been any possible ground for misunderstanding of our desire for a truly neutral Laos, there should be none now."

All this leaves open the potentially most explosive of all the "essentials" of Geneva: reunification. Diplomats and scholars will debate for decades as to whether an unsigned declaration was a binding diplomatic document, or whether the whole promise of general elections in Viet-Nam was a mere sop thrown to the North Vietnamese for their surrender, under Sino-Russian pressure, of vast tracts of territory south of the 17th parallel.

There is a larger dimension to the problem: One cannot be for reunification for Germany and Korea (where the non-Communist population vastly exceeds that in the Communist-held areas) and deny the same right to the Vietnamese (whose northern zone is more populous).

The official American view on this issue seems to be that expressed by McGeorge Bundy in a public interview in April, 1965: "I don't think we ever felt that there was any bar in the long run to working out a future of Viet-Nam which would not necessarily be divided." Or, as another White House aide expressed it more colorfully, but privately: "When the subject [of eventual reunification] came up, nobody fell over the table and vomited."

Obviously, no one has in mind handing over South Viet-Nam to any Vietnamese regime that is, in the American view, a mere Communist Chinese proxy, but some sort of progressive cooperation between the two zones seems not excluded.

There still remains the issue of policing whatever new arrangements might be made, but perhaps here the difficulties are less real than apparent. First of all, the violations against which there must be a guarantee are no longer of the kind which were important in 1954. It is more important to keep down, say, the number of battalion-size Viet-Cong attacks *inside* South Viet-Nam than to watch whether either the United States or China sends jets into Viet-Nam. Joint North–South Vietnamese cease-fire teams under the control of an international supervisory body (as in the case in Palestine) could be useful.

Yet, all the discussions about an international settlement of the Vietnamese problem must not hide the fact that in one essential item the situation may well have changed radically since 1954:

During the First Indochina War there was no question that Ho Chi Minh was the uncontested master of all guerrilla operation throughout Indochina. General Giap's People's Army could enforce a cease-fire and a withdrawal of Viet-Minh forces from south of the 17th parallel without much difficulty.

Whether the Viet-Cong, after eight years of fighting on its own account and after taking tremendous losses, would be willing to give up all that it has gained through fighting and subversion, simply to please the dictates of Hanoi—just as Hanoi gave up the South in 1954 to comply with the long-range policies of its outside backers—is not certain.

After all, it must be remembered, in 1954 both Russia and Red China were putting pressure on Ho to comply with such a pull-out. Today, Peking might well put its pressure on Hanoi in the opposite sense. Or—failing this—Peking might even leapfrog Hanoi in order to help the Viet-Cong sabotage any agreement that Hanoi might subscribe to at the southern guerrillas' expense.

All these considerations must weigh heavily in the balance as policy-makers survey the broken hopes left from the first Geneva agreement on Viet-Nam, and as the dim outlines of yet another negotiated settlement of the same problem begin to appear on the horizon.

PART II

The North:
Two Decades of Revolution

The Communist zone of Viet-Nam, whether omnipresent around every French "enclave" from 1946 until 1954 or in the form of a separate state called the Democratic Republic of Viet-Nam (D.R.V.N.) after the Geneva cease-fire agreements, was first and foremost the product of a small but determined band of excellent guerrilla leaders soon supplemented by vast masses of increasingly well-controlled peasants.

After an initial crisis retrieved with great agility by the aged leader Ho Chi Minh, the North Vietnamese state began to build a state-controlled, semi-industrial economy. A firsthand look at North Viet-Nam clearly revealed the intrinsic strength of the young state and its army, but also its vulnerability in case of an enlarged conflict with the United States.

At present, the D.R.V.N. is a direct partner to the confrontation between the United States and Communism in Southeast Asia, as well as to the confrontation between the Soviet Union and the People's Republic of China. Both roles are difficult at best, and there is some evidence that the split between the pro-Russian and pro-Chinese factions may widen under the pressure of events. It remains to be seen, however, whether such a widening split would improve the position of the United States in the area and reduce the threat of Communist insurgency in Southeast Asia.

7. The Grass-Roots Rebellion

March, 1954

When the provisional government of Ho Chi Minh first gained control of North and Central Viet-Nam during the summer of 1945, it found there the traditional administration as preserved with little modification by the French colonial administration, with its councils of notables (sometimes elected but mostly appointed and hereditary) and elders, presided over at the provincial level by a French administrator. Stable (or stagnant) as it was, this machinery had continued to work even after all the French personnel had been interned by the Japanese, since the small Vietnamese village is generally autonomous by tradition[1] and self-sufficient by economic necessity.[2] The arrival of the young revolutionary elements of the Viet-Minh in the villages had the effect of the proverbial stone in the village pond. In the words of Pierre Gourou, one of the most respected French experts on Indochinese affairs, "armed adolescents have replaced the peaceful councils of notables. This is not necessarily an improvement." It certainly was a drastic change and, in less than eighteen months, did more to alter the political-administrative aspect of the Vietnamese countryside than did the Vietnamese emperors since 938 A.D. or the French since 1862.

While the first attempts at local administration on the part of the Viet-Minh were haphazard, the very fact that village autonomy was so deeply rooted made an ideal breeding ground for the type

[1] An old Vietnamese proverb states: "The power of the Emperor stops at the bamboo hedge." (Each village is generally circled by a bamboo hedge.)

[2] See Paul Mus, "The Role of the Village in Vietnamese Politics," *Pacific Affairs*, September, 1949, pp. 265–72, and his excellent book *Viet-Nam, Sociologie d'une Guerre* (Paris: Editions du Seuil, 1952).

Reprinted, by permission, from *Pacific Affairs* (Vancouver), March, 1954. © 1954 by *Pacific Affairs*. Originally published as "Local Administration Under the Viet-Minh."

of local administration found in the early postrevolutionary years in the Soviet Union. Indeed, "the decentralizing policy practiced by the revolutionary government presented great anaolgies with that applied by the Communist government of Soviet Russia."[3]

As stated in the constitution of 1946, Viet-Nam was divided into three main administrative units (*bo*), with each *bo* divided into provinces, prefectures, districts, villages, quarters (i.e., boroughs), and urban areas. The lower territorial units (up to province) elect People's Councils "by direct suffrage" (Article 58), which in turn elect their own executive committees; while the higher echelon units (*bo* and "interzones," or *lien-khu*, which, though not mentioned in the constitution, have become major territorial units) only elect an Executive Committee by the indirect vote of the People's Councils of its subordinated territorial units.

It is in this particular section of the republican constitution that the parallelism with the Soviet system is quite apparent:

> The general assembly of the Soviet elects from its membership an executive committee. . . . In localities the administrative power belongs to the Soviets, in whose jurisdiction must be all the institutions of administrative, economic, financial and educational characters. . . . All previous orders of local governments . . . must be replaced by respective (regional, provincial, and county) Soviets.[4]

Similarly, the functions of the committees closely follow those described by Lenin in *The Rights and Duties of Local Soviets* with but minor differences. An extremely detailed description of the various local administrative bodies with their relationships and functions was published in the form of a decree on November 22, 1945—i.e., a full year before the promulgation of the constitution.[5] These bodies all had certain common characteristics: first, there was a uniform two-year tenure of office; second, eligibility requirements were liberally interpreted; and third, differences over election results were settled administratively by the next higher

[3] Vu Quoc Thong, *La Décentralisation Administrative au Viet Nam* (mimeo.; Hanoi: Presses Universitaires du Viet Nam, 1952), p. 295.

[4] See *Provisional Workers' and Peasants' Government Gazette* (St. Petersburg), No. 21, January 6, 1918.

[5] *Viet-Nam Dan-quoc Cong Bao* (Official Journal of the Democratic Republic of Viet-Nam; cited henceforth as D.R.V.N. *Official Journal*), Vol. I, Decree No. 63, November 22, 1945, pp. 131–97.

echelon. At every echelon, there was a deliberating body directly elected by the population, the Hoi Dong Nhan Dan, or Popular Assembly; and an executive arm elected by the Popular Assembly from among its own members, along French or Soviet parliamentary methods of procedure, namely the Uy Ban Hanh Chinh, or Administrative Committee.[6]

The Village Popular Assembly (Hoi Dong Nhan Dan-xa) generally contains ten to twenty-five members and five to seven alternates, depending upon the size of the community. Voting requirements are similar to those of the general election, but include in addition a residence requirement of three months prior to the election date. Military and administrative personnel assigned to a given village are considered residents regardless of length of actual residence. Eligibility requirements for candidates include a six-month residence in the village and no exception is made for military and administrative personnel wishing to participate in the election.

The Provincial Popular Assembly (Hoi dong Nhan dan tinh) has twenty to thirty-five members and five alternates, with each district (*huyen*) represented proportionally to its population. All voters registered on the village rolls within the province are automatically eligible to vote and, surprisingly enough, there are no residence requirements (Article 35). The law does not specifically authorize military and administrative personnel to participate in such elections, but this seems to have been a mere oversight on the part of the legislators. In actual practice, such personnel fully participate in local and national politics, as under the Soviet system.

Municipal Popular Assemblies (Hoi Dong Nhan Dan Thanh Pho, or Hoi Dong Nhan Thi-xa): the Regional Administrative Committees[7] were given the power to create or to dissolve municipalities,[8] and eight cities were given autonomous municipal status throughout Viet-Nam: Hanoi (the capital), Haiphong, Nam-Dinh, Vinh, Ben-Thuy, Hue, Da-Nang (better known under the French

---

[6] For the reader unfamiliar with Vietnamese administrative units, the following are the most recurrent: xa (village), huyen (district), tinh (province), thi xa ("big village," e.g., city), khu (zone), and ky (region).

[7] There are three regions (*ky*) in Viet-Nam: North, Central, and South.

[8] D.R.V.N. *Official Journal*, Vol. I, Art. 1 of Decree No. 77, December 21, 1945.

name of Tourane), and Saigon-Cholon. Voting requirements were the same as in the village assemblies and eligibility requirements were as liberal as those of the provinces. Military personnel were specifically authorized to vote and to be elected.[9]

The Administrative Committees (Uy Ban Hanh Chinh), as stated above, were the executive branch of local government at every level, but at the same time must "carry out orders issued by higher authorities"—e.g., the central government or the next higher territorial echelon. The Administrative Committee is also "responsible to higher authorities" before it is responsible "to its own People's Council."[10]

There were generally five echelons of Administrative Committees: the three named above and the district and regional committees, whose duties were at first strictly administrative and which were elected not by the population at large but by the administrative committee of the subordinate territorial echelons.[11]

The Administrative Committees had the following characteristics: (1) Each had one chairman, one vice-chairman and one secretary. (2) All were elected by indirect suffrage, with separate elections for the three above-named posts, with the exception of the Regional Committee, where all elections took place at the same time in one single vote. (3) Tenure of office is generally two years, with the exception of the Regional Committee's, where the tenure is three years. City borough (thanh pho) committees are elected for one year. (4) Conditions of ineligibility or incompatibility include husband and wife, a parent and two children, three brothers or sisters on the same committee. Likewise, while military and administrative personnel were eligible, they could not retain their official functions while serving on the Committee.[12] There are, however, strong indications that the latter regulation is not strictly observed.[13] (5) The Administrative Committees are generally quite

[9] Ibid., Art. 6.
[10] D.R.V.N. constitution, Chap. V, Arts. 59 and 60.
[11] Vu Quoc Thong, op. cit., p. 296.
[12] D.R.V.N. Official Journal, Arts. 64 and 65 of Decree No. 63, November 23, 1945.
[13] Even at the highest echelon, elected members of government fill at the same time administrative posts: Ton Duc Thang, President of the Permanent Commission, is Special General Inspector of Political and Administrative Affairs, and one of his colleagues on the Commission, T. Q. Phiet, is Chairman of the UBKC at Quang-Nam.

small. At village level they include five members, including its president, vice-president, treasurer, and secretary, and a commissar in charge of security matters, as well as two alternates. At district level, there are only three regular members and two alternates. The Provincial and Municipal Committees are similarly organized. The Regional Committee, like the local committees, has five regular and two alternate members.

While it cannot be denied that the various local administrative bodies were originally endowed with wide powers within their territorial limits, those powers were progressively curtailed as the republican government consolidated its position in the country. A circular from the Ministry of Interior (whose powers resemble more those of the Soviet Ministry of Interior than those of the U.S. Department of Interior) specifically states that all orders and regulations issued must be in full accord with similar decisions of every higher echelon, a provision which practically nullifies whatever legislative power there was in the hands of the local assemblies except on very narrow local issues.[14]

Likewise, even on local issues, any decision taken by a local unit of government has to be passed on to the next higher echelon for approval, and is inoperative in the meantime. If after a delay of five days, the District Committee (in the case of a village) has expressed no objection, the decision becomes operative. However, in the case of a decision affecting communal property, the tacit agreement of the higher echelon is not sufficient and specific approval has to be secured. Some questions considered strictly local matters from the Western point of view (local taxes, budget, public works, etc.) even require approval of the next higher echelon, the Provincial Administrative Committee.[15] In turn, provincial administrative tasks require the ratification of the regional authorities—with a fifteen-day delay before implementation—and the region cannot approve the majority of the legislative acts of its provinces without prior referral to the full Council of Ministers.[16]

The cumbersome nature of such an administrative structure is obvious. Indeed, it successfully amalgamates the worst aspects of rule by committee with those of "democratic centralism" while the

[14] D.R.V.N. *Official Journal*, Art. 66 of Decree No. 63, November 23, 1945.
[15] *Ibid.*, Art. 70.
[16] *Ibid.*, Art 85.

paucity of communications and trained personnel soon creates administrative bottlenecks at the higher echelons, thus seriously disrupting the national governmental process.

To sum up, the committees at various echelons have the duty to control the activities of the subordinate committees and assemblies; to approve certain decisions made by subordinate levels of administration; and (in the case of the regional committees) to decide appeals of the communal administration against decisions of the provincial authorities, and to promulgate the legislation necessary for regional application of nationwide decisions of the central government. Also, both the regional and the provincial committees have the right in an emergency to call on the help of the armed forces stationed in their territories—subject, of course, to later endorsement of the measure by the central government.

The outbreak of hostilities on December 19, 1946, did not immediately bring about a change in the administrative structure of the territory controlled by the republican government. A few months later, however, both the need for a strong integration of the whole population into a system of total war and for better ideological control brought about the suspension sine die of the Popular Assemblies and the "merger" of the Administrative Committees at every echelon with the local unofficial "Resistance Committees" of the Dang Lao-Dong (Viet-Nam Workers' Party) and Lien-Viet (League for the National Union of Viet-Nam). The former was created in February, 1951, to succeed the old Indochina Communist Party dissolved in 1945. The Lien-Viet includes all youth and patriotic organizations in the Viet-Minh area. The Viet-Minh merged with the Lien-Viet in 1951, but its name has remained in general use.

In other words, every administrative committee—and many at that time were still not entirely in the hands of the Viet-Minh— was manned simply by a cadre of appointed political officials. The new committees thus created were named Uy Ban Khang Chien Hanh Chinh (UBKCHC), or "Committees for Resistance and Administration," followed by the unit of its administrative level ("UBKCHC-xa," or "Village Committee for Resistance Administration," etc.).

As the war spread over greater areas and many sectors fell into French Union hands during the early stages of the campaign, the republican government decided to create administrative units that were integrated with the military commands, particularly in sectors contiguous to French-held areas. This brought about the creation, on an informal basis at first, of "zones" (*khu*) and groups of villages, districts, or provinces, i.e., territories of overlapping territorial units lumped together under a single administrative authority generally articulated with the local military command zones. These units are known as "interzones," "interprovinces," etc. (*lien-khu, lien-tinh*, etc.) The region (*ky*) seems to have been abandoned as an administrative unit in favor of the zone (*khu*) and interzone (*lien-khu*).

One cannot say, however, that government by legislation has entirely disappeared from the territory of the Republic. According to Viet-Minh reports in January, 1954, the National Assembly of the Democratic Republic of Viet-Nam which had not met since 1946, convened in North Viet-Nam during the first week of December, 1953. Out of 444 members, 177 attended and ratified the land reform decree of May 20, 1953, which thus becomes the law of the land.

The republican government still seems to rely upon popular elections for the nomination of the *administrative* members of the UBKCHC. A decree of February, 1948, shows that the committees of Viet-Nam were classified into three categories according to their political reliability:

Category A. Villages entirely under the control of the Government. Universal suffrage should be applied to them (if it does not hamper the good execution of military operations).

Category B. Villages not entirely under the control of the Government, or (though within the controlled zone) could not participate in universal suffrage without gravely prejudicing military operations (*résistance*). Only persons of both sexes belonging to Peoples' Troops (*Dan Quan*) or National Salvation Units (*Cu'u Quoc*) may participate.

Category C. Villages situated in enemy territory.[17]

Three years after the outbreak of the hostilities, the republican government apparently accepted the idea that the war was going

[17] Document captured by French Union Forces in Gia-Dinh province (South Viet-Nam) on May 10, 1948. Parentheses in original text.

to be protracted, and promulgated a special set of regulations designed to reinstate the Popular Assemblies in a somewhat streamlined form. A series of decrees on the "Organization of Power during the Period of Resistance"[18] contains, substantially, the following innovations:

> Article XII. Should the Communal Popular Assembly make a decision *contrary to higher orders*, this order is not only annulled . . . but the UBKCHC of the district will issue a warning. Should the Communal Assembly refuse to comply, the Provincial UBKCHC may pronounce its dissolution.
>
> Article XIII. After dissolution of the Assembly, the provincial UBKCHC . . . shall *designate* a provisional committee.

The two legislative texts do not show whether the designated committee would eventually be replaced by a new elected committee. Other articles take cognizance of the increasingly difficult situation in transmitting legislation for higher approval and the various transmittal periods are therefore increased from five to eight days (Article XXIV),[19] while another article now specifically provides for higher approval of the nominations of UBKCHC chairmen at all levels (Article XXXIV).

The administrative load falling on the average village in the republican government zone exceeds anything a community of similar size would have to bear anywhere outside the Iron Curtain and seriously burdens the available personnel. In one typical example, the Tien-Hai district in North Viet-Nam, the UBKCHC chairman assumes "full responsibility" for everything; the vice chairman is in charge in the absence of the chairman and is also the town "sheriff"; the secretary is in charge of all the paperwork and keeps the minutes of the committee sessions; together with the chairman and vice chairman (the secretary acting as recorder) they constitute the judicial committee, the basic unit of the judicial system.

One member of the committee is in charge of the finances; another of "economic problems" (direction of the village cooperative

---

[18] D.R.V.N. Decree No. 254/SL of November 11, 1948, and Regulation No. 82/SD of March 13, 1949.

[19] This excessive paperwork constantly traveling to and fro throughout Viet-Nam is one of the major sources of French Union intelligence. Lately, local authorities have complained against this "bureaucratism."

and checking of goods smuggled in from the French Union zone); a third, of Peoples' Troops, guerrillas, and the watch service; a fourth, of education, public works, and road maintenance. The District Committee found that the fourth man was not fully occupied and in addition entrusted him with running the compulsory labor service of the village.

There can be no doubt that the average Vietnamese villager, already harassed by his unusual struggle with the elements to earn his livelihood and by the ever-present threat of enemy air raids or ground attacks, has lost much of his erstwhile eagerness to participate in the always festive occasions of political meetings, elections, and discussions.

The republican government had to find out for itself that elections and meetings can be too much of a good thing and that, past a certain point, agricultural work and war production would suffer. The switching of such meetings to night hours, while it afforded additional protection against air raids, also deprived the farmers of sorely needed hours of sleep. Certain districts soon reported that a good part of the population considered an election as a sort of "compulsory labor." On the other hand, a report from Hadong province in North Viet-Nam (a province that is theoretically almost entirely controlled by French Union and Viet-Nam nationalist forces) shows that during the 1951 elections for the provincial UBKCHC, 33,336 voters out of a registered 51,517 went to the polls.[20]

Still, there can be no doubt that the republican government under the control of the Viet-Minh has succeeded in establishing at least the substructure of what could have become a decentralized democratic government. It is too early to say whether the experiment failed because of the lack of adequate cadres or because it was never meant to succeed.

[20] The Viet-Minh report fails to state, however, that there are about 600,000 inhabitants in that province.

8. Crisis in the North

January, 1957

Events in the Near East and Hungary have obscured the fact that the Communist government of the Democratic Republic of Viet-Nam has undergone a period of upheaval that shook the foundations of the regime and is likely to have serious consequences in the future. Like the crises in Hungary and Poland, the final outbreaks were desperate attempts by the population to find relief from extremely harsh political and economic measures.

In the area of Viet-Nam under the control of the Democratic Republic, particular emphasis had been placed during the past two years upon the total elimination of the landowners through a land reform program in three phases: (1) "mass mobilization," or psychological preparation of the population for mass trials and elimination of the landlords and rich peasants; (2) liquidation of the landlords and rich peasants and expropriation of large estates and lands belonging to churches, pagodas, and "traitors and colonialists"; and (3) the redistribution of land to the landless peasants, along with the beginning of land collectivization.[1]

Land reform proceedings were not handled by the regular administrative organs of the government, but were entrusted to specially created land reform committees attached to the administration at every echelon and topped by a Central Land Reform Committee with Premier Pham Van Dong as chairman. Other members of the committee included Truong Chinh, Secretary General of the Dang Lao-Dong, and Ho Viet Thang, Vice Minister of Agriculture and Forestry. Nonjudicial "trials" of landlords

[1] For a detailed treatment of the land reform procedures, see Bernard B. Fall, *The Viet-Minh Regime* (2d ed.; New York: Institute of Pacific Relations, 1956), pp. 118–35.

Reprinted from *Far Eastern Survey*, January, 1957. Originally published as "Crisis in North Viet-Nam."

and other peasants guilty of owning too much land were held throughout the northern zone with the help of Special Land Reform Tribunals and mobile land reform teams. In the words of a responsible French news source, the land reform "was carried out in an excessively brutal manner by inexperienced cadres mostly originating from the armed forces, who had only received a few weeks' training [in land reform problems] prior to being sent into the villages, their heads full of badly assimilated theories."[2] Communist sources themselves have vividly described land reform "trials" of landlords.[3]

The reforms, already handicapped by the manner in which they were carried out, happened to come when North Viet-Nam was suffering from a succession of bad crops due alternately to typhoons and floods, with the result that the food situation in the area—delicate enough in normal times—was further aggravated and resulted in occasional clashes with the land reform teams in the Hanoi region as well as in the "rice basket" province of Nghé An and Thanh Hoa. On June 29, 1956, *Nhan-Dan* (*The People*), organ of the Dang Lao-Dong, admitted that "besides the agitators who have sabotaged the land reform . . . a certain number of persons not classified as landowners . . . have opposed themselves to the people. . . ." However, the situation had deteriorated beyond the point where words alone could help.

On August 17, 1956, President Ho Chi Minh himself, in a letter addressed to "Our Compatriots on the Farms," admitted that "errors had been committed in realizing the unity of the peasants [and] . . . in the reform of agricultural organizations, as well as in the agricultural taxation policy," and promised redress to those who had been erroneously classified as landlords or rich peasants or who had been otherwise wronged by arbitrary decisions of Communist cadres.

New and better trained cadres (*can-bo*) were dispatched to various points of tension to redress the most urgent cases of injustice; several hundred landowners were released from various prison

[2] Georges Chaffard, "Le gouvernement nord-vietnamien doit affronter à son tour le mécontentement populaire," *Le Monde* (weekly ed.), December 5, 1956.
[3] See the review of Joseph R. Starobin's *Eyewitness in Indochina* in *Pacific Affairs*, September, 1954, pp. 284–85.

camps and greater freedom of discussion was allowed, at least for a time. But here, as in Poland or Hungary, the government was not fully able to control the change of policy. Now that at least a partial failure of the land reform was a matter of public record, a scapegoat had to be found: the Central Land Reform Committee was singled out for public blame.

It remains as yet a matter of conjecture whether events in Eastern Europe and Viet-Nam coincided accidentally or not. However, it is already apparent that the D.R.V.N. had chosen the month of October, 1956, for a house-cleaning that was long overdue. Within a period of less than four weeks, several important meetings of the Council of Ministers took place in Hanoi, along with extraordinary sessions of the enlarged Central Committee of the Lao-Dong, the Central Military Committee, the Central Committee of the "Viet-Nam Fatherland Front," and of the Vietnamese Youth Union, to name but a few.

Actions were taken on both a political and administrative plane. The Lao-Dong's Secretary General, Truong Chinh, severely criticized himself for the shortcomings of the land reform program before the Tenth Enlarged Session of the Central Committee of the Lao-Dong. According to a terse announcement of Radio Hanoi on October 29, 1956, Ho Chi Minh was unanimously elected Secretary General of the Loa-Dong in replacement of Truong Chinh. Furthermore, Ho Viet Thang was reduced from member of the Central Committee to the rank of ordinary party member. Le Van Luong, also a member of the ill-fated Central Land Reform Committee and of the Central Committee of the Lao-Dong, as well as head of the Party's Central Organization Board, was demoted to candidate member of the Party's Central Committee.

On the administrative level, Ho Viet Thang and Le Van Luong who, in addition to their party positions had also held the posts of Vice Minister of Agriculture and Director of Administrative Affairs in the Office of the Premier, respectively, were summarily dismissed from these posts.

Conjectures have arisen as to whether this sudden demotion of Truong Chinh and his closest aides has in fact a deeper meaning than merely that of eliminating a group which had become unpopular because of the mistakes committed by the regime itself. In the past Ho Chi Minh and the commander in chief of the Viet-Nam

People's Army, General Vo Nguyen Giap, have been described as representing a "national-Communist" wing of the Lao-Dong, as against Truong Chinh's pro-Peking leanings. In May, 1955, when Ho Chi Minh relinquished the premiership to Pham Van Dong and kept only the presidency of the D.R.V.N. for himself, voices were heard to the effect that the "pro-Peking" faction had won out over the "national-Communist" clique. If this theory were true, then Ho Chi Minh's re-emergence as both the head of state and the chief of the Communist Party would mean a sudden alteration of the whole set of relations existing between the D.R.V.N. and Red China. There are thus far no indications to support such a view, with the possible exception of veiled references to the future prevention of "mistakes due to great-power chauvinsm" in recent talks between Chou En-lai and Pham Van Dong.[4]

To all outward appearances at least, Truong Chinh has not completely fallen into disgrace. He is still a member of the Central Committee of the Lao-Dong and carries out various official functions. For example, he represented the party at the funeral of Major General Nguyen Son on October 21, 1956,[5] and he presented the party politburo's viewpoint on events in Egypt on November 9. Thus his position appears more like that of Malenkov in Russia than that of, say, Rakosi in Hungary.

Throughout the countryside of North Viet-Nam, particularly in the traditionally rebellious areas of the Fourth Interzone (the provinces of Thanh-Hoa, Nghe-An, and Ha-Tinh), the corrective actions of the government came too slowly and too late. A dramatic session of the D.R.V.N. Council of Ministers was held late in October in Hanoi to consider the explosive situation. After an initial attempt at covering up once more the failures of the administration, the government made public the gist of the cabinet

---

[4] Chou En-lai visited Hanoi from November 18 to November 22, 1956, probably to discuss additional economic aid, which the D.R.V.N. needs badly to tide it over the present crisis, and also to re-evaluate relations between the D.R.V.N. and Communist China in view of the new situation in Eastern Europe.

[5] Nguyen Son, alias Hong Thuy (real name Vu Nguyen Dac, born 1908 in Bac-Ninh), was one of Viet-Nam's oldest Communists. A member of the Chinese Communist Party, he fought in China from 1925 until 1945, and participated in the Long March. From 1945 until 1947, he was Chairman of the *Nam-Bo* (South Viet-Nam) Administrative Committee. From 1947 on he was military commander and political commissar of the vital Fourth Interzone.

discussions. In addition to admitting once more the failures of the land reform, the government now admitted that the reformers, in their zeal, had gone beyond the scope and intent of the law: ". . . the land-reform laws adopted by the National Assembly have not been scrupulously adhered to. The laws of the State have not been respected. The regime of democratic legality has been encroached upon." At the same time, the government now deprived the local Land Reform Committees of their virtual life-and-death powers and reduced them to advisory "study organs." A further decree, issued directly by the Office of the Premier on December 4, deprived the Central Land Reform Committee of the right to give direct orders to the lower land reform committees and reserved the power to do so to the Premier himself.

The earlier cabinet meeting also abolished the hated Special People's Tribunals and formally promised redress for excesses committed by such tribunals in the name of justice. Promises were made to overhaul the entire judiciary so as to "insure the people's democratic rights and to strengthen the basis of democratic legality." Furthermore, the government reaffirmed the "supremacy of the National Assembly as an administrative organ" over the various party authorities that had assumed quasi-governmental powers over the years and promised new elections in 1957 for the local legislatures and administrative bodies, since in many areas such bodies either had not been elected at all or had been elected under very unfavorable conditions in 1947 and 1948.[6] Lastly, the government promised an improvement in living conditions for farmers and workers "in keeping with the financial possibilities of the State."

When these facts became known throughout the countryside (they had been broadcast over the government-controlled radio on November 3 and 4), the farmers and small landowners, who for two years or more had suffered under the heavy hand of the local land reform committees, now found officially confirmed what they had known all along: that they had been mistreated by an arbitrary and oppressive bureaucracy. It is only surprising that popular indignation did not express itself in rebellions on an even larger scale than those which eventually occurred in Nghe-An Province after November 5.

[6] See Chapter 7.

Nghe-An and its neighboring provinces have a long record of fierce nationalism. It had fought on longer than any other region against French colonial penetration in the ten-year "Revolt of the Intellectuals" in the 1880's. Ho Chi Minh, Vo Nguyen Giap, and other leaders originated there. It was the landless farmers of the Nghe-An who, in 1930 and 1931, organized village revolutionary committees—conveniently dubbed as the "Soviets of Nghe-An" by Communist propaganda—and marched unarmed against French troops. During the Indochina War of 1946–54, the Fourth Interzone, with its rice surplus, raw materials, and relatively well-educated population, was one of the Viet-Minh's main bastions and one into which no French troops had penetrated since 1946. In fact, the territory was considered so thoroughly permeated by Communist ideas that the D.R.V.N. had begun to establish Soviet-type collective farms there in 1954. That open revolt against the regime should nevertheless take place in this area suggests the depth of popular resentment against the Hanoi government.

The available information indicates that farmers in the predominantly Catholic Quynh-Luu *huyen* (district), thirty-five miles north of the provincial capital of Vinh, when apprised of the new policy of the government, decided to march upon the district headquarters to air their grievances and demand immediate redress. Regional troops of the 325th Infantry Division, in platoon strength, were sent to Quynh-Yen village along with some representatives of the *huyen* administrative committee "to explain to the compatriots the government's policy." However, the indignant populace overwhelmed and disarmed the troops during the night of November 5 and now did to them what had been done to themselves for years: they forced the troops and party cadres publicly to confess their crimes and sign a prepared statement to that effect.

Between November 5 and November 13, the rebellion spread to the whole district, and four columns, totaling perhaps 10,000 rebellious peasants, began to converge upon the district administrative headquarters. There are some indications that by then the rebellion had spread to neighboring districts, but now the thoroughly alarmed Hanoi government decided to commit the battle-hardened 304th Infantry Division to the job of sealing off the insurrectionary area and to crush the rebellion by military force. According to a declaration made on November 29 by President Ngo Dinh Diem, head of the Vietnamese national government in Saigon, a team of the International Control Commission, which supervises the enforcement of the 1954 cease-fire, passed through Quynh-Luu on November 9 and was handed a series of petitions demanding ICC support for the liberation of arrested family members, restitution of illegally seized property, and the right to be informed about world events as well as the right to circulate freely.[7] There is no evidence that this petition was acted upon by the ICC or that a subsequent letter sent by the Vietnamese Government in Saigon to the United Nations resulted in any action by that body.

On November 14, troops of the 304th Division recaptured Quynh-Yen, and by November 22 regained full control of the area. Similar smaller disturbances in the Haiphong area and in the Hong-Quang coal-mining area (where workers had presented grievances against low living standards) were dealt with locally.

There is evidence that local religious grievances were involved in the uprisings. In fact, Radio Hanoi, in an unusual burst of candor, announced on November 22 that "in the agrarian reform, we have committed errors, including errors in the observance of freedom of religion. The people in general and the Catholic citizens in particular want these errors corrected. These are legitimate demands." The government announced simultaneously that 16.9 million *dong* (about $5,000) had been granted for the restoration of Catholic churches destroyed by the war or typhoons in Thanh-Hoa, and that another 31.8 million *dong* had been granted to a Catholic seminary in the area. Reports on the area subsequently made public by the D.R.V.N. placed great emphasis upon the happiness of the Catholics in Nghe-An, and asserted that churches, particularly those of the formerly rebellious area, are "crowded with Catholics coming to prayer." However, the very insistence with which Hanoi news media continued to deny Western reports on the uprising, in general and in detail, until well into January, 1957, shows how much concern this revolt must have caused in government circles.

Another type of unrest which may prove even more dangerous

[7] Embassy of Viet-Nam (Washington, D.C.), *News from Viet-Nam*, December 1, 1956.

to the regime has arisen in the meantime—that of a press which refuses to be entirely gagged. On December 10, *Nhan-Dan* violently attacked another Hanoi newspaper, *Nhan-Van*,[8] published by the Minh Duc Publishing House. In one of the issues of *Nhan-Van* there appeared a story of Tran Dan, a member of the People's Army, whose life was described in such a way "as to make the reader see that a talented and clear life is being trampled upon." Another article, entitled "The Story of a Few Persons Who Committed Suicide," apparently dealt with an actual news item of people driven to suicide by continued persecutions. Among the other "crimes" charged against *Nhan-Van* was to have stated that "the ugly causes of the events in Poland and Hungary are the lack of democracy." And the editorialist of the Communist Party organ candidly admitted that, after having read *Nhan-Van's* descriptions of the regime, one could ask: "Who could love a regime like that depicted in the five issues of *Nhan-Van?*" and cites a group of pupils of the Chu-An High School in Hanoi who, after reading the paper, said: "Inside us we sensed a feeling of doubt and hatred for the [Lao-Dong] Party and the regime which had trampled on a man and stifled literature. . . . We felt that everything we had previously thought about the troops and Communist fighters was wrong."[9] It is thus small wonder that a Presidential Decree was promulgated on December 14 which put considerable restraints upon whatever was left of free discussion. In its preamble, the decree points out that the "press under our regime . . . is a tool of struggle for the people. It must serve the interests of the country and the people, [and] safeguard the People's Democratic Regime."[10]

As the situation appears in January, 1957, the D.R.V.N. has weathered another severe internal crisis—the previous one being the change from the old "Stalin line." In fact, thus far the

---

[8] See "The Ho Chi Minh Way," in *The Economist* (London), January 5, 1957, pp. 38–42.

[9] Xuan Truong, "Opposing Slander and Distortion," in *Nhan-Dan* (Hanoi), December 10, 1956.

[10] *Nhan-Van* apparently did not survive the promulgation of the new law on "freedom" of the press. On December 10, 1956, in perfect timing with the article by Xuan Truong in *Nhan-Dan*, 500 printing workers in Hanoi passed a resolution strongly censuring *Nhan-Van* for its "destructive" attitude. Its next issue, though ready for publication, was never printed. See "The Ho Chi Minh Way," p. 41.

D.R.V.N. has always been able, perhaps because of its peripheral position relative to the center of Communist power, to profit from the crises of its fellow Communist states. In the present case, it was able to prepare the change in its internal economic policies— with minor political concessions thrown in, mainly to appease a few intellectuals and retain the good will of the Asian neutral nations—during the late summer of 1956, without any outside pressure. When the operation was finally made public on October 30, the political and administrative machine was well geared to deal with the changeover, with the Viet-Nam People's Army on the alert to meet such emergencies as the Nghe-An rebellion.

There are solid indications, indeed, that the Army was most reluctant to accept the idea of a changeover under the present circumstances. According to *Nhan-Dan* of November 9, several of the 600 delegates of all major VPA commands who met with General Giap at the session of the General Military Committee "expressed fears that the Central Committee of the Lao-Dong and the General Military Committee did not have full knowledge of the situation prevailing throughout the countryside and among the [VPA] units . . . so they cautioned the congress [of military delegates] against some points in the resolutions . . ." which admitted the past mistakes of the regime. It is not unlikely that the regime now privately recognizes the correctness of this estimate. On the whole, however, the D.R.V.N. regime has again demonstrated its ability to adapt to changing circumstances. Now, after a brief period of comparative relaxation of pressure, the new "hard" line advocated both in Peking and Moscow has found a receptive echo among the rulers of North Viet-Nam, and their intransigent attitude will no doubt be reinforced by the failure of the United Nations and the Western powers to give effective support to the anti-Communist rebels in Hungary.

9. Inside Hanoi

November, 1962

"It took us eight years of bitter fighting to defeat you French in In-dochina," said the slightly built, grandfatherly man with the wispy goatee. "Now the South Vietnamese regime of Ngo Dinh Diem is well armed and helped by 10,000 Americans. The Americans are much stronger than the French, though they know us less well. It may perhaps take ten years to do it, but our heroic compatriots in the South will defeat them in the end."

After a pause he continued, speaking slowly in flawless French and looking thoughtfully out of the high French window onto the manicured formal garden of his palace in Hanoi.

"I think the Americans greatly underestimate the determination of the Vietnamese people. The Vietnamese people have always shown great determination when they were faced with a foreign invader."

The speaker, looking very spry in a tropical uniform, was Ho Chi Minh, the seventy-two-year-old President of Communist North Viet-Nam. . . .

This was my first visit to North Viet-Nam since it had been oc-cupied by the Viet-Minh in 1954, and my first interview with North Viet-Nam's senior leaders. Flying northward in a Boeing Stratoliner of World War II vintage—operated by the Canadian–Polish–Indian Control Commission that is supposed to supervise the 1954 truce—I had thought for a while that the land looked much as it had when I had known it in the days of French rule. In the Red River Delta I could see dark green patches where tree-lined villages nestle between the rice fields of lush light green. But something had changed even here. Some fields no longer are

Excerpted from "Master of the Red Jab," originally published in *The Saturday Evening Post*, November 24, 1962. © 1962 The Curtis Publishing Company.

small, handkerchieflike squares but are far larger than before, with no dikes to interrupt their expanse. They belong to the new collective farms. Communism already has left its mark on the landscape. And as we came in for a landing I noticed the brutal reds of new tile roofs and the glaring whites of factory walls where there once had been nothing but farmland or French forts. Here the industrialization drive of Communism had left its imprint.

Hanoi looked about as it must have looked the day after the French pulled out—no cars in the streets, the city in a state of "brown-out," a few passers-by walking in an eerie atmosphere of silence, as if every noise were filtered through cotton stoppers in one's ears. In the once-fashionable "French" section of town, the stuccoed villas were in disrepair, the shops boarded up, the broad avenues empty. Not a street seemed to have been paved, nor a house repainted since the French evacuated the city.

The car assigned to me, a rickety Soviet Pobieda (Victory), took me to the hotel I had known as the Metropole. Now it was the Hotel Thong-Nhat (Unity). By coincidence I was assigned to a dining table I had occupied nine years ago, number two, and the waiter brought me an example of what a North Vietnamese chef thought French cooking should taste like. It was edible, but I kept thinking of French officers I had known here, one shot down over Langson, another blown up by land mines, and others long dead in the battle against Ho Chi Minh's guerrillas—the battle that Ho had won.

The only people now eating in the seventy-five-table dining room were a Chinese technician, silently manipulating chopsticks, and a Laotian couple. The husband, a colonel, had attended the U.S. Command and General Staff College at Fort Leavenworth, Kansas; he had also fought with the neutralist forces against the Western-backed government during the Laotian civil war. As we ate, the public-address system—perhaps in my honor—switched from a propaganda speech to a scratched record of Glenn Miller's "In the Mood."

This is official Hanoi. There is another Hanoi, full of the bustle of any Asian city, with children swarming around, street merchants peddling duck eggs, and lines forming in front of movie houses. I saw one food queue too—people lined up to buy the Vietnamese equivalent of Popsicles. Here one can see that the average citizen of Hanoi is neither well fed nor starving (in the immediate post-war period of 1945–46, nearly 1 million did starve to death). The basic food staples, rice and fats and sometimes meat, are rationed, but at bearable levels. Adult rice rations vary between 28 and 40 pounds a month. Clothing is rationed, too, at three yards per person per year, and it lacks the gay colors that brighten many Asian street scenes. There are only two basic colors of clothes: black cotton trousers and white cotton shirts. Recently a new color has been added to the output—faded blue. As for more luxurious goods, the shopwindows of Hanoi hold out little more than a promise. They contain such items as Czech tape recorders and Russian cameras—at prices of $600 and more. Even a pair of poorly made shoes costs $8.50, two weeks' pay for an average worker, and Chinese T-shirts cost $1.25.

I was not restricted in moving around Hanoi. I was escorted on official visits by a member of the Foreign Office, but otherwise I was left on my own to go to the local markets or the movies or to visit the few Western missions still sticking it out under virtual quarantine. And although my Vietnamese is awful I found many people in markets and stores who were willing and able to speak French.

The reasons for Hanoi's general shabbiness became more clear when I got outside the city. The cement that does not go into Hanoi pavements apparently goes into five-story apartment buildings and huge factories in places where I had seen only open rice fields nine years ago. There are an electrochemical complex at Viet-Tri, a fertilizer plant at Lam-Thao, a ceramics factory at Hai-Duong, a blast furnace at Thai-Nguyen, and a tungsten mine and ore refinery at Pia-Ouac which also produce uranium for Communist China's future atomic bombs. The whole Communist bloc has pitched in with nearly $1 billion in aid to make the industrialization of North Viet-Nam a Communist success in an area where America is deeply involved. In contrast to China, the industrialization of North Viet-Nam is relatively easy, for it is a nation a little smaller than Missouri with a population of 17 million. A few modern machine-tool plants, for example, can change it from a machine-importing to a machine-exporting country. Its turret lathes already have made an impressive debut at the New Delhi Industrial Fair. North Viet-Nam is not becoming a Japan, but it is acquiring an industrial backbone stronger than that of any non-Communist country on the Southeast Asian mainland. This country is functioning, and developing at a very rapid rate.

The people working in these factories are an extraordinary collection. At the Hanoi machine-tool plant, which produces turret lathes, carpenters' planes, irrigation pumps, and drills, I was surprised to meet a foreman who addressed me in purest French factory slang.

"You're damned right I talk like a Frenchman," he said. "Worked for sixteen years at the Renault plant outside Paris."

Nearby I saw an old Tonkinese woman wearing brown peasant garb, her teeth lacquered black in the traditional fashion, standing at a turret lathe with calipers in her hand. And next to her, as at most machines, was a younger woman. "There are two workers at each machine," I was told, "because the first teaches the second. This way we won't have any trouble when we build the next machine-tool factory."

Glaring errors are still made. A senior official at the all-powerful State Planning Board, which directs the whole North Vietnamese economic machinery, filled me with complaints—including complaints about Red Chinese aid. In the case of the 400-acre Thai-Nguyen steel complex the Chinese had delivered turbines which were so huge that they could not be fitted on any available trains or trucks. Several months went by until the Red River rose high enough for the turbines to be brought upstream on barges. In many plants young engineers freshly graduated from Chinese, Russian, or East German training schools—or, as of this year, from Hanoi's own school of engineering—must step directly into top engineering jobs involving responsibility over thousands of workers.

"It often looks as if a midshipman had been given the command of a cruiser as his first post," said one of the few Western economists in Hanoi. "And it often works out the same way."

The huge Hon-Gay mining complex, which the French ran with 140 technicians and engineers, continued operating for almost seven years under the direction of two Communist cadres. Neither director had an engineering degree. People's Army colonels were in fact the directors of many of the plants I visited. That kind of militarization of industry makes for great labor discipline, but discipline alone cannot replace technical knowledge. This explains the stretch-out of the targets set for the 1958–61 economic plan and the constant lowering of targets set for 1965.

"When we first drew up our plans we just didn't know enough about statistics," said Vo Quang Anh, a leading member of the State Planning Board. "Even for the Five-Year Plan now under way we are still sending our target figures to the individual ministries for evaluation and finding that they are set too high. And now that we know that our population increases by a fantastic half million a year . . ."

That population increase is an obstacle to all economic growth, as it is in all underdeveloped nations, and it means that even a constant increase in food supplies will not end the people's hunger. Yet partition cut off North Viet-Nam from its normal supplies in the South, which used to provide 225,000 tons of rice a year. Today, as I saw in trips around the countryside, every available inch is under cultivation. In areas where rice won't grow, the peasants have planted corn and yams. In the long run, however, North Viet-Nam's hope of success depends on its being able to export industrial goods to such agricultural nations as Burma, Cambodia, and Thailand.

The struggle for economic development requires an almost military discipline, and Ho Chi Minh has succeeded in imposing it on the whole country. At the basic level, six-year-old "Young Pioneers" are taught to "help" their parents "correct their backwardness in economic thinking." Many a small-time black marketeer or would-be political opponent is turned in by his own family or his neighbor's children. On the next level is the Street Committee, theoretically a nonpolitical organization of "mutual help." In actual fact the Street Committee is an unofficial police force which plays on a man's desire to keep the Joneses down with him if he cannot keep up with them. To buy a suitcase, for example, you need an authorization signed by your Street Committee. In other words, you must explain to your neighbors why you might be planning a trip and how you can afford it.

The Street Committee not only keeps a check on every one of the inhabitants within its area but it also sees to it that everyone turns out every day for early-morning gymnastics classes directed by a voice from a loudspeaker. These loudspeakers are everywhere, as are huge posters exhorting people to further achievements on the "production front"; to greater solidarity with the "heroic struggle" of the Cubans, Congolese, Angolans; to continuing hatred of the United States. In fact, "Hate America Month" was officially proclaimed during my stay in Hanoi. All of this establishes an atmosphere like that of George Orwell's 1984—a feeling that Big Brother is everywhere and knows everything.

Aside from the Street Committees for every home, there is the production cell for farms and factories. The production cell sees to it not only that work quotas are met but also that its members are properly indoctrinated. Returning to my hotel at midnight I could often see the night shift at a printing shop, which formerly housed the French newspaper *L'Entente*, sitting together around a dim light bulb while a production-cell member read aloud from the speeches of Comrade Ko-Rut-Sop (Khrushchev).

Above all these low-level organizations there is the Party itself, an elite of faithful believers. North Viet-Nam's Communist Dang Lao-Dong is 800,000 strong, and its membership has gradually shifted from the unsophisticated peasantry to the students and factory workers who constitute the political backbone of the regime. Its leadership, forged over thirty years of bitter struggle against overwhelming odds, is tough and resourceful.

And finally, beyond the party, there is the fearsome Viet-Nam People's Army. The French—who have good reason to know it well—estimate it to be one of the best combat-infantry forces in the world today. It is at the same time a thoroughly political army. Its creator and commander in chief, General Vo Nguyen Giap, declared in his book *People's War, People's Army:* "The People's Army is the instrument of the [Communist] Party and the revolutionary state, for the accomplishment, in armed form, of the tasks of the revolution."

From a 24-man platoon in 1944, the army has grown into a force of 400,000 men, lavishly armed with Soviet automatic weapons. Yet in spite of this modern armament the army has lost none of its incredible agility in cross-country maneuvering. Whatever training I could see in North Viet-Nam—none of it was shown to me deliberately—seemed to confirm that the North Vietnamese were as ready as ever to fight in the swamps and jungles of their country. I saw infantrymen dogtrotting along the roads with full field kits in the blazing tropical sun. I saw officers instructing militiamen

—there are an estimated 2 million of them—in how to attack concrete bunkers. They were not training to fight against an imaginary enemy but against South Vietnamese—and Americans.

As to the loyalty of those troops there is little doubt. The People's Army is better housed and fed than most civilians, and its discharged veterans have high preference for good jobs in the administration and industry. This loyalty was tested on the one occasion when a large group of Vietnamese attempted a rebellion. In November, 1956, at just the time when the Hungarians rose in revolt, 6,000 farmers in Ho Chi Minh's own native province rebelled against the collectivization of their land. Soldiers of the 325th Division unhesitatingly shot down their compatriots and restored order.

In the face of such an awesome control apparatus, reaching from the family to the armed forces, the individual discontented North Vietnamese has almost no chance of rebellion. And any guerrilla movement sponsored by South Viet-Nam would have little chance of surviving in Ho Chi Minh's land.

All this, and more, was in my mind as I faced Ho Chi Minh, the grandfatherly man who still holds Viet-Nam's fate in his hands, and his Premier, Pham Van Dong, fifty-six, who looks exactly like the aristocrat he is by birth. Both men had led Viet-Nam's Communist movement since its inception. Ho Chi Minh, though all too little known in the outside world, is the last of the Old Bolsheviks still in power. He was a senior Comintern agent at a time when Khrushchev was still on a farm in the Ukraine. Unlike many other Communist leaders, Ho has traveled widely. He has been to the United States (he wrote a pamphlet on the shocking conditions in Harlem in 1918). He even served as a pastry-cook's apprentice under the great Escoffier at the Carlton in London. As a member of the French Socialist Party, he was one of the founders of the French Communist Party in 1920. As a Comintern agent, living in Thailand in the disguise of a Buddhist monk, he organized violent dock strikes in Singapore, later turned up in Berlin during the last days of the Weimar Republic, finally began organizing the Vietnamese underground in 1941—with the help of the American OSS.

Ho himself is reluctant to speak of his own past. "You know, I am an old man, and an old man likes to hold on to his little

mysterics," he said to me. When I objected to this, he said with
a humorous twinkle in his eye, "Wait until I'm dead. Then you can
write about me all you want." Nevertheless, before I left Hanoi I
received at my hotel an unsigned five-page typescript which contained some hitherto unknown details about Ho's life, obviously
delivered on the old man's instructions.

Ho has, too, a kind of human vanity and gallantry that one
scarcely expects in an old revolutionary. I had brought him a book
of mine which contained a portrait of him by my wife. "Where?
Where?" he cried. "Let me see it. Providing that she's got my
goatee right . . . providing the goatee looks all right." After
thumbing through the pages and inspecting the portrait he was
pleased. "Yes, that is very good. That looks very much like me."
He looked around him for a moment, then took a small bouquet of
flowers from a vase on the table and handed it to me. "Tell her for
me that the drawing is very good and give her the bouquet and kiss
her on both cheeks for me."

Most of my political questions, however, were answered by
Premier Pham Van Dong. He sounded almost contemptuous of
South Viet-Nam's President Ngo Dinh Diem, whose regime the
United States is trying to uphold. "Monsieur Diem's position is
quite difficult," said Dong. "He is unpopular, and the more unpopular he is the more American aid he will require to stay in
power. And the more American aid he receives, the more he will
look like a puppet of the Americans and the less likely he is to win
popular support for his side."

"That sounds pretty much like a vicious circle," I said.

The Premier's eyes showed a humorous gleam as he said that it
was more than "vicious." "It is really more like a descending
spiral."

There is, I fear, some justification for the Communist leader's
optimism. The French lost Indochina to Ho's guerrilla armies because they had no political program that could win the support of
the peasantry. In South Viet-Nam today, Diem's regime remains a
family autocracy in Saigon, with few reforms in sight, and there is
no indication that it has attracted any real support from the
majority of the people. Without that support, American helicopters and modern weapons cannot do very much. And although
American officials speak of fighting for years against Ho's guerrillas,

I doubt that most Americans realize what such a protracted war really means.

Despite huge sums in American aid, guerrilla depredations have changed South Viet-Nam from an area which once exported as much as 1 million tons of rice to one which has had to import 100,000 tons in 1961–62. Its exports covered only 27 per cent of its imports in 1961, and that figure fell to 18 per cent by mid-1962. South Viet-Nam is becoming, in the words of one American economist, a "nation of mendicants." For Americans, this war means not only an economic drain but a political drain. "Americans do not like long, inconclusive wars—and this is going to be a long, inconclusive war," remarked Premier Pham Van Dong. "Thus we are sure to win in the end."

Could we negotiate a settlement? Ho Chi Minh told me he was ready to negotiate with "any" South Vietnamese regime that was "willing to sit down with us at the same table and talk." Premier Pham Van Dong spoke in more detail. "We are willing to give all the guarantees necessary for the South to get fair treatment. . . . We do not envisage an immediate reunification and are willing to accept the verdict of the South Vietnamese people with regard to the institutions and policies of their part of the country." What this means, in effect, is a neutralized South Viet-Nam, deprived of large-scale American support and vulnerable to Communist subversion. The South Vietnamese and Americans naturally oppose this. . . .

But part of the Western reluctance to negotiate is based on a feeling that the West is on the defensive in South Viet-Nam, that it would be bargaining from a position of weakness. This is true if we continue limiting ourselves to antiguerrilla warfare in the South. One of the most ominous things about North Viet-Nam, as I look back on it, is the air of massive tranquillity—no guards in watchtowers, no airplane patrols. The Hanoi traffic police don't even carry pistols. But the U.S. doesn't necessarily have to let the North Vietnamese remain so placidly confident.

It is one of the paradoxes of the Vietnamese war that the huge American military commitment to South Viet-Nam is not well suited for waging a guerrilla war but provides a strong political bargaining position. For it enables us at least to threaten direct retaliation against North Viet-Nam itself. While Ho's guerrillas in

South Viet-Nam can elude American air power, his factories in North Viet-Nam are extremely vulnerable to it.

The North Vietnamese are very conscious of this. When I spoke to Premier Pham Van Dong I reminded him of the risk of American retaliation against North Vietnamese territory. I reminded him that he had been to North Korea and said, "You saw what American bombers can do." The Premier showed he was aware of the danger. "We fully realize that the American imperialists wish to provoke a situation in the course of which they could use the heroic struggle of the South Vietnamese people as a pretext for the destruction of our economic and cultural achievements. We shall offer them no pretext which could give rise to an American military intervention against North Viet-Nam."

The North Vietnamese genuinely fear American retaliation. They fear it not only because it would wreck their country but because it would raise the specter of Communist Chinese intervention and occupation. Until now, North Viet-Nam's rulers have followed Russian rather than Chinese leadership, and they are aware of China's ambitions for expansion. If we took into account these North Vietnamese fears of outside intervention, I believe we could press more effectively for some kind of truce settlement on terms that would definitely not be a "surrender." We could demand the immediate end of guerrilla fighting in the South and a far more effective international inspection system to police the truce. We may not achieve such a settlement, but I feel very strongly that we have no reason to fear it. And we must clearly realize that the alternative means the bloodshed and misery of a long and probably inconclusive guerrilla war—a war that Ho Chi Minh is well prepared to fight.

10. A Contemporary Profile

July, 1965

The inclusion of the Democratic Republic of Viet-Nam within the scope of military action by South Vietnamese and U.S. forces has suddenly focused world attention on one of the least-known countries of the Communist orbit. Larger geographically than the three Soviet Baltic republics combined, and having—as of 1964—a population of about 18.2 million, North Viet-Nam ranks fourth in both area and population among the countries of the bloc. The D.R.V.N., dating its birth from September 2, 1945, is also the second-oldest "people's democracy" after Mongolia, and it stands alone with Yugoslavia in having come into being without the help of Soviet bayonets or the presence of a larger Communist power.

These factors alone warrant a close study of the North Vietnamese regime, for they suggest a far greater degree of solidity and cohesion than is usually found in a small Communist country. As one French observer has correctly remarked, the D.R.V.N.'s "Communism is not the result of an alien overlay . . . but the product of a long-maturing and hardening process in the course of the anti-French struggle,"[1] and—one may now add—in the equally long fight for the eventual control of South Viet-Nam. The same factors also have a profound influence upon the attitude that Hanoi has thus far taken toward the Sino-Soviet split, as well as upon the D.R.V.N.'s approach to its confrontation with the United States in the South Vietnamese conflict. A look at the historical, political, and economic background of North Viet-Nam will serve to bring the whole problem into clearer focus.

[1] Julien Cheverny, *Eloge du colonialisme—Essai sur les révolutions d'Asie* (Paris: Julliard, 1961), p. 177.

Reprinted from *Problems of Communism*, July/August 1965, published by the United States Information Agency. Originally published as "North Viet-Nam: A Profile."

Like many of the Communist movements in former colonial countries, that of Viet-Nam started abroad—among Vietnamese living in France, Russia, and China. Under the name of Nguyen Ai-Quoc (Nguyen the Patriot), the D.R.V.N.'s present President, Ho Chi Minh, was a co-founder of the French Communist Party when the latter split off from the French Socialist Party in 1920. By 1923, Ho had risen high enough in the French Communist hierarchy to be sent to Moscow as a delegate to the Krestintern (Peasant International), and later to attend the Fifth Comintern Congress in 1924 as a French colonial delegate.[2] It is worthy of note that he intervened very strongly in the 1924 congress debates on two specific points: namely, the importance of the anticolonial struggle (he asserted that Stalin was one of the few Communist leaders who attached proper weight to the colonial question), and the importance of the peasantry in the revolutionary movements of colonial and semicolonial areas. In the latter connection, Dr. Ernst Kux, noted Far Eastern specialist of the Swiss newspaper *Neue Zurcher Zeitung,* observed that Ho had been well ahead of Mao Tse-tung in advancing "the thesis that Communist revolutions in the colonial areas must be carried out by the peasant masses under the leadership of the party." Kux goes on to remark: "Ho's assertion that practical acts and leadership of the revolution are more important than the formulation of ringing theses became the mainstream of his own future activities. In fact, he almost repeated it verbatim at the meeting of Communist parties in Moscow in 1961."[3]

This pragmatic trait has manifested itself throughout Ho Chi Minh's career to this day, and it has also marked the whole approach of the North Vietnamese party leadership to the thorny problem of relations with the party's competing Soviet and Chinese mentors. Ho's personal loyalty to Stalin during the 1930's perhaps explains why he survived the various purges that sent almost all of his early Comintern associates to death or into exile, and there is absolutely no evidence that the North Vietnamese

[2] There is no full-length biography of Ho Chi Minh. The author has attempted a biographical essay in *The Two Viet-Nams* (rev. ed.; New York: Frederick A. Praeger, 1964), pp. 81–103.

[3] Kux, *Die Satelliten Pekings* (Stuttgart: W. Kohlhammer, 1964), pp. 38–39.

Communists ever swerved from their pro-Moscow sympathies until Stalin's death in 1953.

Ho's stay in the Soviet Union in 1923–24 marked the first shift of Vietnamese Communism away from a West European (mostly French) to a more specifically Soviet orientation. His own assignment in December, 1924, to Mikhail Borodin's Soviet mission to Sun Yat-sen's Chinese revolutionary government in Canton as an "interpreter" (actually to work as a Communist organizer of Vietnamese exiles in South China) strikingly underlined this new orientation toward Moscow—the more so because of the Chinese context. Within a few days after his arrival in Canton, Ho addressed a preliminary report to the Executive Committee of the Comintern in which he described his principal future task to be "the unification of various Vietnamese nationalist groups under Communist leadership."[4] The task was not to be an easy one since many of the Vietnamese exile groups either were hostile to the Communist ideology or, if sympathetic, had come into contact with Communist ideas in France and were reluctant at first to accept the authority of the totally unknown Russian-trained Vietnamese organizers in Canton. But the Canton group had several important assets in its favor: (1) it had official Comintern support; (2) it was able to utilize Chinese Nationalist military academies for training cadres;[5] and (3) it had Ho Chi Minh as its leader.

Vietnamese Communist reliance on Soviet and Comintern support only increased after Chiang Kai-shek's break with Moscow in 1927, which led to the expulsion of the Soviet mission from Canton and the near-destruction of the Chinese Communist Party apparatus. Ho and his associates switched operations to the nearby British crown colony of Hong Kong, which offered excellent liaison with the outside world because of its direct location on the shipping lanes to both Western Europe and Vladivostok. It was in Hong Kong that the final differences among the three existing Vietnamese factions of the Third International (there was also a strong Trotskyite group) were hammered out. Confronted with a

[4] *Ibid.*, p. 40.
[5] According to North Vietnamese Premier Pham Van Dong, "more than 200 cadres" were trained during 1925–27 at the Chinese Nationalist military academy at Whampoa and in Russia. *Le président Ho Chi Minh* (Hanoi: Foreign Languages, 1961), p. 52.

communication from the Comintern which stated that the existence of these differences "under present circumstances is a grave error and an even greater danger,"[6] the leaders of the various factions finally came to terms. On February 3, 1930, the Dong Duong Cong San Dang (Indochinese Communist Party, or ICP) was born in the bleachers of a Hong Kong stadium, where the newly constituted Central Committee held its inaugural meeting while a soccer game was in progress.

The ICP soon experienced its first crisis in the course of a peasant uprising in the Central Vietnamese province of Nghe-An— Ho Chi Minh's province of birth—in the spring of 1930. There has thus far been no definitive account of the uprising, and existing sources conflict as to its interpretation. Basically, it grew out of a totally non-Communist mutiny of native soldiers in Tongking (North Viet-Nam), which then spread to the peasantry as a consequence of drastically falling commodity prices caused by the Great Depression. A Vietnamese Communist, evaluating the uprising in 1960, admits to "serious errors"—notably that the rebellion was entirely based on the small peasantry, rejecting the support, on the side of the French, of all other bourgeois elements. That error was, in fact, duly condemned by the Far Eastern Bureau of the Comintern in May, 1931, as "leftish and sectarian" and "not in accordance with the principles of Communism. . . ."[7]

The ensuing repression of the Vietnamese Communist movement rendered it almost leaderless (and well-nigh memberless) for nearly five years until the advent of a popular-front government in France brought a softening of anti-Communist police activity in Indochina. Tran Phu, the first Secretary General of the ICP, was among those arrested by the colonial authorities in Indochina, dying in prison in September, 1931. Ho Chi Minh, who was still in Hong Kong, was arrested there by the British in June, 1931, but was released later that year and went underground in Shanghai before returning to Russia and Western Europe, where he remained until 1938. The ICP's second Secretary General, Le Hong Phong, stayed abroad until the more lenient popular-front policy took hold in Indochina.

[6] *Ibid.*, p. 57.
[7] Tran Huy Lieu, *Les Soviets du Nghé Tinh* (Hanoi: Foreign Languages, 1960), p. 52.

In July, 1936, the ICP Central Committee officially adhered to the "Dimitrov Line" as laid down at the Seventh Comintern Congress and withdrew the slogans "Down with French Imperialism" and "Down with Feudalism." A short period of political collaboration with the French followed, but the honeymoon was interrupted by the Molotov-Ribbentrop pact of August, 1939, and the outbreak of World War II. Le Hong Phong was arrested and died on the guillotine in 1940. By the end of that year, the whole senior ICP apparatus had again withdrawn to China—but not to the areas held by the Chinese Communists; instead, it chose warlord-held Kwangsi Province, bordering on Viet-Nam, as its base of operations.

A new Secretary General, Truong Chinh, was elected by the reconstituted ICP Central Committee in May, 1941. (His real name is Dang Xuan Khu, and his adoption of the pseudonym "Truong Chinh"—the Vietnamese term for the "Long March" of the Chinese Communists—reflects his long-standing personal admiration of the CCP.) Meanwhile, Ho Chi Minh had rejoined the party apparatus in Kwangsi, but had subsequently antagonized the local Chinese warlords by resisting their pressure for integration of the ICP-in-exile with Vietnamese nationalist elements under their aegis. Arrested by the Chinese, Ho was kept in jail from August, 1942, until September, 1943. This presumably left Truong Chinh a fairly free hand to staff the party apparatus with his own men. Although he has never, to this day, attained the popularity and charisma of Ho or of General Vo Nguyen Giap, the victor of Dien Bien Phu, Truong unquestionably played a major role in the ICP's well-organized takeover of the Vietnamese anti-French revolution in the summer of 1945, which he himself has described in a small book that deserves more attention than it usually gets.[8]

It is vital to remember that, unlike any other successful Communist movement, the Vietnamese party fought its way to ruling power in virtual isolation. In Eastern Europe, Soviet troops were always present in the countries where Communist takeovers took place; in fact, they were an essential ingredient. In China, the turnover to the Communists of vast stores of Japanese arms by the Soviet forces in Manchuria was of vital importance to the CCP's

[8] Truong Chinh, *Primer for Revolt: The Communist Takeover in Viet-Nam* (New York: Frederick A. Praeger, 1963).

military success, and the Russian military presence in North Korea ensured the creation of a "people's democracy" there. In Albania, Tito's partisans played the role of Soviet troops elsewhere. In the Viet-Nam of 1945, on the contrary, the D.R.V.N. had no such support from either the Soviets or even the Chinese Communists (then bottled-up in the hills of northwestern China); and connections with the French CP, then just emerging from four years of clandestinity, were probably nonexistent for the simple reason that the first postwar ships to go from France to Indochina only reached Saigon in late September, 1945—and these were troop transports bringing the vanguard of the French Expeditionary Force. In other words, the Vietnamese Communists literally had to play their revolution alone and by ear.

With practical political realism, Ho played down the Communist character of his regime and movement. The ICP was formally "dissolved" on November 10, 1945, and replaced by a Marxist Studies Association under Truong Chinh. For a time, Ho also succeeded in getting his followers to adopt what was openly called the "Brest-Litovsk doctrine," involving readiness to accept a partial and temporary return of French influence to Viet-Nam in order to get rid of a Chinese Nationalist military presence which, by virtue of its sheer numbers, threatened to become permanent. It was largely because the French were unwilling at this stage to consider relinquishment of their colonial sovereignty that the upper hand in Hanoi eventually passed to those who preferred the risk of all-out revolutionary war to the risk of being nibbled to death by ever-increasing encroachments of French military power. Ho's own failure, during negotiations in France in the summer of 1946, to sway even the French CP to support his viewpoint[9] must have heavily influenced his decision to press for a military contest. On December 19, 1946, the First Indochina War broke out. It ended seven and a half years later with the defeat of the French and the Geneva agreement of July 21, 1954, partitioning Viet-Nam at the 17th parallel.

The war with the French in a way simplified some of the prob-

[9] The French CP was then a member of the government coalition in France and had solid hopes of taking over the government. In that event, all French colonial areas would automatically have passed under Communist control. See Chapter 2.

lems of Viet-Nam's Communist leaders. The fact that the struggle was a "resistance" movement against the colonial power made it easier to attract into an *union sacrée* many Vietnamese elements which otherwise would have eschewed association with the Communists. It also removed the ambiguity arising from the negotiations with the French, which had laid the Communist leadership open to charges that it was ready to negotiate away "true" independence for the sake of short-range political gains. And lastly, it permitted the Communists to take some drastic steps in many fields under the guise of strengthening unity and discipline in the war effort.

The first constitution establishing the formal governmental structure of the D.R.V.N. in 1946 was enacted by an assembly from which all but two opponents of the Communists had been removed, but it discreetly made no mention of the Communist character of the state. This document remained in force until 1960, when it was replaced by a wholly new constitution making that character fully explicit.[10] Throughout the period of anti-French hostilities from 1946 until 1954, a Standing Committee of the National Assembly fulfilled all legislative functions, except for the convocation of an Assembly session in 1953 to enact a land reform law. In actual fact, governmental functions were carried out at the central level by Ho's council of ministers, assisted at various subordinate levels by Committees of Resistance and Administration (CRA) combining civilian, military, and party elements.

Wherever feasible, the village-level CRA's were chosen by election. Needless to say, these elections were strongly influenced by the presence of Viet-Nam People's Army troops, although in many instances locally popular village chiefs managed to win positions as committee chairmen. Communist control, however, was ensured by a *can-bo*, who saw to it that the local CRA chairman did not deviate from the official party line. Furthermore, under a decree of November 11, 1948, the government gave the higher-level CRA's more power not only to override decisions by the local committees "contrary to higher order" (Article XII), but also to designate a provisional local CRA to replace a recalcitrant one (Article XIII).

On the political side, the League for Revolution and Independ-

[10] For a full English text of the 1960 constitution, see Fall, *The Two Viet-Nams.*

ence (better known by its abbreviated title of Viet-Minh), which had been created in Kwangsi in May, 1941, was supplemented in May, 1946 by an even broader "united front," including non-Communist elements which had not been part of the émigré groups in China. This new front, the League for the National Union of Viet-Nam, also embraced a large number of subsidiary "national salvation" (Cu'u Quoc) groups, such as Women for National Salvation, Catholics for National Salvation, etc., thus making it appear that the regime had the backing of a broad variety of parties.

External developments brought the next major political change. In December, 1949, Red Chinese troops arrived on the North Vietnamese border, providing the D.R.V.N. for the first time with direct access to the Communist bloc and all that this meant—i.e., plentiful military supplies; a sanctuary for casualties and training camps; and, above all, easy exchange of political delegations with the Communist countries. This made recognition of the D.R.V.N. by members of the bloc more than an empty gesture, and by the end of February, 1950, all the bloc countries, as well as Yugoslavia, had extended such recognition. It meant further that the regime was no longer as dependent as hitherto on the internal support of non-Communist and bourgeois elements.

The result was that in March, 1951, the old ICP was resurrected in the form of a specifically Vietnamese (rather than, as before, "Indochinese," i.e., including Cambodia and Laos) "Workers' Party," or Dang Lao-Dong. Its secretary general was the same Truong Chinh who had previously been ICP secretary general and later chairman of the succeeding Marxist Studies Association. The radicalization of its posture was reflected in a new slogan: "The anti-imperialist and antifeudal struggles are of equal importance."

At the same time, the Viet-Minh was merged into the broader Lien-Viet front, and traditional Vietnamese Communist predominance in the revolutionary movements of neighboring Cambodia and Laos was reasserted through a meeting (March 3–11, 1951) between Ton Duc Thang, later Vice Premier of the D.R.V.N.; Prince Souphanouvong of Laos, the leader of the Pathet-Lao movement; and Sieu Heng, the head of the Khmer [i.e., Cambodian] Liberation Committee. A Communist source provides clear evidence of the importance of the conference:

It was decided to set up a Viet-Nam–Khmer–Lao Alliance which called on the people of the three countries to coordinate their fight to defeat the colonialists. It was on the basis of these decisions . . . that Vietnamese volunteers later entered Cambodia and Laos to fight side by side with the Khmer Issarak forces—by then the Khmer National Liberation Army—and the Pathet-Lao.[11]

The effective satellization of the Cambodian and Laotian Communist movements under Vietnamese aegis was clearly illustrated at the Geneva conference of 1954. There, after some initial skirmishing, the Communist side accepted the fact that the Khmer and Lao "resistance movements" would not be seated at the conference table, and Brigadier General Ta Quang Buu, the Oxford-educated Vietnamese senior military representative, signed the Cambodian and Laotian cease-fire agreements on behalf of the "Khmer Resistance Forces" and the Pathet-Lao.

The Geneva conference signaled the emergence of the D.R.V.N. as a full-fledged power. Its political and administrative institutions were in place, and it boasted a formidable army capable not only of waging a protracted revolutionary war but also of fighting standing battles against relatively well-armed Western forces. . . .

It is still not entirely clear why the D.R.V.N. accepted the compromise of a "temporary" division of Viet-Nam inasmuch as the prospects for the holding of a reunification election within two years, as provided by the Geneva agreements, seemed fairly slim from the outset. Soviet pressure on North Viet-Nam for the sake of improving Russian relations with France—more specifically, for the purpose of inducing Paris to block the creation of a European Defense Community including West Germany—may well have been the main factor behind Hanoi's agreement.

Another probable factor was the pragmatism of the North Vietnamese Communist leadership. Ho Chi Minh has characteristically settled for a safe half-loaf rather than fight to the finish merely to prove a point. Moreover, the consolidation of Communist power in North Viet-Nam after four years of Japanese depredation, one year of Chinese pilfering, and eight years of scorched-earth war with the French was a formidable enough problem to tackle. To

[11] Wilfred Burchett, *Mekong Upstream* ([East] Berlin: Seven Seas Books), pp. 89–90.

be sure, South Viet-Nam's rice surplus would have been of value to the North, but it must not be forgotten that the 1954 agreements provided for unhindered trade between the two zones. The fact that this never materialized no doubt contributed to the D.R.V.N.'s later decision to attempt a settlement by force.

Following the Geneva accords, the D.R.V.N. settled down to the task of transforming itself into a full-fledged "people's democracy." A "Population Classification Decree" issued in March, 1953, had divided the population into distinct social categories, and the regime now proceeded to eliminate all landlords by methods of force and terror reminiscent of the Chinese Communists—and with similar results. Exact figures remain unavailable, but the number of peasants killed during the North Vietnamese "land reform" drives from 1954 to 1956 is variously estimated at between 50,000 and 100,000.

This brutal policy led to the outbreak, in November, 1956, of a veritable peasant rebellion in Nghe-An Province—the same region which had been the seat of the pro-Communist peasant uprising of 1930. Ho stepped in, as he often had before, to save the unity of his movement without making irreconcilable enemies of the losers— in this case, Truong Chinh and the pro-Peking wing of the party, which stood for all-out collectivization of peasant land. Truong himself was dismissed as party Secretary General, though retaining his Politburo seat, while lower-ranking agricultural officials were purged altogether. (Ho assumed the Secretary Generalship himself, occupying the post until 1961 when he relinquished it to Le Duan, a South Vietnamese Communist.) In the ensuing "rectification of errors" campaign, tens of thousands of people were released from prison camps, and the Lao-Dong saw its membership drop from 700,000 to 420,000.[12] It is doubtful that such drastic actions would have been taken had destalinization not been the order of the day, but Khrushchev's speech at the Twentieth Congress of the CPSU in February, 1956, had apparently not fallen on deaf ears in Hanoi. From the Nghe-An outbreaks of November, 1956, until the spring of 1957, the North Vietnamese press freely published graphic accounts of life in D.R.V.N. prison camps—something that was matched only years later in the Soviet Union, and never in Communist China, even during the "hundred flowers" period.

[12] Kux, op. cit., p. 74.

The relative political calm which followed, coupled with a succession of two good crops in 1958–59, made the situation propitious for a gradual changeover from the makeshift wartime pattern of governmental administration to a more permanent system. At the lower levels, the old CRA's were reorganized in 1958, divorcing the military and party elements (at least officially) from the administrative structure. The new machinery of government was patterned fairly closely after the Soviet model, with locally elected People's Councils, each of which in turn picks an administrative committee from its midst. At the village level, the administrative committees are composed of at least a chairman, vice chairman, and secretary, while those for larger administrative divisions are correspondingly more elaborate.[13] Interestingly enough, the functioning of this machinery has been criticized even in the Lao-Dong's own newspaper, *Nhan-Dan*, which charged that members of the People's Councils often fail to listen to the complaints of their constituents and are not familiar with local problems, causing a "loosening of the ties between the government and the people."[14]

In the matter of territorial organization, the D.R.V.N., unlike South Viet-Nam, maintained the established provincial boundaries from the French period, thus leaving the population by and large within a familiar administrative environment. Two "autonomous zones," each embracing several provinces, also were created to accommodate the bulk of the 2.5 million minority tribesmen living in North Viet-Nam: the Thai-Meo Zone (now renamed Tay-Bac, which simply means "Northwest") was created in May, 1955; and the Viet-Bac (Northern Viet-Nam) Zone in August, 1956. Both have their own zonal assemblies and administrative committees, whose chairmen in both cases are former People's Army generals of tribal origin, as well as their own militia forces.

The most important institutional changes, however, affected the central government. From November, 1946, until May, 1960, the D.R.V.N. had operated with the same National Assembly, but the membership of this body had shrunk from 444 to 202 owing to purges of its non-Communist members, the desertion or capture of others during the war, and normal attrition. The low

---

[13] D.R.V.N., Law on the Organization of People's Councils and Administrative Committees of October 27, 1962.

[14] *Nhan-Dan*, November 24, 1962.

standing of the Assembly was evidenced by the passage of a resolution in January, 1957—that is, after the 1956 uprising—requesting that the Assembly's parliamentary immunities be respected and that bills proposed by the executive be presented for legislative approval within the proper deadlines.[15] These complaints led the regime to scrap plans for a perfunctory revision of the original 1946 constitution and to charge the committee appointed for this purpose with framing an altogether new constitution. After a year of preparatory work by the committee, in which Ho took a personal hand, the draft constitution was presented for public discussion in April, 1959, and, after many amendments, was adopted by the legislature on January 1, 1960.

Consisting of 112 articles divided into ten sections, the 1960 D.R.V.N. constitution is set apart from the run-of-the-mill constitutions of the other "people's democracies" by the virulence of its denunciations of the West and the doctrinaire extravagance of its praise of Communism and the personal role of President Ho Chi Minh. The extremely long preamble is a recital of Vietnamese history over the past twenty years and a paean of homage to the "farsighted leadership . . . of President Ho." The latter is vested, in practice, with almost unlimited power, inasmuch as the Vice President, who is empowered by the constitution to "replace the President by proxy [sic] in all of his powers," happens to be Ton Duc Thang, an old and faithful friend of Ho's, who is in his eighties and hardly likely to step into Ho's shoes. The Premier and five Vice Premiers wield very little authority, and the unicameral National Assembly—like its prototype, the Supreme Soviet of the U.S.S.R.—is a mere rubber-stamping body.

North Viet-Nam's judicial system also merits a few comments. While nominally guaranteeing the independence of the courts, the constitution practically nullifies this guarantee by making the courts "responsible" to the People's Councils at each level and placing the Supreme Court under the authority of the National Assembly and its Standing Committee. In addition to the courts, the Constitution makes provision for a brand new apparatus of "People's Control Organs" which seem to combine features of the Soviet Communist Party's "Control Commission," the Soviet Procurator's Office, and the Chinese Nationalists' "Control Yuan."

15 Fall, *The Two Viet-Nams*, p. 140.

The People's Control Organs have both civil and military sections and seemingly are a law unto themselves, except that the Supreme Control Organ (now headed by a reliable old Communist guerrilla leader from South Viet-Nam, Pham Van Bach) is, like all other government organs, nominally subject to supervision by the National Assembly. A law promulgated in July, 1960, gives the Control Organs the power to bring to justice all cases under inquiry, as well as to "suspend prosecution, [to] participate in judicial processes, and [to] appeal judgments of lower courts."

It is readily apparent that the structure of the North Vietnamese state as fixed by the 1960 constitution contains little that offers any real prospects of liberalization. Elections held since the adoption of the constitution have amply confirmed this. The elections of May 8, 1960, for the new national legislature followed the standard Communist pattern, with 99.8 per cent of the voters casting ballots for a total of 458 candidates "competing" for 404 seats. Two small minority parties (Democratic and Socialist), whose existence is tolerated as long as they obediently collaborate with the Communists, were permitted to put up candidates in certain districts (notably in Hanoi) and won a few seats, but for the most part the voters were offered no choice. The latest regular legislative elections, held in April, 1964, brought little apparent change, except for a reduction of the number of seats to be filled to 366, for which 448 candidates ran.[16]

Thus, North Viet-Nam has become a full-fledged Communist state, backed by a strong army and an ubiquitous party. The intellectuals, who enjoyed a brief taste of freedom of expression during the period of relaxed intellectual controls in late 1956 and early 1957, have since been brought thoroughly into line and find themselves literally "frozen out" of any real participation in public affairs. North Viet-Nam's "hundred flowers" period, which took its cue from Communist China, lasted less than six months. Phan-Khoi, one of the most brilliant Vietnamese intellectuals, succeeded in publishing only five issues of a new literary journal entitled *Nhan-Van* ("Humanism")—a wordplay on the name of the Communist daily, *Nhan-Dan* ("Humanity")—before it was banned. As elsewhere in the Communist bloc, the ensuing crackdown covered

16 *Viet-Nam Information Bulletin*, May 30, 1964.

all branches of the arts from painting to music, and the repressive measures taken by the regime ranged from forced self-criticism—as in the case of one intellectual who was obliged to confess to the sin of reading the French liberal newspaper *Le Monde*—to outright trial for subversive activity. Five intellectuals, including one woman, were tried in January, 1960, on charges of having collaborated with *Nhan-Van* and were sentenced to prison terms up to fifteen years. Phan-Khoi himself died before going on trial, and his son, Phan-Thao, died from unexplained causes seven months later. Thousands of other intellectuals, along with high school and college students, have been conscripted into "education-and-work" programs similar to those instituted in Communist China.[17]

Notwithstanding all the confident claims of the D.R.V.N. leadership, the over-all progress of the economy of North Viet-Nam has not lived up to official expectations.[18] This was acknowledged in the 1964 report of the General Statistical Office, which stated that production in several basic branches of state industry "showed relatively slow growth . . . and failed to respond to the demands

[17] Hoang Van Chi, *From Colonialism to Communism: A Case History of North Vietnam* (New York: Frederick A. Praeger; London: Pall Mall Press, 1964), pp. 109–62. Cf. also Fall, *Le Viet-Minh, 1945–1960* (Paris: Armand Colin, 1960), pp. 320–30.

[18] The following table affords some idea of the progress achieved by the North Vietnamese economy in the production of various key commodities, using 1939 figures (adjusted to cover only those parts of Indochina now included in North Viet-Nam) as a basis for comparison. All statistics for later years are based on unverifiable Communist sources, in some cases representing an average of conflicting figures, and hence should be regarded as only a rough approximation. Nevertheless, they serve to illustrate the relatively low level of economic development to date, especially in relation to population growth. Figures for rice, coal, cement, phosphate, and steel are in thousands of tons; for cattle, in thousands of head; for electricity, in millions of kilowatts; and for textiles, in millions of meters.

Commodity	1939	1955	1960	1963	1964
Rice	2,453	3,600	4,146	4,200	4,300
Cattle	1,351	1,084	2,900	2,233	2,326
Coal	2,615	641	2,595	3,300	3,200
Cement	305	9	400	582	590
Phosphate	31	8	65	163	—
Steel	130	0	3	20	50
Electricity	122	53	271	442	530
Textiles	55	39	86	92	—

of a rapidly-growing national economy."[19] However, it is in agriculture that the D.R.V.N. faces its most serious economic problem —a problem aggravated by the fantastic growth rate of the population, amounting to 3.2 per cent, or about a half-million new mouths each year. Tran Huu Duc, former Minister of State Farms and a member of the party Central Committee, wrote in the party's theoretical monthly *Hoc-Tap* (February, 1962) that the "ridicuously low" per capita acreage of available agricultural land posed a "serious obstacle to the raising of living standards." He furthur warned that the problem would become more critical unless about 600,000 hectares (1.5 million acres) of new land could be brought into cultivation by 1965. Not only has there been no such spectacular expansion of agricultural acreage, but about 260,000 hectares of already cultivated rice land were flooded during the heavy typhoons of 1964.

Although agricultural collectivization has been carried forward in North Viet-Nam at a much slower pace than in Communist China, cooperative farms now embrace about 95 per cent of all lowland agriculture. In 1964 there also were some fifty-nine state farms, largely experimental in nature and operated for the most part by the People's Army. Private farming nevertheless continued to account for a substantial proportion of the available food supply and has helped a great deal to prevent the food situation from deteriorating to an intolerable level. In March, 1965, the regime openly admitted that the 1964 rice crop was about 5.1 per cent below the planned level and only 2.1 per cent above the admittedly bad harvest of 1963.

Progress in industrial development has been more satisfactory, but at heavy cost. A basic Three-Year Plan for 1958–60 was never fulfilled, and the first Five-Year Plan (1960–65) had to be extensively scaled downward in 1963 in accordance with a more realistic appraisal of the country's capabilities. Even so, the industrial development program has depended heavily on economic aid from other Communist countries, amounting as of the end of 1961 to $622 million from Communist China, $365 million from the Soviet Union, and $38 million from the East European countries.[20]

[19] *Bulletin du Viet-Nam*, March 15, 1965.
[20] Speech by Le Thanh Nghi, Minister of Heavy Industry, March 18, 1962. No new figures have been made available.

In recent years this assistance has tended increasingly to take the form of loans and trade credits instead of outright grants, augmenting the long-term burden on the North Vietnamese economy. How heavy this burden could become is clearly indicated by the size of the deficits which North Viet-Nam has been piling up in its trade with the Soviet Union; for instance, in 1962, North Vietnamese imports from the U.S.S.R. amounted in value to $54.6 million as against exports to the U.S.S.R. of only $30.1 million.

Apart from the increasing risks attached to its direct involvement in the struggle for South Viet-Nam, the Hanoi regime faces a delicate external problem in keeping its relations with its feuding Soviet and Chinese allies on an even keel. Some outside observers have tended in the recent past to view the North Vietnamese leadership as leaning more and more towards the side of Peking—so much so, indeed, as to make it questionable that Hanoi's former cordial relationship with Moscow can ever be restored.[21] In fact, however, a closer survey of North Vietnamese actions and statements since the Twenty-second CPSU Congress in Moscow suggests that the Hanoi regime has sought to maintain a careful neutrality between Moscow and Peking by means of a balanced "dosage" of gestures towards both sides.

For instance, while in Moscow in November, 1961, Ho Chi Minh publicly extolled the "unstinting fraternal aid" extended to his country by the Soviet Union and the East European countries, neglecting to mention the large-scale aid also received from China. Yet, when China's Chou En-lai left the Twenty-second Congress in a huff, Ho also saw fit to depart from Moscow—though only to tour the Soviet Union rather than to return home. Throughout 1962, Hanoi made repeated pleas for unity within the socialist camp, obviously seeking to avoid having to choose between Moscow and Peking.

North Viet-Nam's widening intervention in the South Vietnamese insurgency has also been viewed by some Western observers as signifying that the Hanoi regime is more wedded to Peking's ideological line of strident anti-Western struggle in the underdeveloped world than to Moscow's more conciliatory position. This, however, would be difficult to substantiate. Various ex-

21 E.g., P. J. Honey, *Communism in North Viet-Nam* (Cambridge, Mass.: MIT Press, 1964), p. 196.

planations have been advanced in the West as to the genesis of the insurgency in South Viet-Nam and the North Vietnamese Communist role in it. Two common theses are: (1) that the whole insurgency began simply as an internal response to the repressive nature of the Diem regime, which left the local oppositionists no choice but resistance or extermination;[22] and (2) that the insurgency was instigated from North Viet-Nam pursuant to a policy decision taken in September, 1960, at the Third Party Congress of the Lao-Dong in Hanoi.[23]

Neither of these theses, however, explains the highly methodical nature of insurgent operations in South Viet-Nam as early as 1957. As this writer has pointed out elsewhere,[24] killings of village officials inside South Viet-Nam reached the figure of 452 by 1957, and these were clustered in certain provinces, suggesting more than a random pattern. In fact, the geographic pattern of these insurgency incidents closely paralleled that of alleged South Vietnamese violations of the 1954 cease-fire charged in North Vietnamese complaints to the International Control Commission, providing a prima facie case for the existence of close coordination between the Communist guerrillas in South Viet-Nam and the North Vietnamese intelligence apparatus. It is also worthy of note that Communist-perpetrated incidents in South Viet-Nam remained at a low level during the 1954–56 period, when there was still talk about the holding of reunification elections (which the D.R.V.N. expected to win), but that such incidents picked up in intensity immediately after South Viet-Nam refused to agree to the holding of the elections in July, 1956.[25]

This leaves still a third hypothesis regarding the origins of the insurgency in South Viet-Nam, namely, that the D.R.V.N., as a Communist state occupying a sensitive position on the outer per-

[22] This view has often been voiced by French writers. E.g., see Philippe Devillers, "The Struggle for the Unification of Viet-Nam," in P. S. Honey, *North Viet-Nam Today* (New York: Frederick A. Praeger, 1962); or Jean Lacouture, "Le F. N. L. est-il bien le 'satellite' de Hanoi?," in *Le Monde* (weekly ed.), April 21, 1965.

[23] Cf. the white books published by the U.S. Department of State in December, 1961, and February, 1965.

[24] See Chapters 13 and 18.

[25] South Viet-Nam based its refusal on the argument that under the existing conditions it would not be possible to hold elections free of Communist influence and with proper international safeguards.

imeter of the bloc, looked upon its South Vietnamese neighbor as a legitimate target for Communist subversive activities, and that the growth of internal tensions there elevated South Viet-Nam from a "random" objective of Communist subversion to a direct "target of opportunity." The North Vietnamese leadership evidently saw little harm in giving first moral and later physical aid to the insurgents, since such aid appeared unlikely to assume burdensome proportions or to entail any major risk of international complications. It probably was only as the United States counter-commitment grew that North Viet-Nam suddenly realized that it was in the process of being drawn into a major conflict.

The Hanoi regime has not, however, shown any intention of backing away from its increasingly burdensome intervention in South Viet-Nam. On the contrary, recent evidence—chiefly in the form of growing numbers of bloc-supplied weapons captured from insurgent forces and the taking of prisoners from such regular units of the North Vietnamese People's Army as the 325th Division—suggests Hanoi's determination, at least for the moment, to press on with its offensive in the South.

From their own vantage point, both the Soviet Union and Red China must have looked upon the whole Vietnamese insurgency at first as a welcome irritant to the United States—and one which promised not to involve them directly since, on the basis of past performance against the French, North Viet-Nam seemed capable of handling the problem by itself with only a minimal amount of bloc aid. The moment of truth came in August, 1964, when American reprisal raids on North Vietnamese patrol-boat bases made it clear that the D.R.V.N. could not defend itself against air strikes, and that Peking had nothing to offer Hanoi in the way of sophisticated aircraft or anti-aircraft missiles—and, in fact, seemed reluctant to become directly involved at this point.

Nor is this apparent reluctance likely to be altogether one-sided, for Sino-Vietnamese relations—regardless of the regime in power in either country—have been notoriously uncordial for something like 2,000 years.[26] Hence, an outright Red Chinese military commitment in defense of North Viet-Nam would no doubt be less

[26] On the historical background of Sino-Vietnamese relations, see Harold C. Hinton, *China's Relations with Burma and Viet-Nam* (New York: Institute of Pacific Relations, 1958).

palatable to the Hanoi regime than was the Red Chinese intervention in Korea in 1950–53 to the North Korean Communists. The North Vietnamese habit, even recently, of boasting of Vietnamese military victories not only against the French but also against Chinese invaders in earlier times clearly indicates how widespread such feelings are even today. Moreover, the obvious inability of Communist China to supply the D.R.V.N. with the kind of advanced weapons it needs in its present plight must have contributed further to swinging the balance of political influence in Hanoi away from Peking towards Moscow. Particularly after the Viet-Cong guerrilla attack at Pleiku in February, 1965, led the United States to intensify air action against North Vietnamese territory, Hanoi's realignment on the Soviet position became no longer a matter of mere ideological or sentimental preference, but one of simple survival. For only the Soviets had the planes and missiles that could save North Viet-Nam itself from destruction, regardless of the effect of such bombings on the guerrilla situation inside South Viet-Nam or on Hanoi's determination to continue supporting the Viet-Cong. Soviet Premier Kosygin's presence in Hanoi at the time of the first American air raids on North Vietnamese soil resulted in a prompt Soviet assurance of all "necessary support and assistance" to North Viet-Nam.

Both Peking and Moscow sought to turn the new situation to their own conflicting advantages. Peking accused the Soviet Union of being slow to fulfill its pledge to go to the aid of the D.R.V.N. for fear of becoming directly embroiled with the United States, while Moscow returned the compliment by asserting that China was blocking the transshipment of Soviet arms to North Viet-Nam—a charge that gained credence from Chou En-lai's assertion that Soviet military supplies to North Viet-Nam would only result in an ultimate American-Russian "deal" along Cuban lines.[27]

In the meantime, Hanoi began to give off "signals" suggesting a softening of its previous "hard" position of uncompromising insistence upon the virtual unconditional surrender of South Viet-Nam to the Viet-Cong. These signals, which began almost as soon as American air raids on North Viet-Nam became a daily occurrence in early March, 1965, appeared in statements by North Vietnamese leaders which first omitted "immediate reunification" as

[27] *The Washington Post*, April 20, 1965.

one of Hanoi's war aims and then ceased demanding the "immediate departure of all U.S. troops" as a precondition for peace.[28]

In mid-April, a high-level North Vietnamese mission went to Moscow, presumably to nail down promises of Soviet support. The very composition of the mission seemed indicative of a victory for Soviet influence in Hanoi over that of Peking. Its leading members were: General Giap, Vice Premier, Minister of Defense, and Army commander in chief, long known as pro-Soviet; Le Duan, the party Secretary-General; and Nguyen Duy Trinh, a South Vietnamese member of the party Politburo and newly appointed Foreign Minister. The joint statement issued following the Moscow talks, on April 17, contained little new in the way of precise Soviet assurances of military support, but it significantly reiterated the newly softened D.R.V.N. position on war aims in South Viet-Nam, adding that the "two parts of Viet-Nam [must] have no military alliances with other countries, and no foreign military bases and servicemen on their territory." This seemed to mean that Hanoi conceded for the first time—at least in principle —that North Viet-Nam was also "neutralizable," and hence not an integral part of the Communist bloc on a par with, say, Hungary or North Korea. It is admittedly dangerous to assume a change of Communist policy on the basis of a single statement, or even of a series of statements; yet, these signs, considered in conjunction with the ingrained Vietnamese distaste for Chinese domination, the effects of United States military pressure, and the impact of the Soviet rift with China, suggest rather strongly that the present leadership in Hanoi might prefer to opt for a solution of the present situation which—in the words of two French commentators— would not make of "the Viet-Nam war the Spanish [civil] war of the atomic age."[29]

To be sure, Red China will always have geography in its favor: it is next door to North Viet-Nam, while Russia is 5,000 miles away. Over the past twenty years, moreover, Moscow has been less than a reliable ally of Hanoi. From 1946 to 1950, it stood aloof from the Viet-Minh struggle against France; in 1954, it compelled

[28] Text of TV interview given by General Giap to Japanese TV, rebroadcast by Radio Hanoi, March 10, 1965.

[29] Georges Chaffard and Jean-François Kahn, "Ho Chi Minh—l'heure de la vérité," *L'Express*, May 30, 1965, p. 53.

Ricefields, buffaloes, and children: the perennial image of peace in Viet-Nam

Birth of a revolutionary: Ho Chi Minh at the French Socialist Congress, Tours, December, 1920

The current leaders of North Viet-Nam plan offensive in 1954 *(left to right)*: Pham Van Dong, Ho Chi Minh, Truong Chinh, General Vo Nguyen Giap

Viet-Minh guerrillas plan a raid in 1947

(Right) Temporary bridges for coolie convoys: one answer to air power

A South Vietnamese Rhade warrior

Communist Party card of a captured guerrilla

Vice President Lyndon B. Johnson visits President Ngo Dinh Diem during his tour of Southeast Asia in 1961

Pacific Stars and Stripes

The new war: American and ARVN pilots prepare for a mission

Mme. Ngo Dinh Nhu

USIS, Saigon   François Sully

The new war:
Viet-Cong
prisoners

Precarious coexistence: President Ho and school girls at Minsk, 1961

The North: work pause for a political lesson
at Viet-Tri electrochemical complex

The North: People's Army militia girls

The author interviewing North Vietnamese Premier Pham Van Dong

The stakes: wars of national liberation . . .

. . . vs. counterinsurgency and containment

the D.R.V.N. at Geneva to accept conditions far less favorable than the military situation warranted; in 1956, it failed to press for the holding of the reunification elections in Viet-Nam; in 1957–58, it made only a perfunctory bid for the admission of the D.R.V.N. to the U.N.; in 1960–62, it failed to press the Laotian campaign to a successful conclusion; and over the whole past decade, it did not provide the D.R.V.N. with the up-to-date military matériel which it supplies to its European satellites, and which might have helped to protect North Viet-Nam from American air action in 1965.

In sum, the North Vietnamese Communists have succeeded in building a solidly entrenched, totalitarian regime, based upon a disciplined party structure and the largest land army in Southeast Asia. On the other hand, North Viet-Nam—like almost every other Communist state—is plagued by a disastrous agricultural situation and cannot find a solution of its acute food problem within the confines of the bloc. It has also become directly engaged in a military contest in which it urgently requires outside support; yet, the availability of such support from Moscow is jeopardized by the Sino-Soviet conflict, while acceptance of large-scale military assistance from Communist China would not only mean committing North Viet-Nam to Peking's alternative of "liberation war *à outrance*," but would also involve sacrificing a relative freedom of maneuver for which Ho Chi Minh and his associates have struggled for almost forty years.

PART III

The South:
Stillborn Experiment?

No matter what its ultimate fate, South Viet-Nam between 1954 and 1966, when viewed a few decades hence, will probably rank second only to the mishandling of the whole China problem as one of the single most incredible failures of American foreign policy.

As the articles in this section will show, South Viet-Nam would have been—even without the aid North Viet-Nam gave to the Viet-Cong insurgents after 1960—an extremely vulnerable country because of its failure to come to grips with the atomization of its own society. Only total blindness or irresponsible ignorance could explain the failure to realize that such strongly structured and motivated groups as the Hoa-Hao and Cao-Dai sects could not be wished out of existence as political factors, but had to be given an acceptable position within the normal political fabric of the country.

It is probably futile to point out that the socio-economic reform programs announced for South Viet-Nam at the Honolulu conference of February, 1966, are much the same as those developed in 1955, 1959, and 1962, and that the earlier ones failed not for lack of funds or the serious problems of insecurity, but simply because the Saigon authorities thus far have not provided the programs with the proper impetus. The same kinds of errors being made now were also reported in 1958, but they were discounted as either irrelevant or as "birth pangs" of an essentially sound long-range program.

Such arguments were perhaps acceptable in the short run as far as the mistreatment of the tribal minorities or the alienation of the large Chinese community was concerned, if, as was asserted, such discriminatory measures enhanced Vietnamese "national consciousness" (in fact, they did not). But they could not be accepted when it was the rise of a coordinated insurgency that was at issue.

Thanks to Ngo Dinh Diem's failure to carry out the promised reform programs, the same peasantry that had helped the Saigon government destroy the armed bands of the religious sects now failed to give the same aid in the government's fight against the resurgent pro-Communist guerrillas. These guerrillas were to have been reintegrated into the nation, but instead had been the object of nationwide hunts whose results, by the sheer exaggeration of their claims, must have involved many non-Communist elements—and did indeed. As early as January, 1956, police-state measures directed against *anyone* who disagreed with the prevailing edicts of the Diem regime forced all opposition into the agonizing choice of self-imposed exile (if rich), total silence (if less fortunate and thus forced to remain in Viet-Nam), or armed resistance.

Those who made (or influenced) Viet-Nam policy at the time were in an apparent quandary: either admit that the Diem regime was unpopular and recommend that it make the radical adjustments necessary to its survival and to the prevention of a major insurrection—of which North Viet-Nam would not fail to take advantage—or deny that the obvious signs of disintegration were only the early warnings of far more dangerous events to come, and hope that eventual improvements in the Diem regime through internal changes could avert a crisis altogether. The denial of the purely military effects of the rising insurgency lasted from 1956 until General Taylor reported his views to President Kennedy in November, 1961. The attempt to deal with the whole problem through little more than trying to persuade the Diem regime to reform itself lasted until Ambassador Frederick E. Nolting departed from Saigon in the summer of 1963. Little can be added to what amounts in retrospect to a catalogue of errors as, one after another, the various socio-economic problems of South Viet-Nam, held in check for over a decade, exploded: the Buddhist sects, the tribesmen, the landless peasantry, and the stay-behind and infiltrated Communist guerrillas, soon to become the National Liberation Front (NLF) or, in South Vietnamese official parlance, the Viet-Cong (VC).

There remains the question of Viet-Nam's fate after an indefinite period of partition. Unlike the two Germanies, which have settled down to a system of precarious political coexistence and economic symbiosis—the shooting of escapees over the Berlin Wall notwithstanding—the two Viet-Nams have remained actively hostile, thanks to provocative policies whose origin was by no means one-sided. The last chapter of this section attempts to draw some conclusions as to the effect of this long-standing division, with no "safety valve" (such as the interzonal trade of the two Germanies, or the two Koreas' common meeting place in Japan), of two parts of a country that needed each other badly.

11. Religion in Politics

July, 1955

The victory of the Vietnamese troops who under Colonel Duong Van Duc planted the red-and-gold flag of the nationalist regime atop the rugged That Son Mountains on June 29, 1955, marked the end of a curious chapter in the history of postwar Viet-Nam.[1] While recent newspaper accounts have, according to their viewpoint, described the sects either as an element of instability that threatened to disintegrate the already menaced nationalist regime in Saigon or as a solid barrier against Viet-Minh infiltration, very little has been said about the men and the beliefs which, along with more mundane interests, bound the sects into quasi-autonomous religious, economic, political, and military "kingdoms."

The Vietnamese have retained what one French observer aptly called *le goût du merveilleux*, a certain proclivity for the supernatural, which has tended to express itself in the rising of new prophets and new religious interpretations of what had become a rather weak and extremely tolerant Buddhism. However, it was only in the chaos that followed the disappearance of the French colonial administration during the last days of World War II that the religious groups began to organize on a territorial basis so as to be able to protect their adherents. As in Europe in the Middle Ages, such semireligious fiefs became centers of relative calm and stability in the midst of a war-torn country where the farmer, though heavily taxed by the various chieftains, could at least find some meager assurance of physical survival as well as spiritual guidance.

---

[1] South Viet-Nam as referred to in this article means only the administrative *ky* (region) formerly known as Cochinchina. The truncated state of Viet-Nam up to the 17th parallel—generally referred to as South Viet-Nam—will be referred to as Viet-Nam.

Excerpted, by permission, from "The Political-Religious Sects of Viet-Nam," originally published in *Pacific Affairs* (Vancouver), September, 1955. © 1955 by *Pacific Affairs*.

Three major groups emerged from the postwar chaos and attained positions of political strength and military importance: the Cao-Dai, the Hoa-Hao, and the Binh-Xuyen.[2]

Cao-Daism has retained much of Buddhism's external pomp and allied it with similar features from Catholicism. Called in Vietnamese *Dai Dao Tam Ky Pho Do* (Third Amnesty of God), but better known as Cao-Dai (High Palace, a paraphrase for God Who Reigns over the Universe), this faith is based upon spiritualism. It assumes that God already has proclaimed two "amnesties": one in the West through Moses and Jesus, and the other in the Orient through Buddha Sakyamuni and Lao-Tse. Both these previous amnesties have taken on human form while in the third, as revealed in the Cao-Dai faith, God has adapted his teachings to the higher evolution of the human spirit and transmits his messages through mediums or other spiritualistic means.

The theory behind the Cao-Dai faith is explained in the following terms by a now-deceased French adherent of the faith, whose books on the subject have the approval of the highest Cao-Dai authorities: "Cao-Daism . . . is destined to the whole Universe, because the message which it carries already is contained in every religion. The multiplicity of religions is not an obstacle to harmony if there is a subtle but nonetheless real bond which serves as point of contact. This subtle but real bond, Cao-Daism, brings it to every unprejudiced person, in all sincerity, in all fraternity, in its message: Life, Love, Truth."[3] . . .

The Cao-Dai terminology and hierarchy borrow heavily from those of the Catholic Church and are replete with cardinals, bishops, monks, and nuns. Furthermore, it has retained more "feudal" aspects in that it provides for a temporal government branch

[2] In fact, prior to the evacuation of North Viet-Nam, the Catholic bishoprics of Phat-Diem and Bui-Chu and the South Vietnamese province of Ben-Tre were as autonomous as any of the above-mentioned sects and were accurately considered as sect areas by certain writers (e.g., Ellen J. Hammer, *The Struggle for Indochina*).

[3] The writer wishes to acknowledge his gratitude to H. H. Pham Cong Tac, Superior of the Cao-Dai, who gave him some of the information contained in this article during the writer's stay at Tay-Ninh, capital of the sect. (*He died in exile in Cambodia, in* 1961.) For an extensive study of Cao-Dai organization and philosophy, see Gabriel Gobron, *Histoire et Philosophie du Caodaisme* (Paris: Dervy, 1949); and Pham Cong Tac, *Le Caodaisme—Phap-Chanh-Truyen* (Paris: Dervy, 1953).

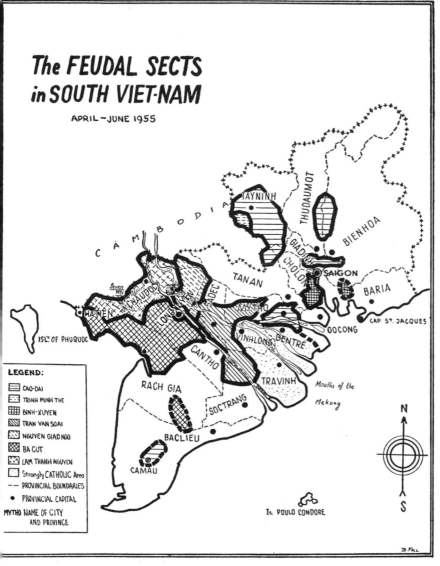

The FEUDAL SECTS in SOUTH VIET-NAM

APRIL – JUNE 1955

LEGEND:

- ▤ CAO-DAI
- ▧ TRINH MINH THE
- ▦ BINH-XUYEN
- ▨ TRAN VAN SOAI
- ▨ NGUYEN GIAO NGO
- ▨ BA CUT
- ▨ LAM THANH NGUYEN
- ☐ Strongly CATHOLIC Area
- – – PROVINCIAL BOUNDARIES
- • PROVINCIAL CAPITAL
- MYTHO NAME OF CITY AND PROVINCE

CAMBODIA

TAYNINH
THUDAUMOT
BIENHOA
GIADINH
CHOLON
SAIGON
BARIA
TANAN
CHAUDOC
Seven Mts
HATIEN
MYTHO
CAP ST. JACQUES
ISLE OF PHUQUOC
GOCONG
VINHLONG
BENTRE
CANTHO
TRAVINH
Mouths of the Mekong
RACH GIA
SOCTRANG
BACLIEU
CAMAU
Is. POULO CONDORE

B. FALL

N
S

FIGURE 3

within the church. Thus, the Cao-Dai at their "Holy See" at Tay-Ninh have the following administrative branches to carry out quasi-governmental functions: the Cuu Trung Dai, which has executive powers and controls the temporal administration and armed forces of the sect; the Hiep Thien Dai, which legislates in religious affairs; and the Co-quan Phoc-thien, a quasi-Western "welfare agency" which takes care of the poor and invalid members of the community. . . .

With the start of World War II, all the Cao-Dai groups turned rapidly toward more and more outspoken forms of anti-French nationalism. Oracles and prophecies announced the early return of Cuong-Dê from Japan and the eventual liquidation of French rule. The French reacted by deporting Pham Cong Tac and several of his closest aides to Madagascar, where they remained until the end of the war. To this the Cao-Dai responded by seeking the aid of the Japanese. Paramilitary groups, such as the "White Caps" and the "Volunteer Interior Forces," began to appear in South Viet-Nam, and for a short time after French power collapsed in March, 1945, the Cao-Dai came close to gaining preponderance over all other groups (including the Viet-Minh) operating in the South. However, in the absence of the Ho Phap, still imprisoned in Madagascar, the subordinate Cao-Dai leaders quarreled and failed to exploit the situation.

When the Viet-Minh gained in power, the Coa-Dai joined it on a basis of mutual respect in fighting the return of the French, at least until June 6, 1946, when Tran Quang Vinh (then the commander of the Cao-Dai armed forces) was made prisoner by the French. He negotiated a truce with the French in exchange for the freedom of Pham Cong Tac and his aides and their return from Madagascar, which took place in September, 1946.

When fighting later broke out between the French and the Viet-Minh, the Cao-Dai at first remained neutral. However, Nguyen Binh, the Communist doctrinaire who led the Viet-Minh in South Viet-Nam, attempted to wage a two-front war in trying to liquidate the sects while also fighting the French, with the result that he pushed the sects into the arms of the French. On January 8, 1947, the Cao-Dai signed a military convention with the French High Command, promising "loyal collaboration" with the French and respect for the laws and regulations of the authorities. In exchange, the French were to arm and pay the organ-ized armed forces of the Cao-Dai, to be composed of "Mobile Brigades" and of garrison troops. This was done, and the majority of the Cao-Dai forces cooperated from then on with the French troops, with the exception of a small group under Trinh Minh The,[4] an ultranationalist who in 1951 took to the hills with a few hundred men.

Politically, the Cao-Dai leaders, having now made peace with the French, sought to consolidate their position by making the suc-cessive nationalist regimes dependent upon their support. Having toyed at first with ideas of an autonomous Cochinchina Republic, the Cao-Dai gave its allegiance to a unified Viet-Nam after the Elysée agreements of 1949 formally gave Viet-Nam its independ-ence, and on May 6, 1950, threw its weight behind Tran Van Huu, Bao-Dai's second premier. At that time, to show goodwill, one Cao-Dai battalion was integrated in the national army.

However, the Ho Phap still had not abandoned his idea of mak-ing the Cao-Dai the dominant power in Viet-Nam. In 1951, the Cao-Dai asked the French to arm and train three full Cao-Dai divisions (about 45,000 men) and demanded three cabinet seats. A refusal of both demands resulted in a military "torpor" of the Cao-Dai, from which they were only prodded by some Viet-Minh attacks on their Tay-Ninh stronghold. Soon, in view of the de-teriorating situation, the French and the Vietnamese Government relented, at least in part; additional Cao-Dai troops were armed and some of the sect's dignitaries, such as Le Van Hoach, soon held high cabinet posts.

The coordination of the military activities of the sects was handled by a French staff section, the Inspectorat Général des

---

[4] For the duration of the hostilities with the Viet-Minh, The remained in his hideout near Tay-Ninh in a sort of loyal opposition to the Ho Phap. His underground broadcasting station, "Voice of National Viet-Nam," regularly attacked the various Vietnamese regimes under the aegis of Bao-Dai and his forces—bearing the resounding name Quan-Doi Quoc Gia Lien-Minh (Inter-Allied National Forces)—and his followers fought a not-too-spirited war against both the Viet-Minh and the French. After the consolidation of the Ngo Dinh Diem government in Saigon late in 1954, Trinh Minh The (who had in the meantime named himself brigadier general) joined the nationalist camp on February 13, 1955, for a price reported to be $2 million. His troops were integrated in the Vietnamese national army. "General" The was killed during the outbreak of fighting in Saigon on May 4, 1955, and received a state funeral.

Forces Supplétives, which paid an allowance to the unit commanders on a per capita basis of actual fighting men available. French liaison officers and training staff were stationed with all major Cao-Dai and Hoa-Hao units. The job of those missions was hazardous enough, particularly with the smaller and less well-organized sect units, whose "war effort" closely resembled banditry. In many cases, such units massacred their French cadres or fought over supplies with a neighboring unit which had invaded the preserve of the first. Lastly, military units of the sects were primarily concerned with acquiring larger fiefs. Hence, a military unit constituted—as formerly in the case of the warlords in China— a considerable commercial asset that could not be squandered on a sudden military operation. This made the sects highly reluctant to fight the Viet-Minh effectively and their troops could seldom be used except in or near their own living area.

Until the end of the hostilities, the sects even had their own officers' school, where their most promising cadres were trained during a five-month course by French and Vietnamese officers. Today the sects may have 3,000 or more officers acquainted with at least the rudiments of modern warfare. This singularly complicates the problem of liquidating the sects' armed forces.

Exceedingly sensitive to changes of the political atmosphere in the country, Pham Cong Tac in 1953 steered the Cao-Dai movement on a strictly Vietnamese nationalist course. Indeed, it seemed for a time during the late summer of 1953, when Premier Nguyen Van Tam's government showed signs of weakening, that the Cao-Dai heads were willing to assume the political leadership of the country. Ngo Khai Minh, the "apostolic representative" of the Ho Phap in France, in fact hinted broadly that "Tay Ninh would offer a solid base for conversations in view of the fact that millions of signatures could back up the signature of the 'pope' Pham Cong Tac"[5] in the case of final independence negotiations between Viet-Nam and France.

The political activities of the Ho Phap increased further during Bao-Dai's ill-fated attempt of September and October, 1953, to rally a majority of all nationalist groups behind him in negotiating with France a "final" Vietnamese independence treaty. A congress of such nationalist groups was to meet at Saigon early in October,

---

[5] *Paris-Presse—L'Intransigeant* (Paris), August 4, 1953.

1953, and hammer out a program to be discussed by the Vietnamese delegation with France. On September 4, 1953, the Ho Phap called a press conference at his Saigon headquarters and launched an appeal for national union in which he managed to praise both Bao-Dai and Ho Chi Minh and to appeal for full independence while not being averse to a close association with France.[6]

The Ho Phap, as one of the members of the organizing committee of the nationalist congress, remained in the political limelight throughout the congress. It was he who read the political objectives of the congress to the press on October 4, 1953, and the block of 17 Cao-Dai seats out of a total of 203 was the biggest given to any of the sects. It is not clear whether the Cao-Dai was finally outbid by other groups in a frantic rush to ask for full independence or whether the demand for full independence which was finally made by the congress (thus backfiring on Bao-Dai and the French) was actually part of a carefully thought-out plan of the Ho Phap to repay the French for his five years in exile. In any case, nationalist support for Bao-Dai failed to materialize at this time, and the Emperor now attempted to tackle the sects and other nationalist groups piecemeal, by inviting the leaders to see him one by one. General Phuong of the Cao-Dai thus was called to Dalat, and so was the Ho Phap, who, on April 9, 1954, issued a statement that he was now "supporting without reservations" Bao-Dai in the latter's "struggle for total independence for Viet-Nam" and "for the liberation of the Vietnamese people from the Communist yoke."[7]

The rapidly worsening military and political situation of the country put the Cao-Dai's promises of full support for the Saigon

[6] In the course of a personal conversation with the writer in the summer of 1953, the Ho Phap stated that one of the major advantages of Viet-Nam's staying in the French Union would be the possibility of resettling a great amount of Vietnamese surplus population in the sparsely populated French colonies in the Pacific and in Madagascar, thus making Viet-Nam a strong partner not in a "French Union" but in a "Franco-Vietnamese Union." At present, there are more than 10,000 Vietnamese in the New Hebrides and New Caledonia, and there is a fast-growing Vietnamese colony in French Guiana. For a report of the Ho Phap's press conference see *Journal d'Extrême-Orient*, September 5, 1953.

[7] Bernard B. Fall, *Political Development of Viet-Nam*, Vol. II: *State of Viet-Nam* (Ann Arbor, Mich.: University Microfilms, 1955), p. 403.

regime to a severe test. When the government of Premier Buu-Loc decided on April 12, 1954, to integrate the armed forces of the sects into the Vietnamese National Army, the Cao-Dai commander in chief, Nguyen Thanh Phuong, addressed a circular to all his subordinates violently attacking the decision, alleging that it had been made without previous consultation with him.

This seems untrue in view of the fact that Phuong himself had had a lengthy conversation with the Vietnamese chief of staff, General Nguyen Van Hinh, on April 5, and in view of the public statements made a few days later by the Ho Phap. In any event, the integration decree remained a dead letter until more than a year later. Because of the disastrous developments at Dien Bien Phu, the Cao-Dai once more changed course. All anti-Communist references were played down to the minimum and on the eve of the fall of Dien Bien Phu, the Ho Phap launched an appeal to both sides for moderation and addressed an open letter to Ho Chi Minh containing the following passage: "You and His Majesty, Bao-Dai, have succeeded in liberating the country. The Vietnamese people are grateful to both of you. However, there remains a problem to be settled: reconciliation between the nationalists and the Communists."[8]

A last outburst of Cao-Dai political activity followed the Geneva conference and the unsuccessful rebellion of the Vietnamese Army Chief of Staff (Nguyen Van Hinh) against Premier Ngo Dinh Diem in the fall of 1954,[9] but, as will be shown later, the Ho Phap adroitly succeeded in avoiding a head-on clash between the Cao-Dai sect and the Diem regime during the brief civil war of April and May, 1955. Backed by a well-disciplined hierarchy and a devoted following of more than 2 million faithful, the Cao-Dai, under the leadership of what many observers call the "shrewdest Vietnamese politician," successfully made the transition from feudalism to the beginnings of organized governmental administration. . . .

The Phat Giao Hoa-Hao sect, better known as the Hoa-Hao, is an example of Buddhist "protestantism" that can be found in

[8] *The New York Times*, May 6, 1954.
[9] See Bernard B. Fall, "Indochina since Geneva," *Pacific Affairs*, March, 1955, p. 7.

many areas in Southeast Asia. Of even more recent vintage than the Cao-Dai—it was created in 1939—the Hoa-Hao sect claims nearly 1,500,000 adherents, mostly concentrated in the highly fertile rice bowl of the Mekong Delta, particularly in the Mien-Tay, the "new West" area of the Trans-Bassac.

Spiritually, the Hoa-Hao philosophy claims to have its roots in the ideas preached by Phat Thay Tay-An,[10] who in the 1830's had predicted the end of the Vietnamese Empire at the hands of "men come from the West." The prophecies survived his death and spread throughout the Trans-Bassac, where it resulted in two Boxer-like rebellions in 1875 and 1913 which nearly unseated the French administration in the Mien-Tay. The whole area, with its many canals, swamps, and rivulets, and the sparsely populated Seven Mountains, remained a favorite refuge for revolutionary elements in South Viet-Nam.

Thus, anti-French feelings needed only a new spark to be rekindled and Huynh Phu So, the founder of the Hoa-Hao sect, provided such a spark. Born in 1919, in the small village of Hoa-Hao (hence the name of the sect), the son of a small notable, his childhood was not remarkable: he was lackadaisical, sickly, and graduated from junior high school only through the influence of his father. His father then sent him to a sorcerer at Nui-Cam, in the Seven Mountains, where So learned magic tricks, acupuncture, and also the teaching of Phat Thay. Still in ill health, he returned to his native village upon the death of his master in 1939. One evening, after a period of extreme nervousness, he walked out of the house, meditated in front of the family altar, and then returned to his family, apparently completely healed. He then began to explain to the startled family members the teachings of Buddha as he saw them. Neighbors gathered, listened, and marveled at his recovery. A new prophet was born.[11]

From then on, So's career closely parallels that of most other prophets: he performed miracle cures with simple herbs and acupuncture, asking for no rewards; he offered his home as a shelter for the poor, preached at street corners and canal intersections. In

[10] "Master Buddha, Pacifier of the West," 1820–1841.
[11] I wish to acknowledge my indebtedness to the excellent unpublished study of the Hoa-Hao made by Major A. M. Savani, French Colonial Infantry, which I was able to consult at the Pacification Commissariat, South Viet-Nam.

March, 1940, he once more retired to Nui-Cam and there wrote his *Sam Gian* (*Oracles and Prayers*). He returned a few months later with a reputation for holiness that began to spread throughout South Viet-Nam. Soon he had a following of more than 100,000 and became known as the Mad Bonze (Dao Khung). In less than one year, So's preachings had created a force with which the French administration had to reckon.

The faith that So preached was temptingly simple in a country where every second person was almost permanently in debt in order decently to worship his gods and ancestors, marry off his daughters, or bury his parents. The Hoa-Hao faith requires no temples or pagodas, no expensive statues or instruments.

Huynh Phu So himself described his philosophy as follows: "The cult must stem much more from internal faith than from a pompous appearance. It is better to pray with a pure heart before the family altar than to perform gaudy ceremonies in a pagoda, clad in the robes of an unworthy bonze."[12] . . .

Such principles, by their very simplicity, were almost as revolutionary in conception as were Martin Luther's in sixteenth-century Europe. So also assailed the social evils that beset his country and forbade the sale of child brides, matchmaking, gambling, and the use of alcohol and opium. . . .

It is hardly necessary to underline the social and political explosiveness of such a philosophy, particularly when it was propounded by a man with the spiritual power and elegance of expression of the Mad Bonze. With France's defeat in June, 1940, So's prophecies took on a political tone and his prediction of a Franco-Japanese war had an end-of-the-world effect on the rice farmers in the Mien-Tay, who began to desert their farms in droves and take to the hills.

The reaction of the French administration was typically short-sighted. It first exiled So from his home area to My-Tho and Cai-Bé, where he promptly made thousands of converts; it then committed him, first to an insane asylum in August, 1940, and later to the psychiatric ward of Cho-Quan Hospital near Saigon, where he converted Dr. Tam, the Vietnamese psychiatrist in

---

[12] Huynh Phu So, *Cach Tu Hien va Su An O Cua Nguoi Bon Dao* (*Rules of the Practice of the Good and on the Attitude of the Faithful*), published fragmentarily by the Hoa-Hao sect, 1945–50. An unofficial translation was made by various French liaison officers with the Hoa-Hao sect.

charge of his case. (Tam, who became an ardent follower of So, was executed by the Viet-Minh in 1949.) Finally declared sane in May, 1941, by a board of French psychiatrists,[13] So was exiled to Bac-Lieu while his most ardent followers were sent to the French concentration camp at Nui-Bara. Bac-Lieu soon became a place of pilgrimage for the followers of the Mad Bonze, whose brushes with the French had merely added to his reputation. In despair, the French finally decided to exile him to Laos, but the Japanese intervened and in October, 1942, forced his release and free return to Saigon, where he remained as their protégé. From then on, the participation of the Hoa-Hao in politics became almost unavoidable.

So successfully avoided the odium of being called a Japanese puppet by prophesying Japan's defeat well in advance and by using his influence to obtain weapons for the Hoa-Hao sect through the Japanese. When Japanese rule collapsed in Indochina in August, 1945, So and his followers were in full control of most of South Viet-Nam south and west of Saigon and unwilling to relinquish authority to the faraway government of the Viet-Minh in Hanoi, or to its local representatives in Saigon.

The period of "coexistence" between the Hoa-Hao and the Viet-Minh was short-lived. The Viet-Minh showed as little understanding of the sects as the French did. On September 8, 1945, a band of 15,000 Hoa-Hao armed with pikes and knives marched on the well-armed Viet-Minh garrison at Can-Tho. In the ensuing bloodbath, thousands of Hoa-Hao were killed, and the brother of the Mad Bonze and the brother of his military commander, Tran Van Soai, were summarily executed along with other Hoa-Hao leaders. The return of the French and the British prevented further largescale reprisals on the Hoa-Hao, but the latter now attempted to repay the Viet-Minh in kind. In the words of a French observer, "the Hoa-Hao had the habit of tying Viet-Minh sympathizers together with ropes and of throwing them into the rivers to drown in bundles. . . . One could see those bundles of bodies floating down the rivers like so many trains of junks, at the mercy of the currents and tides."[14]

Politically, the Hoa-Hao, with their wonderfully simply social-

---

[13] A French doctor diagnosed him then as "a little maniacal, very ignorant even in Buddhist practices, but a big talker."

[14] Cited in Fall, *Political Development of Viet-Nam*, II, 458, n. 60.

religious program and their good record of nationalism presented a serious danger to the Viet-Minh in its attempt to monopolize the nationalist label for itself and for the northern parties then in the Viet-Minh government coalition. In a move reminiscent of the East European "people's democracies," the Viet-Minh attempted to establish a National Unified Front of all religious groups. Huynh Phu So participated in the Front, but after a few months it was dissolved by the Viet-Minh in July, 1946, when it became clear that neither the Hoa-Hao nor the Cao-Dai would let themselves be steered along the Viet-Minh line.

It was then that So decided to enter politics openly. On September 21, 1946, he created the Viet-Nam Social Democratic Party (Dan Xa, for short). Such an act in the face of the Viet-Minh's attempts to eliminate all independent parties sealed his fate. While So retained his post as a member of the Viet-Minh's Executive Committee for South Viet-Nam, relations between the Viet-Minh and his increasingly warlordlike field commanders worsened again. On April 16, 1947, the Mad Bonze was invited by the southern Viet-Minh leaders to a "conciliation meeting." He was waylaid on his way, executed, and his body hacked to pieces. His remains were never found.

The Viet-Minh's unwillingness to compromise[15] and its outright stupidity in dealing harshly with the sects at a time when it needed every ally it could get, threw the sects into the arms of the French and gave the latter control over wide areas of South Viet-Nam which they could never have hoped to conquer militarily. Following the pattern which they had initiated with the Cao-Dai, the French signed a military convention with the Hoa-Hao on May 18, 1947, less than a month after the killing of the Mad Bonze.

After So's death, the Hoa-Hao clearly showed signs of disintegration into smaller baronies. The main reason for this is probably to be found in the less solid religious underpinning which the Hoa-Hao sect has, as compared with that of the Cao-Dai. Moreover, the Cao-Dai, with its strong hierarchy and accumulation of wealth and, above all, its head start of twenty years of organization,

---

[15] The two Viet-Minh leaders at that time in the South, Tran Van Giau and Nguyen Binh, were both Moscow-trained and rigidly adhered to a basic pattern of action without regard to local conditions. Binh was later removed from command and killed in an ambush.

had a centralized leadership which the young Hoa-Hao sect could not expect to match, now that it had lost its magnetic leader. To this day, no religious personality has emerged from the Hoa-Hao sect who could hope to become the spiritual successor of the Mad Bonze. There remained only the various military chieftains. Their *raison d'être*—for themselves—was to maintain their exalted positions and material privileges, and—for the French—to fight the Viet-Minh. Hence, with the end of the hostilities the Vietnamese Government had no reason further to tolerate the existence of the Hoa-Hao as separate units of government. But the Hoa-Hao chieftains did not understand this hard fact before it was too late. . . .

Politically, the Dan Xa, So's political party, continued dormant. So's father was selected to take over the spiritual guidance of the sect "in the absence of the Leader"—for the Hoa-Hao cling to the belief that the Mad Bonze will eventually return alive to the sect. Together with Nguyen Giac Ngo, So's father attempted to create a Hoa-Hao "third force." Soai's troops began to desert and on October 24, 1948, Ba Cut once more took to the swamps. However, the French had decided to make Soai their man, and it was he who received the bulk of the equipment supplied to the Hoa-Hao, including several cars and a light amphibian plane. Lam Thanh Nguyen and the other sect leaders felt slighted again, particularly after Emperor Bao-Dai chose So's father as a member of his own Privy Council. Another Hoa-Hao internal struggle began, ending only in 1950 when the Vietnamese Government, slowly rising to its task, began to allot what amounted to "territories" to the various Hoa-Hao leaders. Small feuds still took place (particularly between Soai and Nguyen, each kidnapping the other's family members) and culminated in Soai's staging an amphibious landing in Nguyen's area. Again, the French intervened and by 1952 the Hoa-Hao fiefs were "frozen" in their boundaries and the Vietnamese Government began to place its own civil administrators throughout the Mien-Tay, an arduous process which suffered many reverses and is still far from complete.

From the foregoing, it seems clear that the Hoa-Hao were neither a unified political force nor a solid religious front like the Catholics or—to some extent—the Cao-Dai. The Hoa-Hao fiefs were first and foremost exceedingly profitable economic enterprises for their leaders, many of whom have acquaintances in high government circles. Soai and his fellow leaders, for example, controlled the bulk of rice purchasing and milling operations in the Bassac area, through the SOCACI, his own corporation, duly incorporated by the Vietnamese Government after a series of highly irregular but very successful interventions by influential persons. The crop was sold by the farmers to Soai below market prices and the latter stored it until the end of the season (when prices are high) and then sold it to big enterprises in Saigon at huge profits.[16]

The second major source of income of the Hoa-Hao leaders was the operation of gambling establishments or the collection of protection money from operators of such establishments. One can only imagine the disastrous effect of such a state of affairs upon the prestige of local underpaid Vietnamese administrators who stood no chance of enforcing their regulations upon such barons—assuming that they were not outright creatures of the warlords, as was often likely.

Here again, the situation differed from one fief to another. The hapless farmers under the rule of the maniacal Ba Cut fared worst, for the latter is given to fits of incredible cruelty and has no sense of public duty. Next were the fiefs of Soai, where farmers were practically "taxed" into starvation in order to satisfy Soai's and his wife's greediness. Lam Thanh Nguyen, while still making a handsome profit, is more amenable to the ideas of good government. He has invested part of his revenues in good roads, has reduced the rents of his own farmers, and built about 100 schools with more than 170 teachers in his area. He also returned their properties to the Catholic villages enclaved in his zone of influence. Nguyen Giac Ngo, likewise, not only ruled his area in a normal fashion, but voluntarily relinquished the administration of his area to the national government before he was compelled to do so under threat of force. Both Lam Thanh Nguyen and Nguyen Giac Ngo had their troops recently incorporated into the Vietnamese national army (though they retain a certain amount of control over their areas), thus paving the way to an eventual liquidation of the Hoa-Hao problem.

---

[16] For example, at the end of August, 1953, when rice prices began to rise above normal in Saigon, French official sources estimated the rice stocked by Lam Than Nguyen at 20,000 tons, while Soai already had sold 12,000 tons and was hoarding another 40,000 tons for later sales.

The last of the sects in South Viet-Nam can hardly be called "political-religious," for it professes no particular religion nor does it advocate a particular political program. "In American terms, it would mean transforming 'Murder, Inc.' into a unit of the National Guard and raising the gang leader to the rank of brigadier general."[17] The name Binh-Xuyen is that of a suburb of Cholon and the leader of the group is Le Van Vien, who was before World War II a chauffeur in the French colonial administration. In the chaotic days after the Japanese defeat, Le Van Vien, also known as Bay-Vien, gathered around himself a band of river pirates who operated along the marshy stretches of the river, working at first with the Viet-Minh against the French. In fact, the Binh-Xuyen are even considered responsible by some for the 1945 massacre of 150 French women and children in a Saigon city block where they had been interned by the Japanese.

However, when the Viet-Minh lost ground in South Viet-Nam, Bay-Vien made his peace with the French and the Saigon regime, particularly after Nguyen Binh, the Viet-Minh leader who already had liquidated the Mad Bonze, issued a similar invitation for a "conciliation meeting" to Bay-Vien.[18] In June, 1948, short of supplies and funds, Lai Huu Tai, his contact man, received a promise from the French Deuxième Bureau (Intelligence) in Saigon that the Binh-Xuyen would receive official recognition of their "sect" status in exchange for their submission. Bay-Vien acquiesced, immediately began dabbling in politics, and soon became a well-known political figure in Saigon. His troops occupied small zones along most of the roads leading out of Saigon, where for years they continued to levy "road safety taxes" on cars and buses as well as on small farmers bringing their produce to market.

Bay-Vien himself rose to the position of director-general of one of Asia's largest gambling establishments, the Grand Monde in Cholon, and, simultaneously, to the rank of brigadier general in the auxiliary forces. Enjoying the personal favor of Bao-Dai, the Binh-Xuyen reached their apex in 1953, when in the National Congress of October they received nine seats—more than the

---

[17] Fall, *Political Development of Viet-Nam*, II, 436.
[18] Huet-Handache, "Les Binh-Xuyen et leur Chef," in *Le Monde*, April 5, 1955.

labor unions, the professional groups, the Buddhists, or the mountain populations.

It became clear, however, that with the shift of Viet-Nam's problems from the military to the civilian field after the Geneva ceasefire, the national government at Saigon had to find a means of accomplishing the full integration of the various sects into the body politic of the country. As has been noted, the sects were, first and foremost, commercial undertakings. It is thus hardly surprising that Premier Diem at first attempted to attack the sect problem by buying the allegiance of various sect leaders. There are indications that the method proved successful in certain cases, with American financial help.[19]

For others—particularly Bay-Vien and Ba Cut—the price of allegiance (a doubtful item at best) would have had to be a share in governmental power: in the case of Bay-Vien, the control of the Saigon police, with its files, its fingerprint and passport records, and the means of "squeezing" bribes from thousands of people; in the case of Ba Cut, almost total sovereignty over one of truncated Viet-Nam's richest rice areas. Soai, too, held out for such an exemption from governmental control, and for a brief period—had the initial moves been successful—it appeared likely that the Cao-Dai would have joined in the attempt to make the Diem regime bow to the wishes of the sects.

From the sects' point of view, the situation since the armistice had seriously deteriorated: French subsidies had nearly completely stopped and by January 1, 1955, the Diem regime had full control over such subsidies. The same applied to all logistical support of the armed groups of the sects: the flow of arms and other equipment was reduced to a trickle, if not stopped altogether. The sect chieftains' main resource (their troops) dwindled as the men began to desert in order to support their families. On the other hand, the reduction in American and French financial aid to the Vietnamese Government made it necessary to reduce the existing Vietnamese army by half. Hence, transfer of the sect troops into the regular army on a mass basis was well-nigh impossible. The sects now became an economic and social, as well as a political, problem.

At first, unsure of the national army, Premier Diem—who also had committed the mistake of staffing most major government posts with his relatives or fellow Catholics—had yielded to the

[19] C. L. Sulzberger, in *The New York Times*, December 20, 1954.

combined pressures of Bao-Dai and the French and was obliged to accept several Cao-Dai and Hoa-Hao leaders as cabinet ministers. Tran Van Soai himself became Minister of State. However, the sects recognized the precariousness of their own position as long as they were not in full control of the Saigon government and openly continued to conspire against the very regime of which they were members. A Unified Front of National Forces was created early in March, 1955, which grouped all sects into a loose anti-government coalition. Again, the Ho Phap appeared in the political limelight. Emissaries were sent to Cannes to ask Bao-Dai to remove Premier Diem, but, without awaiting Bao Dai's reply, the sect leaders (the Ho Phap and General Nguyen Thanh Phuong for the Cao-Dai, Soai and Ba Cut for the Hoa-Hao, Bay-Vien for the Binh Xuyen, and Trinh Minh The on behalf of his "dissident Cao-Dai") on March 21, 1955, sent an ultimatum to Diem, giving him five days to broaden the government.

On March 25, before the expiration of the ultimatum, Diem requested the sect leaders—most of whom still were officially members of his government—to visit him in order to discuss their grievances. In the words of a government spokesman: "It is up to the sects to show some humility and take the first step, or we shall destroy them, beginning with that of Bay-Vien."[20]

On the following day, the four Hoa-Hao and four Cao-Dai cabinet members resigned from the Diem government, and only a group of second-string sect leaders presented the sects' counter-proposals to Diem. The major point of those proposals was that the executive power of the government was to shift from Diem to a five-man council of which Diem was to be merely a member. Such a proposal was unacceptable to Diem. He refused to bargain on such a basis and, in retrospect, it can be said that the sects entered into open conflict with Diem a few days after the propitious political moment had passed. Indeed, such a heterogeneous group as the sect leaders could not retain for long a single consistent political line without squabbling. The Hoa-Hao and Cao-Dai soon accused the Binh-Xuyen (whose power, based on Saigon itself, was more directly menaced by Diem than that of the other sects) of forcing them into an open conflict with Diem, whom they knew to be backed by the United States. The Cao-Dai, as ever sensitive to changes in the political atmosphere, backed out of the brewing

[20] Lucien Bodard, in *Paris-Presse*, March 27, 1955.

conflict on March 29, preceded by Trinh Minh The and soon followed by smaller Hoa-Hao groups, so that when the final show-
down came between the sects and the national government, the
Binh-Xuyen found themselves almost isolated. It is not yet clear
who fired the opening shot in the battle and the point is unimportant. It is, however, certain that Premier Diem's palace was
shelled by mortar fire on March 31. The final battle for the control
of South Viet-Nam and, hence, for all of Viet-Nam south of the
17th parallel, had begun.

It is needless to describe the details of the brief but bloody civil
war which ravaged South Viet-Nam for weeks following. The
Binh-Xuyen, encircled in several dispersed garrisons throughout the
Saigon-Cholon area, broke after several days of severe fighting,
during which the native city borough of Khanh-Hoi was burned to
the ground, and after both French and American leaders in Saigon
had attempted to mediate between the adversaries. For a few days
also, food supplies for the 2 million inhabitants of the Saigon-
Cholon urban area were blockaded by Hoa-Hao sympathizers who,
otherwise, remained neutral in the first phase of the battle. The
position of the French in the matter was strange. Needless to
say, the anti-French statements made by Diem's entourage had
antagonized them; on the other hand, it is equally certain (and in
this the French apparently had the backing of General Lawton
Collins, President Eisenhower's special ambassador to Viet-Nam)
that a civil war in the midst of a densely populated city could
benefit no one. Vietnamese sources alleged that French army
officers turned over equipment to the Binh-Xuyen in the middle of
the fighting[21] and most American newspaper reports tended to
follow the viewpoint that "the French have used the sects . . . to
undermine the government of Premier Diem."[22]

On the other hand, the French rejoinder is that they had been
"framed" by Vietnamese nationalists who, according to French
sources, have inflated a single incident involving one vehicle beyond all proportions.[23]

[21] The New York Times, May 7, 1955.

[22] Joseph Buttinger, "Are We Saving South Vietnam?," Supplement to The
New Leader, June 27, 1955, p. 8. See also France-Observateur (Paris), April
14, 1955.

[23] The Washington Post and Times Herald, May 8, 1955.

By the middle of May, Bay-Vien's troops were completely eliminated from the Saigon-Cholon urban area and pushed back into the river swamps where they had begun their pirates' career ten years before. The government forces, now flushed by their successes, pushed more boldly towards their main objective, the Hoa-Hao "kingdoms" in the Mekong rice bowl.

On May 29, 1955, both Soai and Lam Thanh Nguyen let it be known that they were ready to negotiate a surrender, but by now Premier Diem needed a military victory more than a surrender and he was in a position to fight the demoralized sect remnants to the finish. He replied by outlawing Tran Van Soai and Ba Cut and branding them as ordinary criminals. Soai's troops put up a last show of resistance for the river passages at Can-Tho and Vinh-Long, but even the presence of Generals Nguyen Van Hinh and Nguyen Van Vy (former Bao-Dai-appointed commander in chief of the Vietnamese army) could not bolster the sagging morale of the sect fighters, deprived of military supplies and regular pay for several months. By June 18, Soai's forces had been cut to pieces by nationalist attacks and by the defection of several battalions. On the following day, Soai, Vy, and Hinh crossed into Cambodia. A few days later the nationalist forces concentrated their strength on Ba Cut, still holding out in his Seven Mountains redoubt. He gave up that position almost without a fight to flee into the marshy plains of Ha-Tien. On June 30, 1955, all organized sect resistance throughout South Viet-Nam had ceased.*

Does this mean that any threat of rebellion against the Diem regime is definitely wiped out? Far from it. The armed remnants of the sects are still able to carry on extensive harrassing operations, just as the Viet-Minh did after the French reoccupied South Viet-Nam in force in 1945, but it is unlikely that they will ever regain even part of their erstwhile political strength. As anachronistic in present-day politics as the dinosaurs were at the approach of the ice age, the sects had to disappear in the face of Viet-Nam's evolution toward a unified national state.

---

* *Ba Cut was captured in 1956 and guillotined by Diem; but four Hoa-Hao battalions stayed in the field until Diem's death, after which they joined the Saigon regime.*

12. Danger Signs

May, 1958

On July 11, 1957, a group of armed men machine-gunned to death seventeen occupants of a bar in Chau-Doc, South Viet-Nam. On September 14, the district chief of My-Tho and his whole family were stopped in broad daylight on a main highway and killed in cold blood. On October 10, a bomb thrown into a cafe in Saigon's Chinatown Cholon wounded thirteen persons, including two plainclothes Security Police members. On October 22, thirteen American servicemen were injured in three bombings directed against American installations in Saigon. On February 12, 1958, a Vietnamese Army truck was ambushed on a main highway near Saigon and its occupants killed. And on March 6, 1958, the Saigon newspaper *Dan-Chung* (*The Population*) announced that "our people are fleeing the villages and returning to the cities for fear of Communist guerrillas and feudalistic officials."

These are items culled from hundreds of similar incidents reported over the past six months in the South Vietnamese press. They clearly express a trend which has been developing over the past year and one which is hidden from the casual foreign observer behind a screen of immaculate refugee camps, model nurseries and schools, and store displays in Saigon overflowing with Western consumer goods, from nylon shirts to tape-recorders, hi-fi sets, and shiny automobiles.

In spite of a most generous measure of American financial (more than $1 billion in the past four years) and political support, the South Vietnamese Government of President Ngo Dinh Diem is faced today with growing insecurity in the countryside and an economic crisis which threatens to wipe out most of the benefits

Excerpted, with permission, from "Will South Vietnam Be Next?," originally published in *The Nation*, May 31, 1958. © 1958 by The Nation Associates, Inc.

this country derives from the aid program of the International Co-operation Administration (ICA). Without this aid, South Viet-Nam would, beyond a doubt, have collapsed long ago. This is not the place to discuss how and why South Viet-Nam became an ex-clusive American responsibility after having been French-controlled for one hundred years. Suffice it to say that the government of President Ngo Dinh Diem, which took over from the French at the time of the 1954 cease-fire and partition, had the wholehearted support of the United States. As a British journalist termed it recently, American aid to the small country became one of "the biggest Santa Claus" operations of all times.

To understand the effect of this aid, its mechanism must be briefly explained. About 80 per cent consists of merchandise ex-ported directly to South Viet-Nam. This merchandise, sold through normal commercial channels, "generates local currency"—Wash-ington "officialese" for the fact that the local population buys such merchandise with its own currency. This currency, minus normal commercial profits, is deposited in a counterpart fund, out of which the receiver government covers the expenses for various projects approved jointly by the local United States Operations Mission (USOM) and the government. (More than $200 million out of an approximate total of $250 million a year of U.S. aid goes into the support and maintenance of the ten-division Vietnamese army and other security forces.) The remaining 20 per cent of the total aid is given Viet-Nam in "hard currency" (i.e., dollars) granted for outright purchases in the United States and other countries, or may consist in part of currencies of third countries which owe money to the United States and from which Viet-Nam desires to make certain purchases.

During the past fiscal year, American aid to Viet-Nam supported the whole cost of the Vietnamese armed forces, nearly 80 per cent of all other government expenditures, and almost 90 per cent of all imports. And this is not all. In terms of personnel, American com-mitments are equally far-reaching. USOM provides for American technical help in every field of activity. Michigan State University, under a million-dollar-a-year contract to ICA, runs the administra-tion school and trains the police; U.S. educators write the country's textbooks; American medical personnel trains nurses; a "private" American-Vietnamese association runs English-language courses for Vietnamese officers. And a vast U.S. Military Assistance Advisory Group (MAAG)—its exact size classified but including well over a thousand officers and men—trains the Vietnamese army, navy, and air force.

In addition, there are the regular, fairly large, staffs of the U.S. Embassy, the Information Service (USIS), and of several private American charitable agencies which have provided the Vietnamese with more than $30 million worth of clothing, drugs, and food over the past four years. There are dozens of private engineering and other firms on subcontract to USOM, each with its vehicles conspicuously marked with the firm name and a U.S. insignia. There is the Alhambra, an air-conditioned movie theatre exclusively reserved for U.S. personnel and *verboten* to Vietnamese; there is the *Times of Viet-Nam,* a weekly produced by a former American information officer operating under a Vietnamese name; and, above all, there is the PX, providing the American colony with all the amenities of American life. The Navy supply ship which brings in those goodies does not, like all other commercial ships, berth in the port of Saigon, but is unloaded right at the end of Saigon's busiest thoroughfare under the eyes of hundreds of Vietnamese bystanders.

And here, precisely, lies the nub of the situation. "Don't the Americans ever buy anything from us?" is the standard complaint of Vietnamese merchants. "We can't live on selling soda and ice to the Americans," say the café owners, sadly contemplating their American customers with their hip flasks of American whiskey. "They don't like our food," says the restaurant owner, "they say its unsanitary." These are the more obvious signs of a real breakdown of the country's tenuous economic fabric, due to a total misreading of the role which the Americans and Vietnamese expected each other to play in the rebuilding of the country's economy. The Americans saw their role limited to giving the country an economic start and to keeping its armed forces strong enough to deter Communist aggression from North Viet-Nam. The Vietnamese, on the whole, wanted to get rid of the French but *without* losing the benefits of having 270,000 customers—the French Expeditionary Force—spread throughout the countryside, buying soap and cigarettes from the local merchants, eating Chinese soup at the village shop, paying for local services such as laundry-washing, dating the local girls. The countrywide spread of purchasing power now has disappeared and has not been replaced, with serious consequences for the whole economy, but particularly for the back country, which in no way shares the artificial prosperity of Saigon. The disappointment is real and growing, and neither American nor Vietnamese officials have thus far had the courage to attempt to explain the state of affairs to the Vietnamese or, for that matter, to Washington. Or, when the truth *is* brought home, as it was last year in an excellent report by Clement Johnston, President of the U.S. Chamber of Commerce, or as it is at present by Leland Barrows, the Director of USOM–Viet-Nam, who was recently called to Washington to testify on Viet-Nam's economy, it is buried in government channels. In his unclassified report, Mr. Johnston stated:

> The number of American jeeps, American uniforms, American faces, which one encounters on the principal streets of the principal cities [of Asia] seems disproportionately large to a native population that has an innate distrust or resentment of anything alien or nonnational. . . .
>
> If the American presence is over-obvious we will inevitably be made the scapegoat for failure or shortcomings in which we had little or no part.

This is exactly what has happened in South Viet-Nam. Incidents between Vietnamese and Americans, most of them carefully hushed up in the press, occur frequently enough, even if one disregards the repeated bombing of American installations—the U.S. library in 1955, the Ambassador's residence in 1956, a hotel and the library again in 1957—which may be the work of professional terrorists. The bulk of them involve MAAG personnel who, like their colleagues in Taiwan, are in no way subject to local jurisdiction.

"What do you expect us to do?" said one MAAG officer to this writer last summer in Viet-Nam. "We aren't an occupation force, you know. Our guys are spread in small packets throughout the countryside, wearing civvies, living in the local hotels. It's a miracle that they don't get into any real trouble. And if they *do* get into trouble, they're shipped out to the Philippines for courts-martial. If convicted, they'll serve their time in the brig there or, if the offense is serious, in the United States. In any case, the Vietnamese don't know what happens to them. They probably think we just whitewash all the cases, as the Commie propaganda tells them." . . .

But the foregoing factors would constitute only minor frictions if America's $250-million-a-year gamble had proved successful otherwise. The hard fact is, however, that Viet-Nam's economy today is steadily deteriorating. With the lone exception of rubber, it is below even the pre–cease-fire level, not to speak of the prewar level. Rice exports slumped from 1.3 million tons pre-World War II to about 350,000 tons during the years of the war with the Communist Viet-Minh. Even in 1954, when the Communists occupied much of the countryside and levied heavy "taxes" on the peasants, exports of rice totaled 778 million piasters.* In 1955, the first year of peace, and without the drain of exporting rice to the usually deficient (now Communist) North, exports slumped to 313 million piasters. In 1956, exports dwindled to *nothing*, and in 1957, despite formal government assurances of a surplus of 300,000 tons, only about 195,000 tons were exported. The 1958 crop is already faced with a disastrous drought and all rice exports were stopped by government order this month.

Land reform, widely hailed as giving the small farmer a share in his country's economy, has bogged down in red tape and inefficiency, and is not even keeping pace with the natural growth of the farming population. In the field of business, particularly, the whole program has failed to come up to expectations. The process of "generating local currency" as a source of funds for various projects puts both the Vietnamese and American governments at the mercy of what the public is willing to spend its money on—and the Vietnamese public seems to prefer hi-fi sets, cameras, wrist watches, and American cigarettes to tractors and lathes. During 1956–57, Viet-Nam, a traditional food exporter, purchased agricultural products totaling about $33 million, including $7 million for rice products, $11.2 million for milk, and $300,000 for fresh fruits. Compared to $800,000 allocated for tractors and industrial vehicles, $7 million were spent on private cars and $5.5 million on tires and tubes for them. This agricultural country imported $2

---

* *The exchange rate from 1953 to 1961 was 35 piasters per U.S. dollar; from 1961 to 1965, it was 71 piasters per dollar; and as of September, 1965, it was 119 piasters. The "free market" rate was 180 piasters in early 1966.*

million worth of fertilizer, but imported $6.5 million worth of cigarettes and tobacco. One-fifth of total aid funds—about $45 million—was spent on textiles. Lastly, $141,000 were spent on importing—firecrackers!

The market is saturated with consumer goods of all kinds which the Vietnamese are no longer able to buy. Merchandise is left to rot on the docks by importers who haven't the money to pay for it.*

Last summer, ICA imported U.S. agricultural surpluses of milk, wheat, flour, and corn. Like all Asians, the Vietnamese are not fond of milk, prefer rice to wheat, and detest corn. Yet, at the same time, American charitable agencies imported vast quantities of these same surpluses for free distribution to the refugees, who immediately resold them for whatever the market would bear. The bottom fell out of the cereals market, importers went bankrupt, and observers witnessed the odd spectacle of private American charity apparently "torpedoing" an American government aid program. Similar occurrences are increasing in number. On January 30, 1958, Viet-Nam had a stock of typewriters sufficient to cover its needs for five years and a stock of calculating machines (including 450 electric calculators) sufficient to cover its needs for eight years. Neither of these items can be successfully stocked in the tropics for so long a time.

In the field of textiles, where the imports compete with a small, struggling, native industry, the result has been a disastrous price slump, with goods selling below cost. Stocks on hand are sufficient to give about two suits of clothes to every Vietnamese man, woman, and child, not counting an additional 23 million yards of cloth which were due to arrive by the end of March, 1958.

Obviously, the "commercial import program," designed to generate local currencies" in order to finance a large standing army and long-range economic development, is definitely *not* a solution for an underdeveloped area such as Viet-Nam. On the contrary, it channels whatever little capital is available into goods that at best are useless, and are sometimes actually injurious, to a weak economy. Shiny big cars, for instance, create a long-term dependency upon dollar-paid spare parts, tires, batteries, and gasoline which

---

* *It still happens in 1966.*

the local economy can ill afford. In Viet-Nam, this dependency has gone from bad to worse. The amount of imports covered by exports *decreased* from 27 per cent in 1956 to 21 per cent last year, while the amount of imports in the same period *increased* from 7.5 billion piasters to more than 10 billion. In other words, after four years of peace and American aid the Vietnamese economy, far from "paying its way," is going downhill at an increasingly rapid rate.

The same may be said of the state of security throughout the countryside. Even President Ngo Dinh Diem, after two years of official silence on the matter in Saigon (and loud optimism on the subject abroad), acknowledged in a press conference during his state visit to Manila last March 22 that "there had been a renewal of Communist subversive activities in South Viet-Nam." Within a few months, given the rapid spreading of ambushes and killings of minor government officials, and the increasing economic difficulties, this may be an understatement.

To be sure, the regime is reasonably secure, and the Communists in the North have their own problems, such as the peasant rebellion which coincided with the Hungarian revolt. As to politics, warning is due against any starry-eyed illusion about "democracy" in South Viet-Nam. President Ngo Dinh Diem was elected by a 98.2 per cent vote and opposition journalists in Saigon, as reported recently in *The New York Times,* tend to "vanish" and their newspapers to be wrecked by well-coached mobs. Thus, since democracy cannot be the criterion, the government must be judged on its efficiency in "keeping the trains running on time" (i.e., giving the country a fair amount of good administration and economic development).

Empty slogans such as "economic independence"—a myth not even the advanced countries can well afford—are bandied about in Viet-Nam and used to wreck what is left of French and Chinese economic footholds in the country, while at the same time shining offers are made for new (i.e., American) capital to enter the picture.

Economic planning is haphazard, unencumbered by the specialized knowledge required for sound planning. South Viet-Nam has none of the basic requisites of an industrial nation: coal, iron, power, skilled labor, and markets. Yet the industries launched were exactly those it needed least: a watch-assembly plant which, after one year of operation, recently closed its doors; a scooter-assembly plant, a sewing-machine assembly shop, etc. On the other hand, a French-built rubber-products plant capable of producing a full line of goods from locally made rubber was allowed to close down for lack of a modest modernization loan. Year-long dickering went on between Viet-Nam and the Renault, British Ford, and Volkswagon firms for the establishment of an auto-assembly plant in Saigon; the three firms finally gave up in the face of Vietnamese demands while little Cambodia, next door, with far fewer resources, now has an assembly shop for the French 2-horsepower Citroen trucks.* Viet-Nam now seeks to build a sugar-refining industry to cover all its potential sugar needs (about 60,000 tons a year). But, according to American experts, it would take it as least ten years to establish the sugar-cane resources to feed such an industry—and meanwhile in the neighboring Philippines, half of a very efficient American-built sugar industry lies idle.

These are the hard facts, and they are not very pretty. But they must be revealed now, while it is not yet too late to change course. The change cannot be undertaken in Saigon, but must be carried out in Washington in the face of probable opposition by the well-established "Vietnamese lobby." The United States cannot afford yet another defeat in Asia without losing whatever remains of Asian confidence in the West's ability to understand and cope with Oriental political, economic, and social problems.

Perhaps the time has come to reappraise the impact of the vast commercial import programs upon the economies of underdeveloped areas—in Latin America and the Middle East, as well as in Asia. It may be that despite their temporary usefulness as pump-primers, these programs, which have become the favored American form of foreign aid, in the long run create more problems than they solve. What if the local populations exhaust their needs for "hard" consumer goods, or just find them too expensive? This phenomenon, we are told, is at the root of the present American recession. How much more vulnerable to the same phenomenon is an underdeveloped economy!

With a rival Communist regime in the North watching South Viet-Nam for every sign of internal weakness, neither the United

---

* *It closed down in 1961.*

States nor, for that matter, France, the Colombo Plan countries, and the U.N. (all of which operate smaller aid programs in behalf of Saigon), can afford to take a "devil take the hindmost" attitude in this corner of Southeast Asia. For in this case the hindmost are the landless farmer and the jobless worker. And they made up the Communist shock troops who defeated the French at Dien Bien Phu.

13. The Birth of Insurgency

July, 1958

We have underestimated the chances of the South. It is good, for a journalist and for others as well, to have the opportunity to acknowledge this. We did not believe in Monsieur Diem, but in two years of effort he has dispelled this pessimism. We may not like the political style of the regime or find in the personality of its leader certain traits which displease us, but is it still our business? In spite of all our reservations, a reality emerges here which we can no longer ignore: the Republic of Viet-Nam has taken substance as a State. We must fully take into account its existence and its importance.[1]

The above opinion, by one of France's most astute journalistic observers of the Far Eastern scene, in one of France's most influential newspapers not hitherto noted for its sympathies for the government of President Ngo Dinh Diem, is the more remarkable as the same journalist, writing in the same newspaper in 1954, held out little hope for South Viet-Nam even to survive as a political entity until the plebiscite deadline set (by the Geneva cease-fire agreement) for July, 1956. With a very few exceptions, no French observer of the Vietnamese scene deviated from Guillain's judgment until after the 1956 deadline passed without incident, and only a very few American writers gave South Viet-Nam more than an even chance until after Ngo Dinh Diem's spectacular victories over the political-religious sects in the summer of 1955.[2]

Once the South Vietnamese Government had proved that it was able to survive the immediate trials ahead, attitudes changed rapidly, particularly in the United States. From an almost unknown exiled politician in 1953, Ngo Dinh Diem became the miracle man

---

[1] Robert Guillain, "Le Vietnam et Nous," *Le Monde*, December 25, 1957.
[2] See Chapter 11.

Excerpted, with permission, from "South Viet-Nam's Internal Problems," originally published in *Pacific Affairs* (Vancouver), September, 1958. © 1958 by *Pacific Affairs*.

of 1956, in many American eyes not unlike the late President Mag-saysay of the Philippines. The South Vietnamese Government, still dismissed in Asia as either a French or an American puppet at the time of the 1955 Bandung conference, is now a respected member of the Far Eastern community of nations. Burmese Premier U Nu, during a visit to Saigon, found President Ngo Dinh Diem "charm-ing," and the country "efficiently run." The reception accorded Ngo Dinh Diem in New Delhi in November, 1957, was almost as cordial as that which he had received a few months earlier in Washington. And when Christian Pineau, France's Foreign Min-ister, visited Saigon in March, 1958, and extended to Ngo Dinh Diem an invitation for an official visit to the French capital (coupled with a visit to the Catholic pilgrimage of Lourdes),* the South Vietnamese regime could look with rightful pride upon the series of diplomatic successes which it had achieved by its own efforts. . . .

In order to understand the development of South Viet-Nam since the 1954 cease-fire, it is useful to divide the intervening years into three major periods: (1) the liquidation of the colonial heritage, including the implementation of the armistice; (2) the consolidation of the regime within its present boundaries and institutions; and (3) the reconstruction of the country's economic machinery and its development within the new context of full independence. The first period lasted from the accession of Ngo Dinh Diem to power on July 7, 1954, to the military defeat of the rebel sects and the termination of the refugee exodus from North Viet-Nam, in May-June, 1955. The second period includes the resettlement of the northern refugees (about 860,000),[3] the reor-ganization of the National Army into a coherent fighting force, the establishment of the Republic of Viet-Nam as heir to the regime of ex-Emperor Bao-Dai, and the beginning of an agricultural re-form. The third, and current, phase may be said to have begun with the proclamation of the republican constitution in October, 1956.

[3] Various estimates exist of the number of refugees evacuated. The above figure, given the writer in a communication by Mr. Bui Van Long (former Commissioner General for Refugees of the Vietnamese Government), does not include French Army troops evacuated from North Viet-Nam.

* *Diem failed to follow up on the French invitation.*

Reports on South Viet-Nam by Western observers have generally stopped at phases one and two, for the former includes the always emotionally appealing story of the plight and evacuation of the anti-Communist refugees from North Viet-Nam, while the latter permits the observer to dwell upon the truly remarkable achievements of urban improvement, resettlement of refugees, the re-establishment of daytime security, and the liquidation of French influence in the country. Thus, the general picture of South Viet-Nam abroad generally errs in two ways: most American (and now some French) sources tend to paint a picture of the situation which concentrates exclusively on the bright spots; while on the other hand, a minority of sources of American, French, or Vietnamese origin, opposed to President Ngo Dinh Diem for a variety of reasons,[4] generally deny the regime any claim to successful achievement. Both groups generally focus on certain aspects: the pro-Ngo Dinh Diem sources generally overemphasize the fact that one now can travel unmolested throughout much of the country—an impossible feat four, or even three, years ago—and that Saigon, previously endowed with a certain amount of open vice like almost all large cities, now seems to be free of it. The other group generally seeks its arguments in the limitations on civil liberties and in the police-state aspects[5] of the regime, forgetting that no other regime in Viet-Nam has thus far been able to do better and that, in the present circumstances of competitive coexistence with a Vietnamese Communist regime, full-fledged democracy might in the short run work in favor of the side with the better political machine. . . .

One political by-product of France's disinvolvement in Viet-Nam had unexpected, but severe, economic repercussions. This was the rapid withdrawal of the French armed forces from the area, whose numbers dropped from about 278,000 at the time of Dien Bien Phu to nothing by July, 1956. These French forces, spread throughout the countryside and relying far more on local goods and

---

[4] Neither of these groups is meant to include the Communists who, for obvious reasons, are against the very existence of a non-Communist Viet-Nam.

[5] Such as Presidential Ordinance No. 6 of January 11, 1956, which stipulates that "by decision of the President of the Republic upon proposal by the Minister of the Interior, may be sent to concentration camps . . . all persons considered as dangerous to national defense or collective security." Article 2 of the same ordinance limits assignments to concentration camps to a duration of two years.

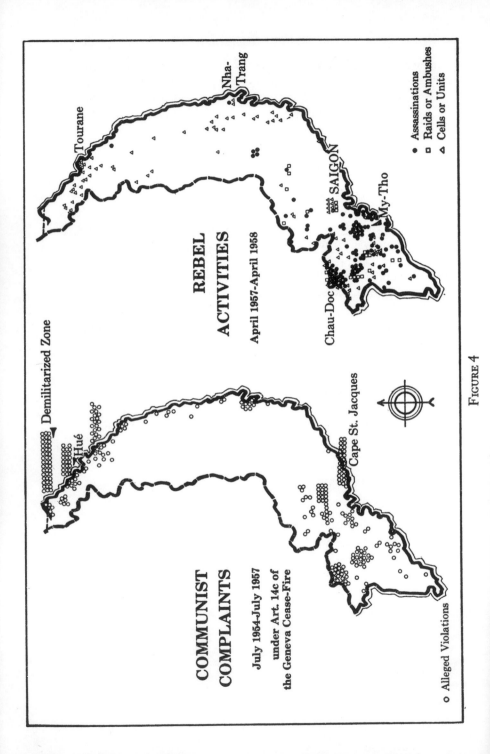

COMMUNIST
COMPLAINTS

July 1954-July 1957
under Art. 14c of
the Geneva Cease-Fire

Demilitarized Zone

Hué

Cape St. Jacques

o Alleged Violations

REBEL
ACTIVITIES

April 1957-April 1958

Tourane

Nha-
Trang

SAIGON

My-Tho

Chau-Doc

• Assassinations
□ Raids or Ambushes
◁ Cells or Units

FIGURE 4

services than was usually imagined, constituted an economic stabilization factor of no small importance. The expenditures of these troops, who ate much local food and used thousands of local clerks, mechanics, servants, or communications operators, contributed greatly to the wartime prosperity which, financially at least, was less artificial than is generally believed. Arguments that the Indochina War was financially expensive to Viet-Nam are often nonsense; since the Vietnamese currency was then linked to the franc bloc, the shock of all inflationary pressures eventually had to be absorbed by the French treasury at home. This was understood by the United Nations economic survey mission to Viet-Nam in 1956, the final report of which noted that "inflation caused by the French Expeditionary Force was re-exported to France, and repatriation of funds to France was one of the stabilizing elements of the region's financial policy."[6] With the disappearance of this "built-in" purchasing power—further aggravated by a corresponding decrease of the Vietnamese National Army from about 250,000 men to 150,000—the local market found itself facing a huge wave of imported products which had to be absorbed by a local economy suddenly deprived of any chance of increasing its resources. The 1954–56 *Activity Report* of the United States aid mission to Viet-Nam explains the problem in the following terms:

> At its height in fiscal year 1955, the program was sustained by a budget of 320 million dollars, nearly two dollars for every person in America and more than 26 dollars for every one of the approximately 12 million population of Free Viet-Nam. . . . In Viet-Nam, more than 85 per cent of 1955's 320 million dollars was brought into the country as goods to be exchanged for local currency, which went into a special account used to support the major part of the projects implemented jointly by the U.S. Operations Mission and the Vietnamese Government.[7]

The magnitude of the problem, in terms of both dollars and of its impact upon the local economy, remained at about the same level in 1956 and 1957, about 80 per cent of the aid being financed through goods imports, while about 15 per cent was imported directly through the grant of U.S. currency to the Vietnamese Gov-

[6] *Les Perspectives du Développement Economique au Viet-Nam* (New York: United Nations, 1956), p. 456.
[7] USOM–Viet-Nam, *Activity Report*, June 30, 1954–June 30, 1956, p. 8.

ernment. Another 5.5 per cent of the aid consisted of goods imported from France through a triangular system of exchange.[8] It must be remembered, lest one assign blame where blame is not due, that in countries where the military aspect of the aid program is extremely heavy (as it is in South Viet-Nam and South Korea), the *size* of the over-all program often has little relation to the economic capabilities of the country. The so-called force goals (i.e., the number of military units planned to be activated and maintained on a basis of varying readiness by virtue of U.S. aid) are set at high-level conferences of the U.S. Defense Department.[9] The International Cooperation Administration must then provide the necessary economic underpinning to the country to help it meet its force goals, with purely economic long-range undertakings necessarily assuming a role of secondary importance. Thus far, the only practical way to find the necessary local currency for both the military and the economic projects has been the method of "counterpart fund financing."

This system has worked satisfactorily in the developed economies of Western Europe, whose relatively high per capita income permits the absorption of considerable amounts of consumer goods. In Viet-Nam, however, where the estimated per capita income lies in the vicinity of U.S. $130 per year, it was obvious that the financing of a large army (which absorbs well over $200 million out of an approximate total of $260 million which South Viet-Nam received during 1957–58) and of a minimum program of economic development could not in the long run depend merely upon what the individual Vietnamese is willing to absorb for his personal consumption. For, unless his individual earning power were to increase steadily, thus permitting him to purchase ever greater quantities of imported goods, there was bound to come a point where his limited resources (or needs, for that matter) would simply bring

[8] France received agricultural products from the United States and repaid by allowing South Viet-Nam to purchase goods in France to the amount owed the United States by France.

[9] For a brief explanation of the "force goal" concept, see *The Military Assistance Program of the United States*, U.S. Senate Special Committee to Study the Foreign Aid Program (Washington, D.C.: Government Printing Office, 1957), pp. 100–108. It must be emphasized that, in many cases, the U.S. force goal is more conservative than what the recipient country's leadership desires. South Korea is a prime example of this.

the import program to a halt. Or should the flow of merchandise continue—as it does—without stop, then the goods would simply pile up, unsold, in the shops and warehouses. This is precisely what has happened in South Viet-Nam since the spring of 1957, bringing about not only a crisis in the very concept of counterpart financing, but an even greater crisis in the Vietnamese economy itself. The merchants are faced with a glut of unsaleable goods—even though most of them are now advertised at prices far below those paid in the country of origin or even by the Vietnamese importer and some of them, in addition, have practically priced out of existence certain important branches of the Vietnamese industry. . . .

The import-export figures for the past three years are eloquent proof that the Vietnamese economy not only has not recovered its pre-World War II levels, but that in almost all categories production has slumped even below pre–cease-fire levels. Rice (with rubber the mainstay of South Viet-Nam's exports) reached an average annual export level of over 800,000 tons in 1899–1903, 1.2 million tons by 1913 and 1.5 million tons for the period between 1913 and 1941.[10] World War II brought a breakdown of the export trade (although Japan still took an important part of all rice exports until 1943, when cargo space became scarce), but by 1951, in spite of the fact that the Viet-Minh guerrillas controlled much of the countryside, exports had climbed back to 360,000 tons and approximately maintained this level through 1954 in spite of the deteriorating military situation. Rice exports for 1955, however, fell to below half those of 1954 and exports for 1956 were almost nil (a token export of a few thousand tons replaced by imported American surplus rice).

With peace now fully restored for more than two years, Vietnamese agriculturalists were called upon by Ngo Dinh Diem to make a special effort in 1957. In his "Double-Seven"[11] anniversary speech of 1957, the President stated that "we are planning to export 300,000 tons of rice this year; one-half was already exported."[12] As it turned out, less than 190,000 tons were exported, and even this

[10] Haut Commissariat de France en Indochine, Centre d'Information Economique, *Bulletin Economique de l'Indochine*, LX, No. 1 (March, 1952), 59.

[11] The anniversary of the accession of President Ngo Dinh Diem to power on July 7, 1954.

[12] *Viet-Nam Press* (English-language daily news bulletin, Saigon), July 9, 1957, p. 7.

effort resulted in a rise of internal rice prices. Prospects for 1958 are extremely poor, in view of a bad drought, key provinces having already reported 50 to 80 per cent losses of their crops.[13]

South Viet-Nam's rubber, which is mainly produced on large French-owned plantations and accounted for 62.5 per cent of all South Vietnamese exports in 1957, has maintained its production level but, owing to continuous strikes for higher wages, can no longer compete with world rubber prices. Even France, a year ago South Viet-Nam's largest rubber buyer, now has turned to importing Malayan rubber, and rubber prices accordingly slumped from one dollar to 65 cents a kilogram on the Saigon market.[14]

As an American writer pointed out a year ago, "trade and the budget have thus been linked closely and both have registered serious deficits—in 1955 and 1956, $175 and $275 million respectively. . . . In dealing with these deficits, it [South Viet-Nam] has been entirely dependent upon American aid."[15] In spite of some attempts at austerity, South Vietnamese imports have risen by 25 per cent (from 7.5 to 10 billion piasters), while coverage of imports by exports has risen only by about 7 per cent.[16] The Vietnamese Government and its American friends both in Saigon and in the United States have recently given vent to feelings of frustration, because they apparently feel that the United States aid program is unsatisfactory in size, administration, and emphasis. Thus, in recent months, many persons in the U.S. interested in Vietnamese affairs received several reprints and pamphlets showing the apparent "success" of the sizable Communist industrial build-up in North Viet-Nam, with the clear inference that similar programs in South Viet-Nam were not being pushed forward with similar determination.[17]

[13] *Phong Thuong Mai Saigon*, issues of February and March, 1958. Rice exports were stopped in May, 1958.

[14] *Buoi Sang (The Morning)*, March 7, 1958. French rubber concerns in Indochina also own plantations in Malaya; thus, the switch in markets does not hurt them particularly.

[15] Ellen J. Hammer, "Progress Report on Southern Viet-Nam," *Pacific Affairs*, September, 1957, pp. 229–30.

[16] *Dan-Chung (Population)* (Saigon), March 7, 1958. According to this source, the 1957 trade deficit amounted to $210 million.

[17] See releases by the American Friends of Viet-Nam (New York), February, June 13, and June 25, 1958; translation of Tibor Mende, "Les Deux Viet-Nam," in *Esprit* (Paris), No. 6 (June, 1957); and *Vital Speeches*, issues of

To be sure, administrative techniques are always subject to improvement, but it must have been both embarrassing and painful to U.S. aid officials in Washington and Saigon to see their programs (which, for better or for worse, *did* save South Viet-Nam) openly criticized by Ngo Dinh Nhu, brother of President Ngo Dinh Diem and his highest political adviser, in an exclusive interview with the French economic weekly *La Vie Française* (May 15, 1958). In a somewhat curious editorial, the English-language *Times of Viet-Nam* reprinted in full the paragraphs most critical of American aid policies, after prefacing them with a passage explaining that the interview had not been "cleared for publication" by Counselor Nhu, and then added an editorial statement saying that "although it is not officially confirmed, we believe that the above quoted passage *does* accurately express the Counselor's views. At the very least, it reflects common opinion of those Vietnamese who must cope with the problems involved in the administration of American aid."[18]

The gist of the Vietnamese complaints is that there simply is not enough American aid for the kind of large-scale industrialization programs which some Vietnamese and Americans (though not most experts) believe will rapidly raise the country's living standards. The ICA thus finds itself in the unenviable role of being the man in the middle between big force goals with their financial requirements, and Vietnamese desires for both a large army and a flourishing economy.

What, then, are the prospects for an ambitious industrialization program? This point has been raised time and again by both idealistic Vietnamese and Americans, the proposed plans being the more grandiose as their authors were less acquainted with the realities of the economic situation in the country. Most plans formulated by professional foreign economists have thus far not met with favor in Saigon, for they were generally far too modest to carry with them a political impact commensurate with their economic feasibility. Industrialization plans, either nationwide or by branch of industry, have been made—from the French "Monnet-Bour-

---

June 1, 1957, December 15, 1957, and April 1, 1958; all reprinted or reissued by the American Friends of Viet-Nam.

[18] *Times of Viet-Nam* (Saigon), June 7, 1958. *Italics in original.*

goin" plan of 1947 to various American, Japanese, West German, and United Nations plans in 1956, 1957, and 1958. These do not include South Viet-Nam's own Five-Year Plan[19] which was to be launched in 1957, but aroused so much controversy that it was finally ordered off the headlines by a laconic communiqué of the Presidency: "The Five-Year Plan is being studied at present. It will be officially published once it has been approved by the Government."[20]*

In actual fact, little has been done to industrialize the country even within the limits of its present capabilities. A completely needless watch-assembly plant was opened in 1955 for intermittent operation. A coal mine has begun operations at Nong-Son (Central Viet-Nam) with an expected output of about 15,000 tons a year; and a "Vietnamese Petroleum Company" (it carries an English name in its original form), which was launched in the summer of 1957 and immediately hailed as a "great step forward to economic independence," is now being investigated for a swindle involving 100 million piasters.[21] Several appeals have been made, particularly in the United States, for the investment of private capital in South Viet-Nam and an American-Vietnamese Investment Guaranty Agreement was signed in Washington on November 5, 1957, to provide additional inducements to potential investors.[22] A special meeting for such potential investors was organized in New York City by the American Friends of Viet-Nam, in February, 1958. But it is doubtful whether, in view of the present economic conditions in the United States, much private American capital can be mobilized for long-range, low-return investments such as those needed by Viet-Nam. An Industrial Development Center (IDC), designed to help Vietnamese businessmen to plan industries, was set up by ICA in Saigon in 1958.

In the field of agricultural development, expectations for a more

[19] In a brief description of the Five-Year Plan, distributed "for information only," the program cited includes some agricultural colonization projects, as well as some industrialization in the field of coal mining, sugar refining, and paper milling. Electrification, through the building of two dams, is also to be pushed.

[20] *Viet-Nam Presse* (French ed.), July 19, 1957, p. 1.

[21] *Dan-Chung*, April 11, 1958.

[22] Mimeographed copies in English and French of the agreement are available to the public at the Department of State, Washington, D.C.

* *It never was.*

rapid normalization of production would have been justified, but, as has been shown above, have not been fulfilled for a variety of reasons. Reapportionment of land (which is what is actually meant by "land reform" in South Viet-Nam) was particularly feasible and desirable in South Viet-Nam, where 45 per cent of all arable land was in the hands of owners of estates totaling 50 hectares or more, and where only about 12.5 per cent of the available arable land was owned by smallholders.[23] While timid attempts had been made during the administration of Nguyen Van Tam in 1953, credit for a comprehensive land transfer law must go to the republican government. Promulgated as Ordinance No. 57 on October 22, 1956, the regulation[24] provided for the transfer to smallholders of all land holdings over 100 hectares (260 acres). Landowners may also retain "for purposes of ancestor worship" an additional 15 hectares.

Estimates of the total land area available for reapportionment range from about 727,000 hectares[25] to almost 1 million hectares. The agrarian reform program has been hailed as being the major single step the South Vietnamese administration has taken to counteract Communist propaganda; yet, even sympathetic observers have said that the program, though moving ahead, is doing so "perhaps not with the urgency that some of its adherents would like to see for it."[26] This at the time was a decided understatement, for after nearly two years of the reform program only 35,700 hectares had been transferred to 18,800 farmers, a total of about 4 acres per family.[27] In fact, the whole program bogged down in its

[23] A hectare is about 2.6 acres. For studies on the South Vietnamese land reform problem, see Price Gittinger, "Vietnamese Land Transfer Program," *Land Economics*, May, 1957; his "Rent Reduction and Tenure Security in Free Viet-Nam," *Journal of Farm Economics*, May, 1957; and David Wurfel, "Agrarian Reform in the Republic of Vietnam," *Far Eastern Survey*, June, 1957.

[24] As was explained to this writer by a high Vietnamese official, the land reform was promulgated as a decree rather than a law (which would have to be debated by the legislature) in order to forestall its being filibustered or circumvented by fictitious transfers of land titles to relatives.

[25] Gittinger, *op. cit.*

[26] Hammer, *op. cit.*, p. 228.

[27] *Viet-Nam Presse*, July 15, 1957, p. v. In recent months, however, according to *The Asian Student* (San Francisco), June 10, 1958, land reform has been speeded up. It was reported in *La Dépêche du Cambodge* (July 9, 1958) that 148,445 hectares had been transferred to 64,877 farmers as of May 24, 1958.

early stages, for the landowners refused for nearly a year to come to terms with the government as to a fair price to be paid for the land, and the issue was finally settled by administrative fiat. Therefore, the lands which thus far were parceled out to the land-hungry farmers consisted mostly of plots which had been abandoned by their Vietnamese (or, in the majority of cases, French) owners. France, in fact, is expected to make a major contribution to the land reform program by using funds of the economic aid which it provides for South Viet-Nam to buy up French-owned lands and turn them over to the Viet-Nam Government.*

Yet, one agricultural project—a combination of land reapportionment and land reclamation—was to stand out as a shining example of what could be done in the field of social and economic rehabilitation of large groups of landless farmers: the Cai-San project. As the 1956 USOM *Activity Report* explained, "the name 'Caisan' stands for more than a project alone. Caisan is a symbol of the new country's determination to shelter people who linked their future with that of the free government. It exemplifies the purpose of American aid which is to help people help themselves" (p. 27). USOM devoted more than $10 million and 100 tractors—one of the largest concentrations of motorized agricultural implements ever used on a single project in Asia—to prepare 30,000 hectares of fallow rice land to receive 40,000 refugee settlers. Cai-San became the magic word for a successful program. Photos were distributed, showing the individual farmers receiving title to their plots of land, and emphasis was laid upon the fact that, from landless peasants, the refugees had become owners.

However, in January, 1958, the provincial governor of Kien Giang, which includes Cai-San, appeared at the settlement with an escort of Civil Guards to explain to the farmers that the word "distributed" used in their land contracts was not to be confused with "definitely granted," and that they owed rent or purchase payments to the "rightful owners" of the land. Needless to say, the situation became explosive, the refugee farmers claiming that they had been "duped" by the authorities. Vietnamese newspapers took up the cudgels for the farmers, and even the government-owned newspaper *Cach Mang Quoc Gia* (*National Revolution*) felt con-

---

* By 1966, still another land reform was under way—with similar agonizingly slow results.

strained to explain that "there is no question about giving the land back to the owners of Cai-San," but that "in order to have land, one must buy it, if it were only for a symbolical price."[28] Apparently, the situation is far from settled, for riots in Cai-San, involving more than one hundred refugee farmers and former owners, were subsequently reported in the Saigon press.[29] . . .

Certain problems concerning South Viet-Nam's internal security, though kept out of public notice during the past three years, may soon loom large again. Much has been said, especially in American publications, about the improved administration of the country, and particular emphasis has been laid upon the fact that the present South Vietnamese administration has been the product of nationwide elections held in 1955. This overemphasis on formal processes rather than political facts can, at least in part, be attributed to the application of an American scale of values to an alien situation. But one independent European journalist with more than passing experience in Asia, whose other articles were given wide distribution by the South Viet-Nam Government, described this attitude in a brief paragraph:

> As usual, the Americans go about their business in dead earnest. Having decided to transplant their variety of democracy into this forgotten corner of Asia, they rejoice in every gesture of "democracy" as only a mother could rejoice in the progress of her child. The greater majority of the Americans in Viet-Nam very sincerely believe that in transplanting their institutions, they will immunize South Viet-Nam against Communist propaganda. In fact, they do this with great tact.[30]

One example of this cultural transference is the new South Viet-Nam constitution, proclaimed on October 26, 1956, which borrows largely from the American example, but which also contains some elements of the French constitution of 1946. On the whole, however, and making due allowance for the political immaturity of the population, more could have been done to give the system a more

[28] January 17, 1958.
[29] *Ngon-Luan* (*Opinion*), April 8, 1958.
[30] Tibor Mende, *op. cit.*, p. 933. His article on extensive industrialization in North Viet-Nam has since been widely distributed by the Southern authorities as an example of the aid program they desire the United States to implement in the country.

effective, if not more representative, character. Although the constitution now has been operative for nearly two years, the Supreme Court (or Constitutional Court, as it is called) has never been appointed—thus depriving the country of any check on the constitutionality of government actions—and the Economic Council has likewise remained in limbo.[31]

One other defect which must be remedied soon is the obvious powerlessness of the National Assembly. This should *not* be understood to mean that the Assembly is a one-party group in which the opposition is entirely gagged. On the contrary, it has developed a very vocal opposition group over the past two years and its sessions exhibit a refreshing give-and-take. But this very willingness of the Assembly to do its job well seems to emphasize its powerlessness. The most important issues of government business are simply never submitted to it for discussion but—like the land reform, for example—simply promulgated by presidential decree. Thus, the legislative record of the South Vietnamese National Assembly over the past two years is somewhat less than impressive. It includes such laws as the adherence of South Viet-Nam to the International Atomic Energy Agency; the creation of an "eye bank" for corneal transplants; the confiscation of the property of former Emperor Bao-Dai and his closest associates; and, more recently, the introduction of a widely opposed bill abolishing not only polygamy but (for all practical purposes) divorce—in a country which is nine-tenths Buddhist and one-tenth Catholic. Small wonder that the Assembly is often taunted in the press for lack of real authority.

The Vietnamese press, however, has really benefited from a greater measure of freedom over the past two years. Official censorship over Vietnamese-owned newspapers is said to have been discontinued; only imported or foreign-owned publications published in Viet-Nam are still subject to censorship (the latter including at present the French-owned *Journal d'Extrême-Orient* and *France-Asie* and the partly American-owned *Times of Viet-Nam*). This does not mean that opposition newspapers can be published with-

---

[31] *Tu-Do* (*Liberty*), April 3, 1958. According to *Tin-Dien* (*The Message*) of June 17, 1958, two bills have been filed with the National Assembly for the creation of a National Economic Council. (*It finally took the Diem regime until 1961 to create the Council, which never functioned and disappeared when the regime was overthrown, in 1963.*)

out danger; several newspapers were wrecked by mobs; two of them were later sued for "libel" by government agencies. The major opposition newspaper, *Thoi-Luan* (*Chronicle of the Times*), was finally driven out of existence after a trial of its publisher under a press law which may punish "sabotage of public order" with sentences up to and including death. Phan Quang Dan, an American-trained M.D. and South Viet-Nam's most vocal opposition leader, was implicitly accused of being the author of the most inflammatory articles, some of which appeared in the form of "open letters to my Deputy" (i.e., member of the National Assembly). The article which finally brought about the demise of the publication contained a broadside attack against nearly every aspect of the regime.[32] The trial of the publisher, however, was open to the public and freely reported in other newspapers. The following excerpt from the interrogation of the defendant, Mr. Thien, by the president of the tribunal is of interest:

President: "Why did you make pro-Communist propaganda, outrage the nation, and say that our constitution was not as good as that of the [North Vietnamese] Communists?"

Whereupon Mr. Thien [the publisher] speaks of Article 98 of the constitution which permits the President of the Republic to suspend the exercise of civic freedoms, thus putting the constitution of Viet-Nam in a state of inferiority.

The President reproaches Mr. Thien with having written that persons had been arrested and their trace never found. He invites him to cite names. Mr. Thien seems embarrassed but as he is pressed by the President, he replies: "The *doc-phu* [mandarin of governor's rank] has been arrested a few days ago, and there are other names which I would not like to cite, but here is a letter which may be illuminating." Mr. Thien hands a letter to the President, who reads it and no longer insists.[33]

Nonpolitical news, such as items on the economic situation, and on security conditions in the countryside, however, are reported quite extensively throughout the Vietnamese press. All this cer-

[32] *Thoi-Luan*, March 1, 1958.
[33] *Ngon-Luan*, March 14, 1958. A new paper, *Nguoi Viet Tu-Do* (*The Free Vietnamese*), has taken the place of *Thoi-Luan*. It recently was sued for libel in the highest Vietnamese court for having said that the court system was not yet "fully democratic."

tainly amounts to criticism, if not to opposition in the Western sense. Certainly it is unlikely that all critics of the regime, as certain sources have complained, remain in their position for motives of personal interest rather than out of any concern for the future of their country and appear to have little appreciation of the sense of public responsibility. As a matter of fact, the most effective critics of today are in many cases men who were close collaborators of President Ngo Dinh Diem during his first two years in office and who are not usually suspected of egotistical motives.

There is a certain contradiction in the simultaneous assertions that there is peace and normal activity in the countryside of South Viet-Nam and in the justification of police-state measures because of the threat of internal subversion by still-existing Communist and sect guerrillas. This contradiction arises, however, mostly in the view of the Western observer. To the Vietnamese on the spot, the *resurgence* (rather than the continuance) of rebel activities has become a fact of life with which he has to cope on an increasing scale over the past twelve months. The extent and rise of this insecurity need not be explained in subjective terms which may be biased according to the particular viewpoint of the observer. It can be simply plotted, as in Figure 4 (see page 172), for which daily newspapers or non-secret reports provide the basic raw material. The left-hand map, showing the geographic distribution of Communist complaints to the International Supervisory and Control Commission about alleged South Vietnamese violations of civil rights of "Former Resistance Members," is interesting not because of the number of complaints but because of their location. A perusal of the complaints (the writer has read them all) shows that they are sufficiently precise in their details to have been based upon information given to the Communist North Vietnamese authorities by Viet-Minh agents who have remained behind in the South after the armistice or who have been infiltrated into the area since. This is further confirmed when one compares these data with the right-hand map showing the actual location of recent rebel activities: all major areas of rebel activity also provide the major source of Communist complaints to the ISCC. The conclusion is inescapable that there must be some coordination between the rebels and the North Vietnamese Government.

As to the security situation throughout the Vietnamese countryside, it would be fallacious to compare, as most superficial observers do, the present state of security with that prevailing at the time of the battle of Dien Bien Phu, or in 1955, during the battle against the political-religious sects. Vietnamese in general consider the period between the proclamation of the republic and the promulgation of the constitution (October, 1955–October 1956) to have been the high point in the regime's popularity and countrywide security. The precarious economic situation, however, is regarded as a contributing factor in the present deterioration.

Guerrilla activities in South Viet-Nam during 1957 and 1958 no longer represent a last-ditch fight of dispersed sect or Communist rebel remnants. On the contrary, they have taken on a pattern of their own which is quite different from that followed by the Viet-Minh during the struggle against the French. While the wartime Viet-Minh forces generally limited themselves to the intimidation of the local administrators (village chiefs, notables) into a state of "positive neutrality," the new terrorists seek out the local police chiefs, security guards, village treasurers, and youth leaders and kill them in as spectacular a manner as possible. It would be pointless to describe here the hundreds of cases reported in detail in the Saigon press, but in general they document the fact that the objective of the rebels—gradual "insulation" of the central authorities from direct contact with the grass roots—was achieved. At that time, there was not yet any serious interference with accurate reporting about the state of the population to the central authorities. Various Saigon newspapers sounded the alarm as early as the fall and winter of 1957: "Today the menace is heavier than ever, with the terrorists no longer limiting themselves to the notables in charge of security. Everything suits them, village chiefs, chairmen of liaison committees, simple guards, even former notables. . . . In certain areas, the village chiefs spend their nights in the security posts, while the inhabitants organize watches."[34]

> The most urgent need for the population today is security—a question to which we have repeatedly drawn the attention of the authorities.
>
> Spectacular assassinations have taken place in the provinces of An-Giang and Phong-Dinh [in the Mekong Delta]. In the village of

[34] *Thoi-Luan*, December 15, 1957.

Thanh-My-Tây, armed men appeared in the dead of night, awakened the inhabitants, read a death sentence, and beheaded four young men whose heads they nailed to the nearest bridge. . . .

The security question in the provinces must be given top priority; the regime will be able to consolidate itself only if it succeeds in finding a solution to this problem.[35]

These views were not merely figments of the journalistic imagination. By early spring 1958, insecurity had made sufficient strides for the reappearance of the once-dreaded pattern of desertion of isolated villages. President Ngo Dinh Diem himself expressed concern over the developments during his visit to the Philippines in March, 1958, and more recently, in his May Day message, "urged those who once lived on farms in the countryside and were forced to abandon their age-old way of life . . . to resume their former occupation in order to boost the nation's farm production."[36]

Viet-Nam's cities are calm, save for isolated bombings such as those directed in October, 1957, against American personnel. Main roads can be traveled, although isolated vehicles in the Bassac area are warned to stay in town after 6 P.M. The Vietnamese Government has recently reacted against the widening growth of insecurity by some successful antirebel operations and the capture of several Communist rings in the provincial administration of such key areas as Ben-Tré and My-Tho, one of which included several journalists from Saigon and members of the film industry.

One of the problems arising in this connection is that of the overconfidence previously displayed by the authorities as to their ability to "convert" Communists into genuine "nationalists."

[35] *Tu-Do*, December 17, 1957. In the U.S. Senate hearings on the 1959–60 foreign aid program, Admiral Felix B. Stump, U.S. Commander in Chief, Pacific, reported on March 21, 1958, that the South Vietnamese authorities "are still having trouble in some areas" and then testified in secret as to the exact extent of the disturbances (*Mutual Security Act of 1958*, p. 120). In testimony released in August, 1958, by the House of Representatives Subcommittee on International Operations, Elbridge Durbrow, U.S. Ambassador to Viet-Nam, stated that "the Communists and sect remnants have regrouped and stepped up their terrorist activities in the past several months," and that "because of the terrorist activities in the fertile [Mekong] Delta area, the peasants, through fear or intimidation, cannot till their fields properly." (*Foreign Aid Construction Projects*, pp. 864–65.)

[36] *News From Viet-Nam*, May 16, 1957, p. 4.

While beyond a doubt many such conversions are genuine, others are not, and those have hurt the republic rather badly. A particularly obnoxious case was that of Dai-Loc, a farming area in Central Viet-Nam, where 360 such "ex-Communists," released from an internment camp barely four months before the incident, arrested more than a thousand inhabitants of the area as "Communist agents" and sent them to nine "re-education centers," while another 160 were incarcerated and some of them beaten.[37] Needless to say, the authorities finally stepped in and re-established order, but this sort of free reign given to individuals whose conversion from Communism is still very much open to question has led to reports of Communist "re-infiltration" in certain government services and agencies.

It is certain that a re-examination of the policy of extreme leniency towards former Communist cadres is indicated, while at the same time more leniency should be shown to individuals whose sole crime consists of having chosen the right side too late. Both actions will contribute to relaxing the atmosphere in Saigon.

South Viet-Nam in 1958 thus finds itself at a crossroads. It is now an independent state, and, given the limitations imposed upon it by its precarious economic and military position, it is a free agent. American aid may be essential to keep South Viet-Nam from collapsing within a few months, but American advisers in Saigon are no more than advisers, and their advice is in many cases only heeded when it does not clash with the views of the South Vietnamese presidency. As *Time* magazine, once Ngo Dinh Diem's staunchest supporter, remarked caustically, "put simply, Diem is still taking U.S. money by the millions, but less and less U.S. advice."[38] This relative independence from outside pressure is both a political asset and a dangerous liability for South Viet-Nam. In terms of foreign policy it contributes to the standing of the regime among the noncommitted nations of Asia, and there are strong indications that it already has done so. But in terms of internal policies, it places all responsibility for failure directly on the central authorities, with no opportunity left to blame French colonialism or other foreign interference for the difficulties confronting the country.

[37] *Tu-Do*, January 17, 1958.
[38] *Time*, August 26, 1957, p. 25.

No mention has been deliberately made in this article of the extremely delicate problem of the Chinese minority in Viet-Nam, whose bringing-to-heel by Ngo Dinh Diem has created more problems than it has solved;[39] nor of the problems of Vietnamese foreign relations. The issues raised here are those which the South Vietnamese Government now must face and settle alone, if they are to be settled at all.

Ambitious "paper" industrialization projects must be replaced by more modest but concrete achievements.[40] Since the cost of maintaining the Vietnamese National Army controls in fact the magnitude of the budget (and of the counterpart import program), more earnest attempts will have to be made to "cut out the frills" from the army without cutting its combat efficiency. Vietnamese Army pay scales are now among the highest in Asia and in some cases higher than those paid to troops in NATO; their reduction to a lower level would free considerable funds for economic development while decreasing the demand for imported consumer goods. A greater effort should be made to place good civil servants in field positions instead of keeping them in staff positions in Saigon, so as to provide the central government authorities with the necessary feedback to enable them to make sound decisions based upon real situations. Less effort might, on the other hand, go into prestige projects, such as the creation of lawns and miniature golf courses in the already beautiful city of Saigon.

The government of South Viet-Nam has in many fields deliberately departed from the established mold, and this is laudable. It has, at the price of great sacrifices, "Vietnamized" itself and the country. But this Vietnamization must not stop at the slogans which cover the walls, the signs of the Chinese shops, and the language in which courses are taught at the law school. It must consider the development of the economy and of the country's political life in line with the needs of the majority of the population—and that population, for a long time to come, will be devoted to rice farming to an overwhelming extent. Better social services for the farmers need to be given top priority in all government pro-

[39] See Bernard B. Fall, "Viet-Nam's Chinese Problem," *Far Eastern Survey*, May, 1958, pp. 65–72.
[40] For an optimistic view, see Tillman Durdin, "Saigon Planning Big Export Gain," *The New York Times*, July 3, 1958.

grams, and promises made to the peasantry, once given, should be fulfilled. . . .

Ngo Dinh Diem's administration, after four years of American training in nearly every field, now begins to show a modicum of orderly, if not yet very efficient, development. But there are disturbing signs of loss of contact with the people in certain areas of the countryside, and there—as the Nationalist Chinese found out—is where wars may be lost in Asia.

14. The Montagnards

"They have no social traditions, no tombs, no altars." That incredible statement—a sheer anthropological idiocy if applied to
any human society—can be found in the leading paragraphs of a
United States Information Service booklet on Viet-Nam's 700,000-
odd mountain tribal people, published in Saigon in 1962 for the
guidance of Americans who had to work with them. It explains
why, after ten years of being deeply committed in that country,
Americans are still "taken by surprise by recent events in Viet-
Nam."

Yet the problem of South Viet-Nam's mountain minorities has
been part of the Viet-Nam problem for the past decade. Called in
American parlance *montagnards* (a French word, but one the
French never used in this connection), these tribesmen represent
the aboriginal population of the area, which is largely of Malayo-
Polynesian and Mon-Khmer stock. It was gradually pushed back
into the hill areas of the whole Southeast Asian peninsula when
the more sophisticated Thai (that is, Laotian, Siamese, and Burmans) and Sino-Mongoloid (Vietnamese) ethnic groups penetrated the area from the north about 1,000 years ago. Oppressed
and despised by the lowlanders, who called them and treated them
as slaves and savages (to this day the general Vietnamese term
for the tribes is *Moi*, i.e., "savages"), the tribesmen greeted the
arrival of white colonizers with unalloyed relief. That is why during
World War II the pro-Allied guerrillas in Burma were all Kachin,
Chin, and Karen, while the lowland Burmese (the Burmans) were
pro-Japanese; and why to this day in Viet-Nam an American
Special Forces' man's best introduction to the Vietnamese tribes-

Excerpted, by permission, from "Who's Who in Vietnam?," which originally
appeared in *The New Republic*, October 17, 1964. © 1964 by Harrison-Blaine
of New Jersey, Inc.

men is his white face: the French also had treated the tribes fairly and many of the village chiefs are former French Army sergeants.

How far-reaching is the sympathy for the white man as a "buffer" between the tribes and the lowlanders became clear in an almost comical episode in 1888–90. A French adventurer sought to imitate the "White Rajahs" of Borneo, had himself proclaimed "Marie I, King of the Sedangs," and began to issue stamps, medals, and titles of nobility in the name of his ephemeral realm. It took the French colonial administration several campaigns to persuade the tribesmen that the "White Rajah" from Paris was the real one.

The struggle for independence brought the tribes into the twentieth century. Although representing less than 5 per cent of the South Vietnamese population, they occupy more than 60 per cent of the country's territory, and their vast holdings completely hem in the lowland Vietnamese in compact "pockets," particularly in Central Viet-Nam (see Figure 5). The French trained separate Vietnamese units made up almost entirely of tribal troops and officered in the lower ranks by rapidly trained tribesmen. Some specially selected lowland Vietnamese also served with them. One of them was Le Kan Kim, who became chief of staff of the 4th Mountain Division in 1951. It was he, now one of the four allegedly "neutralist" generals under house arrest, whom Premier Nguyen Khanh wanted to use during the September, 1964, tribal rebellion to negotiate with the tribesmen. The "young Turks" (or, rather, young wolves) from among the military around Khanh prevented this, although Kim is one of the few officers the tribesmen know and trust.

When the late Ngo Dinh Diem took over Viet-Nam, his solution for the tribesmen was "equality" with the lowland Vietnamese and their "integration" with them. Diem's American advisers, so far as they had ever bothered to try to understand the problem, thought of it in terms of the American Indian problem—which it closely resembled, except that the mountain tribes had no taste for genocide and looked to North Viet-Nam for an alternative. To the mountain tribes, as they saw it, "equality" turned out to be an absolute right of the lowland Vietnamese to colonize the hill areas and to drive the tribesmen into the most inhospitable areas left over; and "integration" turned out to mean closing the tribal

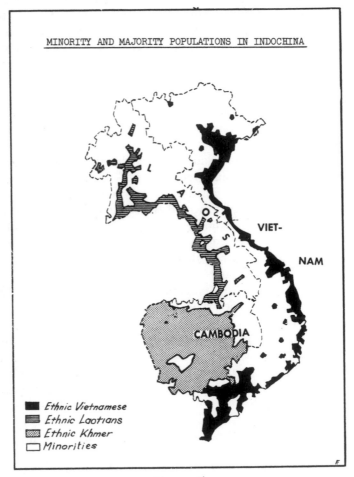

FIGURE 5

schools where classes were taught in native dialects lovingly trans-
literated into Latin script by French missionaries. As early as June,
1957, the foremost American scholar in that field, Gerald C.
Hickey, reported back to the U.S. aid mission in Saigon that the
mountain tribes were bitterly discontented with the new regime of
Diem: "The Vietnamese talk equality," Hickey quotes a group of

tribesmen, "but they don't mean what they say . . . in their hearts, they want to dominate us. They are colonialists. . . . They don't mean it when they call us 'brothers.' Even little Vietnamese call Mountaineers [civil servants] '*moi*'. . . . Under the French the schools were better. The Vietnamese have better schools, but the Mountaineer schools only get worse—no money, no teachers, and no directors."

And Hickey also warned the U.S. mission in Saigon that the Communist Viet-Minh had taken along with them in 1954, when Vietnam was divided, thousands of Southern tribesmen and the elite of the leaders; and that they were infiltrating back (already in 1957!) trained lowland propagandists who not only spoke the local dialects but who even broke their front teeth and wore loincloths to conform with local mores.

Mr. Hickey's advice went as unheeded as that of Frederic Wickert, then a psychology professor at Michigan State, who two years later, after a personal survey among the tribesmen, reported: "The tribesmen see themselves starved to death. They feel that the Vietnamese are letting diseases, such as smallpox, kill them off. Too, they feel that the Vietnamese are trying to force them to give up their culture." And Wickert also warned of the Communist infiltrators who "do not assume the superior airs that too many Vietnamese officials in tribal country do."[1]

But all warnings (including the author's, which paralleled those of Hickey and Wickert) fell on totally deaf ears. One unabashed apologist for the Diem regime dismissed all this well-meant advice as a "passion for finding fault with everything done by the Vietnamese," and defended his own hopelessly rosy view of the tribal situation by saying that he owed his insights "to the man who has both a greater knowledge of and a deeper concern for the minorities than any other person in Viet-Nam—President Ngo Dinh Diem himself." It is on the basis of that sort of poppycock that policy was made in Saigon (and Washington) about an extremely sensitive problem. The results are here for everyone to see.

On the Communist side, the tribal problem was handled differently: two "autonomous zones" were set up in North Viet-Nam, where tribal leaders—though of course solidly "boxed in" by Com-

[1] See Richard W. Lindholm, *Vietnam—The First Five Years* (East Lansing, Mich.: Michigan State University Press, 1959), pp. 126–40 *passim*.

munist cadres—deal with the local affairs of their own territory, with the help of tribal civil servants and even a tribal militia force. In Hanoi, an Advisory Council on Minorities is headed by Major General Le Quang Ba, a Thai tribesman, who was a full division commander in the war against the French (the present Saigon regime rarely allows a tribesman to receive even a lieutenant's commission); the council advises the central government on all matters affecting the tribes. A central Minorities School in Hanoi (which also trains tribesmen from South Viet-Nam) provides the tribal areas with well-indoctrinated and able administrative officers, teachers, and public health personnel. Nothing like this has been tried in South Viet-Nam.

How well the Communists succeeded among the Southern tribesmen became obvious in mid-1961, when full-fledged 2,500-man Communist mountain regiments began to appear in the hill areas. In its two-volume study on Communist aggression in South Viet-Nam published in December, 1961,[2] the State Department mentions casually (and apparently without at all realizing the importance of the fact) that members of the Viet-Cong's 120th Regiment, commanded by Colonel Y-Bloc, had been identified and captured. Y-Bloc is a *tribal* name and the 120th Regiment is a Hre tribal regiment. By 1963, all the other Communist tribal regular units which had slowly strangled the French in the highlands were also back in business: the 108th, the 126th, and the 803d regiments, made up of Jarai, Rhade, and Bahnar tribesmen. Communist radio propaganda, couched in mountain dialects, had begun as early as 1956; South Vietnamese radio programs addressed to the tribesmen began four years later. And while Saigon still preached the hollow myth of "equality," the Communists were preaching the heady idea of autonomy for the mountain zones.

A Communist document captured by American advisers in 1963 explicitly sets forth these promises, which were also included in the "Liberation Front" program of 1960, but which were now made even more appealing: "The nationalities have the right to maintain or change customs and habits, use language and script, develop a national culture of their own. . . . The localities with minority peoples living concentrated are allowed to form them-

---

[2] *A Threat to the Peace: North Viet-Nam's Effort to Conquer South-Vietnam* (2 vols.; Washington, D.C., 1961).

selves into autonomous regions, after the homeland has been entirely liberated and the government will fall into the people's hands."

Considering the treatment the tribes have been getting from Saigon for ten years, that program carries great emotional appeal, and "after the homeland has been entirely liberated" is a clear invitation to the tribes to join the Communist lowland Vietnamese in the war against the South Vietnamese Government. Even a hill tribe flag suddenly appeared: green-red-black with three white stars representing the major tribal groupings, and completely different from the red-and-sky-blue VC flag—no doubt to make the promise of later autonomy more real. This flag was waved by tribal soldiers at their American advisers when the former mutinied around the hill town of Ban Me Thuot on September 22.

The position of the U.S. Special Forces in all this is unenviable. For three years, the Special Forces had slowly rebuilt tribal confidence, with as little interference (even from the CIA, which at first controlled their operations) as possible. By June, 1962, much of key Darlac Province had been cleared. Thirty-six Special Forces detachments began fielding *montagnard* strike companies. On July 1, 1963, the Special Forces also assumed control over the Civil Irregular Defense Groups (CIDG), the equivalent of village militia units in the hill areas, and the Viet-Cong began to feel the effect of the pinch on its transit lines to Laos and North Viet-Nam. Surely, the Vietnamese war was not going to be won in the tribal areas (it is in the Vietnamese-inhabited Mekong Delta that the outcome will probable be decided, if anywhere), but the progressive clearing of the vast mountain areas would have helped immensely.

But on May 15, 1964, orders came to integrate the American-run Special Forces units into the Vietnamese Army corps in whose area they operated; and Vietnamese lowland officers and noncoms, who hitherto had been sedulously kept away from the tribesmen, began to take over command. The effects were not long in coming. *Montagnard* units deserted en masse in many places, sometimes after murdering lowland Vietnamese cadres, and often taking along their high-powered American weapons. Some camps were betrayed from within by disaffected tribal units; others were attacked by VC units backed by tribal deserters.

Finally, during a tense week beginning on September 22, the

tribesmen showed the full effect of years of Vietnamese mistreatment, official American misunderstanding, and clever Communist
propaganda. They temporarily occupied Ban Me Thuot, seized its
radio transmitter to clamor for autonomy, raised their new flag
over the Special Forces camps and massacred sixty of their Vietnamese officers. The alien Americans had to step in as negotiators
between the "Vietnamese" tribesman and their lowland "brothers." The Special Forces were compelled to play an uncomfortable
role which the tribesmen may well construe as a betrayal of their
interests in favor of Saigon.*

As long as the Vietnamese Government clings to the fiction of
"integrating" the tribes against their will, the military advisers who
work with the tribesmen—and who know that the tribesmen will
fight only for the right to live undisturbed—will always sooner or
later clash with the too-well-insulated policymakers, who have
never understood the emotional appeal of local autonomy, and who
seemingly believe that a human being has to have a seersucker
suit and an advanced education to be entitled to social traditions,
tombs, and altars.

---

* *This may well have come true in the meantime. In September, 1965, there
was another rebellion of mountain tribal Strike Force units, in the course of
which many tribal leaders moved to neighboring Cambodia. In the battles
around the Special Forces camps of Plei-Me (November, 1965) and A-Shau
(March, 1966), many of the Strike Force tribesmen deserted their American
Special Forces advisers.*

15. The Agonizing Reappraisal

February, 1965

The disintegration of South Vietnamese society, precipitated by the Diem regime's dictatorial policies but carefully plastered over until its demise, has now come into the open and manifests itself in student riots, government paralysis at most levels and in many areas, Buddhist demonstrations, and war-weariness among many South Vietnamese Army (ARVN) units. Pro-government successes may still be best measured in "kills"—23,500 for the year 1963[1] —rather than in provinces or districts made safe for unfettered local elections or for effective economic improvement.[2]

The "strategic hamlet" program, launched with great fanfare in March, 1962, and designed (in slavish imitation of a Malayan pattern totally inapplicable to Vietnamese conditions) to protect the villagers and their chiefs from Communist control, was a shambles by the time Diem died, although that truth had been hidden from the outside world, and in part probably from Diem as well. Probably one of the few side benefits of Diem's demise was that it set in motion a reassessment of Viet-Nam's internal situation and occasioned a series of brutally frank studies (most of which are still unavailable to the public), which showed clearly how badly the situation had deteriorated. Of the 8,500-odd strategic hamlets— now rebaptized "New Life Hamlets"—officially declared to be in

[1] Military Advisory Command—Viet-Nam, *The Observer* (weekly), March 21, 1964. The same source credits 7,500 of those kills to fixed-wing aircraft.

[2] While this is totally forgotten today, local elections took place in war-torn non-Communist Viet-Nam in January and June, 1953. The 3,650 elected town councilors were (predictably) anti-French in their majority, a few even were open "neutralists," and one successful candidate—in Saigon—was a Trotskyite Marxist. But it was felt in Saigon that the gain in representatives was worth the gamble. The by then hopeless military situation prevented further exploitation of that initial gain.

Excerpted, by permission, from "Vietnam: The Agonizing Reappraisal," which originally appeared in *Current History*, February, 1965. © 1965 by Current History, Inc.

197

existence, less than 1,500 were viable. In a misguided effort to boost their hamlet construction "score," some provincial governors had declared a hamlet "strategic" when it had received a few strands of barbed wire and a few old hunting guns; while others had exerted dire pressure on the population to provide free construction services for jobs that should have been remunerated. The result was that a joint American-Vietnamese report of January, 1964, openly stated that "the war cannot be won unless immediate reforms are made at the village level."[3] At year's end, no reforms had been undertaken.

In the urban areas of Viet-Nam, nine years of total denial of political expression were followed by a typical "decompression" problem. Viet-Nam's students and Buddhist leaders, hitherto silent, gave the country what could almost be called a case of the political "bends." In their attempt to create a South Vietnamese regime which (having represented them not at all for nine years) would represent them only and in full, they went to an anarchical extreme.

It should be obvious by now that in the present state of affairs in South Viet-Nam, *everything* is Communist-infiltrated. In 1951, Bishop of Saigon Chassaigne had to dissolve the Sao-Mai Boy Scout units of the Saigon area, because they were Communist-infiltrated. In the kind of fratricidal war being fought in Viet-Nam, even family bonds prove little: Buddhist leaders Tam Chau or Tri Quang may have brothers in North Viet-Nam; but so have Generals Duong Van Minh and Nguyen Khanh. And it was Madame Ngo Dinh Nhu who proudly admitted, three months after her husband had been murdered along with Diem, that he had indeed contacted Viet-Cong leaders and was undertaking negotiations, allegedly for their surrender.[4]

As for the Buddhists of Viet-Nam, it would be totally futile to argue in detail with those who hold the view that the Buddhists are the sole channel of Communist infiltration in South Viet-Nam.[5] In the case of Viet-Nam's "Buddhists,"[6] persecution was

[3] *The Saigon Post*, January 20, 1964.

[4] *Le Nouveau Candide* (Paris), February 13, 1964.

[5] See Marguerite Higgins, "Ugly Americans of Vietnam," in *America*, October 3, 1964; or *Time*, December 11, 1964.

[6] "Buddhists" in Viet-Nam include all the Confucianists, ancestor-worship-

real, but it was not new, nor, for that matter, one-sided. The myth of Vietnamese religious tolerance, sedulously built up by the Diem regime and some of its foreign admirers, does not stand serious examination. One of the most compelling reasons for French intervention in Viet-Nam in 1845–47 was precisely that the Vietnamese emperors, Thieu-Tri and Tu-Duc, were engaging in wholesale massacres of Vietnamese Catholics. An American Catholic source averred that "in the persecutions of the last century, tiny Viet-Nam had 100,000 martyrs, far above any single nation's quota [*sic*] since the early Roman persecutions."[7] Independent Vietnamese and French sources confirm this. Under the French, the pendulum swung the other way and kept on swinging that way under Diem.

As early as 1952, Vietnamese sources began to complain that French-armed Catholic militia forces, rather than fighting the Communists, preferred to use their weapons to "plunder pagodas, demolish temples, and convert by force the population."[8] And exactly nine years later, in July, 1961, a Western observer, though sympathetic to the Diem regime, was to report than an ARVN military operation failed to capture Communist insurgents but, in the process, destroyed rural villages in Tra Vinh Province of the Mekong Delta: "The following month, after the army had retired leaving thousands of unhappy peasants behind it, Buddhist bonzes petitioned the province chief in Tra-Vinh against the shelling of hamlets and pagodas and to demand the release of their imprisoned fellows. Some months later their leader, Superior Bonze Son Vong, appeared on the lists of the central committee of the Viet Cong's National Liberation Front."[9]

That case, from personal observation, was not unique; and discrimination in favor of Catholics throughout the Diem administration was sufficiently widespread for *Informations Catholiques Internationales* to devote almost a whole issue to it (and to its long-range danger for the Vietnamese Catholic community) *before*

---

ers, Cao-Dai and Hoa-Hao sect members who do not explicitly reject Buddha, as do the Catholic, Protestant, and Muslim minorities in Viet-Nam.

[7] *Catholic Digest,* February, 1962, p. 17.

[8] Van Thanh, "L'auto-défense des villages: base de la pacification du Nord-Vietnam," *Orient-Occident* (Paris), November, 1952, p. 19.

[9] Denis Warner, *The Last Confucian* (London and New York: Penguin Books, 1964), p. 153.

the outbreak of the Buddhist demonstrations in Viet-Nam.[10] All
that did not prevent the departing American ambassador, Frederick E. Nolting, from declaring, as he left Saigon in the summer
of 1963, that he had never seen "any evidence" of anti-Buddhist
persecution while in Viet-Nam.

In sum, the religious tensions racking South Viet-Nam in 1964–
65 are not new, nor are they directly ascribable to some particularly
evil phenomenon. Rather than being the *cause* of South Viet-
Nam's internal malaise, Buddhist obstreperousness is a clear *symp-
tom* of disintegration of the South Vietnamese social fabric. This
does not mean, of course, that the Communists do not seek to exploit that situation: they exploit every other South Vietnamese
weakness as well, and probably most of all the dissension among
the senior military leaders and the absence of some sort of consensus among Saigon's politicians. . . .

Clearly, a heavy legacy was left by the Diem regime to its successors. Its worst shortcomings are precisely *not* in the largely irrelevant conventional military field, but in what it did (or what it
allowed to happen) to relations between parts of the Vietnamese
population by its constant playing-off of one group against another:
refugees vs. indigenous South Vietnamese; *montagnards* vs. lowlanders; Buddhists vs. Catholics; pro-French vs. pro-Americans;
the army vs. the civilians; the peasantry vs. the city dwellers. These
wounds, deeply imbedded in the society, prove harder to heal than
military losses.

This may at times be difficult to understand for people to whom
"stability" seems to be the only yardstick of government effectiveness[11]—they apparently forget that the world recently has seen
several "stable" governments disappear overnight, from Batista's
in Cuba to Khrushchev's in Moscow. These same observers would
do well to remember that it was the Vietnamese *army* (not the
Buddhists or the students) that twice tried to murder Diem, in
November, 1960, and February, 1962, before finally succeeding
in overthrowing his regime in November, 1963. There is perhaps
no grimmer evidence of the loss of control which had already over-

[10] *Informations Catholiques Internationales* (Paris), No. 188 (March 15,
1963).
[11] Joseph Alsop, "King's Log and Stork," *The Washington Post*, December
16, 1964.

taken the Diem regime in March to May, 1963 (i.e., *before* the Buddhist clashes), than the map (see Figure 6), based on official documentation,[12] indicating the extent of Communist tax collections throughout South Viet-Nam. In all but three provinces, the Viet-Cong was collecting taxes of some kind or another; and in twenty-seven provinces Communist taxation proceeded on a formalized basis, with bond issues, tax tables, and proper receipts.

While it is always risky to state a case on the basis of might-have-beens, the realities of the situation on the ground inside South Viet-Nam, even six months before Diem's overthrow, indicate that an even more brutal collapse of South Viet-Nam might well have occurred had the regime survived the November, 1963, coup. The ARVN might have split for good into loyal and disloyal elements, and Ngo Dinh Nhu (as his wife asserted in the above-mentioned article) might have negotiated both his brother and South Viet-Nam into neutralism; or, failing this, might well have joined the rebels with his own Republican Youth movement transformed into *maquis* forces. Those who might reject such a possibility would do well to ponder the example of the American-trained and American-advised Kong-Le forces in Laos: overnight they smashed the United States–backed right-wing regime and later joined the Pathet Lao pro-Communist forces in an alliance that lasted just long enough to destroy all American hopes for a right-wing Laotian regime.[13] In South Viet-Nam there are ample numbers of civilian and military candidates for a "Kong-Le gambit."

Throughout 1964, the situation inside South Viet-Nam worsened considerably by every yardstick of insurgency measurement, from actual battle casualties to tonnage of rice falling into Viet-Cong hands; from the size of the enemy units to the desertion rate of the ARVN forces; from the reduction of United States advisory forces promised in October, 1963, to the steady increase of American reinforcements until the 25,000-men mark was probably reached by early 1965. The losses of village officials through assassination, which had reached a peak rate of 4,000 a year in 1960–61,

[12] U.S. Operations Mission, Saigon, *Resources Control Survey—Vietnam,* June 14, 1963 (declassified January 1, 1964). The same survey also indicated that control measures were noneffective or nonexistent in sixteen provinces; and only six were rated as "acceptably effective."

[13] See Arthur Dommen, *Conflict in Laos* (New York: Frederick A. Praeger, 1964).

REPUBLIC OF VIET-NAM

Areas taxed by Viet-Cong March-May 1963

From Marcus G. Raskin and Bernard B. Fall (eds.), *The Viet-Nam Reader* (New York: Random House, 1965). By permission of the publisher.

FIGURE 6

had reached the figures of 429 killed and 482 abducted between January 1 and November 15, 1964—i.e., a rate of about 1,000 a year. The cumulative loss of such officials since the beginning of the insurgency in 1957 in all likelihood is now in excess of 15,000— or almost one per village.[14][*]

That makes the chances of a liquidation of the insurgency through simple military repression, as in the case of the Mau-Mau in Kenya, somewhat dubious. The recognition of this fact is by now almost unanimous. Yet it has brought about two exactly opposite viewpoints on how to terminate the Second Indochina War. One, mostly limited to the liberal end of the spectrum, urges a rapid disengagement of the United States from the conflict;[15] the other argues for a heavier involvement, culminating—if need be—in a full-scale Korean-type ground war in North Viet-Nam.[16] An even more extreme view holds that the Viet-Nam affair could be transformed into a "golden opportunity" to "solve" the Red Chinese problem as well, possibly by a Pan-Asian "crusade" involving Chinese Nationalist, Korean, and Japanese troops, backed by United States power as needed.

Other "options" or sub-options have cropped up in recent months and have no doubt been entertained at various government levels with varying degrees of success, or have been discussed in the press. In most cases, however, the arguments failed to take into account some of the obvious difficulties inherent in the military aspects of such an escalation; almost none hinted at the price that would be exacted in blood, treasure, or world-wide political complications for the implementation of any one of the options offered.

To "play through" the full set of options would be tantamount to attempting to define the total number of color, trim, power-plant, and body variations in which a major car model is available: diplomatically, it will eventually make a great difference if an air-

[14] Jack Foisie, in *Los Angeles Times*, November 16, 1964. The same newspaper, over the signature of Ed Meagher, reported on July 26 that "the Viet-Cong guerrillas have lost the initiative."

[15] National Committee for a Sane Nuclear Policy, "Southeast Asia and Vietnam," press release of October 16, 1964 (2 pp., mimeo.).

[16] William Beecher, "U.S. Readies Data: Could Serve To Justify 'Escalating' War on Reds," *The Wall Street Journal*, November 18, 1964.

[*] *Official U.S. sources spoke in March, 1966, of a total of 61,000 village leaders killed since 1958, or about 5 per village. (Cf. Douglas Pike, "How Strong Is the NLF?," The Reporter, February 24, 1966.)*

craft of American manufacture used to bomb the Ho Chi Minh Trail in Laos (a) is of the Laotian, South Vietnamese, or American air force; (b) is piloted by a Laotian, a Vietnamese, an American, or a mercenary in the pay of one or all of the three; (c) is propeller-driven (authorized under the provisions of the 1954 Geneva cease-fire) or jet-propelled (forbidden under that treaty); and (d) carries a normal complement of fragmentation bombs and machine guns; napalm, weedkilling chemicals, or low-yield nuclear weapons.* The alternatives presented below are merely for reference, and do not pretend to be exhaustive. They are, briefly: (1) "walking away," (2) negotiating "out," (3) negotiating while fighting on, (4) "diplomatic judo," (5) fighting on under the "ground rules," (6) escalation-by-proxy, and (7) harassing the "sanctuary." . . .

The West in general, and the United States in particular, are thus left in the throes of a dilemma aptly described by Walter Lippmann as the choice between "unattainable victory and unacceptable defeat." As the year 1964 ended, the consensus seemed to converge toward a more or less temporary stabilization along the lower reaches of points 5 to 7 of the above scale. The advantage of such an approach is that it stays within the realm, for good or ill, of what has already been experienced; and there exist some remote chances that alternate approaches by third parties on both sides may bring about a "thaw" in the presently frozen positions.

Some sources aver that Hanoi and Peking, and these two and the Liberation Front, may not be as unified as it appears on the surface. The usually reliable Le Monde expert Georges Chaffard reported in November, 1964, that Peking might be in the process of "leapfrogging" Hanoi with the NLF to take over directly the backing of the latter's operations. Chaffard (echoing other French views) feels that Hanoi, now truly worried about an extended American "spasm-reaction" or a deliberate shift toward policy ranges 7–8 of the above scale, might be willing to settle for a compromise that neither Peking nor the NLF find acceptable.[17]

Approaches made by Dr. Pham Ngoc Thach (a South Viet-

[17] Georges Chaffard, "Par-dessus Ho Chi Minh," L'Express, November 15, 1964.

* Some of these nonnuclear phases were, of course, implemented.

namese guerrilla leader during the First Indochina War and now Minister of Health in the North Vietnamese Government) to Vietnamese exiles in France during a recent visit seem to have echoed a similar tendency.

If such a fissure indeed exists within the Asian Communist complex involved in Viet-Nam, then perhaps application of a solution within the 3–4 range of the above scale could become conceivable without endangering the ever-fragile and volatile South Vietnamese political-military gossamer. As often before, American policies —indeed, the West's whole position—in Southeast Asia are at a crossroads. But that crossroads is dangerously close to the point of no return.

16. The Scars of Division

July, 1964

The partition of sovereign states is neither a new phenomenon nor a rare one. A number of nations whose ethnic homogeneity had been taken for granted—such as Germany, France, or the Scandinavian countries—are found to have large and well-established minority groups. Or, vice versa—and this is the case which applies to Viet-Nam—it is clear that certain well-established national groups inhabit several distinct polities.

Such cases as that of the Kurds, split among Iraq, Turkey, Iran, and Syria; or of the French, spread over France, Belgium, Switzerland, and Italy's Aosta Vale, are well known. What differentiates the Kurdish from the French case is that in the latter one can hardly speak of a "Pan-French" feeling. Among the Kurds, however, that feeling does exist. In other cases, the "pan" feeling, once acute, eventually dies down, as it apparently now has in Eire, where the return of Northern Ireland to the Free State no longer is considered a do-or-die issue. In fact, the emergence of about fifty Afro-Asian nations, not one of which is ethnically, culturally, or linguistically homogeneous, has just about laid to rest whatever was left of the Wilsonian illusion about national self-determination. The rule now seems to be that a nation is whatever the over-all political situation in its area allows it to be, and nothing else. In fact, the technical means of mass transportation or mass extermination now available make it relatively easy to match a territorial amputation with a corresponding expulsion or liquidation of that part of the population which no longer fits the national or ethnic image (or illusion) being imposed by the ruling group.

Viet-Nam fits somewhere in between the above. There were

Reprinted, by permission, from "Sociological and Psychological Aspects of Vietnam's Partition," *Journal of International Affairs*, Vol. XVIII, No. 2 (1964), pp. 173–87.

exoduses, expulsions—the difference between the two being the absolutely compulsory aspect of the latter—and exterminations. It is asserted that in North Viet-Nam close to 50,000 "landlord" and "bourgeois" representatives have died in various labor camps and through summary sentences handed out by land reform tribunals; and in South Viet-Nam at least a like number of opponents, from members of Buddhist sects to highly respectable non-Communist dissenters, were sent to concentration camps where grim climatic and health conditions insured a high casualty rate.

Thus, the political criteria established for the partitions which came to the fore after World War II brought about a *social* aspect to the partition in addition to the usual *territorial* and *ethnic* aspects. Since the ringing down of the Iron Curtain, "bourgeois"[1] elements tend to flee to the West first, followed only much later by other social elements, thus leaving behind a society that is more "proletarian," poorer, and deprived of many of the skills (doctors, engineers, administrators) which the departed bourgeoisie represented. This is even truer in an underdeveloped country such as Viet-Nam than it was in Eastern Europe. The cleavage, involving classes and religion as well as political allegiance, becomes deeper than it ever has been before as the "amputated" society has to build a new leadership class almost from scratch. In the Communist zone of Viet-Nam, leadership is made up from the revolutionaries who have grown up in the war against France, supplemented to a very small extent by returned *émigrés*, none of whom holds a key job thus far. In South Viet-Nam, leadership—under the rule of the late Ngo Dinh Diem—was in the hands of an active regional and religious minority, the Northern and Central Vietnamese Catholics. In fact, there was a saying in South Viet-Nam that in order to succeed one needed the "Three D's": Diem (i.e., connections with his family), Dao (i.e., religion, that is, Catholicism), and Dia-phuong (i.e., province, that is, originating from the proper Central Vietnamese area). The revolutionary juntas of Generals Duong Van Minh and Nguyen Khanh had the merit of

[1] The term "bourgeois" is used here in the relative sense in which the Communists use it. Thus, in North Viet-Nam, where the average, individually owned plot of land measured about an acre, the owner of four acres was a "landlord"; in South Viet-Nam, where land is abundant, landlords owned hundreds and even thousands of acres.

at least being both largely Buddhist-Confucianist and South Viet-namese—i.e., "indigenous."* Thus, both Vietnamese societies already have, for better or for worse, begun a process of social "restratification" which has left deep marks upon their present political and economic structures.

It seems difficult, at first glance, to provide a statistical under-pinning for the assertion that fundamental changes have taken place in the divided Vietnamese societies. Both regimes, however, have provided us with some figures which—though far from being comparable—indicate to a certain extent the depth of social change which already has taken place.

In South Viet-Nam the major problem consisted of absorbing the 860,000 refugees from North Viet-Nam. Of those, about 700,-000 were farmers, 88,000 were fishermen, and the remainder—businessmen, government employees, and professionals—came from urban areas. Ethnically, all but about 20,000 were lowland Viet-namese; in terms of religion, over 600,000 were Catholics. The fact that these people had been willing to move from their home areas to escape Communism was correctly interpreted to be a sign of implicit loyalty to the Diem government. The high percentage of Catholics further guaranteed their loyalty to a government domi-nated by Catholics but ruling a largely Buddhist-Confucianist country.

The Catholic refugees, resettled in easily accessible areas, mostly around Saigon and along major roads, became the political shock troops of the regime, providing the cheering crowds that for so long fooled American official visitors about the popularity of Diem and the "safe constituencies" which unfailingly elected regime-approved candidates by 99 per cent majorities. Mme. Ngo Dinh Nhu was "elected" by such a refugee constituency. But in addition to their Catholicism, the refugees had some other disturbing quali-ties in the eyes of their southern Vietnamese hosts. The North Vietnamese refugees, by virtue of demographic pressure, harsher climate, and smaller available land acreages—and also by virtue of the fact that, for centuries, they had to bear the brunt of Chinese invasions—are of a tougher fiber, work harder, and are

* This became less true with General Nguyen Cao Ky's regime of 1965–66, which was again northern-dominated.

"pushier" and "grabbier" than the easy-going Cochinchinese. The result was that the newcomers soon held many of the choicest positions throughout the government and the economy. In the Institute of National Administration, for example, which until 1962 functioned with the help of American advisers from Michigan State University, the latter found that all but an infinitesimal number of the staff positions were held by Catholic northern refugees, while all the menial positions (cleaning women, porters, etc.) were held by South Vietnamese.

Such cleavages finally came out in the open when the spreading guerrilla war began to put heavy stresses on the social fabric. By stressing their support of the poor peasantry, the Viet-Cong (a South Vietnamese pejorative term for the guerrillas) clad themselves in a Robin Hood role and profited from the existing country-vs.-city and northern Catholic refugee-vs.-southern Buddhist aborigine tension. A few figures illustrate the extent of the problem. Whereas in North Viet-Nam prior to the Communist takeover 98.7 per cent of all agricultural holdings were tilled by their owner, this was the case with only 64 per cent in South Viet-Nam. And in South Viet-Nam, 2 per cent of the landowners owned 45 per cent of the land, while in North Viet-Nam 98.2 per cent of all farmers owned five hectares or less.[2] The inequalities of land distribution in the South, unrelieved by a succession of poorly executed land reforms, contributed a great deal to making the Viet-Cong cause far more popular than Communist propaganda alone could make it.

When the Ngo Dinh Diem regime made the additional mistake of mishandling what was, at the beginning, a seemingly trivial incident with the Buddhists (a question as to whether or not Buddhist flags could be flown on Buddhist holidays), all the proper conditions were met for a major conflagration. A wave of civil disobedience set in, demoralizing the administration and also affecting the armed forces—the latter more, perhaps, than the civilians—and culminating in the overthrow of the Diem regime and the murder of Diem and his brother Nhu on November 2, 1963.

The new military regimes of Generals Minh and Khan at least had the merit of superficially "southernizing" the Saigon regime.

---

[2] Department of Agriculture, *The Agriculture of Indochina* (mimeo., Washington, D.C., 1950), pp. 11–15. See also Fall, *The Two Viet-Nams*, pp. 308–9.

But it is too early to tell what effect this will have in re-establishing some sort of rapport between town and country in South Viet-Nam. After all, there are only 300,000 South Vietnamese out of 14.5 million employed in nonagricultural pursuits (the Vietnamese army not included), and of the 14.5 million, all but 2 million live in small villages and hamlets that are readily accessible to the guerrillas. South Viet-Nam's eventual survival may, in the long run, depend upon whether Saigon succeeds in re-establishing some sort of dialogue with its own hinterland. Whether this will be possible under present conditions is doubtful.

Social change in the Communist zone of Viet-Nam was deliberate. A large part of the bourgeoisie had, as was shown, fled southward in 1954 and thus saved the Ho Chi Minh regime both the bother and the onus of large-scale purges. The flight, likewise, of close to 700,000 farmers also provided the Communist regime with abandoned land to be reapportioned in the initial land reform program without undue upheaval.

A Population Classification Decree which established pseudo-scientific and almost racial criteria for classification as a "landlord," a "rich farmer," or—down the line—a "landless worker,"[3] set into motion a whole process of social antagonisms which the regime deliberately used for the purpose of establishing total population control. The result of the application of the Population Classification Decree was that each social class was assigned a specific economic level. Based on agricultural acreages, it was also applied in the cities through a complicated system of similar criteria.[4]

As becomes obvious from even a brief glance, this redistribution of land was totally meaningless from the purely agricultural viewpoint. The net result of the land reform was chaos, as no one but the rich farmer—who, with a family of five, kept a hectare of land—had a remote chance of making ends meet with the land he received. Also, farmers about to lose their land failed to till it

[3] Decree No. 239/B. TLP of March 2, 1953. There were, for example, complicated criteria by which a saltpan owner of a given production level could be assimilated to a landlord; and specific conditions were set for the transference of social "class" level to a spouse of a different category, etc.

[4] Bernard B. Fall "A 'Straight Zigzag': The Road to Socialism in North Viet-Nam," in A. Doak Barnett (ed.), Communist Strategies in Asia (New York: Frederick A. Praeger, 1963), p. 217.

Average Acreages Before and After Land Reform
in North Viet-Nam
(*in hectares*)

Social Class	Before	After
Landowners	.65	.10
Rich farmers	.21	.21
Middle-level farmers	.12	.17
Poor farmers	.05	.14
Agricultural workers	.02	.15

properly. Those who were landless and hoped to receive a piece of land ceased to work for their landlords and waited for the over-worked and ill-trained land reform teams to do their work. This explains the brief peasant rebellion which flared up in North Viet-Nam in November, 1956, and which compelled Ho Chi Minh to fire his Communist Party chief, Secretary General Truong Chinh, who had been in charge of the land reform program.

The eventual outcome of land reform in North Viet-Nam was, however, the collectivization of much of the land, as the farmers found it progressively more difficult to survive on their individual plots. A secondary consequence was that some of the new landless farmers became free to be used as industrial and coolie labor on the ambitious irrigation, railroad, and industrial projects. Even so, the change from a primarily agricultural to a semi-industrial or semi-urbanized society has been arduous. There was a total of 520,000 North Vietnamese classified as "artisans" in 1959. When the Communist regime began its rule in North Viet-Nam in 1954, there were only 10,000 industrial workers, 700 "technicians," and 23 engineers in the whole country.[5] When the targets for the 1961–65 Five-Year-Plan were set at the Party's Third National Congress in Hanoi in September, 1960, the graduation of "25,000 cadres . . . from higher educational institutions and approximately 100,000 from intermediary [*sic*] vocational schools"[6] was

[5] Jeanne Delattre, "L'economie vietnamienne au debut de son premier quinquennat," *Economie et Politique* (French Communist Party monthly) (Paris), June 1961, p. 22.

[6] Le Thanh Nghi, "Socialist Industrialisation," in *Third National Congress of the Viet-Nam Workers' Party* (Hanoi: Foreign Languages Publishing House, 1961), III, 147.

among them. At the same time, an increase of the total industrial labor force by 200,000 was also announced.

The political importance of that new urbanized proletariat was made clear in the final resolutions passed by the Congress, one of which read that the "Party must, by means of increased education given the working class, unceasingly enhance the sense of their vanguard role and their leading responsibility."[7] The "eliteness" of the industrialized proletariat appears doubly enhanced—as this writer observed on the spot in North Viet-Nam in 1962—by the fact that many factory workers and cadre personnel are discharged Peoples' Army soldiers and officers whose absolute loyalty to the regime has been tested in combat.

To be sure, this restructuring of North Vietnamese society has not yet reached the political elite itself. As in most other first-generation Communist countries, it is still made up of scions of the bourgeoisie and even the nobility. President Ho Chi Minh's father was a small mandarin; Premier Pham Van Dong's father was a high mandarin who once held the rank of chief of cabinet to the Vietnamese emperor, and Pham Van Dong himself is a graduate of Nationalist China's Whampoa Military Academy; Phan Ke Toai, Vice Premier until 1963, was the Viceroy for Tong-king under Emperor Bao-Dai. In the last published study on that problem, made by the Lao-Dong itself in 1953, it was pointed out that out of 1,855 key positions in the Party, 1,365 were held by intellectuals or "scions of the bourgeoisie," while only 139 were held by "workers." From what is known of the present senior leaders—and their past is pretty much a matter of record—there is little indication that a shift of *actual* power toward the urban proletariat has taken place. However, there exist the beginnings of the development of the famous "new class" of party bureaucrats: men who have never held another job but that of a Communist Party official. Le Duan, since 1960 Secretary General of the Party, fits that description, although he did for a time command guerrillas against the French during the First Indochina War.

In sum, then, the two separated zones of Viet-Nam have, ten years after their division (which initially was designed to last only two years), developed societies different from each other in some

[7] *Third National Congress* . . . , I, 243.

respects. In the South, the preservation of the existing economic system and of a large part of the traditional administrative cadre[8] has made such changes less apparent. The overthrow of the Ngo Dinh Diem regime by the military, however, may well bring about the progressive demise of the pre-eminence of the mandarin bureaucracy. The earlier version of the military junta under General Duong Van Minh attempted "coexistence" with such traditional mandarins as the civilian Premier, the *doc-phu* (provincial governor) Nguyen Ngoc Tho. But the junta under General Nguyen Khanh, which took over on January 31, 1964, represents a new breed of Vietnamese non-Communist leadership: it is younger, had not reached maturity under the traditional mandarin system with its French colonial overlay, and thus is not bound by a moral obligation to "play the game." In its general outlook the junta probably is not too far apart from the party bureaucrats who are about to take over in North Viet-Nam.

In both systems, the rice peasant still represents about 80 per cent of the total population—and he has hardly changed at all. He resists being confined to southern "strategic hamlets"—or "new life hamlets"—just as much as he resists being collectivized in the North. And that, perhaps, is an encouraging sign for later developments in both zones.

The psychological effects of partition are far harder to define[9] and even more difficult to assess in a measurable way. In one of the rare studies dealing with the influence of historical change on the individual, it has been indicated that "men who share an ethnic area, a historical era, or an economic pursuit are guided by common images of good and evil. Infinitely varied, these images . . . assume decisive concreteness in every individual's ego development."[10]

In other words, depending on an individual's identification with his national group and area, the partition of his territory may be

[8] Roy Jumper, "Mandarin Bureaucracy and Politics in South Viet-Nam," *Pacific Affairs*, March, 1957, pp. 47–58.

[9] I wish to acknowledge here the kind help given me by Dr. Joseph Noshpitz, a psychiatrist practicing in Washington, D.C., in explaining to me certain of the problems involved and in directing me toward relevant literature, including an unpublished manuscript of his own.

[10] Erik H. Erikson, "Ego Development and Historical Change," *Psychological Issues*, I, No. 1 (1959), 18.

considered a temporary inconvenience or, at the other extreme, as drastic as the amputation of his own limbs. Some groups are so rooted to their territory as to prefer extermination to exodus. Others are willing to accept any change of citizenship or religious allegiance if this be the price of remaining in their home area— even when considerations of property play no major role. In other cases, to accept exodus is considered the higher patriotism.

In such cases, where the division affects a formerly homogeneous cultural area such as North America in 1783, Germany and Korea in 1945, and Viet-Nam in 1954, the choice of allegiance must be made according to far more tenuous criteria: those involving a different political-economic system within an originally similar cultural environment. In the case of North America, the choice existed in both directions and, with a few minor excesses at the local level, did not involve much personal harm to those who chose to remain loyal to Britain and moved to Canada. In the case of Germany, there exists at least the free choice of moving *from* the West *to* the East (and until the erection of the Berlin Wall, a "safety valve" existed for movement in the opposite direction); in Korea, the temporary advance northward of the U.N. forces in 1950 gave many North Koreans an opportunity to move southward with the troops. And even Communist China, during the 1962 famine, relaxed its border controls around Macao and Hong Kong. Only in the case of the two Viet-Nams did the temporary cease-fire line harden into an almost airtight fence crossed only by military infiltrators. It is no exaggeration to say that today Viet-Nam is the "most divided" of all divided countries.[11]

In the face of such a total cleavage, radical changes of psychological outlook (individual as well as collective) were a foregone conclusion. First of all, the very source of the creation of both regimes left the South with a decided feeling of inferiority: its regime had *lost* the Indochina War along with the French. The

---

[11] One will, of course, evoke the example of Israel here. Israel is *isolated* from her Arab neighbors, but very little prevents Jews in Arabic countries from moving to Israel. In the case of Korea, neighboring Japan provides a handy meeting ground for Koreans from both sides of the fence. No such "neutral ground" exists nearby for the Vietnamese to maintain meaningful relations beyond the dividing line. Mail is reduced to a few hundred cards each way. There are no economic exchanges whatever, while the two zones of Germany trade with one another to the extent of $500 million a year.

North had defeated both on the battlefield—"fair and square." The Geneva conference of April–July, 1954, gave a pathetic illustration of this. When the South Vietnamese Government, with American encouragement, refused to sign the cease-fire agreements making the division of Viet-Nam into two zones official, the French Premier, Pierre Mendès-France, turned toward his South Vietnamese colleague and asked whether the Vietnamese people wanted to continue fighting the war all by themselves. The answer to that was obvious and thus the division of Viet-Nam proceeded over the protests of the Saigon regime.

The 1954 cease-fire also brought about the departure of the French from South Viet-Nam both as a military and a political factor. The South Vietnamese could hardly have achieved this by themselves. What made it inevitable was, of course, France's defeat at the hands of the Viet-Minh. No matter what his official propaganda says, every South Vietnamese, including (or, perhaps, particularly) the peasant in the village, knows that it was the Viet-Minh who compelled the "colonialists" to leave—not his own government in Saigon. That is indeed a heavy psychological burden to bear—and Saigon must bear it.

The South Vietnamese counterargument clearly plays up to the strong Vietnamese feeling of national unity. It berates Hanoi regularly for having condoned the division of the country for reasons of political opportunism. It also brings out the fact that on March 6, 1946, the then Viet-Minh–dominated pan-Vietnamese government signed accords with the French, allowing for the peaceful return of French garrisons in exchange for the explicit recognition of internal autonomy. Making short shrift of eight years of brutal war between the Viet-Minh and the French, this is the basis for still very much alive charges of "colonialist-Communist collusion"—such as the "neutralism" issue now being considered as one way of settling the South Vietnamese insurgency problem.

With regard to reunification, both regimes claim, of course, to represent Viet-Nam "from the China Gates to the Camau Peninsula" (the latter being Viet-Nam's southernmost tip), and the phrase can be found in the constitutions of both regimes. However, like its East German ally,[12] North Viet-Nam has adopted a

[12] Cf. Gerhart Hammerbacher, "Die volkerrechtliche Problematik der Rechtsstellung konnationaler Flüchtlinge in geteilter Staaten unter besonderer

more flexible attitude in the matter and is willing to concede the temporary coexistence of two separate and sovereign states maintaining *de facto* relations with each other. It is, for obvious reasons, impossible to tell whether that North Vietnamese flexibility represents anything more than a tactical decision made by a small leadership group. But that view is likely to be correct. The Fatherland Front, created by Hanoi in 1955 supposedly to advocate an early reunification, has been very much played down in recent years. This is in exchange for encouragements given to a South Vietnamese Front of National Liberation whose avowed aim is to create a separate but neutral South Vietnamese state.[13]

At an individual level, the advent of Communism in North Viet-Nam forced the large Catholic minority there to make some crucial identity decisions, the foremost being whether to stay in its home area or to flee south, where the practice of its religion would be encouraged. This was possible because the southern chief of state, Diem, was a Catholic. As has been shown, 600,000 Catholics, out of a possible total of 800,000 in all of North Viet-Nam, chose that path.[14] In South Viet-Nam it is now admitted that close to 100,000 people elected to go north of the dividing line. How many of them went because of their absolute allegiance to the Viet-Minh, and how many simply because their superiors told them to do so, is unknown. Propaganda on both sides stressed the intolerable conditions that would prevail after final division: religious intolerance and poor living conditions in the North; political reprisals even against non-Communists in the South.

Once the division was final, 300 days after the cease-fire, both regimes settled down to the creation of separate polities. That also meant, in effect, the creation of at least temporary substitute national myths likely to command the allegiance of the population under their respective control. As can readily be imagined, in the

Berücksichtigung Vietnams," *Integration* (Liechtenstein: Vaduz, 1960), p. 232, n. 65.

[13] Fall, *The Two Viet-Nams*, pp. 439–43.

[14] The northern Central Vietnamese provinces of Thanh-Hoa and Nghe-An also have strong Catholic minorities, variously estimated at about 400,000. Having been under effective Viet-Minh control since 1945, however, their population simply never was able to make a choice. Its feelings can be guessed at by the fact that in several villages petitions were handed to Canadian members of the International Control Commission asking for authorization to go south. They were not acted upon by the Hanoi regime.

North the two main themes are the "struggle for socialism" and the struggle against "American imperialism." Up to the present time, Hanoi has abstained from making its populace too well acquainted with the subtleties of the Sino-Soviet dispute as regards the war in South Viet-Nam. But a definite commitment of North Viet-Nam may well become inevitable;* it would then become an additional facet of the "struggle for socialism" myth.

In the South, myths along with institutions had to be built from scratch. While the northern regime transferred its whole administrative system quite readily from the jungle to Hanoi, South Viet-Nam's Ngo Dinh Diem had to contend at first with the hard fact that in his zone "government" as such simply did not exist. Aside from the Communist-controlled areas there were three large sectors controlled by "politico-religious" feudal sects who brooked no secular infringement of their privileges; and the French in effect controlled most of the military and economic levers. The Vietnamese army was hardly more than a warlord's force, with its own chief of staff obeying the civilian government when it suited him to do so. And it did not very often. It will redound to Diem's lasting merits, whatever his faults may have been, that he did succeed in creating a state out of this chaos, a state whose authority was largely accepted for at least five years.

The Diem regime clearly realized that it still lacked true psychological appeal and that a competitive myth had to be created. An attempt at couching it in popularly acceptable terms occurred in December, 1962, when the Saigon government, in conjunction with American psychological warfare advisers, began to devise a "surrender plan" designed to divert all but the hard-core Communist guerrillas from the Liberation Front. The lead paragraphs of the draft text give a clear idea of the problem involved:

> The Vietnamese Communists . . . have always sought to usurp the fruit of the work of the Nationalist members of the Resistance War;[15] they continue today to claim they led the Resistance War.
> . . . through flattery they have deceived the people of the North, [the] cadres and their relatives and the regrouped people [i.e., those who went north after July, 1954].
> The success of the Resistance War was due not to the leadership

[15] The Vietnamese term for the First Indochina War.

* *As of mid-1965, regular North Vietnamese troops were identified operating in South Viet-Nam.*

of the Communists but to the work of the Nationalist members of
the Resistance. . . . The insurrection of September 2, 1945, was
the work of the Nationalist members of the Resistance.

It is noteworthy that the Diem regime apparently even claimed
the proclamation of the Communist-led Democratic Republic of
Viet-Nam on September 2, 1945, to the credit of mythical "resistance" fighters. But, at the same time, it failed to mention the
proclamation of independence under Japanese aegis made by Emperor Bao-Dai on March 11, 1945. The *reductio ad absurdum* of
that line of reasoning was finally reached when Saigon propaganda
not only credited the whole anticolonial war to the "nationalists,"
but to a particular class of them—the landlords. That came out
clearly in an article written by a usually sophisticated writer who
was led to describe the Viet-Cong insurgency in South Viet-Nam
in the following terms: "In 1959, agents of the Viet-Cong began
trying to re-establish their position in the villages. . . . Their chief
talking point concerned land that the peasants had taken over
*while the landlords were away fighting the long war against the
French.*"[16] [Italics added.]

The mind balks at the thought that Dien Bien Phu was con-
quered by a horde of 50,000 irate landlords. But the invocation of
that mythology by the Saigon government lent it (a) the aura of
sharing in the victory against the French ("nationalism"); (b) a
justification acceptable to Americans for its harshness toward the
peasantry; and (c) a rationale for lumping together the "nasty"
peasants with the French colonials.

It is equally obvious that so hoary a mythology is difficult to
accept even by the peasants who comprise 90 per cent of the
population. They know full well who fought the French and who
did not. It also explains why psychological warfare appeals based
on such palpable untruths fail to be very effective. But the need to
"prove" their nationalism has remained with the military juntas that
succeeded Diem. The bulk of the junta officers had started their
careers in the French Army and had fought the Viet-Minh under
French command. This explains the virulence of recent charges by
junta chairman General Nguyen Khanh that he is the victim of a

[16] Robert Shaplen, "A Reporter in Viet-Nam," *The New Yorker*, August 11,
1962, p. 56.

"colonialist plot" to murder him: like the peasants under the French, he now is threatened by "colonialism." If the argument is accepted at face value by a large segment of the South Vietnamese population, then the exploitation of this issue is worth the deterioration of relations with France which it brings in its wake.

This South Vietnamese psychological weakness in relation to the "colonialism" issue also explains the difficulties experienced by American advisers. The Vietnamese at every level are fully aware of their utter dependence upon the United States for their everyday survival—politically, militarily, and economically. Thus, the only way to assert their "independence" is to resist American advice. This became, in the last months of the Diem regime, a veritable mania and a policy in its own right. Sometimes the emphasis on dependence was unwittingly increased by basically well-meant American actions. For example, while the formerly British-led colonial areas—even those which fought the British, such as Israel, Kenya, and Cyprus—maintained much of the authority-associated military symbolism, in South Viet-Nam that symbolism was almost totally destroyed.

French-type uniforms and insignia were replaced by American ones, even when the latter, in view of differences in climate, proved less suitable. To cite just one instance, the wide-brimmed jungle hat, which the French themselves had taken over from the Australians, was replaced by the smart-looking American stiff-crowned field cap; the latter, however, does not protect a jungle-going infantryman from the monsoon rains or the tree leeches that fall into his collar.[17] The total similarity of U.S. and South Vietnamese uniforms has been much exploited in Communist Vietnamese propaganda as physical proof of the total subservience of the Saigon regime to its American "masters." In a similarly helpless situation with respect to the Soviet Union, the East German regime has chosen the totally opposite tack: its military uniforms are line-for-line copies of the old Reichswehr[18] uniforms in order to emphasize the otherwise rather doubtful "Germanness" of the Ulbricht regime. West Germany, which does not suffer from

[17] *The Washington Post*, August 20, 1961.
[18] The Reichswehr was the name of the German Army under the Weimar Republic. It wore somewhat modified German Imperial Army uniforms of 1918 which were further modified by the Wehrmacht under Hitler.

similar inferiority complexes, has been able to stick to variants of American military clothing. North Viet-Nam, on the other hand, has adopted a modified Chinese adaptation of the standard Russian uniform, but has retained for its field forces the olive-green fatigues and distinctive woven helmets well known since the days of the First Indochina War.

In one more field, the two Vietnamese regimes have evolved in different ways. While North Viet-Nam superimposed its political-administrative structure on the existing French-created provincial structure, Diem utterly destroyed the latter and replaced it with new provinces of his own design. The result is that the Communist peasant operates within a familiar administrative milieu: he goes to the same county seat as before for his taxes, loans, seeds, or schools, while his southern counterpart is never sure from one moment to the next to what higher authority he is physically subordinated. Since the Diem regime created sixteen new provinces in five years and literally changed the boundaries and names of almost all the others, it can readily be imagined how difficult it is in such an environment to create the local loyalties so necessary to bind a rural society together.

Lastly, as the two Viet-Nams drift further apart through the civil war and their allegiance to different power blocs, their very language undergoes increasingly marked changes. In the North and in the South, the strictly technical vocabularies necessary to teach engineering or chemistry take their foreign roots from the sources closest to them—French and English in the South, Chinese and Russian in the North. If one adds to this fact the existence of a strong regional accent and vocabulary, it is not inconceivable that within a few decades—should partition continue—direct communications between northern and southern Vietnamese might become as difficult as between Frenchmen and Italians rather than as between Americans and Englishmen or East and West Germans. The reason for this is that in the case of the two Anglo-Saxon nations cultural interchanges never stopped and that in the case of the two Germanies the bulk of the modern technical vocabulary was largely developed by the time partition came. In Viet-Nam, both zones began to develop such a vocabulary in the vernacular only after partition.

In conclusion, the sociological and psychological effects of partition can be both favorable and deleterious to the divided nation, just as offshoots of plants can often grow stronger than the original plant itself. In the case of the Anglo-Saxon "partitions" into separate American, Australian, New Zealand, and British entities, the effect of partition was certainly positive in all fields. In the case of the post-World War II partitions into Communist and non-Communist zones of one and the same country, only West Germany has thus far come out ahead, although it is hardly possible to gauge the sum of hidden complexes—from fear of the Russians to hatred and revenge—that are at present covered by the façade of the German "economic miracle."

In the case of Viet-Nam, the problem of partition affected a nation that had hardly begun to exist in the modern sense of the term. The Communist zone can claim to its advantage two key factors: its prior inception and its military victories. In fact, the Communist regime can, strangely enough, invoke even the argument of "legitimacy," since the last emperor, Bao-Dai, transmitted to it his legal instruments of power after formally abdicating in August, 1954. The South was born out of defeat and revolt—not victorious revolution. There is no ideological or political underpinning behind it except that of anti-Communism. But the score is not entirely negative. The demise of Diem, with the concomitant departure from power of his largely northern Catholic entourage, has considerably "southernized" the Saigon regime. The junta leaders' reconciliation with the religious quasi-Buddhist sects which are aboriginal to the South may give the new military rulers more roots in the country than Diem had cultivated in a decade. The apparent playing down of the northern refugees' role as a political pillar and the cessation of their coddling through special privileges may yet add further to the rise of a specifically "southern" nationalism.

And that, added to such obvious appeals as higher living standards and outside support from the United States, will have to serve as "patriotism" until some better defined national *raison d'être* can be developed, or partition ends.

PART IV

The Unseen Enemy

Hostile countries usually evoke clear-cut images in one's mind, and the central issue of the war is focused in convenient symbols: Hitler and the swastika, Tojo and the "rising sun" flag, Stalin and the hammer and sickle, and so on. But in Viet-Nam, the enemy has remained strangely diffuse: The peasant garb worn by the guerrilla does not lend itself to the kind of hated image that the Nazi uniform, with its jackboots and steel helmets, did; and the spindly grandfather figure of Ho Chi Minh is not convincingly caricatured as a blood-thirsty ogre.

Yet the combination of dedicated leadership and effective guerrilla tactics can have fearsome military effects, as the French were the first to find out. Ambush patterns known in 1953 and described soon thereafter are still utilized to this day in South Viet-Nam. What surprises is that the mistakes made by the French continue to be repeated, although infinitely superior American firepower at least mitigates their effect.

But the central question remains: What *is* the Viet-Cong? Is it really little else but the Hanoi regime in exportable format? Or is there enough regional—if not national—consistency to it to provide it with objectives separate from those of its North Vietnamese supporters? There are no ready answers, but I have at least attempted here to formulate the question and examine the possible answers.

On the other hand, there is, first and foremost, the Viet-Nam People's Army (VPA)—North Viet-Nam's combination of jungle-going regulars and well-trained reserves. It is they who may well, at any moment, change the whole character of the Viet-Nam conflict from a local, if severe, counterinsurgency problem to a major war with incalculable long-range consequences to the peace of the world.

Neither the Viet-Cong nor the VPA could forever resist the amalgam of massive firepower, modern logistics, and large American-led armies that the Western effort in Viet-Nam could become. But they may go down in history as the forces that stymied the world's largest power for a decade or more.

And no other power on earth has thus far been able to make a similar claim.

17. *Communist Military Tactics*

When on May 7, 1954, at about 5 P.M., Platoon Commander Chu Ba The of the Viet-Nam People's Army (VPA) planted the red flag with the gold star of the Communist-led Democratic Republic of Viet-Nam atop the headquarters bunker of Dien Bien Phu, a new era opened in Asian warfare. An army that had begun its existence ten years ago as a small guerrilla force had annihilated in open combat the cream of a well-trained Western army equipped with nearly all modern implements of war short of atomic weapons.

This Communist victory stemmed from two different roots. One lay in the tactics of the French Union Forces during the last year of the war;[1] the other in the terrain and in the People's Army itself —its organization, training, and tactics. . . .

The VPA is composed of three different combat echelons. The hard core of the VPA is composed of its approximately ten regular divisions—nine infantry and one "heavy" artillery and engineering division. They are known as the Main Force (*chu-luc*). It is they who bore the brunt of all major operations between 1950 and 1954: the border offensive of 1950, the 1952 offensives into northwestern Viet-Nam, the stabs into Laos in 1953, and, finally, the liquidation of the airhead of Dien Bien Phu. The *chu-luc* units of the VPA are well equipped and its infantry battalions had a distinct superiority in firepower—particularly in the field of 81-mm and 122-mm mortars—over the opposing French units.

Not all regular units operated along the main battle lines. For example, during 1953 and 1954 a sizable part of the 320th Infantry Division, VPA, along with the 42d, 46th, and 50th independent regiments, operated well within the French Union lines in support

[1] See Chapter 3.

Excerpted, by permission, from "Indochina: The Last Year of the War: Communist Organization and Tactics," *Military Review*, October, 1956.

of regional and semimobile militia battalions (*Tieu-Doan Tap Trung Tinh*). Those regional units form the second-echelon troops. They have neither the training nor the equipment for large-scale maneuvering, but their superior knowledge of the terrain makes them extremely useful as scouting or screening units for infiltrated regular units.

Lastly, the third combat echelon was composed of the locally raised militia units (*du-kich*). It is the *du-kich*, unrecognizable because they wear no uniforms and continue to live in their native villages, taking up arms for a specific mission only, who do most of

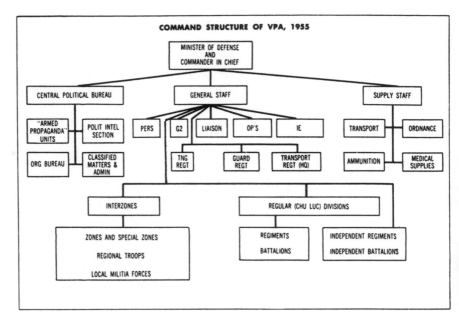

FIGURE 7

the communications sabotage, local espionage, sniping, reconnoitering, and who, in the past, often fought costly rear-guard actions to permit the escape of cornered regular units.

As a glance at an organization chart of the VPA shows (see Figure 7), the political control apparatus within the VPA is extremely important. Indeed, General Vo Nguyen Giap, the D.R.-V.N. Vice Premier, Minister of Defense, and Commander in Chief of the VPA since its inception, openly declared that "the military is the [Communist] Party's essential arm for the attainment of any political aim."

There exist cells of the Viet-Nam Dang Lao-Dong in every VPA platoon. At platoon level there are "political agents" reporting on all signs of political weakness to their own political commissar (*chinh-uy*) who is attached to every unit at battalion level and above.

The political commissars of the VPA have far-reaching powers even in the field of military strategy and tactics. A D.R.V.N. decree of 1950 created "Front Command Committees with Political Preponderance" in which the views of the political commissar on a given tactical situation prevail over those of the military commander and deputy commander of the unit. It is obvious that under such conditions the VPA military commander is little more than a tool of his own political machine, with little chance of deviating from a given line. However, frictions between the political commissars and the military commanders occur. The author spoke in 1953 to a Communist officer who had deserted from the VPA side after *successful* completion of an operation, because he had been criticized in front of his troops by the commissar for "errors" he allegedly had committed.

This constant political indoctrination has made over the VPA soldier from an illiterate peasant into an efficient fighting machine, much in the fashion of the Chinese Communist as described in a thorough study by Lucien-Max Chassin, the former Commanding General of the French Far Eastern Air Force: "In the day's work of the Red soldier, the Marxist political lesson plays as important a part as the arms manual. Taken in hand by intelligent leaders, the armed peasant rapidly becomes a fanatic, an apostle of the new religion."[2]

This fanaticism could be found in many units of the VPA, in the militia forces as well as among the regulars. "Death Volunteer" units whose members would throw themselves with a load of explosives, "kamikaze" fashion, against a French tank or against the firing slits of bunkers, proved particularly effective in attacks against fortified positions and were difficult to neutralize. Feats

[2] *La Conquête de la Chine par Mao Tse-tung* (Paris: Payot, 1951), pp. 232–33.

of the Death Volunteers, along with others emphasizing strict obedience to orders, are often played up in D.R.V.N. propaganda to its troops, such as the following incident: "During the attack against the French post of Vinh-Trach, the comrade company commander gave an order to the comrade in charge of the BAR to rise and to fire upon the blockhouse. The comrade rose immediately although he was to be sacrificed before he could even fire a shot."

It is obvious that Western fighting methods are not particularly well adapted to cope with an enemy using such tactics, and until the end of the war in Indochina, French unit commanders throughout Indochina were haunted by the problem of having to cope with a Death Volunteers attack.

In October, 1950, at the end of the first Communist offensive, which had cost the French their string of forts along the Chinese border, General Giap held a staff study with the political commissars of the VPA's crack 98th Infantry Regiment, in the course of which he developed the outline of the operation he was going to fight so successfully over the next four years:

> During the first and second phase we gnawed away at the forces of the enemy, in the third phase we must annihilate them. . . .
>
> In order to pass over to the general counteroffensive (GCO) the following conditions must be met:
>
> Superiority of our forces over those of the enemy.
>
> The international situation must be to our advantage.
>
> The [local] situation must evolve in our favor.
>
> . . . we shall benefit from foreign aid in order to pass over to the GCO [but] merely to count upon such help would be proof of subjectivism and light-mindedness.
>
> . . . other factors may also play in our favor: [French] difficulties in political, economic, or financial matters; protest movements against the war in the [French and Vietnamese nationalist] army and among the people.
>
> When we shall have reached the third phase, we shall use the following tactical principles to fulfill our strategic mission:
>
> Mobile war, as principal activity.
>
> Guerrilla war, as a secondary activity.
>
> Positional warfare, also secondary.
>
> *The counteroffensive phase:*
>
> . . . the third phase may last over an extended period because we

need time, but our possibilities in receiving aid from abroad will also be quite extensive.

It might be considered a tribute to Giap's remarkable military acumen—he is a French-educated high-school professor with a Ph.D. in history and no formal military training—that he was able to carry through his plan to the last iota in less than four years. On the other hand, it must surprise the military reader that the French High Command—which had been in possession of Giap's plan since late 1952, when a copy of it was captured by French paratroop raiders—had in no appreciable way reacted to meet the new challenge. . . .

In Indochina, prevalent types of terrain have brought about four major types of guerrilla warfare: urban terrorism, rice-field and swamp warfare, hill and mountain warfare, and jungle warfare.

Of the four, the first is in no way different from similar operations in other parts of the world. In Viet-Nam it was particularly effective in view of the latent sympathies of a large part of the population with the terrorists, providing them with shelter and intelligence. . . .

The second type, fought in the marshy and waterlogged rice flatlands which include nearly all of Viet-Nam's populated areas, large cities, and major communications lines, can be considered as the "local specialty," and is radically different from any of the guerrilla tactics thus far described in available U.S. Army Field Manuals.

Throughout most of the Vietnamese flatlands—and also those of much of China, Indonesia, Thailand, Cambodia, and Burma—communications are limited to the tops of dikes of varied construction, with the smallest barely wide enough for a column marching single file, while the largest often may carry a double-track motor highway or railroad. Such communications lines proved to be the number-one target of Communist guerrillas in Indochina. Their success either in destroying them or in maintaining them in a constant state of insecurity robbed the French Union Forces of nearly one-third of their combat personnel, not to speak of the gigantic effort it required from the engineering and signal units diverted from other tasks to road and telegraph-line rebuilding.

Guerrilla attacks in Viet-Nam, however, were not limited to the roads themselves but also included the convoys that circulated on them. Ambushes generally took place (see Figure 8) in an open stretch of field broken by some bushes or hedges, or an old pagoda. Hand-triggered mines were used to disable the lead vehicle, thus immobilizing the convoy. The rear-guard vehicle was dealt with similarly, or was destroyed by rocket launcher (bazooka) or mortar fire. Once the convoy is pinned down, the stage is set for its general attack.

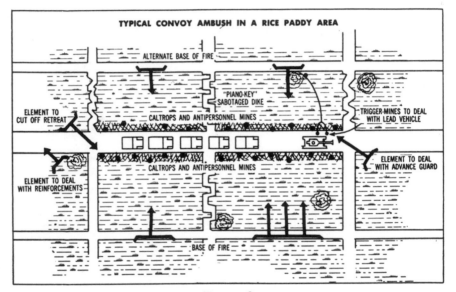

TYPICAL CONVOY AMBUSH IN A RICE PADDY AREA

ALTERNATE BASE OF FIRE

"PIANO-KEY" SABOTAGED DIKE

ELEMENT TO CUT OFF RETREAT

CALTROPS AND ANTIPERSONNEL MINES

TRIGGER-MINES TO DEAL WITH LEAD VEHICLE

ELEMENT TO DEAL WITH ADVANCE GUARD

CALTROPS AND ANTIPERSONNEL MINES

ELEMENT TO DEAL WITH REINFORCEMENTS

BASE OF FIRE

FIGURE 8

According to American practice in such a case—which was also French practice in the early stages of the war—the escorting units of the convoy detrucked and took cover in the road ditch opposite to the apparent line of enemy fire.* In Viet-Nam such a procedure usually led the detrucked unit into terrain that was either mined or heavily spiked with caltrops of a crude but very effective type, and also exposed to enemy fire from a secondary base. If

---

* *Incredibly, that procedure was still recommended in the* Marine Corps Gazette *in January, 1962!*

panic ensued, the convoy usually could be considered a total loss.

It became French standard practice to take cover atop the dike under the vehicles themselves and to concentrate the fire of the heavy weapons of the convoy on major enemy targets while radioing for help. Air support in such cases proved particularly effective, since the enemy generally was deployed in a clearly defined target area. Counterattacking a Communist ambush with infantry forces of the convoy itself was considered as costly and of little value since every dike provided a natural covering position for retreating enemy forces. In clement weather, helicopters and light planes flying as convoy scouts proved effective in foiling ambushes; however, this was only possible in view of the fact that the enemy in Indochina had no air force of his own and, until Dien Bien Phu, was not believed to possess an effective anti-aircraft artillery.

Hill and mountain guerrilla warfare was widely practiced by Communist units in the tribal Thai areas and in Laos. The terrain most suitable for such operations is that covered with six-foot-tall elephant grass. As in the case of jungle warfare, units generally had to progress single file and thus were unable to bring their weapons to bear upon an enemy only yards away. In such terrain, air reconnaissance was well-nigh useless, unless the aircraft hovered practically at grass-top level, in which case it was extremely vulnerable even to small-arms fire. The usual countermeasure against that type of ambush was to avoid beaten paths wherever possible, and to have a light scouting screen deployed on both sides of the column. However, only larger columns have the necessary manpower to do so, and since the scouts then must hack their own path through the brush, the risk of losing them piecemeal may outweigh that of progressing in a body. The best method seems to be to separate the column into several elements sufficiently apart to make their falling together into an ambush unlikely, while still being close enough to each other for mutual support in the case of an attack against one of the column elements.

Jungle warfare in Indochina followed the usual rules with which American forces in Burma and the Pacific became familiar during World War II. Perhaps it may be useful to stress here again the overwhelming ineffectualness of combat airpower in that type of operation. Roads hacked in the jungle by thousands of Communist slave laborers over a distance of more than 300 miles supplied the four VPA divisions operating in the Dien Bien Phu area with probably more than 100 tons of ammunition and food a day.

In spite of total French mastery of the air, French air reconnaissance photographs throughout the entire Indochina war told an eloquent story of the capacity of the Communist logistical system to switch rapidly from truck convoys to hordes of human porters. When three regular VPA divisions broke through 200 miles of jungle in less than 15 days in January, 1954, and cut Indochina in half for nearly 2 weeks, they did so *without using a single motor* vehicle, but were supported by a logistical lifeline of coolies stretching all the way from the Thai border back to the hills of South China. In the words of a French officer: "Not even an atom bomb could have helped us; assuming that it would have hit one of their coolie trails, they would merely have bypassed 'ground zero' and hacked themselves a new path through the jungle."

However, the type of political-military guerrilla warfare fought by the Communists within the main French Union position, the Red River Delta, proved to be the operation that, more than Dien Bien Phu, finally broke the back of the French war effort in Indochina. As the author has stated elsewhere: "Depleted of their best troops for the sake of Dien Bien Phu, the French garrisons in the delta now had to face the brutal reality that their high command had refused to face for the past five years; the fact that it was the adversary who had effective control of most of the Red River Delta."[3] . . .

It is worthy of note that precisely the southern area of the Red River Delta which was already so heavily infiltrated in 1953 was the first to be evacuated by the French when, after the fall of Dien Bien Phu, they began to retreat toward the Hanoi-Haiphong "lifeline," with 80,000 to 100,000 Communist guerrillas swarming around them, sabotaging their supply lines and attacking their convoys. By then the French within the delta were, in the apt image of a French officer, like *des grumeaux dans la soupe*—"bread crumbs in the soup"—and fighting degenerated into a series of small-size Dien Bien Phu's as French garrisons desperately fought their way out of trap after trap in an effort to keep their communications lines open.

[3] *The Political Development of Viet-Nam—V-J Day to the Geneva Cease-Fire* (doctoral thesis; Ann Arbor, Mich.: University Microfilms, 1955).

In other words, efficient Communist guerrilla warfare behind French Union lines had already weighted the scales of war heavily in favor of the VPA before Dien Bien Phu, and even before the development of the Navarre Plan.

It but remains to attempt to draw some general conclusions from the way the Communist Viet-Minh fought its war against the French in Indochina. From the over-all point of view, the VPA command has not evolved any particular tactical formula that had not already been field-tested by the Chinese Communists in their fight against the Chinese Nationalist forces of Generalissimo Chiang Kai-shek.[4]

However, they have successfully adapted those general principles to local conditions and have made best use of their basic weakness in heavy equipment by simply transferring the entire war to a level of fighting which largely nullified the French weapons monopoly in the field of aviation or armor. The danger of the West's simply "pricing" itself out of the field of conventional warfare by an overreliance upon superweapons must be faced and met today from Korea to Indochina, and from Egypt to Algeria. Experience shows that a series of brush fires is harder to combat than one single major blaze—and one may be just as deadly as the other.

[4] Lieutenant Colonel Robert B. Rigg, "Red Parallel: The Tactics of Ho and Mao," *The Army Combat Forces Journal*, January, 1955.

18. The Viet-Cong

April, 1965

Much has been said and written lately about the war in Viet-Nam, the bombs and the aircraft that are being used, and the large political issues that are involved. But relatively little is being said by either side about the furtive enemy who actually holds much of South Viet-Nam's terrain and effectively administers perhaps as much as 50 per cent of the country's rural population.

To the South Viet-Nam Government in Saigon, the enemy is simply the Viet-Cong, or VC ("Vietnamese Communist"). To the United States and its closest allies, the VC is an Orwellian unperson. It simply does not exist, except as an emanation of North Viet-Nam's People's Army and its political masters in Hanoi. The State Department has recently devoted a whole white book to proving that, by contrast with such guerrilla wars as Greece, Malaya, or the Philippines, "the war in Viet-Nam is *not* a spontaneous and local rebellion against the established government. . . . In Viet-Nam a Communist government has set out deliberately to conquer a sovereign people in a neighboring state."[1]

If that view were entirely correct, then the whole Viet-Nam insurrection would be little else but an invasion from the outside, like Germany's aggression against Poland; and any measures taken against North Viet-Nam would fall within the inherent right of a nation to self-defense against attack.

The insurrectionists in South Viet-Nam must, for obvious reasons, convince the world of the opposite—namely, that they represent a genuine uprising against a series of unpopular regimes and are willing to offer the South Vietnamese people a valid alternative both to the current Saigon regimes and to domination

---

[1] Department of State Publication 7839, released February, 1965.

Reprinted, by permission of the Editor, from "Vietcong: The Unseen Enemy in Vietnam," *New Society*, April 22, 1965.

by Hanoi. For the time being, neither the United States (and Saigon) nor the guerrillas (and their backers in Hanoi) seem to have made their case to the point where it carries full conviction. That may be mainly so because the actual truth lies somewhere in between the two views.

First of all, it must be understood that armed opposition to the Ngo Dinh Diem regime inside South Viet-Nam, in one form or another, had never ceased between Viet-Nam's partition in 1954 and the demise of the Diem regime in November, 1963. Apart from the Communists, there existed in South Viet-Nam a variety of political-religious sects, such as the Hoa-Hao and the Cao-Dai; and at least one well-organized, semipiratical band, the Binh-Xuyen, which never fully surrendered to the South Viet-Nam Government.[2]

The Binh-Xuyen were soundly beaten in May, 1955, at the outskirts of Saigon and were finally cornered in the Rung-Sat swamps a few months later. But some of the Hoa-Hao units held the field for years in the western plains of Viet-Nam. Four Hoa-Hao battalions—called Le-Loi, Bay-Dom, 104, and 117—though hard pressed at times, were never fully destroyed. Battalion 104, under the command of "General" Truong Kim Cu, was finally cornered in 1962, in a pincer operation between Viet-Cong Battalion 510 and the South Viet-Nam army's Seventh Division with its American advisers. Its members were slipped into neighboring Cambodia for internment. The other units joined hands with the South Viet-Nam army after Diem's overthrow and now hold for Saigon the same terrain which they held against it for nine years.

In the absence of any kind of legal opposition, even for the staunchest anti-Communists, all opposition to the Diem regime had perforce to be conspiratorial and, sooner or later, of a true "resistance" nature. This was true long before Communist subversion became a major menace to South Viet-Nam, and before North Viet-Nam had any logical reason to "invade" South Viet-Nam. Diem's Presidential Ordinance No. 6 of January 11, 1956, provided for the indefinite detention in concentration camps of anyone found to be a "danger to the state." This went far beyond the preventive-detention acts so dear tó some Commonwealth countries. The ordinance was followed by other repressive acts

[2] See Chapter 11.

which hit harder at non-Communists than at Communists, whose apparatus was better geared to clandestine operations.

Between the partition of 1954 and July, 1956 (the date originally set for a reunification election between the two zones by the Geneva conference), the Communist network in South Viet-Nam retained a prudently calm attitude. About 80,000 raw recruits and dependants had left for areas north of the 17th parallel. What stayed behind were an elite guerrilla cadre force of perhaps less than 5,000 and the traditional left-wing elements in Saigon. In Saigon, as late as 1953, a Trotskyite was elected to the city council, and even Diem's brother Nhu ran a Catholic Labor Movement for Peace.

As President Eisenhower was to remark in his memoirs later, every responsible observer estimated that the North Viet-Nam leader, Ho Chi Minh, would win even an uncoerced Pan-Vietnamese election by 80 per cent of the popular vote. With elections only two years away, there was no reason for the Communists to risk precious cadre personnel on short-term adventures.

This is exactly what the later leader of the National Liberation Front of South Viet-Nam (NLF), a Saigon barrister named Nguyen Huu Tho, meant when he explained to the Australian Communist writer Wilfred Burchett: "There were mixed feelings about the two years' delay over reunification but the general sentiment was that this was a small price to pay for the return to peace and a normal life, free of foreign rule."

Nguyen Huu Tho had first become involved in politics in March, 1950, when he led a student demonstration in Saigon against the presence of three American warships on a courtesy call to the French. He paid for this with three years' detention in the northern mountain town of Lai-Chau. In August, 1954, he set up what in Communist parlance is called a "legal-struggle" organization in the form of a Committee of Defense of Peace and the Geneva Agreements, whose aim was to keep up the pressure on the South Viet-Nam Government of Diem, as well as on the still-present French, to make sure that the Geneva agreements would be observed.

But Diem had already made up his mind not to observe the agreements (which South Viet-Nam had not signed), and his repression against all oppositionists also covered Nguyen Huu Tho's peace committee and the local branches it had set up in various provincial towns.

On November 11, 1954, security police closed in on the peace committees and arrested their members. These included Nguyen Huu Tho, who now found himself jailed in the Central Viet-Nam detention house at Tuy-Hoa. He escaped only in 1961, after his appointment as President of the NLF.

"We had no idea that time," Tho told Burchett in 1964, "but we had created the embryo for the National Liberation Front, set up more than six years later."

When the South Viet-Nam Government, with the open encouragement of most Western powers, defied the July, 1956, deadline for elections, it was obvious that a struggle to the death would ensue with Hanoi, unless Hanoi could be made to see that it was to its advantage to coexist with a southern rival too strong for overthrow through subversion. That could have happened if the Diem regime had chosen a set of policies which would have provided it with maximum popular support and left the Communists reduced to the role of an ineffectual harasser. The regime did exactly the opposite.

By a presidential decree of June, 1956, Diem abolished elected village councils and mayors. This imposed directly on the Viet-Nam peasantry the dictatorial regime which he already wielded at the center. In March, 1957, the regime openly violated the last restraints placed upon it by the Geneva agreements with regard to reprisals exercised against "former resistance members"—that is, ex-guerrillas of the Viet-Minh who had fought against the French, and many of whom were not Communists. Such highly respected non-Communist French observers as *Le Monde's* Jean Lacouture and Philippe Devillers aver that, faced with physical extermination along with the sect units, some of the former Viet-Minh guerrillas simply banded together for survival. In Devillers's words, "the overriding needs of the world-wide strategy of the socialist camp meant little or nothing to guerrilla fighters being hunted down in Nam-Bo [South Viet-Nam]. . . . Hanoi preferred diplomatic notes, but it was to find that its hand had been forced."

The actual situation probably lay somewhere in between: Hanoi, to be sure, was distressed about what was happening to its faithful followers in the South. But other Communist regimes had abandoned failing guerrilla movements before: in Greece, Azerbaijan, Indonesia, Malaya, and elsewhere. In the case of Viet-Nam, however, Hanoi may well have made the judgment that: (a) the South Viet-Nam Government was in the process of alienating its own people to such an extent that even a modestly encouraged and supported guerrilla movement could well succeed in overthrowing it; (b) Saigon's American advisers were so blinded by Diem's "successes," and so oblivious to the real weaknesses of the situation, that a rebellion might succeed before the cumbersome American apparatus could shift into high gear.

As events were to show, the plan almost worked. How well it did, even without outside aid, is best shown by the progressive shift in village official killings between 1957–58 and 1959–60. The new guerrillas began to take over control of the only thing worth holding in a revolutionary warfare situation: people, and rural people at that. With a method showing long-standing professionalism, the guerrillas first established "resistance base areas" in certain Mekong Delta provinces such as Chau-Doc and My-Tho. They then proceeded to seal off Saigon from the rice-rich and densely populated delta area.

But terrorism was not the whole program. There was sound propaganda, like the "Three Withs" program ("a good cadre lives with, eats with, works with the population"), some modest reforms, and even a measure of physical improvement.

In his remarkable book *Mission in Torment*, John Mecklin, America's chief information officer in Viet-Nam during the critical 1962–64 period, writes about a village called Binh Yen Dong, only twenty miles from Saigon. The village had "gone Viet-Cong" without apparent coercion, and a study was made of how the process had worked. As it turned out, the NLF had forced a local landlord to allow the farmers to take a short cut through his property to the village well, which until then they had been forced to reach via a detour.

Organizationally, the movement rose apace. In March, 1960, the Nam-Bo Resistance Veterans Organization met in hiding and issued a proclamation in which it announced that it had taken up "arms in self-defense." At the Third Congress of North Viet-Nam's Lao-Dong, held in Hanoi on September 5, 1960, Le Duan, the party secretary and a former leader of the Viet-Minh in the South, issued a report which for the first time took cognizance of the "southern people's revolutionary struggle" and advocated the creation there of a "broad national united front against the U.S.–Diem clique." And on December 20, 1960, on the day after the fourteenth anniversary of Ho Chi Minh's uprising against France, a provisional Central Committee of southern resistance leaders created the National Liberation Front. The guerrilla movement had matured into a full-fledged revolutionary apparatus.

The newborn NLF led a very shadowy life for almost two years, although its military arm, the People's Self-Defense Forces, began to roam far and wide throughout South Viet-Nam. By May, 1960, the situation had deteriorated enough for the Saigon government to report to the International Control Commission set up by the Geneva agreements that the "southern liberation forces" constituted a "grave menace for peace."

Statistics now began to pile up inexorably: 452 village chiefs were lost by South Viet-Nam in 1957–58. By January, 1960, they were being lost at the rate of 15 a week. On May 22, 1961, President Kennedy told Congress that minor officials were being killed in Viet-Nam at the rate of 4,000 a year (11 a day).

The guerrillas' strength was estimated at 3,000 in 1959. By mid-1961 they were 15,000, half of them fully armed. There were 35,000 hard-core elite troops by January, 1965, in addition to 60,000–80,000 "local force" guerrillas. By April, 1965, the Pentagon had revised the figures to 45,000 and 100,000, respectively, grouped in five or six regimental-size units—about 60 battalions and more than 150 companies.*

In terms of administration, the killed or fleeing officials of the Diem administration were replaced by administrative committees, soon capped by district and provincial committees of the NLF. By February, 1962, the movement was ready to present itself to the world in the course of a clandestine congress attended by over 100 delegates. Whether by coincidence or design, the congress was convened just a few days after the United States had set up its Military Advisory Command in Saigon—just as the NLF had originally proclaimed its existence one month after Diem had almost been overthrown, in November, 1960, by his own best paratroops.

According to published accounts, the NLF congress grouped not

---

* *The March, 1966, estimate for VC forces was 237,000.*

only former Communist resistance members but also other elements from the Vietnamese Democratic Party and the Radical Socialist Party, both of which, like all non-Communist Vietnamese political organizations, represented almost nothing. There also had appeared on the scene a small but openly Communist party, the People's Revolutionary Party (PRP), created in December, 1961, as well as an Afro-Asian Solidarity Committee, a Saigon-Cholon Peace Committee, representatives of minority tribes and of various front organizations such as the Liberation Writers and Artists' Association, etc. None of these could claim much of an established following. But some of the people present had excellent reasons for being there, such as Superior Bonze Son Vong, from the Mekong's Vinh-Binh Province.

The thoroughly respectable Denis Warner tells Son Vong's story in his book *The Last Confucian*. In July, 1961 (that is, long before anyone spoke of Buddhist persecutions in Viet-Nam), a South Viet-Nam Army unit had swept through the province "leaving thousands of unhappy peasants behind it," and the Buddhist bonzes of the province had vainly petitioned against the indiscriminate shelling of hamlets and pagodas and the imprisonment of many of the Buddhist priests. "Some months later," says Warner, "their leader, Superior Bonze Son Vong, appeared on the lists of the central committee of the Viet-Cong's National Liberation Front."

The NLF congress proceeded to establish a central committee of fifty-three members, thirty-one of whom were elected then, while another twenty-two seats were kept open for representatives of "mass organizations, political parties, and groups of personalities which will join the front in the future." Some of the names published corresponded to aliases of unknown persons, but others were known South Viet-Nam politicians.

Nguyen Huu Thu was made President of the NLF. There are also five Vice Presidents: Dr. Phung Van Cong, a French-trained doctor who had fled Saigon in 1960; Vo Chi Cong, a Communist survivor of France's Poulo-Condore island prison; Ybih Aleo, a French Army–trained mountain tribesman who is also chairman of the Tay Nguyen (*Montagnard*) Autonomy Movement; Huynh Tan Phat, a Saigon architect who is also secretary general of the Democratic Party; and, finally, Superior Bonze Son Vong, who happens also to be a member of the important Cambodian minority living in South Viet-Nam. The Central Committee also includes a Catholic, Josef-Marie Ho Hue Ba; a Cao-Dai leader; and other personalities deemed to make the committee "representative."

Several changes have occurred in the make-up of the NLF since its inception. Its erstwhile secretary general, a journalist styled Professor Nguyen Van Hieu, became roving ambassador for the front in various uncommitted countries and was replaced in his post by Huynh Tan Phat. This was said to have been a concession to the more moderate elements of the Front. Phat in turn had been replaced as vice president by a tough military commander, Tran Nam Trung, who is the highest-known leader of the Communist PRP, with the rank of assistant secretary general, and who also is the representative of the People's Self-Defense Forces in the NLF presidium. Burchett describes him in fact as the "Liberation Front's military chief."

The program of the Front is by now well known and need hardly be repeated here. Much has been made in some quarters of the fact that the program in itself is quite moderate, which is true. Its ten points make hardly any doctrinaire references to the United States and none whatever in favor of Communism. Its points dealing with foreign policy restate the Geneva agreements' position on South Viet-Nam's nonengagement in military alliances, and re-unification is left to later negotiations rather than to an iron-clad two-year provision as provided for in 1954. It must be remembered, however, that this program represents at best a set of "electoral promises." After all, North Viet-Nam had a constitution until 1960 that embodied phrases from the American Declaration of Independence. It was changed for a strikingly doctrinaire document once North Viet-Nam had been made secure for its regime.

A significant fact in the Front's existence is—and this point may well be argued in favor of the theory of its being a total puppet of the North—that it has failed to transform itself into a "liberation government." To be sure, it has quasi ministries, but they are significantly known as "committees" (Committee on Military Affairs, External Affairs, Information and Education, etc.) and are not attributed to a single person. The NLF representatives abroad—in Algiers, Havana, Cairo, Jakarta, Berlin, Prague, and, recently,

Moscow and Peking—do not claim diplomatic status though they probably could do so in certain countries. This may simply be caution born out of previous dire experience, when such "liberation governments," too hastily constituted, collapsed or were (as with Cambodia's Khmer Resistance Government in 1954) simply negotiated away.

In the American official view, there can be no doubt that the NLF is nothing but a suboffice of the Reunification Commission operating under the Council of Ministers of the Hanoi government. The State Department white paper has elaborate charts that demonstrate ties with Northern military and political agencies.

But to many people that can only be part of the story. There is, for example, the high-ranking spokesman of the Front who told *Le Monde's* Georges Chaffard that the NLF had got along without the North for "a long time" and would "prefer to settle our affairs among 'Southerners.' " And he added something that many a resistance fighter will fully understand: "We have not fought all these years simply to end up by installing a new set of dictators in place of the old."

It is this aspect of resistance war that seems to be too often overlooked in the case of the NLF. One does not fight for eight long years, under the crushing weight of American armor, napalm, jet bombers and, finally, vomiting gases, for the sheer joy of handing over whatever one is fighting for to some bureaucrat in Hanoi, merely on the say-so of a faraway party apparatus. The NLF *and* South Viet-Nam have both had to pay a heavy price for NLF victories. Officially, the U.S. Army Chief of Staff, General Harold K. Johnson, claims that 75,000 Viet-Cong were killed between 1961 and February, 1965. Agence France-Presse, on the basis of earlier Saigon reports, stated that casualties between 1957 and 1961 amounted to 29,000 on the government side and 66,000 on the Viet-Cong side. This is not too far off the NLF's own claim that more than 160,000 South Vietnamese (on its side, presumably) have thus far been killed in this war.*

There has been increasing evidence of differences in view as well as in tone between Hanoi and the NLF, just as there have been between Hanoi and Peking or Moscow. Thus, an important policy statement issued by the Front on March 22, was seriously toned

* *See p. 312 for up-to-date statistics.*

down by Hanoi. In recent weeks there have been reports from Paris that Peking, fearing that Hanoi may weaken under the impact of American pressure, has attempted to "leapfrog" it by dealing directly with the Front through the NLF delegation in Peking and through emissaries in Laos and Cambodia.

Yet, it is on this slender reed of hope—that is, that the whole Southern guerrilla movement would wither away if only it were abandoned by North Viet-Nam—that the whole present American policy of bombing North Viet-Nam into submission seems to be based. On the basis of the available evidence, one may well wonder if that calculation is not somewhat too simple to be entirely true.

19. The New Communist Army

September, 1965

On March 15, 1954, on top of Hill Gabrielle overlooking the valley of Dien Bien Phu, Master Sergeant Bensalem Abderrhaman of First Company, Fifth Battalion, Seventh Algerian Rifles, had spent his last ammunition and the small-boned but tough North Vietnamese regulars of Regiment 88, 308th People's Army Division, were now all around him in their green fatigues. They wore short, quilted jackets to protect them against the morning cold of the mountains, palm-leaf pith helmets covered with camouflage netting in which they had stuck leaves and branches from the surrounding foliage, rubber-soled sneakers with broad cleats, and cheap-looking, thin web belts and pouches in which they carried spare ammunition, grenades, and perhaps a fist-sized ball of cooked rice as an emergency ration.

But beyond Sergeant Abderrhaman's trench, there were perhaps 800 more of them—dead or dying, where French machine guns and artillery had mowed them down. A Communist officer, recognizable by the fact that, in addition to the standard infantryman's equipment, he carried a map case slung over his shoulder and had a fountain pen in his breast pocket, ordered the sergeant and his remaining squad in good French to get moving northward, across the barbed wire, to the rear of the Communist position.

"How do you want us to get across the barbed wire and the minefields?" inquired the sergeant.

"Just walk across the bodies of our men," said the officer. As the Algerians and Frenchmen began to pick their way across, the column came to a sudden halt before a dying Viet-Minh, as the Communist soldiers then were called. He looked up and his lips were moving.

Reprinted, by permission, from "If Ho Chi Minh's Army Moves South in Force," *The New York Times Magazine*, September 5, 1965. © 1965 by The New York Times Company.

"Get going," said the officer. "You can step on him. He has done his duty for the Democratic Republic of Viet-Nam."

As he was telling me this almost ten years later in Algiers, Ben-salem Abderrhaman—who had later joined the anti-French Algerian liberation movement and is now one of the assistant chiefs of staff of the Algerian Army—said to me:

"You know, me and the other Algerians—we were very impressed."

That episode is not untypical, perhaps, of the kind of tough-minded fanaticism that has made the North Vietnamese People's Army (Quan-Doi Nhan-Dan) one of the best infantry combat forces in the world, capable of incredible feats of endurance and raw courage even against vastly superior firepower and under the worst physical conditions. And as the recent large-scale fighting in South Viet-Nam at such places as Binh-Gia and Dong-Xoai has shown they may well have provided more than the inspiration—most certainly the training and in many cases the cadres—for similar abilities displayed by Viet-Cong regulars even when faced with American-built armor and high-powered jet bombers. At a time when an ever-enlarging American commitment of troops to South Viet-Nam may well be suddenly matched by the appearance on the battlefield of division-sized VPA units, a brief attempt at examining what makes the North Vietnamese *bo-doi*—the "basic infantryman"—tick, what makes him so effective and, thus far, so much superior to all his enemies, French, Laotian, and South Vietnamese, is surely in order.

First of all, exactly how large is this threat, coming as it does not from the multitudes of China, but from a nation of fewer than 18 million? In proportion, as well as in absolute figures, the VPA is one of the largest armies of the Communist bloc. From a thirty-four-man platoon created by its present commander, General Vo Nguyen Giap, in December, 1944, it rose to seven 10,000-man divisions in 1954 (reinforced by about 230,000 semiregulars and guerrillas) and then to a twenty-division force by 1956. In March, 1965, Senator Birch Bayh, Democrat of Indiana, on the basis of information available to the government, stated that the VPA now numbered 490,000 troops.

In addition, there exists a large reserve backup covering all men up to the age of forty-five, divided into two classes: the first includes all men who have completed their two years of compulsory military training, as well as trained women specialists; the second comprises the untrained men subject to being called up. The Class 1 reserves have weapons and equipment in local armories and can be mobilized at a moment's notice. Reports and photos recently released from North Viet-Nam show such units doing duty with anti-aircraft batteries shooting down U.S. planes over North Viet-Nam. At least a half-million men can be included in that category.

North Viet-Nam also has a large, well-armed police and border-control force under Brigadier General Pham Kiet, commander of the People's Armed Security Forces. Finally, a countrywide propaganda campaign, begun since the American raids started in February, 1965, and termed the "Three-Ready Drive" ("ready to fight, ready to join the army, ready to go wherever needed"), is said to have netted 1.5 million volunteers. Against this well-honed force behind the Viet-Cong, battered South Viet-Nam fields a war-weary 300,000-man regular army backed up by as many paramilitary troops—and 100,000 Americans. . . .

The primacy of political ideology shows clearly in the VPA's training schedule. Political education in one form or another—films, lectures, inspirational plays by the army's theatrical troupes, or basic education for still-illiterate soldiers—takes up almost 50 per cent of the total training time. The rest is spent on the use of explosives and on camouflage techniques, along with small-unit tactics. A good part of the field exercises take place at night and under adverse weather conditions. The lowland Vietnamese is a born *swamp* fighter—not a jungle fighter (a fact which Americans in South Viet-Nam often seem to overlook). The fact that the Viet-Cong and the VPA have also become excellent jungle fighters is truly attributable to nothing but training and indoctrination born out of necessity. But at no time is the soldier and officer allowed to forget that he is a political soldier first and foremost.

Should he ever forget this fact, his unit's political commissar, the *Chinh-uy*, will remind him of it, and there is one at every unit level above the company. In every platoon, moreover, there is a political cadre and in every company at least one party cell. The Army Political Directorate is a key post of the VPA General Staff. When the Sino-Soviet split deepened and the North Vietnamese civilian and military leadership showed signs of splitting into pro-Peking and pro-Moscow factions (with the bulk of the North Vietnamese leadership, including General Giap, leaning toward the latter), the then head of the Political Directorate, General Nguyen Chi Thanh, turned out to be leaning toward Peking. He soon found himself running the Ministry of State Farms.

There is, of course, another, more personal, reason for the VPA leadership's almost automatic distrust of a too-close alliance with Red China—and for about the same reasons that De Gaulle mistrusts an "integrated" European army. Any close alliance with the Chinese People's Liberation Army could result only in the eventual absorption of the smaller army into the bigger one. And Giap and the other proud VPA generals, who led their jungle-going divisions victoriously into Laos and Cambodia in 1953–54, beat the French in an open siege at Dien Bien Phu, ruined America's hopes for Laos in 1960–62, and could well drag the United States into a Korea-type war, have no reason to give up in South Viet-Nam today their independent and relatively secure positions for the dubious pleasure of becoming subordinate leaders of a Chinese satellite force.

Furthermore, the North Vietnamese believe they have the manpower necessary to defy a push coming from South Viet-Nam even if backed by the United States—and the kind of sophisticated equipment they would require to put a stop to the American air raids, such as SAM missiles and MIG-21 jets, can be provided in meaningful quantities only by Russia, not by China.

The origin of the VPA's senior officers is fairly variegated. Some are the product of the French colonial army and, in fact, had served so long in it that they were entitled to retirement pay— which they duly claimed when France set up a mission in Hanoi in 1954 (the French pension law being what it is, she paid). Others came from the Chinese People's Liberation Army or even the Kuomintang; or simply had learned their trade in the long years of guerrilla warfare against the French. Only a very few, including Giap himself, come from what could be called the bourgeoisie, and that is understandable: in Viet-Nam, as in China, the military profession was rated very low, and even a Communist, while he would not hesitate to fight for his ideology as a guerrilla, would not lightly remain a military professional in peacetime.

Thus most of the division commanders, such as Generals Hoang Minh Thao, of the 304th, Vuong Thua Vu, of the 308th, or Le Trong Tan, of the 312th, rose from the resistance; Lieutenant General Chu Van Tan and Major General Le Quang Ba, both now retired, were *montagnard* chieftains whom the Ho Chi Minh regime (contrary to what happens in South Viet-Nam) successfully won over to its cause. There are at least three complete *montagnard* divisions in the VPA; one, the 324th, is made up of tribal units from the southern plateau area where much of the fighting is going on. Then there are such "political" generals as the former head of the Army Political Directorate, Nguyen Chi Thanh; or Ta Quang Buu, an Oxford-trained intellectual and former chief scout, who signed the 1954 Geneva agreements as a brigadier general of the VPA.

But above all, there is Giap himself. Born in 1912 just north of the 17th parallel, Giap is a stockily built man whose glowing black eyes betray his otherwise imperturbable mien. One French observer once dubbed him a "snow-covered volcano."

After high-school studies in Central Viet-Nam, in the course of which he joined an anti-French nationalist youth movement, Giap studied law and history at Hanoi University and joined the Communist Party in 1937. Upon earning a graduate degree in 1938, Giap married the daughter of a Vietnamese professor and both he and his wife became active Communist militants. When the French cracked down on the Communists after the signature of the Hitler-Stalin pact of 1939, Giap fled to China, but his wife was arrested and died in prison in 1943. Their only child died soon thereafter.

Giap already had come to the attention of Ho Chi Minh for his grim determination and his organizational ability. That led Ho to entrust him with the organization of the first Communist guerrilla forces. When the Democratic Republic was proclaimed, Giap was for a time its Minister of Interior—i.e., in charge of police—and as such, in charge of the bloody purges that decapitated Vietnamese nationalism for years to come. He also was in charge of negotiating some of the difficult agreements with the French, which later failed.

At one time, in 1946, his French counterpart was France's present Minister of Defense, Pierre Messmer, who, barely a few months earlier, had been a prisoner of Giap's own Viet-Minh guerrillas. It was Messmer, with whom Giap was finally on a familiar "thou" basis, who was to tell later on how Giap, one evening over a drink, suddenly leaned forward and began to tell in a quiet voice about his youth, the death of his wife and child, and his hatred for those Frenchmen who had done this to him. Yet, Giap added, he was willing to swallow his feelings for the sake of his country. Messmer, in turn, told Giap how his own aide had been killed by poison while in Viet-Minh hands and how he had been "propelled across the Red River Delta by *coups de pied au derrière*," all while Giap was Minister of the Interior; and how he also was willing to forget the past. Both men were overtaken by events: the negotiations broke down and their countries were at war a few months later.

It is not clear to this day whether it was Giap himself or other extremists who finally pushed Ho Chi Minh into the war, but the cold mathematics of the situation in 1946 were in favor of Giap's advocating it—after all, the French were still weak and they were bound to get stronger as more reinforcements arrived from France, while Giap's forces could count on no outside support whatever. During that period, Giap is quoted as having said to a friend: "Every minute hundreds of thousands of people die all over the world. The life or death . . . of thousands of human beings, even if they are our compatriots, represents really very little." By the time the Indochina War was over, the Communists had probably lost more than a half-million men and the French had lost 172,000. Since 1961, the Viet-Cong is said to have lost 102,000 dead, while South Viet-Nam's army has lost 28,000. Probably 100,000 civilians have lost their lives at the hands of both sides.

The professional worth of VPA leadership and of the *bo-doi* is clearly proved on the basis of past performance. However, in the past the issues were always clear-cut. At first, the VPA was fighting the French colonials. Since national independence was at issue, many patriotic Vietnamese of non-Communist viewpoints fought on the Viet-Minh side, including many Catholics from the Hanoi area. The fighting in Laos in 1960–62 involved relatively small forces from the 335th and 316th Divisions, many of whose men were of the same Thai *montagnard* ethnic stock as the tribesmen on the Laotian side, and the war thus took on an ethnic lowland-vs.-upland coloring that was only too dimly perceived on the out-side.

But the battle in South Viet-Nam is of a different texture alto-gether: the Communist soldier for the first time has the choice between *two* Vietnamese regimes and to all appearances he some-times prefers what he sees to what he has got north of the 17th parallel. There have been many cases of reinfiltrated former South Vietnamese who took the first chance to desert from their new Viet-Cong units simply to go home and see their families whom they had not seen for ten years. Others have simply grown ten years older and, in their late thirties and early forties, simply can-not face up once more to perhaps ten years of jungle warfare, this time in the face of a murderously effective technology which the French never possessed. That kind of war takes the enthusiasm and fanaticism of youth—and that probably is the reason why recent captured infiltrators are very young; not that the North Vietnamese have "run out" of available regrouped Southerners.

On the other hand, there are the others: the vast majority of People's Army regulars who stoically took French napalm bombing and artillery and kept coming at French prepared positions and who now, as officers and senior noncoms, keep filtering southward to join the Viet-Cong. Their interrogation reports (which may be colored to suit their captors) and, above all, their private diaries, which are often found on their bodies, provide a fairly good idea of their state of mind. Life on the march for months over jungle trails is tough, food is poor, and sometimes there are even gripes about excessive paperwork. But the regular feels sufficiently sure of himself to break army regulations on the keeping of private diaries in front-line conditions, and he also inscribes in them his pride in his primary mission: the "liberation" of South Viet-Nam. . . .

Both officers and men are swayed temporarily when faced with new situations or tactics. The massive use of helicopters baffled them for a while, but soon North Viet-Nam began to broadcast detailed flight characteristics, weaknesses, and strengths of various helicopter types. There was an initial fear of the M-113 armored personnel carriers until it was found out that their aluminum skin is easily pierced even by rifle bullets. Most recently, Hanoi in-formed the combatants in the South not to be overawed by B-57 jet bombers: "Their wings are full of fuel and they burn easily when hit. The recent Vietnamese Government setbacks, such as in Quang-Ngai and Dong-Xoai, seem to indicate that the VPA has once more adapted itself to a changed situation, and in the recent battle with United States Marines at Chu-Lai, Viet-Cong regulars fought against massive firepower and withdrew in good order despite heavy casualties.

The availability of American firepower demands a rapid destruction of the opponent by a massive "punch" of weapons and infantry and a rapid dispersal afterward in order to avoid high losses through American aerial pursuit, in deference to Mao's rule: "We are against guerrillaism [i.e., the belief that the revolution can be won by guerrilla warfare alone] but for the guerrilla character of the Red Army"—that is, lightness of units, ease of dispersal and concentration, etc. That, apparently, still holds true for the VPA divisions north of the dividing line, which are still organized on the 10,000-man model and still are capable, if the need arises, of trading their Soviet-modeled Chinese trucks for long lines of human coolie supply columns.

Informed Western observers are in fact surprised at how little heavy "conventional" equipment the VPA has received over the past ten years from its Communist allies. Such armor as there is appears limited to obsolescent Soviet amphibious tanks and light armored reconnaissance vehicles. The artillery is of the Soviet medium type, although captured American 105-mm howitzers from Korea and the French Indochina War are still available and some regiments may use the old faithful American 75-mm pack howitzer, of which there was a plentiful supply in China. The infantry's backbone is the "SKZ"—the recoilless rifle, of which even the wartime guerrillas produced an impressive array in their own small factories. Light ground-to-ground rockets of the World War II Soviet "Katyusha" type have been in North Viet-Nam since the battle of Dien Bien Phu. That fact, along with the existence of a great many radar sites in North Viet-Nam, could well mean that the North Vietnamese should not have found it impossible to provide trained personnel to serve the more sophisticated SAM-2 anti-aircraft missiles recently provided in limited quantities by the Soviet Union.

The North Vietnamese Air Corps—there is no separate air force as such—was limited until very recently by the Geneva agreements, since, unlike South Viet-Nam, it had no airplanes whatever at the time of the 1954 cease-fire. Thus, until 1962, it was largely limited to Czech-built light reconnaissance craft, Russian or Chinese copies of obsolete twin-engine transports of the DC-3 type, and a few light helicopters of the Soviet Mi-4 (Hound) type. In recent weeks, perhaps thirty or more obsolete MIG-15 and MIG-17 fighters were reported at the Phuc-Yen airbase north of Hanoi. Some of them, obsolete as they may be, shot down two American F-105's in April. And in May perhaps eight Il-28 Badger light jet bombers, roughly equivalent to the British-designed B-57 Canberras stationed at Bien-Hoa in South Viet-Nam, were sighted in the North. All this is not terribly impressive right now, but there is absolutely no reason to believe that a fairly large number of qualified North Vietnamese jet pilots have not been trained over the past thirteen years in Eastern Europe and China, nor that a conversion from obsolete jets to advanced MIG-21's, should they become available, would present an insurmountable problem.

The North Vietnamese Navy (which also does not exist as a separate service) is just as puny. Before the Gulf of Tongking incidents of August, 1964, in the course of which North Vietnamese gunboats fired at U.S. Navy destroyers, it was known to have had two submarine chasers, about thirty light gunboats and sixteen Chinese-built PT boats. Since last year, the United States has reported at least twenty of those craft as sunk, two by naval gunfire in 1964 and the rest by recent air raids. East Germany has provided North Viet-Nam with a small fleet of fishing trawlers that could be used as picket ships and minelayers. But perhaps far more important is a huge "mosquito fleet" of small wooden junks sometimes equipped with powerful engines. According to recent U.S. reports, this must be something like the tactical surprise of the year: Contrary to earlier assurances of an "airtight" coastal control, it now turns out that much of the smuggling of weapons and infiltrators does not come via the jungle-shrouded Ho Chi Minh Trail, but via these coastal junks sneaking southward from cove to cove. In recent weeks, U.S. Coast Guard cutters have been sent to South Viet-Nam to attempt to deal with that unusual aspect of naval warfare.

A major debate now goes on among Western observers as to

whether Giap and his associates actually believe that, in order to win a revolutionary war against a conventional force of the present Vietnamese-American type, the insurgent in turn must resort to an escalation of conventional warfare—precisely as Giap himself did at Dien Bien Phu. An American military analyst who had fought with Mao's forces in World War II and had observed the Viet-Minh as early as 1953, stated in 1955 that "Viet-Minh foot mobility has been of the highest order [and] is the Asian rebuttal to machine-age war." And General Lucien-Max Chassin, who commanded France's Air Force in Indochina, raised as early as 1954 the question as to whether, by deliberately depriving North Viet-Nam of heavy weapons, its major Communist allies did not compel it "to practice warfare methods which are capable of stalemating the most modern Western armaments short of mass-destruction weapons." That situation may well be in the process of occurring right now.

There are examples on both sides of the argument: in Malaya and the Philippines insurgent forces were defeated without either side resorting to large-scale warfare; in Algeria and Cyprus the insurgents won their point without ever leaving the primary guerrilla stage, while their opponents used everything from tanks to jets.

It was the North Vietnamese party ideologist, Truong Chinh, who, in a recent article in the VPA's daily newspaper, most clearly expressed the VPA's present strategy:

> We are determined to reject bourgeois military views, including the revisionist [i.e., Russian] views making much of the role of nuclear weapons and lowering the political role of man in modern war. . . .
>
> People's war, not modern weapons and techniques, decides victory because war is the most acute form of struggle between man and man . . . and not between various kinds of weapons and techniques which cannot spontaneously oppose one another. Weapons, no matter how keen they may be, [can only] be handled and used by man.

And General Giap somewhat earlier presented an evaluation of what actually rides on the outcome of the Viet-Nam war—and no one in Washington is likely to quarrel with him:

> South Viet-Nam is the example for national liberation movements of our times. . . . If it proves possible to defeat the "Special War-

fare" tested in South Viet-Nam by the American imperialists, this
will mean that it can be defeated everywhere else as well.[1]

As the war now gains in intensity and the American commitment grows by leaps and bounds, it becomes highly doubtful
whether the North Vietnamese political and military leadership
can in the long run avoid an escalation of its own commitment
and whether, in that case, it can sustain the struggle, as it did
against the French, without a massive arrival of Chinese "volunteers" or Russian technicians.

If, on the other hand, the Vietnamese problem may now be
moving slowly toward the conference table and a probable compromise of sorts rather than an outright American and South
Vietnamese victory, then this can be imputed as much to the
existence of the North Vietnamese People's Army, with its largely
untapped strength, as to the successes of the Viet-Cong inside
South Viet-Nam.

[1] *Nhan Dan* (Hanoi), July 19, 1964.

PART V

The West at Bay

As the Viet-Nam problem grew into its present magnitude, there developed among long-time observers a distinct feeling of *déjà vu* —the impression of once more going through a situation that already has been played or even replayed several times.

There is the constant stream of high-level visitors to Saigon— which had its counterpart even in French days—who strenuously try to reach the realities of the situation by reducing the physical distance between themselves and the problem at hand. Apparently, they forget that the very officials who escort them around Viet-Nam are those who write (or wrote) the reports they read in Washington (or Paris).

The internal stresses described in Part III and the rising guerrilla threat described in Part IV posed ever greater dangers because of the lack of realistic response in Saigon. Jean Lacouture, in his recent *Viet-Nam: Between Two Truces** wrote: "War generally entails extraordinary legislation; one can say that here extraordinary legislation entailed war." By the time the full extent of the disintegrating situation was realized (assuming that it was at some point prior to the February, 1966, Honolulu conference between American and South Vietnamese leaders—which is not certain), the West had painted itself into a corner in Southeast Asia. The alternatives, equally unpalatable, resembled inauspiciously those which faced the Western alliance at the time of the French siege of Dien Bien Phu: constantly increasing escalation under "open

* New York: Random House, 1966.

end" conditions, or ignominious surrender of a regime and country one had, in Kennan's words, "adopted as a protégé."

Slowly, the West went, as is described below, the full circle of the 1954 crisis, but with roles strangely inverted: the United States in France's position as the main and hard-pressed combatant (though, of course, in a far better military position); Britain in America's earlier position as a reluctant ally in a seemingly unpromising military situation; and General de Gaulle's France echoing almost verbatim the warnings addressed in 1954 by British Prime Minister Churchill to his allies not to upset the détente and the chances for a peaceful settlement of the crisis with a hasty escalation. There was one difference, however, which neither Britain nor France fully understood, and that was the ability of the United States to prosecute the war even in the face of only lukewarm foreign support for the operation.

Yet, here again it was easy to foresee that even a massive military effort could hardly solve *all* of Viet-Nam's most pressing problems, even if that effort could keep some sort of a non-Communist government in power. The real problem was, as a recapitulation of events leading to the Second Indochina War clearly shows below, that "institutionalized [socio-political] fetters and vices would soon bring about the same defects." This seems to have been realized in 1966 at Honolulu and by such exponents of the civilian counterinsurgency approach as General Edward Lansdale.

But in Viet-Nam, reform programs have a strange way of changing character as they go from the drawing board to the rice paddy.

20. The Stakes in Southeast Asia

November, 1962

It is too early to point to a precise date which might serve as a milestone for the decline of the West's power in Southeast Asia. Some observers point to the Anglo-American defeats of Singapore and Corregidor of 1942 as a landmark similar to the loss of Constantinople to the Turks in 1453. Others point to the French defeat at Dien Bien Phu in May, 1954, as the event that marked the end of an era.

Dien Bien Phu was much more than a lost military engagement and even more than simply the death knell of French colonialism in Asia. Just as Singapore and Corregidor showed that a non-Western nation could defeat Western nations with their own type of weaponry, Dien Bien Phu showed that a *revolutionary warfare* force could defeat on the open field of battle a far better equipped conventional force. In Korea, a conventional Communist force had been checkmated by likewise conventional American, Korean, and United Nations troops; Dien Bien Phu showed the way to Communist victories elsewhere, beyond the twin deadlocks of conventional war and nuclear war.

The Geneva cease-fire conference which followed the Indochinese debacle left the map of Southeast Asia drastically changed. North Viet-Nam down to the 17th parallel became the regroupment area for the Viet-Minh forces of Ho Chi Minh and blossomed into a full-fledged Communist state. South Viet-Nam, racked by administrative disintegration, feudal sects, and the sudden influx of 860,000 refugees from the soon-to-be Communist areas, seemed moribund.[1] Laos, twice almost overrun by Viet-Minh

[1] For a balanced study of South Viet-Nam during the early post-1954 period, see John W. Lindholm (ed.), *Vietnam—The First Five Years* (East Lansing, Mich.: Michigan State University Press, 1960).

Reprinted, by permission, from "Southeast Asia: The West at Bay," *Current History*, November, 1962. © 1962 by Current History, Inc.

invasions,[2] was in no position to resist Communist demands for a regroupment area made up of the two northern provinces of Phong-saly and Samneua with a connecting corridor between them, in which a Communist-dominated administration under Prince Souphanouvong maintained full control and an embryo of an autonomous armed force.

Only Cambodia, endowed more by luck than design with an able leadership under the authority of its king (now Prince) Noro-dom Sihanouk, was able to maintain both its independence and unity. Sihanouk had succeeded in disentangling himself from the French colonial administration—thus avoiding the stigma of being branded as a "French puppet" like his Vietnamese neighbor, Bao-Dai—and in showing a great deal of courage in standing up to the great powers at Geneva in 1954 when the latter were ready to carve up Cambodia like the other two states of Indochina in order to provide for a Communist regroupment area.

In a diplomatic rear-guard battle that no doubt will remain a classic in diplomatic annals, the Cambodian delegation fought for almost seven hours on July 20, 1954, to save the unity of its coun-try. Finally, at 3:43 A.M. of July 21, dour Soviet Foreign Minister V. M. Molotov yielded to the Cambodian negotiators, who thus saved not only the unity of their country but also (and this is much too often forgotten these days) the right to maintain an American military mission on their soil.[3]

The creation of the Southeast Asia Treaty Organization (SEATO) in Manila on September 8, 1954, included the three non-Communist Indochina states under the "protective umbrella" clause of its Protocol, thus ensuring them of a measure of external aid in case of renewed aggression. This move, along with the grad-ual improvement of the Western position in Malaya (where the

[2] In January–May, 1953, Communist Vietnamese Divisions 308, 312, and 316 stabbed via Samneua at Xieng-Khouang and Luang Prabang, while Divi-sion 304 attacked the Plaine des Jarres hedgehog position. In December, 1953–April, 1954, Divisions 304, 308, and 312 attacked further north in the direc-tion of Muong-Sai, while Divisions 304 and 325, in a daring 400-mile raid through mountains and jungle, cut Indochina in two on Christmas Day, 1953, wiped out nearly all French positions in southern Laos, and laid siege to the northern Cambodian towns of Voeune Sai and Siempang.

[3] Cf. Bernard B. Fall, "Cambodia's International Position," *Current History*, March, 1961. See also Jean Lacouture and Philippe Devillers, *La fin d'une guerre*.

Chinese terrorists had finally been driven into the deep woods) and the Philippines (where the reform administration of Ramòn Magsaysay was taking hold) restored a certain favorable balance in Southeast Asia. That balance, however, was to prove precarious.

The end of the Indochina War brought about the removal of the French as a political factor in Southeast Asia. When American aid payments began going directly to the Indochinese states as of January 1, 1955, and the last French troops left Saigon in April, 1956, French influence in the area fell to its lowest point in 100 years. That disappearance of France also paved the way for the reopening of old wounds and the settling of old scores—and those came very soon. In fact, the very absence (at least for a short time) of direct Communist pressure made the reappearance of such local but violent disputes a more important factor than they would have been otherwise.

Most of those disputes dealt—and still do late in 1962—with the re-establishment of the *status quo ante* 1863, i.e., the date when the French colonial influence began to make itself felt throughout the peninsula. Prior to that date, the situation looked roughly as follows: in a series of successful wars fought during the latter part of the eighteenth century, Siam (now Thailand) had taken over much of the Laotian-held Korat Plateau. In a last bitter war with the decaying kingdom of Vientiane in 1828, it had literally destroyed the little country and had put the whole Mekong valley south of Luang Prabang under its effective control. The southern Laotian principality of Champassak also became a Siamese protectorate—a situation which prevailed until the establishment of the French protectorate in 1893.

The Vietnamese emperors also had not remained idle. Several Vietnamese wars with the kings of Luang Prabang in the sixteenth and seventeenth centuries had brought the vitally located kingdom of the Tran-Ninh (which includes the famous Plaine des Jarres) under Vietnamese control. This was followed by an actual protectorate as of 1831, in the course of which many Vietnamese moved across the mountain passes into Laos.

Neighboring Cambodia had suffered a similar fate at the hands of the Siamese and Vietnamese. At the beginning of the nineteenth century, Cambodia was little more than a Siamo-Vietnamese condominium, whose kings had to secure the consent of both

Bangkok and Hue, and Cambodian attempts at rebellion were ruthlessly put down. As of 1818, Cambodia, like Poland in Europe, had been completely split up into Siamese and Vietnamese provinces with colonial governors of the neighboring nations directly administering them and alien immigrants dispossessing the native Cambodians of their soil and even of the names of their cities.[4] The boundary between the Siamese and Vietnamese zones of control ran roughly south of the Great Lake, with the capital of Oudong in Siamese hands and with Siamese army units holding the mountain uplands in today's Central Viet-Nam as far east as Kontum and Pleiku. Cambodian cities such as Stung Treng and Siempang were known as slave markets, where the Siamese bought and sold Cambodians and mountaineers as late as the 1850's.

Thus the arrival of the French constituted for both the Laotians and the Cambodians a last-minute respite from a fate that would have been by and large tantamount to total disappearance as national entities; just as the United States in 1919 was largely responsible for the reappearance of Poland and Czechoslovakia as national units. And like those two states, Laos and Cambodia have been ever since in the uncomfortable buffer position between two far larger and far more dynamic neighbors. To put it in one simple sentence: The survival of Laos and Cambodia as independent states depends, regardless of the additional Communist threat, upon the willingness of one or several outside powers to assume responsibility for their protection against their stronger neighbors.

During 1960–61, the failure of the United States to play this role in Laos[5] has resulted in a reassertion of North Vietnamese control over much of that country—a situation which, regardless of the Communist character of the Hanoi regime, any Vietnamese would consider "historically correct." In the case of Cambodia, Prince Sihanouk late in 1962 actually seeks to obtain a similar guarantee

---

[4] It is noteworthy of the Orwellian type of history-writing that has been the fashion with regard to Cambodia that Joseph Buttinger's massive *The Smaller Dragon: A Political History of Vietnam* (New York: Frederick A. Praeger, 1958) completely fails to mention Vietnamese colonialism in Cambodia. Saigon (formerly Prey-Nokor) became Vietnamese only in 1698, and the Camau Peninsula only in 1757. The Cambodians—over 500,000—who still live there, are one of the sources of insecurity in some areas of Viet-Nam today.

[5] Cf. Bernard B. Fall, "Reappraisal in Laos," *Current History*, January, 1962.

against encroachments upon his country by America's Thai and South Vietnamese allies. Needless to say, the open promise of such a guarantee would add a certain strain to American relations with Thailand and South Viet-Nam. The Russians, not hemmed in by similar considerations, gave such a guarantee by backing a Cambodian request for a fourteen-nation conference to safeguard Cambodia's neutrality.[6] On the Western side, the French also followed their own traditional policies as "re-creators" of Laos and Cambodia: President de Gaulle endorsed the idea of an international conference on Cambodian neutrality in a personal letter addressed to Prince Sihanouk early in September, 1962.

The question has often arisen as to whether the Cambodian leadership (e.g., Prince Sihanouk) is "too naïve" to understand the reality of the Communist threat, in the face of which the encroachments of both Thailand and South Viet-Nam must be considered as decidedly minor. The reasoning of the Cambodians—and this includes, as far as is possible to judge, a great many outside the governing élite—is based on the stark facts of their history of the past 200 years. It was expressed to this writer by Prince Sihanouk several times during the past year and runs roughly as follows:

> We are aware of, and concerned with, the threat which the Communist powers represent. However, it has been our observation that in the case of a Communist takeover, be it in Eastern Europe or in Asia, the national *entity* of the country thus taken over is preserved. The Poles are Poles and the Czechs are Czechs and are ostensibly governed by people of their own kind.
>
> If we were to be swallowed up by the Thai and the Vietnamese tomorrow, we would purely and simply disappear as a *people*, not to speak of Cambodia as a national unit, just as the kingdom of Champa[7] has disappeared; and would become anonymous provinces of our neighbors. Within a generation, even our language and culture would be wiped out and there would be no more Cambodians.

It is not important whether or not Thailand or South Viet-Nam would *really* completely swallow up Cambodia or merely amputate

[6] *Pravda*, August 28, 1962.

[7] Champa was a kingdom occupied by a Hinduized seafaring nation along the Vietnamese shoreline between the 18th and the 11th parallels. The Chams were totally destroyed in 700 years of war by the conquering Vietnamese. There exist only about 20,000 Chams today in South Viet-Nam.

several of its key provinces, although the leaders of both countries have made several statements to the effect that they desired such boundary changes. The essential point in the present situation is that Cambodia has a *real* fear of partition and that, in such circumstances, Communist domination must of necessity appear to it as an evil of less permanent a nature than genocide.

Here again, a comparison with Poland, with its long tragic tradition of being divided among its neighbors, is not without interest: under the Communist regime, Poland at least can maintain sufficient cultural and ethnic integrity to await perhaps an eventual liberalization of the bloc system. In the meantime, it survives as a national unit. Under the Nazi administration, Poland had disappeared (with Soviet help, let it be noted) as a national unit, and the Poles were purely and simply slated for extermination. When the alternatives become as crude as national subservience or genocide, the choice, unfortunately, becomes obvious.

This old quarrel has taken on increasing bitterness as internal stresses both in Thailand and South Viet-Nam make the existence of an external issue desirable to the rulers in Bangkok and Saigon. By late in 1962 it also has become a major factor in the relations between the United States and the three countries primarily concerned.

The argument that none of the countries in the area is absolutely essential to American defense has relatively little impact on the over-all issue that the Communists apparently have found Southeast Asia a propitious battleground where they can demonstrate U.S. inability to stand up to the enormous stresses of revolutionary war. In the first round of that war, the American-supported French lost the battle. In Laos, General Phoumi Nosavan's overmotorized, overarmed, and overpaid right-wing forces met one defeat after another in spite of lavish American aid and 800 military advisers. In Malaya, a hard core of 475 Chinese terrorist guerrillas still holds the field in the Thai-Malayan border area—no doubt on higher orders, since it would have no trouble whatever in filtering across Thailand or Burma to South China.[8] It ties up better than 100

---

[8] In recent months, the leader of the Chinese terrorists in Malaya, Chin Peng, spent a holiday in Bangkok and returned to his jungle stronghold without being apprehended. Chin Peng, originally trained by the British to fight the Japanese, received in 1946 the Order of the British Empire for his wartime guerrilla activities.

times its own strength of Malay, British, and Thai troops, thus fulfilling its disruptive task even in this quiescent theater.

In South Viet-Nam, less than 25,000 full-time guerrillas and infiltrated North Vietnamese regulars tie down more than 400,000 South Vietnamese soldiers and militiamen of various kinds, in addition to 10,000 American specialists recruited in many cases from the elite Special Forces. Here again, the 20-to-1 tie-down ratio of regulars versus guerrillas constitutes a heavy drain on scarce manpower (not to speak of the war's cost, which is currently set at $1 million a day), at little expense to the Communist bloc.[9]

All this spells a real challenge to the United States and one which the United States has decided to face up to in South Viet-Nam, regardless of cost. In spite of the usual press statements northern Southeast Asia has no direct military value: Laos really is not a "road" to anywhere, and it is not South Viet-Nam but Cambodia that shields the vulnerable parts of Thailand. But the "denial value" of the area is enormous: the neutralization of Laos and the difficulties in South Viet-Nam have renewed Thai fears of American disengagement to the point that certain Thai leaders (such as, in September, 1962, General Prapas Charusathien) have made statements which could well be construed as at least indicating an increased interest by Thailand in following a policy of noncommitment. The recent negotiations between Bangkok and Hanoi about further repatriation (without choice as to destination, let it be underlined) of Vietnamese refugees in Thailand to Communist North Viet-Nam and increased Soviet trade with Thailand may be straws in the same wind.

With Southeast Asia no longer under American control, India's position would become well-nigh impossible. What Indonesia's attitude then would be is anybody's guess. In other words, the negative stake of denying the adversary access to further Southeast Asian real estate is truly an important one. It is the denial value of

[9] According to an Agence France-Presse report released in Saigon on July 31, 1962, and passed by South Vietnamese censorship, the South Vietnamese forces lost during the first six months of 1962 a total of 2,588 weapons to the Communist guerrillas, while capturing only 2,148. While the ratio of captured to lost weapons improved since 1961, it still permits the Communists to re-supply themselves largely out of South Vietnamese booty rather than through costly supply convoys from their North Vietnamese sanctuary, which are reserved to scarce heavy weapons and hard-to-get drugs.

the area which inspires policy-makers in Washington to accept the battle on almost any terms, regardless of whether the Ngo Dinh Diem or any other regime is "popular" or not. In fact, the present trend is to go so far as to say that popular support is not particularly relevant to the outcome of a guerrilla war.[10]

So far, experience has shown that popular support is a vital factor in a revolutionary war, but this does not exclude the possibility of the discovery of radically new methods of counterinsurgency in which popular support can be replaced by technological or tactical innovations. In any case, both views are being put extensively to the test in South Viet-Nam today. Victory or defeat in that war, therefore, will influence the West's over-all position in most underdeveloped areas where Communist-inspired revolutionary warfare is likely to challenge it.

One of the most interesting aspects of the present preoccupation with revolutionary warfare is the state of semantic confusion into which it has thrown everybody even remotely interested in the subject. The number of self-styled experts who suddenly are selling their services to the government in that field, and of civilian agencies and branches of the armed services which suddenly develop "unconventional warfare capabilities" (and that includes almost everyone except perhaps the Women's Army Corps) is equally impressive. It involves, of necessity, much waste of effort, much duplication, and much laborious rediscovery of facts which the British and French, with their wide-ranging experience in that field, had lying around gathering dust in their file drawers for years. Thus, a few words of semantic clarification may be required

[10] W. W. Rostow, Chairman of the State Department's Policy Planning Council, stated in June, 1961, in an address to the Special Forces School at Fort Bragg: "In my conversations with representatives of foreign governments, I am sometimes lectured that this or that government within the free world is not popular; they tell me that guerrilla warfare cannot be won unless the peoples are dissatisfied [sic]. These are, at best, half-truths." (*Marine Corps Gazette*, January, 1962, pp. 48–49.)

The same point was made sometime later by Roger Hilsman, Director of the Office of Intelligence Research of the State Department, in his preface to the American edition of General Vo Nguyen Giap's *People's War, People's Army* (New York: Frederick A. Praeger, 1962): "Guerrillas do not need majority support from the entire countryside. They can operate effectively even if some of the populace is hostile and the rest indifferent."

in order to understand in full the Communist challenge in Southeast Asia.[11]

Much has been said of late about "unconventional warfare," "special warfare," "guerrilla warfare," "insurgency," "political warfare," "national liberation wars," "bandit war"—to name a few. All of them in one way or another succeed in conveying the idea of violence. Only one of them, political warfare, conveys the idea of a simultaneous nonmilitary struggle; to the point, in fact, where the military facet of the term almost disappears. In the view of this writer, only the expression *revolutionary warfare* gives full credit to both the military and dynamic political aspects of the struggle which we are facing.

The expression was originally used in its present meaning by Mao Tse-tung in his key study *Strategic Problems of China's Revolutionary War*, first published in 1936. The French, who were first faced with the problem on a large scale, adopted the same term. It was a French professor at the Ecole Supérieure de Guerre, Colonel Gabriel Bonnet, who, in a book that is totally ignored in the United States, defined revolutionary war as "the application of guerrilla warfare methods to the furtherance of an ideology or a political system."[12] That definition does fully take cognizance of the essentially *political* use to which those guerrilla warfare methods are put when used by the Communists rather than by us.

On the Communist side, the military target is always chosen according to its political impact. On our side, the enemy revolutionary warfare fighter seems to be the major target, if not the only one. *The military "kill" becomes the primary target—simply because the essential political target is too elusive for us, or worse, because we do not understand its importance.** Intellectually, of course, this is realized at top level, as is evidenced by a remark made by President Kennedy to Stewart Alsop in a much-quoted interview in the *Saturday Evening Post:* "What they're doing at Fort

---

[11] This writer discusses the whole problem more extensively in *The Two Viet-Nams*.

[12] *Histoire des guerres insurrectionnelles et révolutionnaires de l'antiquité à nos jours* (Paris: Payot, 1958).

* *No change has occurred as of early 1966.*

Bragg [the Special Forces School] is really good, but, in the final analysis, what is needed is a political effort."[13]

Yet at the operating level, the view seems still to be that the Viet-Cong maintain their control solely through armed terror;[14] and thus, that "counterinsurgency" or, *in fine*, counterterror, will turn the tide against the adversary. That is wishful thinking at best. Mao Tse-tung himself warned against this in his previously mentioned book when he admonished his military commanders that they must be *"against* guerrillaism in the Red Army, yet *for* its guerrilla character [italics in text]."

What is being practiced right now on our side is "guerrillaism." Small-unit warfare is the rage; men are being trained for every contingency likely to arise in the jungle. But it is doubtful whether they (or anyone else on our side) can convince the Vietnamese peasant that the Communist program of land reform, neutralism, and above all, peace, is merely a propaganda ploy. The Vietnamese will have to do that explaining themselves; no one can do it for them. Here again, the Communist leaders are not loathe to prescribe the proper recipe. As early as September, 1947, Truong Chinh, then Secretary General of the Vietnamese Communist Party, warned of "those who tend to rely on military action [alone and] believe everything can be settled by armed force. They don't mobilize politically. They are unwilling to give explanations and try to convince the people to side with them."[15]

Thus, the Communist challenge in Southeast Asia has yet to be faced on its *real* terrain: that of ideas, policies, and down-to-earth effective administration.* Thus far, that struggle seems to be limited to conventional "psychological warfare" operations whose overuse throughout the world has worn off their novelty on both sides, and to an attempt at whipping Western opinion into line by intimidating foreign journalists and professors.[16] Neither tactic has been particularly successful.

In addition, there is always the ominous shadow of Communist

[13] Stewart Alsop, "Kennedy's Grand Design," *Saturday Evening Post*, March 31, 1962.

[14] Rostow, *op. cit.*, p. 49; Hilsman, *op. cit.*, p. xxv.

[15] Truong Chinh, *La résistance vaincra* (new ed.; Hanoi, 1960), p. 71.

[16] *Newsweek*, September 10, 1962; *Harper's Magazine*, September, 1962.

* *No change has occurred as of early 1966.*

North Viet-Nam behind whatever happens in the Indochinese peninsula. As this writer could see for himself during a visit there in July, 1962 (which included personal interviews with Ho Chi Minh and his Premier, Pham Van Dong), North Viet-Nam is likely to be a tough and determined "adversary-by-proxy" in what can in all honesty be called the Second Indochina War.

As one surveys the situation in Southeast Asia in the fall of 1962, there are few evidences that the situation is clearly turning in the West's favor. Recent attempts by the United States to patch over intra-area disputes between Cambodia and her neighbors have unfortunately failed because of insufficient pressure on all concerned to come to reasonable terms, either through direct confrontation, mediation, or under United Nations auspices. This will only make Cambodia's case for a fourteen-power conference on the subject more pressing and the conference itself more unavoidable.

Much is often made of the "stability" of the governments in the area. The re-establishment of such stability, where it is said to be lacking, is being made a primary target of policy, and its achievement hailed as a major feat. In my view, the trouble with the Western position (and not only in Southeast Asia) has been, in fact, too much of that false stability which in many cases does little else but hide advanced governmental sclerosis. For almost six years, from 1954 until 1960, the Communists gave the West a breathing space in the area. Only now does it become clearly apparent how badly that time has been used, or rather misused. In spite of lavish aid expenditures, none of the countries concerned achieved the Rostowian "takeoff" stage. In fact, it is doubtful whether they achieved pre-1939 living standards on a general countrywide basis.

In the underdeveloped areas of the world, and in Southeast Asia in particular, the Communists are riding the crest of a revolutionary wave which the peoples of those areas would have generated even without their presence. In the words of President Kennedy in his Special Message to Congress in May, 1961: "They seek an end to injustice, tyranny and exploitation. More than an end, they seek a beginning. And theirs is a revolution which we would support regardless of the Cold War, and regardless of which political or economic route they should choose to freedom."

Considering the present situation throughout the whole Indochinese peninsula, a more literal application of President Kennedy's exhortation might come closer to meeting the political requirements of the situation than anything else that is being done at this moment.

21. Full Circle, 1954–64

This is the time of tenth anniversaries in Indochina: on May 7, 1954, Dien Bien Phu fell after fifty-six days of grueling battle; on the same day the cease-fire conference opened at Geneva; and Viet-Nam was partitioned at the 17th parallel on July 20.

And precisely as a decade ago, the non-Communist regions of Viet-Nam are teetering on the brink of disaster, their battle-weary troops kept in the fight by a "thin red line" of white military professionals. Even the speeches of the to-the-bitter-enders have not changed. On April 16, 1954, Vice President Richard Nixon suggested that "we must take the risk now by putting our boys in [to Indochina]," and on April 16, 1964, Presidential-aspirant Nixon was quoted as advocating "military strikes against Communist bases in North Viet-Nam and Laos." On May 29, 1950, *Time* assured its readers, on the basis of French estimates, that ex-Emperor Bao-Dai needed "time to organize an effective government [and] train an army and militia that can restore order in the villages," and on March 26, 1964, U.S. Secretary of Defense Robert McNamara assured the world that the chief of the South Vietnamese military regime was "vigorously rebuilding the machinery of administration" and that the "security forces of Viet-Nam will be increased [and] their effectiveness and conditions of service improved." The French, through *Time*, assured the world that, given generous amounts of American aid, they would win in Indochina in three years. The same timetable for victory was also given by Mr. McNamara in 1963. But by March, 1964, he had revised his estimates to the point where he candidly admitted that the war in Viet-Nam might not even be over after "the first thousand days" of the Johnson Administration.

Reprinted, by permission, from "1954–64—Full Circle in Vietnam," *The Spectator*, May 8, 1964.

Strangely enough, the only *new* element in the Viet-Nam equation is that of the attitude of two of its minor actors: Great Britain and France. Whereas Britain in 1954 sought peace at almost any price in Southeast Asia, even if it meant (as it did) abandoning a major ally, France, in the direst straits, the same Britain in 1964, ruled by the Conservative Party just as it was ten years earlier, advocates a "hard-line" policy on Viet-Nam that is perhaps a shade to the right of the present views of the American administration. Conversely—and the irony of the situation must be underlined to be properly savored—France in 1954 was ruled by a center party coalition dominated by the *jusqu'auboutiste* Foreign Minister Georges Bidault, who bitterly resented the restraining role which Britain played upon American intentions to provide at least air support to the hard-pressed French. As Sir Anthony Eden later explained in his memoirs, Britain opposed such joint allied action as a threat against Red China because it would have left the allies with the awful choice of having to "withdraw ignominiously or else embark on warlike action against China." Ten years later, with a conservative regime ruling France, it was the lonely French Foreign Minister, Couve de Murville, who presented the "Eden line" to the other seven members of the Southeast Asia Treaty Organization's ministerial meeting at Manila, only to be almost hooted down by the other members of the conference. And both Lord Carrington, Minister Without Portfolio, and Keith J. Holyoake, the Prime Minister of New Zealand, demonstratively went directly from the SEATO meeting to Saigon to express the full support of their respective governments for General Nguyen Khanh, Premier of the Saigon military regime.

All those contradictory statements, estimates, and policies are, of course, the result of a decade during which unbounded enthusiasm for the "greatest little guy in Asia," Ngo Dinh Diem, replaced coolheaded appraisals of the rapid deterioration of the situation inside South Viet-Nam; and where unabounded faith in some ill-applied and shopworn techniques of "pacification" and population "control" replaced some deep thinking on how to win over that population without first having to sear it with napalm bombs.

Until the inspection mission of General Maxwell D. Taylor in October, 1961, the rapid spreading of Communist-inspired revolutionary warfare was purely and simply denied, as were the idiotic policies of the Diem regime which provided a relatively small hard core of regular guerrillas with a ready mass of peasant and student recruits driven into the *maquis* for want of a legal opposition. Unbelievably, a book published early in 1962 in America by a group of former advisers to Diem, affirmed with a straight face that the "clearly relaxed relationship" between the Saigon traffic police and the populace "suggests that accusations of authoritarianism" against Diem "lack solid substance";[1] just as a senior American military commander in Viet-Nam testified somewhat earlier to a Senate committee that there were in all of South Viet-Nam only a few "bandit remnants." When well-organized guerrilla units finally routed whole Vietnamese Army battalions, it had to be recognized that a war was going on and that the Vietnamese Army (for eight years prepared to fend off a conventional, Korea-type invasion) was hardly in shape to win it.

The result was a crash program, in the course of which every counterinsurgency trick known was tried at least once: weed-killing chemicals to destroy the vegetation in which the guerrillas were hiding (it did not work too well); high-speed automatic weapons; amphibious armored personnel carriers; rocket-armed helicopters— all were made available in fantastic quantities. Soon there were at least 16,000 American military advisers in Viet-Nam who of necessity became more closely involved in actual combat operations as the situation deteriorated. By mid-April, 1964, they had suffered over 1,100 casualties, of which 205 were deaths in action.

On the civilian side, 1962 brought the beginning of the strategic hamlets program, designed to break the insurgents' control over 7 of the 12 million peasants (out of an estimated 14 million inhabitants) of South Viet-Nam. Ideally, a strategic hamlet included perhaps 1,200 inhabitants whose houses, conveniently grouped together around a school, a well, and a fortified watchtower and surrounded by a moat and breastworks covered with barbed wire, would separate the peasant sheep from the guerrilla wolves. That ideal was rarely reached.

[1] Wesley Fishel, "Problems of Democratic Growth in Free Vietnam," in Fishel (ed.), *South Vietnam Since Independence* (Glencoe, Ill.: The Free Press, 1961), p. 25.

In all this, Britain's successful counterguerrilla operations in Malaya had become the example. More than an example, a fetish. "It worked in Malaya—by God, it's going to work here" was the slogan in Saigon in 1962. And to make sure that the copy would fully conform to the model, a British advisory team, headed by the former Secretary for Defense of Malaya, R. K. G. Thompson, was imported directly to participate in the planning and execution of the project. In view of what has happened in Viet-Nam since, the transposition of the Malayan example could not have been more disastrous—for of course the *economic* and *social*, as well as political and military, conditions under which the Malayan operation succeeded, did not in the least exist in Viet-Nam. In Malaya the terrorist element rested on the Chinese minority; *ipso facto*, any Malay or Indian inhabitant of Malaya (about 55 per cent of the total) could be reckoned as loyal or even actively unsympathetic to the terrorist cause; in Viet-Nam both the population and the guerrillas are of exactly the same stock. Indeed, even the infiltrators from North Viet-Nam are former southerners who left in 1954 and are now returning: they know the topography of the area they fight in and they speak the proper South Vietnamese dialect. In Malaya, home-grown food is scarce and almost totally unobtainable in the jungle. In Viet-Nam food grows everywhere and food denial or control programs have thus far proved total failures; in fact, the guerrillas allow rice from the areas they occupy to go to Saigon for export since the "taxes" they levy provide them with handy cash.

In Malaya, there was no "active sanctuary" next door since the only contiguous country, Thailand, was staunchly anti-Communist. In Viet-Nam, North Viet-Nam openly supports the guerrillas, Laos is a complete sieve, and Cambodia, in view of its persistent bad relations with Saigon, makes no particular effort to halt guerrilla operations in hard-to-survey border areas. The record of all guerrilla wars since 1940 shows that the guerrilla cannot readily be defeated as long as the "sanctuary" plays its role. In Malaya, the Communist Party had not even had time to indoctrinate the Chinese segment of the population before it was forced underground. In Viet-Nam, the Communists have had twenty years to indoctrinate much of the countryside without ever being effectively challenged by a competing philosophy. Certainly the French colonials could not come up with one; and all Diem's philosopher-brother Nhu could come up with was a "personalist" philosophy whose liberal Catholic tenets have found no major echo in France (where they originated in the 1930's) and which certainly no Buddhist Vietnamese rice peasant could understand. In Malaya, Britain's own forces, reinforced by Malays, Gurkhas, Dyaks, Fijians, Australians, and New Zealanders, fought a poorly armed force without access to outside supply lines for thirteen years at a strength ratio of 30 to 1 in their favor. In South Viet-Nam today, the Vietnamese and Americans fight a well-armed guerrilla force having ample outside support at a strength ratio of 4.5 to 1.

Yet, in the United States as well as in South Viet-Nam, wherever counterinsurgency planning is being carried on, the Malayan example is being trotted out as a last shining ray of hope that there is a satisfactory military solution to the Viet-Nam war. No one, it seems, is willing to face up to the fact that the situation in these two countries is radically different—and that the tried-and-true methods that worked so well in Malaya do not seem to yield the same kind of satisfactory results in Malaysia's North Borneo territories, where Indonesia provides her infiltrators with precisely the kind of support the Viet-Cong gets.

To win, then, militarily in South Viet-Nam—and that is the only kind of solution that is at present envisaged in Saigon, Washington, and, apparently, in London as well—will take an incredibly larger effort in Viet-Nam than is being made at present. Assuming that such an effort were to be made and that such "civilian" factors as loyalty of the population, war-weariness, the possibility of new coups in Saigon, etc., could be disregarded (and of course they couldn't), the military bill to pay would look about as follows: (1) increase of South Vietnamese forces from about 500,000 to a 10 to 1 ratio with the guerrillas—i.e., 1 million men; (2) increase of the American advisory force from its present 16,000-man level for an already-trained force to a cadre corps for 500,000 raw levies, i.e., about 60,000 Americans (an army corps, half the size of the European French component of the French forces in Indochina ten years ago); (3) a concomitant increase of expenditure in Viet-Nam from the present approximately $750 million a year to perhaps $1.5 billion—at a time when the total foreign aid budget is hardly likely to clear the $3 billion* hurdle.

Instead, the effort now contemplated under the new "McNamara Plan" of March, 1964, provides for a modest increase in the American advisory force, an increase of the Vietnamese Army by 50,000 men (of which 15,000 would barely replace last year's casualties), and the delivery of some better aircraft, such as the propeller-driven Skyraider, to Viet-Nam. In other words, the war effort in Viet-Nam is being at best, sustained (assuming that the military situation does not worsen, which it has in recent weeks), but is not being increased to a point where victory not only becomes possible, but at least *politically credible*.

That is possibly what Couve de Murville was referring to in diplomatic language at the SEATO Council meeting when he said on April 14, that, "in spite of the considerable efforts deployed by the United States to save Viet-Nam—efforts which France admires—the situation there has reached the point where in many places governmental authority is no longer exercised." In other words, if the military effort is not made of the stuff necessary to win, then a solution must be found in other fields. But Britain, already dangerously overextended in Cyprus, Aden, and East Africa, and in need of American support in Malaysia, supported the paragraph of the SEATO communiqué which stated that "defeat of the Communist campaign is essential not only to the security of the Republic of Viet-Nam but to that of Southeast Asia." All the other SEATO members—none of which is likely to be able to contribute anything but symbolic units to the American effort in Viet-Nam—followed suit, save France.

The next months will no doubt prove which of the two British policies on Indochina—that of Churchill and Eden ten years ago, or that of the present Prime Minister—will have been the more correct under the prevailing circumstances. Charles de Gaulle, albeit belatedly, seems to agree with Churchill.

---

* *Here the writer was far too modest in his estimate. Eventually, American appropriations in Viet-Nam were to exceed $15 billion for fiscal year 1966. And the problem remained no nearer solution.*

22. The Roots of Conflict

January, 1965

As this article is written, an insurgent group which originally had engaged in little else but lightly armed banditry has blossomed out into a full-fledged national liberation movement; and, as ten years earlier, its effects have outstripped by far its own Vietnamese national context to affect the whole Indochinese peninsula, including Thailand.

Much has been written, on both sides of the ideological fence, about the Vietnamese emergency that is wholly or partly inaccurate. The present situation in Viet-Nam is not due entirely to North Vietnamese aggressiveness, nor can the blame be laid fully at the feet of the oppressive and woefully inefficient Ngo Dinh Diem regime. The truth, as almost always in such cases, lies somewhere in between. A case can probably be made for the assertion that the mistakes of the Diem regime gave rise to enough discontent for the ever-watchful North Vietnamese Communists to attempt to give that discontent a shape and dimension which would turn the situation to their advantage. And that they would succeed so well at their enterprise as they have so far must be credited to the erroneous estimates of the Indochina situation made in many Western chanceries since 1954.

The origins of the Second Indochina War are deeply rooted in the way the First Indochina War ended at Geneva in July, 1954. Although politically negotiated, the Geneva agreements were a military cease-fire, signed on both sides by the representatives of the military commanders: General Delteil for the French Union High Command, which also controlled the Vietnamese and Laotian national armies, and General Ta Quang Buu for the Viet-Nam

Reprinted, by permission, from "The Roots of the Conflict," *International Affairs* (London), XL, No. 1 (January, 1965).

People's Army, the Khmer Resistance Forces, and the Pathet-Lao fighting units.[1] Since Cambodia had had operational control over her own forces as of October 1953, General Nhiek Tioulong of the Forces Armées Royales Khmères signed separately for Cambodia.

At the time no feeling of incongruity was apparent at the thought that on each side (with the exception of Cambodia) one foreign power signed the cease-fire for the local military forces. After all, barely a year earlier, a United States admiral had signed the Korean cease-fire at Panmunjom on behalf of the United Nations side by side with a North Korean and a Chinese Communist general officer; and the Rheims cease-fire with Nazi Germany was surely binding on all the small Allies even though the Poles, Czechs, Norwegians, and Nicaraguans personally had no hand in it. In the case of the Geneva cease-fire, however, two countries refused to join in the Final Declaration—the United States and South Viet-Nam; although, in separate statements, the United States affirmed that she "will refrain from the threat or the use of force to disturb" the agreements, while South Viet-Nam promised "not to use force to resist the procedures for carrying the cease-fire into effect."

The Final Declaration (an apparently unsigned document in the official text)[2] stipulated that Viet-Nam as a whole would be reunified through "general elections [to] be held in July, 1956, under the supervision of an international commission." But almost from the start the Ngo Dinh Diem government in Saigon repeatedly declared itself "not bound by the Geneva agreement signed in contempt" of Vietnamese national interests. The dissolution of the French High Command in Indochina—that is, the actual signatory of the cease-fire—on April 26, 1956 (before the July, 1956, deadline) provided some grounds for Saigon's argument that it was not bound by the obligations signed by a French general on its behalf. Although there was, for a brief moment, a vague feeling that such an attitude was, in all logic, incompatible with the presence of the Indian-Canadian-Polish International Control Commission, good sense eventually prevailed and the Diem regime, on the eve of the

---

[1] Cf. full text in *Further Documents Relating to the Discussion of Indochina at the Geneva Conference* (Cmd. 9239).
[2] *Ibid.*, pp. 10–11.

July, 1956, deadline, established what its Foreign Secretary Vu Van Mau, called *"de facto* cooperation" with the ICC.[3]

By doing so, South Viet-Nam, in her own view and in that of most Western observers, had in fact availed herself of the benefits of the cease-fire negotiated at Geneva. However, she had not assumed any of the responsibilities laid down as regards political relations with the northern rival state. In fact, northern proposals to establish *de facto* economic and postal relations with South Viet-Nam approximately equivalent to those between West and East Germany were turned down by Diem personally because "we cannot entertain any Communist proposal as long as we do not have evidence that they place the interests of the Fatherland above those of Communism."

A somewhat different light on events in 1956 was recently shed by Edgar Ansel Mowrer, who asserted, in May, 1964, in bilingual *Réalités* (in an article which, remarkably, failed to appear in the English edition), that commando raids into North Viet-Nam were launched by South Vietnamese troops "with such success that around 1956 Ho Chi Minh refused to hold the impartial plebiscite provided for the two Viet-Nams . . . when he saw that he was certain to lose it."

Either way, it was certain that after the July, 1956, deadline the North Vietnamese Communist regime had little reason to treat South Viet-Nam with kid gloves. What could have possibly deterred it from beginning an extended campaign of subversion was what deterred similar attempts in the other two divided countries, Germany and Korea. In the former, that deterrent was the solidity of the German economic and political fabric even before the rebirth of West German armed might; and in the latter it is a 600,000-man standing army of such strength (and directly backed up by U.S. ground forces on the cease-fire line) as to make any attempt at undermining it through pinprick attacks a fairly hopeless enterprise.

Viet-Nam south of the 17th parallel at first possessed neither of those two assets, but the acquiring of economic and political stability was within her power, and provision of an adequate military shield for her was within the means of her allies. In the end, she

[3] *News from Viet-Nam,* August 18, 1956.

was to get neither. Contrary to all the mythology on the subject—
for instance, that "the years 1956 to 1960 produced something
close to an economic miracle"[4]—South Viet-Nam's economic recovery had floundered badly. In the words of Denis Warner, an
Australian observer who was otherwise inclined to view events in
South Viet-Nam with considerable optimism: "The much-vaunted
rural help program did not exist. Land reform was a flop. Industry
was insignificant."[5] Administratively, South Viet-Nam's government purely and simply resisted any deep-seated reforms. In spite
of extensive American help in that field, the Vietnamese bureaucracy remained largely mandarin in outlook, and the overlay of
corruption and political favoritism which emanated from the Ngo
Dinh family only made matters worse. And finally, there was the
matter of the poor, misled, badly equipped and badly trained
Army of the Republic of Viet-Nam (ARVN).

The departing and beaten French had left the ARVN a shambles, despite the fact that some of its units had fought heroically
(and many say, better than now) alongside the French to the
bitter end. Until 1954, most of the technical and staff services of
the ARVN had been handled directly by the French Union Forces,
and no Vietnamese officer had actually commanded more than a
regiment in combat. With the changeover to American advisers
and matériel, the ARVN also changed its whole military purpose.
Until 1961, the defense of South Viet-Nam was based on the assumption of a Korean-like across-the-parallel attack. The secondary
assumption then was that, as in Korea, such an open onslaught
would have to be dealt with by the SEATO coalition specifically
created in September, 1954, for that purpose—if not by the United
Nations. In such a case, the mission of the ARVN was simply to
delay the advance of the Communist invaders long enough for the
Allied counterthrust to come into play; say two to three weeks.
That, so the assumption went, could be handled by a 100,000-
strong Vietnamese force abundantly provided with armor and
artillery. Paramilitary forces needed for the control of the countryside were either disbanded or left without American aid or training.

[4] *A Threat to the Peace: North Viet-Nam's Effort to Conquer South Viet-
Nam* (Washington, D.C.: Government Printing Office, for the Bureau of
Public Affairs, 1961), Part I, p. 5.
[5] *The Last Confucian*, p. 114.

The effects of what I have elsewhere called the "Korean trauma"[6] were not long in coming and also aroused the concern of other observers. Colonel H. C. B. Cook, a former British military attaché in Saigon, wrote in 1962 that Vietnamese officers talked to him about the "American-type war we train for and the Indochina War we will have to fight."[7] That concern, as I know from personal experience, was also shared by his American and French colleagues at that period. But by the time the Second Indochina War reached such proportions as to make itself felt on the Vietnamese military, it already had been going on for a considerable while.

Much has been said in the West in recent years about guerrilla warfare that has no application whatever to the South Vietnamese situation—and that particularly applies to the British experience in Malaya.

What is being faced in Viet-Nam is *revolutionary warfare.* In revolutionary warfare, small-war tactics are being used as the physical environment warrants, but for a political purpose and in a highly politicized environment. That is why the British "won" (after thirteen years) in Malaya and decisively "lost" in Cyprus and Palestine. In the case of Malaya (or the Mau-Mau case, for that matter) the insurgents had not truly succeeded in politicizing their civilian environment in their favor. Thus, tactics used in Malaya were not successful in Cyprus and are not, to all appearances, in South Viet-Nam, as the near-disastrous experience with the "strategic hamlets" showed. The Communist adversary, on the other hand, had made his judgment very early in the game on what particular target within the South Vietnamese body politic would yield him the highest dividends in *effective population control*—not military supremacy. And that target, as during the First Indochina War, was the village administration, since 85 per cent of the Vietnamese population lives in village units of about a thousand souls.

The following two maps clearly show what this meant to the French in the Tongking Delta in 1953, one year before the military disaster at Dien Bien Phu. Personal investigations then carried out

---

[6] *The Two Viet-Nams.*
[7] "Shaky Dyke Against Red Flood," *The Bangkok Post,* March 15, 1962.

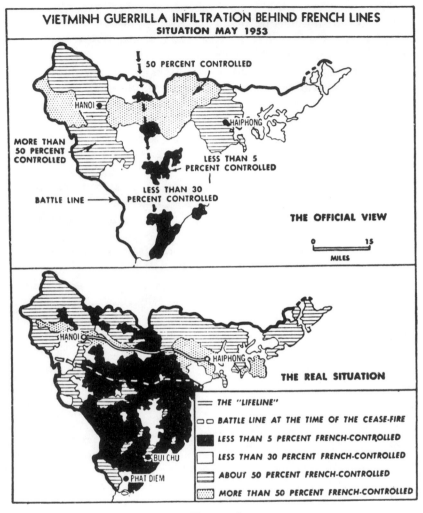

VIETMINH GUERRILLA INFILTRATION BEHIND FRENCH LINES
SITUATION MAY 1953

50 PERCENT CONTROLLED

HANOI

HAIPHONG

MORE THAN
50 PERCENT
CONTROLLED

LESS THAN 5
PERCENT CONTROLLED

BATTLE LINE

LESS THAN 30
PERCENT CONTROLLED

THE OFFICIAL VIEW

0   15
MILES

HANOI

HAIPHONG

THE REAL SITUATION

THE "LIFELINE"
BATTLE LINE AT THE TIME OF THE CEASE-FIRE
LESS THAN 5 PERCENT FRENCH-CONTROLLED
LESS THAN 30 PERCENT FRENCH-CONTROLLED
ABOUT 50 PERCENT FRENCH-CONTROLLED
MORE THAN 50 PERCENT FRENCH-CONTROLLED

BUI CHU

PHAT DIEM

FIGURE 9

showed that in May, 1953, the 180,000 French Union troops in North Viet-Nam fully controlled 1,803 villages and towns out of a total of approximately 5,780; another 1,843 were considered "unsafe," and the remaining 2,143 were under effective Communist control. In the province of Hung-Yen, located in the center of the Tongking Delta, three townships out of 511 were in French-Nationalist hands by March, 1954. Those villages had by and large been wrested from non-Communist control through a variety of tactics ranging from the assassination of the village chiefs to friendly persuasion of the villagers.

The same efficient tactics were employed four years later against South Viet-Nam, and with the same resounding success. The fact that this was not recognized in time is the great tragedy of South Viet-Nam's present plight. Yet, the signs were clearly visible for everyone who wanted to see them. Field research in South Viet-Nam in 1957 already showed disquieting evidence of a deliberate "kill-pattern" of village chiefs (see insert of Figure 10) and officials: they were not killed in random fashion—as in the case of widespread banditry or lawlessness—but in certain key provinces obviously destined to become "resistance bases." I was to report in 1958 that "guerrilla activities in South Viet-Nam during 1957 and 1958 no longer represent a last-ditch fight of dispersed sect or Communist rebel remnants. On the contrary, they have taken on a pattern of their own [including] gradual 'insulation' of the central authorities from direct contact with the grass roots."[8]

That this view was far from being accepted is shown by many statements made then and later by many experts in Vietnamese affairs. Professor Wesley Fishel, an American former senior civilian adviser to the late President Diem, averred in August, 1958, that South Viet-Nam "can be classed as one of the most stable and peaceful countries of Asia today." Another adviser, Wolf Ladejinsky, dismissed the insurgent effort as being the work of "local Viet-Minh agents in remote areas."[9] A highly reputable British observer, Mr. P. J. Honey, stated as late as 1963 that "by 1959 . . . President Diem had consolidated his position and effectively

---

[8] "South Viet-Nam's Internal Problems," reprinted here in Chapter 13.
[9] "Vietnam: The First Five Years," *The Reporter*, December 24, 1959.

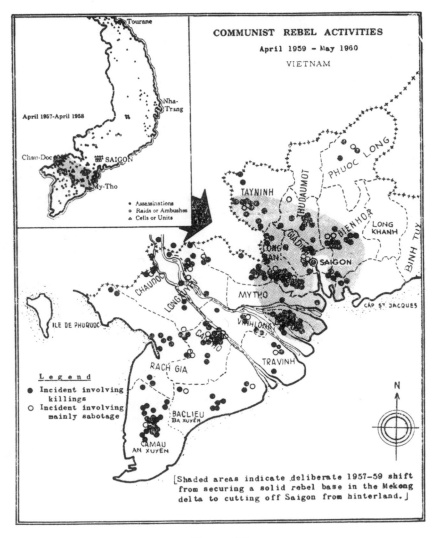

COMMUNIST REBEL ACTIVITIES

April 1959 – May 1960

VIETNAM

April 1957-April 1958

• Assassinations
□ Raids or Ambushes
△ Cells or Units

Legend
● Incident involving killings
○ Incident involving mainly sabotage

[Shaded areas indicate deliberate 1957–59 shift from securing a solid rebel base in the Mekong delta to cutting off Saigon from hinterland.]

FIGURE 10

silenced most of the opposition to his regime."[10] What had indeed been silenced was what could have become the "loyal opposition" in Viet-Nam; the Communist cadres on the other hand, were playing havoc with the local administration. A few figures will give an idea of what is meant. During the year 1957, a total of 472 small officials were killed by the Communists, according to a statement made by President Diem himself. That figure about doubled during 1958–59, and, according to a conservative American source, "since the middle of January [1960], terrorists led by Communists have been killing on the average fifteen government officials of South Viet-Nam each week."[11] On May 25, 1961, the late President Kennedy, in an address to both Houses of Congress, stated that the Communists (Viet-Cong) in South Viet-Nam had killed "4,000 civil officers" during the previous year, or more than ten a day.

In other words, by the time the VC became an open military challenge to the South Vietnamese regime and its American advisers, they had (contrary to what the CTs had been able to do in Malaya) literally taken over effective control of much of the South Vietnamese hinterland from the legal government. This was also confirmed by a former U.S. government adviser in Viet-Nam, Professor Robert Scigliano, who stated that by late 1962, "the Communists had in fact extended their influence, in varying degrees, to about 80 per cent of the Vietnamese countryside."[12] It is, therefore, highly immaterial to attempt to trace back Communist intentions at subverting South Viet-Nam to a particular meeting of the North Vietnamese Communist Party Central Committee in May, 1959, or to a particular resolution of the same party's Third National Congress, held in Hanoi in September, 1960. Long before those dates the Second Indochina War had assumed its basic pattern, and those misguided Western readers of Mao Tse-tung who may still be seeking to interpret events in Viet-Nam according to a supposedly unswerving adherence to Mao's three steps, appear to forget that revolutionary wars can be lost

[10] *Communism in North Vietnam* (Cambridge, Mass.: The MIT Press, 1963), p. 67.
[11] Peter Martin, "Where Reds are Trying to Grab Another Country," *U.S. News and World Report*, May 2, 1960.
[12] "Vietnam: A Country at War," *Asian Survey*, January, 1963.

without the insurgent resorting to mobile warfare with large units: Cyprus and Algeria are recent examples. Again, by applying civilian rather than unrealistic military standards of effective control—such as in the field of taxation—the present situation in South Viet-Nam appears to show striking parallels to the situation which prevailed in the Tongking Delta under French aegis in 1953. A map prepared by the U.S. AID Mission in Saigon to cover the period between March 23 and May 15, 1964—that is, *before* the outbreak of Buddhist discontent—clearly shows that the Communists had been able to establish a highly-organized tax-collection system in South Viet-Nam as well. (See Figure 6.)

In the face of that kind of generalized threat, the actual military threat was comparatively secondary, despite its more spectacular and newsworthy aspects. Here again, as ten years earlier, the military setbacks assumed a certain gravity only because they occurred against a background of political disintegration. Dien Bien Phu, as a military setback, involved only 4 per cent of the French battle force and the equipment lost was replaced by U.S. aid deliveries even before the battle was over. But what made Dien Bien Phu the disaster it became was that the Vietnamese civil administration was then, as now, on the verge of countrywide collapse.

But even so, it is unlikely that South Viet-Nam's armed forces could, over a long period of time, sustain the battle casualties they suffered during 1963 and 1964, which were well over 1,000 a month, and which reached, during September 1964, 3,240, as against 1,740 Communist casualties.[13] At such a level of attrition, the 50,000 new recruits that were to be raised for the ARVN under a new plan developed by Secretary of Defense McNamara in March, 1964, would hardly permit the replacement of losses suffered, and only with human material that surely would be less efficient than the army regulars lost previously. And since at least 5 million South Vietnamese are, according to official figures, under more or less permanent Communist control (and thus are hardly likely to respond to mobilization orders), South Viet-Nam cannot even count on that last-ditch resource of almost any Asian country engaged in war: unlimited human supplies. Communist North Viet-Nam, with a population of 18 million as against the South's

<hr>

[13] U.S. Military Assistance Command—Viet-Nam, *The Observer*, October 11, 1964. Government losses rose to 1,595 a week in mid-October, 1964.

14.5 million, and with the additional southern population under VC control, does not, of course, face that sort of problem even in the event of a conventionalization (or "Koreanization," as some say) of the Second Indochina War. That explains why various South Vietnamese regimes have pleaded for Allied troop reinforcements on the ground, in addition to the large-scale aid in matériel which already has been provided.

But aside from the extremely serious fallacies in the field of military counterinsurgency, the major errors made in the Second Indochina War have been administrative and political. In an excellent book, which unfortunately has remained untranslated thus far, a senior French colonial official who writes under the pen name of Julien Cheverny stated as early as 1961: "The Americans forget [in Viet-Nam] that Tocqueville once said that the most critical moment comes for a bad government when it starts reforming itself." And with a prescience of admirable clarity, Cheverny noted further:

> They forget that . . . Chiang Kai-shek, Sarit Thanarat, or Ngo Dinh Diem could argue with perfect reason that their successors would hardly be better than they are—should they be overthrown— since the institutionalized [socio-political] fetters and vices would soon bring about the same defects. It is not enough to change men to change regimes. To call upon returned exiles who have regained a political virginity in their retreat; upon the least corrupt if not the most honest; and upon faceless technicians whose importance is suddenly blown up out of proportion, does not solve anything. In Korea and Viet-Nam, attempts will be made to provide the illusion of renovation that way, for some time.[14]

It is in that precise sense that those "realists" who now regret Ngo Dinh Diem's murder of November 2, 1963, and the consequent demise of his regime, argue the case for a continuing succession of "strong" South Vietnamese governments. And failing to find these, they proclaim that American support for Diem's overthrow (for that support is now clearly established),[15] was a "mistake" due in large part to misguided American idealists.[16] What

[14] Cheverny, *Eloge du Colonialisme*, p. 262.

[15] David Halberstam, "*Coup* in Saigon: A Detailed Account," in *The New York Times*, November 6, 1963.

[16] Marguerite Higgins, "Ugly Americans of Viet-Nam," in *America*, October, 1964.

those pseudo realists apparently seem to overlook is that during the last years of the Diem regime, communications between Diem and his people had completely broken down. A continuance of that regime for any greater length of time merely would have assured a general uprising of the pro-Buddhist majority of the population or, worse, a "triangular" war between rival military factions and the Viet-Cong.

Even Senator Mike Mansfield, once known as the "Godfather of Ngo Dinh Diem," acknowledged as early as February, 1963, that South Viet-Nam was "less, not more, stable than it was at the outset," and "more removed from, rather than closer to, the achievement of popularly responsible and responsive government."[17] Thus, while the assassination of Diem and his brother Nhu (another brother, Can, was later executed by firing squad) can hardly be considered a desirable way of changing South Viet-Nam's government, the demise of that regime was as fore-ordained as a Greek tragedy.

But so pervasive had been the Diem regime during its nine years in power that all its successors have suffered from its taint: the new military leaders owed their prominence to Diem, and the civil servants their jobs to their cooperation with Ngo Dinh Nhu's civil servants' organization or his secret Can-Lao party. And precisely as Cheverny had predicted, there was an understandable hesitation on the part of the United States policy-makers, once Diem had been removed, to upset matters further by a truly revolutionary purge. In the face of Viet-Cong infiltration, it was feared that such a purge could only play into the latter's hands and thus completely destroy what was left of orderly government in South Viet-Nam. The net result was piecemeal reshuffles of civilian personnel and military commanders, with changes repeating themselves over and over again as pressures mounted against officers or civil servants who displeased their local charges by being of the wrong political, religious, or regional background; or by being, on the contrary, too well-liked and thus dangerous to the men in power in Saigon.

Much has been said about the artificiality of the Buddhist disturbances of 1963–64, which led to the downfall of Diem and, to a

17 *Viet Nam and Southeast Asia*, Report to the Committee on Foreign Relations, U.S. Senate (Washington, D.C.: Government Printing Office, 1963), p. 8.

certain extent, to the fatal weakening of his second successor, Major General Nguyen Khanh. Certain observers (notably, in the United States, those of right-wing persuasion) have argued that Viet-Nam was not even a Buddhist country, and have provided statistics showing that perhaps only one-fifth of all Vietnamese are truly Buddhist, while the remainder range from animists to Confucianists to Catholics. That argument is, of course, as specious as it would be to confuse the number of churchgoers with that of nominal "Christians" in a Western country. While there may only be a relatively few organized Buddhists in Viet-Nam, all but the Catholics, the animists, and the 30,000 Muslim Chams will *react as Buddhists* if they feel that their religion is challenged. And in Viet-Nam south of the 17th parallel that represents 12.4 out of approximately 14.8 million people.

In the case also of the Vietnamese Buddhists, the myth was allowed to take hold that Viet-Nam had always been a haven of religious tolerance. That, of course, is totally inaccurate. In the earlier part of the nineteenth century, close to 100,000 Catholics had been murdered in Viet-Nam by the imperial regime, and to come to the help of the Vietnamese Catholics was in fact the pretext for the eventual Franco-Spanish intervention in Viet-Nam in 1858. The subsequent French colonial regime accorded preferred status to Catholic institutions of all kinds, including—during the First Indochina War—Catholic militia forces, which were armed first and armed better than their Buddhist counterparts. In fact, there were open complaints in North Viet-Nam in 1952 that Catholic village militia units, rather than fighting the Communist Viet-Minh, used their weapons to "plunder pagodas, demolish temples and convert by force the population."[18] The succeeding Diem regime slanted government operations further in favor of the Catholic minority. The net result was that the regimes which followed the overthrow of Diem in turn condoned extensive harassment of Catholics, including the total destruction of two Catholic villages near Da-Nang on August 24, 1964, and the sacking of a Catholic newspaper and high school in Saigon in September. In the face of threats by Father Hoang-Quynh, chairman of the Central Committee of Struggle for Catholicism, to set up

---

[18] Van-Thanh, "L'auto-défense des villages: base de la pacification du Nord Viet-Nam" in *Orient-Occident* (Paris), November, 1952, p. 19.

Catholic self-defense groups, talks were held late in 1964 in Saigon to reach an understanding between the two religious communities.

Another major South Vietnamese failing in communal relations has been that of relations between Saigon and the tribal aborigines, commonly referred to as *montagnards*. Under the French colonial regime, the tribesmen had, like their British-administered counterparts in Burma, led a life sheltered from the depredations of a too-rapid influx of lowland majority control. In North Viet-Nam, the Communist regime, for purely practical reasons, left the tribes a measure of local self-government in autonomous zones. In South Viet-Nam, on the other hand, policies were pursued which, so the tribesmen felt, would lead to their eventual extinction, or to their total absorption into the majority population at the expense of their own culture and freedom. American warnings on that score remained unheeded by the Diem regime. Hence, it became a relatively easy task for the Viet-Cong to infiltrate the mountain tribes by presenting them with an alternative policy which explicitly provided for the creation of self-governing tribal areas in South Viet-Nam.

The fact that the American Special Forces, out of sheer necessity, began to train and equip *montagnard* "Strike Forces" further accelerated the politicization process of the tribal elites. On September 20, 1964, parts of strike units belonging to the Rhade (or E'de), one of the most sophisticated tribes, rebelled and for a time took over the important mountain city of Ban Mé Thuot. While a combination of American entreaties and South Vietnamese firmness succeeded in quelling the rebellion for a time, its leaders nevertheless proclaimed a movement of the Forces Unifiées de Lutte pour la Race Opprimée (FULRO) with its own flag and with aims which, while somewhat scornful of the Viet-Cong, are essentially based on hostility towards the South Vietnamese and their American advisers. The next few months will show whether the tribesmen of South Viet-Nam will become as deadly effective in their resistance to South Viet-Nam as the Nagas were in their opposition to New Delhi. In that case, the resulting complications may further increase the already heavy burden resting upon the men in Saigon.

But the real test of South Viet-Nam's (and the United States') ability to withstand the pressures of the Second Indochina War is going to come in the political field. Yet it is precisely in that field that the whole first year after Diem's overthrow can be written off, at best as a total loss or at worst as a fatal step backwards. It was one of the United States' leading experts in the field of counter-insurgency, Major General Edward G. Lansdale, who wrote, in October 1964, about past American attempts at "engineering a great patriotic cause led by some universally loved Vietnamese of American selection," adding that "this type of puerile romance should not be attempted in real life."[19] But this was precisely what was done.

Even a casual perusal of official statements about Diem and his successors shows literally hundreds of examples of attempts to "sell" them to their own people (and to America's allies abroad) on the basis of sterling qualities that they either did not have, or had only in minute quantities. Thus, when it became obvious that the Vietnamese urban areas were seething with discontent against Diem, the standard reply was that while admittedly unpopular among the "urbanized intellectuals" Diem was extremely popular among the peasantry. The fact that over 60 per cent of the peasantry was no longer under government control apparently was ignored. For a few weeks after November, 1963, the virtues of General Duong Van Minh ("Big Minh") seemed without parallel (and later experience showed that *he*, at least, enjoyed genuine popularity), until, on January 30, 1964, he was overthrown by Major General Nguyen Khanh on the basis of allegations that Minh and his closest collaborators were tools of a French plot to deliver South Viet-Nam to the Communists. That plot, first invented by an American columnist during the dying days of the Diem regime, was later shown to be, at best, unprovable; and in October, 1964, the generals were reinstated in their ranks and senior staff positions.

Nguyen Khanh in turn was the object of a press build-up of vast proportions and endowed with a reputation for "tough-mindedness," political acumen, strong will, and strategic genius as well as grass-roots popularity that later events failed to substantiate. An attempt at ramming through, in the wake of the Tongking Gulf incidents of August, 1964, a state-of-emergency decree, and a new

[19] "Viet-Nam: Do We Understand Revolution?," in *Foreign Affairs*, October, 1964, p. 82.

South Vietnamese "charter" (the 1956 constitution having been declared invalid in November, 1963) failed in the face of renewed street rioting in the major cities. There followed several weeks of confusion, in the course of which Khanh expressed his desire to take a long "vacation," was declared to be in a state of mental exhaustion by one of his vice premiers and fell out with some of his military and civilian supporters. A short-lived military *coupette* on September 13–14, 1964, led by Brigadier Lam Van Phat and troops of the 7th Division, delivered Khanh almost completely into the hands of the younger officers to whom he owed his survival. While officially he continued to be billed as a strong man essential to any viable South Vietnamese government, it was obvious that he had passed his apex: Khanh promised to surrender power to a civilian government formed on October 31, 1964, on the basis of a new charter previously worked out within thirty days by a seventeen-man group of Vietnamese elder statesmen.

The new regime, with Phan Khac Suu, an ailing agricultural engineer who had been jailed by Diem, as president, and Tran Van Huong, a former prefect of Saigon-Cholon, as premier, exactly filled Julien Cheverny's earlier-cited formula of the returned exiles, the least corrupt, and the faceless technicians. Like its predecessors, the new regime promised a return to representative government in the unspecified future and in the meantime appealed to "national discipline." Its inauguration under the disastrous effect of a devastating bombardment by Communist mortars of the U.S. Air Force base of Bien-Hoa, twelve miles from Saigon, which destroyed or damaged thirty aircraft (the majority of which were Canberras), did not speak well for its long-term chances of survival.*

This estimate of the South Vietnamese situation, based on verifiable data rather than wishful thinking or personal opinions, has deliberately avoided taking into account such unassessable elements as rivalries between Vietnamese generals and civilian politicians, or the possible negative or positive influence of Buddhism or of the South Vietnamese trade unions. Yet, on the basis of the known and verifiable facts alone, it can be stated that the chances of a Western success in South Viet-Nam similar to that achieved by Britain in Malaya or by the United States in the Philippines are, for the time being, somewhat remote. In both

* It lasted from November 1, 1964, until January 27, 1965.

Malaya and the Philippines there was a very early recognition of the nature of the problem, and a fairly rapid build-up of economic, social, and political counterforces. In Viet-Nam, such recognition was absent, and similar steps now being taken there meet with commensurately little success.

Realization of that fact has produced (and in part with the advice of British experts from Malaya now attached to the United States Military Advisory Command in Viet-Nam) a new strategy designed to re-establish, through military means, the security conditions necessary for the various civilian reforms to become established. There is nothing basically new about that strategy. Many other specialists in that field have advocated variants of it in the past.[20] But in the past it has required a ratio of pacification forces versus insurgents that is simply not available in Viet-Nam today. In Malaya, British and Malayan forces had achieved a superiority ratio of 50 to 1; In Cyprus, British forces had achieved a 110 to 1 ratio, and in Algeria the French had reached 10 to 1. The present ratio in South Viet-Nam is 4.5 to 1; and the French ratio in the First Indochina War was an incredibly low 1.2 to 1, which (all other matters being equal) would suffice to explain France's ultimate defeat.[21]

Obviously, then, an unconditional surrender victory over the Viet-Cong—if that is what is contemplated—will sooner or later require *political* decisions in Washington, and perhaps London as well, as to how the South Vietnamese war theater is to be provided with the requisite troop ratio if South Viet-Nam's manpower and, above all, cadre reservoir, cannot provide it.

This leaves the political or military observer of the Vietnamese scene with the temptation to look for solutions that might perhaps be less costly in manpower, such as naval or air intervention against North Viet-Nam. The temptation, assuredly, is great, for North Viet-Nam is no guerrilla base but an organized state with conventional targets such as cities, industries, and railroads. But such a policy raises two questions, at least: (1) would not such a

---

[20] See, for example, David Galula, *Counterinsurgency Warfare* (New York: Frederick A. Praeger, 1964); Roger Trinquier, *Modern Warfare* (New York: Frederick A. Praeger, 1964).

[21] The figures for Malaya are based on *Handbook to Malaya and the Emergency* (Singapore: Public Relations Office, 1953); and for Cyprus on the *New Statesman*, September 18, 1964.

policy have the net effect of "unleashing" upon sorely pressed South Viet-Nam a large part of North Viet-Nam's regular combat divisions, whose deadly effectiveness needs no additional substantiation;* and (2) could such an operation be attempted without a Red Chinese counterescalation which, in turn, could bring Russia into the conflict as an albeit reluctant supporter of her Asian Communist allies? All firm answers to both questions are hardly more than wishful thinking.

However, the possibility that the United States might adopt such a course (or subvariants of it) must have been driven home to Hanoi by the incidents in the Gulf of Tongking in the summer and autumn of 1964. And the *political* use of that incipient American naval and air strength in the Far East for a diplomatic confrontation with North Viet-Nam can certainly not be excluded; for North Viet-Nam must be fully aware of her own fate in a Korean-type engagement: partial or total destruction of what she has painfully built in ten years of socialist construction, and a Communist Chinese military occupation for perhaps a decade, merely to settle down eventually on the same cease-fire line as before.

To be sure, previous diplomatic encounters with the Communists have left the United States, in particular, with the impression that the West usually gets the worst of the bargain. That, of course, may be true if the West allows itself to be maneuvered into a position where it has nothing to negotiate but its own surrender. This is not yet the case in South Viet-Nam. But there are indications that North Viet-Nam, and perhaps even Communist China, are betting on a possible internal collapse of organized government in South Viet-Nam, in which case that country may well fall into the hands of a National Liberation Front regime by default. The example of the collapse of the Chinese Nationalist regime on the mainland in the autumn of 1949 serves as a grim reminder that countries can be lost to revolutionary warfare even without having been first negotiated away at the conference table.

* *It did, apparently.*

PART VI

The Second Indochina War

Two types of warfare died in 1965–66 in Viet-Nam, in both the North and the South: Counterinsurgency was one of them, and the national war of liberation was the other. They were both killed by the sheer mass of American firepower thrown into the conflict.

It does little good to judge a war from the comfort of a study if one wishes to understand its impact upon the country in which it is fought, upon the combatants who are engaged in it, and upon the population which is its helpless victim. What makes the war in Viet-Nam in one sense curiously impersonal is that it is fought on both sides by many people who have only a dim perception of what it is all about. There are hundreds of prisoner interrogations on record to show that many of the NLF guerrillas have no concept of Vietnamese nationhood and that to them the whole war is a series of ground-level engagements fought for very personal motives: to obtain land, to chase away the foreigners. Rightness and justice (or their absence) come up more often than Marxism-Leninism.

On the anti-Communist side, the enemy is something seen furtively through pilot's goggles at high speed, a gray shadow on the infrared sniperscopes, a blip on the antipersonnel radar. In death he becomes little more than a child-size human being, and as a prisoner he resembles the thousands of peasants who surround the Westerner everywhere in the country.

On a higher plane, the whole rationale of the war becomes

logical only if one involves geopolitical doctrines of "containment" of Communist China in the explanation and reduces the effects of the war to the hard statistics whose sole claim to reality is their seeming precision. Yet even a brief glance at those figures, as will be found in Chapter 24, shows up their futility in many cases, their inaccuracy in others, and their meaninglessness most of the time.

A period of high tension is never a propitious time for a backward glance. But it becomes clear now that 1965 will, in all probability, have to be marked down as the year in which the so-called "hawks" were in control of events on both sides most of the time. If the war lingers on much longer, that year may well be looked back upon as a period of lost opportunities by all those who failed to press for acceptable alternatives before positions had hardened beyond redemption and before massive military inputs—American as well as North Vietnamese—had become commitments in their own right, requiring no further justification.

As an observer who surveys the situation from the vantage point of more than a decade of experience in the area, one cannot help but ask whether the tragic past history of Viet-Nam is not about to repeat itself—not, as is commonly believed, because Americans do not remember history or because Communists do not believe it applies to them but because, on the contrary, both antagonists have learned some of its lessons only too well.

23. The Impersonal War

October, 1965

"Bernard Fall . . . is now convinced that American air and fire-power will carry the field."

Newsweek, September 27

"They have made a desert, and have called it peace."

Tacitus, Life of Agricola

It was during one of the quieter periods of his stormy tenure as Ambassador to Viet-Nam that General Maxwell D. Taylor developed the theme that there was not *one* Viet-Nam war, but forty-four: one for each of the provinces of the country. It was a good public relations line, and it lived through at least one or two state-side TV shows before dropping out of sight. The fact remains that there are many kinds of war that are being fought in Viet-Nam, often in one and the same place—from the Dr. Strangelove missions flown by B-52 superbombers designed to carry H-weapons, to the *punji* stakes covered with human excrement planted by the Viet-Cong in the middle of a path in the hope that they will pierce a GI's boot and give him a festering wound.

But there are not forty-four wars in Viet-Nam and there never were. There are vast areas where rice-paddy-and-swamp wars are fought; other areas where ridge-running prevails, as it did in the Appalachians during the French and Indian Wars; and, finally, there are even a few areas where one can engage in the kind of jungle-fighting familiar from Late Late Show films dealing with Guadalcanal. All this gets fairly abundantly reported in the American press, particularly when it involves U.S. troops and thus allows the citation (with nickname, age, and home town) of as many men as space and local interest permit. Of course, there are also the

Reprinted, by permission, from "Vietnam Blitz: A Report on the Impersonal War," The New Republic, October 9, 1965. © 1965 by Harrison-Blaine of New Jersey, Inc.

Vietnamese, on whose territory—the hardnose term is "real estate" —the war is fought. The Vietnamese fall into two categories: the Viet-Cong (also known as VC, Victor Charlie, Charlie, or "the Congs"), and "our" Vietnamese, for whom there are no particular nicknames, except perhaps "our allies," or "the friendlies"—both terms followed by a guffaw.

As human beings, neither type of Vietnamese appears to be any longer of great importance. The VC is almost never seen close up; he leads a shadowy existence in deep forests and grottoes, displays no unit insignia even when he wears a uniform, carries no dog-tags by which to identify him, manages to bury his weapon before he is found dead on the battlefield; and pushes his uncooperativeness with our side to the point where he—contrary to more normal armies, including the North Vietnamese when they were fighting the French—constantly changes unit numbers. This · hopelessly fouls up Intelligence estimates, order-of-battle reports, and other EEI's (elements of essential information). The "off-again-on-again" Northern 325th Division may well be an example of such totally unorthodox and highly unfair camouflage tactics. For all anyone knows, only a few small segments of that ten-battalion force may have been "in-country," as one says in Saigon. As of the time I left, a few days ago, no Intelligence officer was ready to swear that the 325th as a unit had joined the battle in South Viet-Nam.

It is an old rule that to know your enemy is a good step forward to defeating him. Yet to most Americans (even those who fight them), the VC remain faceless and often nameless. There are no "Wanted" posters in Viet-Nam offering rewards for the capture of Communist leaders. There are such posters, however—now in tatters but still quite prominent—offering rewards for the capture of various non-Communist losers of Saigon military coups. This impersonality (or depersonalization) of the enemy merely reflects how this war is being fought. When one expects to destroy the opposition through massive use of firepower from afar, regardless of whether it is from aircraft, artillery, or naval turret guns, it becomes totally irrelevant to know who the leaders of the Liberation Front are, or whether a given VC unit commander is a local boy or from a North Vietnamese cadre. For all one knows, the chairman of the Liberation Front could work as a clean-up boy in a U.S. mess hall in Bien-Hoa and nobody would recognize him.

In the same sense, the "friendlies" have become irrelevant. What happens (or who happens to be in power) in Saigon has largely become unimportant. Thanks to the sheer enormity and multifariousness of the American commitment, it is now possible to just about do anything without the approval or the cooperation of the Vietnamese. A few months ago, as long as "Arvin" (shorthand for ARVN, the Army of the Republic of Viet-Nam) troops were required to mount an operation, American advisers had to plead with often reluctant local commanders. Now, if need be, a whole operation can be mounted from stem to stern without involving a single Vietnamese. The Chulai operation was typical of this: It was American-planned and executed, and the plan was kept a secret from the Vietnamese to prevent the notorious "leaks" for which Saigon is famous. American power also has become great enough to stave off just about any kind of military disaster. When a helicopter-borne outfit of the 101st Airborne was erroneously put down in the midst of a VC assembly area a few days ago, the result should, under normal circumstances, have been unmitigated disaster. During the French Indochina War that happened several times to misdropped paratroop battalions, who invariably made a futile but heroic last stand and got wiped out because there were no reserves available and, above all, insufficient airborne firepower to make the area around the cut-off unit unlivable.

Today in Viet-Nam, there is *so much* of everything available that almost any kind of military error, no matter how stupid, can be retrieved on the rebound. In the case of the recent battle near Ankhe the misdropped unit was reinforced by other helicopter outfits and progressively surrounded by a protective wall of American firepower until the enemy, unable to maintain his position, broke off contact. At Bongson, on September 24, the VC overran a government outpost, but in the "reaction" operation they allegedly lost 600 men—500 of whom were killed by American aircraft. Against that kind of slaughter, the teachings of Mao Tse-tung, superior tactics, popular support for the VC, or, conversely, poor motivation among the Arvins and patent ineptness among many of their officers, and even the "mess in Saigon" are totally irrelevant. If tomorrow morning Mickey Mouse became prime minister of

South Viet-Nam it would have precious little influence on the men of U.S. Army Task Force Alfa (in fact, a full U.S. Army corps in everything but name) or on the fighting ability of the U.S. Third Marine Division.

Much has been said about the use of B-52's in a counter-insurgency operation or, as it should properly be called, a revolutionary war. Joseph Alsop, always willing to swallow uncritically every official handout on Viet-Nam, has again assured us in a recent column that the B-52's are necessary to destroy "deeply dug-in" VC installations, thus making a few underground bunkers covered with sandbags and bamboo look like the Siegfried Line.

His words had hardly appeared in print when the Air Force switched targets on Alsop and flew three raids into the Mekong Delta, followed by several raids along the Central Viet-Nam shore. The Mekong Delta is so flat, and the water table so high, that one cannot dig a pit privy without hitting water. It is well-nigh impossible to build underground positions there. And, as official population-density maps of Viet-Nam clearly show, the delta has (with the exception of a single district out of perhaps 30) an average population density of about 250 people per square mile, with one belt of districts across the whole delta reaching the fantastic density of 1,000 *people* per square mile! With an average bomb load of 500 tons per 30-plane raid and a known bomb dispersion of about 2,000 yards by 1,000 yards for such a raid, the effects of such a bombardment on a heavily populated area can readily be guessed.

Yet this consideration, too, has become irrelevant, because it presupposes that hate or love for Saigon or the acquiescence of the Vietnamese population in its own fate is important. In the view of many of the *Realpolitiker* in Saigon and Washington, this is no longer true. Even the old-fashioned military view that a given target must be attained or destroyed before the operation can be called a success no longer holds. The B-52 raids (or "in-country" raids by smaller aircraft) do one thing regardless of whether they hit a VC installation or a totally innocent and even pro-government village—they keep the Viet-Cong on the move, day and night, in constant fear of being hit. Gone are the days of large and even comfortable jungle hospitals above ground; of the VC rest camp with warm food, clean clothes, and a good swimming hole; of the large ammunition depot and weapons repair plant with electric generators chugging away peacefully. The heavy bombers have changed all that. The VC is hunted down like an animal. His wounded die unattended. A VC combat unit returns from an operation only to find its camp area destroyed and its painfully amassed rice and ammunition reserve shattered.

And now there are research figures (for this is the most operations-researched conflict in human history) to back up the allegations of success through firepower. Before February, 1965—that is, before the United States began to use jets inside South Viet-Nam— only about 2 per cent of VC deserters cited air action as a reason for leaving their side. Since then the rate has risen to 17 per cent. Indeed, as many an informed observer in Saigon will concede, what changed the character of the Viet-Nam war was *not* the decision to bomb North Viet-Nam; *not* the decision to use American ground troops in South Viet-Nam; but the decision to wage unlimited aerial warfare inside the country at the price of literally pounding the place to bits.

There are hundreds of perfectly well-substantiated stories to the effect that this merciless bombing hurt thousands of innocent bystanders and that one of the reasons why few weapons are found in many cases is that the heaps of dead in the battle zone include many local villagers who didn't get away in time. And every observer in Viet-Nam meets several American officers who will curse loudly every time they hear a jet overhead, because it again means an invisible objective hit blindly—for an F-105 travels far too fast to see what he hits and must be guided on his target by a "FAC"— a Forward Air Controller in a spotter plane. The same goes for the incredible wastage of artillery ammunition. "In my area," said an American provincial adviser to me, "we shot a half-million dollars worth of howitzer ammunition last month on unobserved targets. Yet the whole provincial budget for information- and intelligence-gathering is $300."

In another instance known personally to me, a plantation hospital had been pilfered by the VC. When informed of that fact by a plantation official, the immediate reaction of the local command was *not* to pursue the retreating VC with troops—always a tiresome and risky affair—but to propose the laying-down of an artillery barrage on the plantation area. "I had the devil's own time dissuading them from it," said the plantation official later. "After all, we have 9,000 workers and 22,000 women and children here."

Here again, operations research comes to our rescue. Thus far, interrogations seem to show that there is no *positively* hostile association between the devastation wrought upon the countryside, and the United States or the Saigon government. In the words of one of the experts, the aerial attacks on the villages "of course cause unhappiness, no doubt on the part of the villagers, [but] do not cause them automatically to become VC's. In fact we have never met one who has become a VC as a result of this." But perhaps the answer should have read, "who has been willing to admit that he has become a VC as a result of this." Be that as it may, and punchcard stacks to the contrary, a high-level mission was sent to Viet-Nam a few days ago to investigate the effects of that massive firepower on the Vietnamese. It will probably split along service lines.*

The usual reply to all this is that Communists, too, kill civilians. They have murdered local officials (more than 400 since January, 1965), bombed the U.S. Embassy, hit a Saigon restaurant with a mine that killed and maimed more than 20 people, and so on. That is perfectly true. But their ability to do harm is immeasurably smaller than that of the other side, and there is no doubt in anyone's mind, and that includes the Intelligence specialists in Saigon, that the VC are deliberately keeping terrorism at a low level because of its psychologically adverse effects. If the VC set its mind to it, it could go on a rampage that would leave most Vietnamese urban centers a shambles (and it may yet do so if pushed back into the terrorism phase of guerrilla war as its field operations fail), but it has not thus far.

Another aspect of the progressive irrelevance of the human aspect of the Viet-Nam war is the universally callous attitude taken by almost everybody toward the crass and constant violations of the rules of war that have been taking place. The long-suffering (and far too long silent) International Red Cross finally addressed an appeal in July, 1965, to both sides, exhorting them to live up to the Red Cross and Geneva agreements; and it was hardly an accident that Secretary of State Dean Rusk chose August 12, 1965,

---

* *It was not released, but new guidelines on aerial bombing were issued. Their effect is unknown.*

the sixteenth anniversary of the Geneva Convention on War Victims, to reaffirm America's adherence to the treaty, which was fully ratified by the United States Senate. Both North and South Viet-Nam also have ratified it.

As personal questions to both American and Vietnamese unit commanders have shown (and I made a point of touching on the subject with most of them), there is only the vaguest idea among them as to what exactly *is* covered by the 1949 Convention; in the few cases where the terms "rules of war" meant anything at all, the officer concerned very often confused the rules of land warfare of The Hague with the Geneva Convention on Prisoners of War of 1929, the 1949 Convention, the Red Cross Convention, and the American Code of the Fighting Man. Several officers would argue that the VC were all "traitors" and thus could be shot out of hand, in yet another misinterpretation of the laws covering treason. But in that case, following the logic of the State Department's assertion that the North Vietnamese are "foreign aggressors," North Vietnamese regulars caught inside South Viet-Nam would have to be treated as regular POW's, as were American pilots until now if shot down over North Viet-Nam. Needless to say, no such distinction was made between North Vietnamese regulars and VC regulars, nor between both of them and the VC guerrillas: they are all being treated under the same appalling conditions. The attitude of "this isn't *our* war; it's a Vietnamese war" could hold as long as U.S. combat troops were not operating on their own and taking prisoners all by themselves. Now, this is no longer possible and the Viet-Cong are in the position of virtually bulldozing the United States into accepting responsibility for what happens to prisoners; they can shoot in reprisal American POW's whom they hold whenever America's Vietnamese ally executes VC prisoners, as just happened in Danang. Two American servicemen had to pay with their lives for that gratuitous gesture. The September 29 announcement by Hanoi that henceforth American pilots caught in the North will be treated as "war criminals" is a direct consequence of Washington's lack of foresight on the POW problem.

If total disregard of signed treaties is allowed to continue, then the Viet-Nam war will degenerate to an ignominious level of savagery far below that experienced in other guerrilla wars since World War II. During the French Indochina War neither the

Viet-Minh nor the French were exactly models of knightly behavior, but one-armed M. Durand, the Swiss IRC representative
in Saigon, could be seen visiting the camps where the French
held their POW's. And while virtually 70 per cent of all Frenchmen in Communist camps died from the brutal climate and
disease alone, only a very few ever complained of deliberate inhu-
manity. Indeed, in such savage fighting areas as the Vietnamese
Mountain Plateau, the 803rd People's Army Regiment was often
known to leave French wounded on a jungle trail, with their wounds
attended, to be picked up by their own side; and the same happened in the no-holds-barred battle of Dien Bien Phu.

The real moral problem at issue in Viet-Nam is that of torture
and needless brutality to combatants and civilians alike. The issue
has been sidestepped in the United States, or worse, simply ignored as not being an "American" problem. When the famous
newsreel was shot showing Marines burning down houses with
cigarette lighters, the reaction among officialdom in Saigon was
not so much one of distress that the incident had happened as one
of furor at reporters for seeing and reporting it. To have the Secretary of the Navy try to explain the act by dubbing the village
of Camne a "facility developed by the Viet-Cong" hardly raises
the moral stature of the whole operation. Yet, since then, charges
of unnecessary brutality have again come out of Viet-Nam. On
September 11, 1965, the *Saigon Daily News*, a newspaper published entirely for the English-speaking Western community of
Viet-Nam, showed on its front page a large photograph of American servicemen standing with drawn weapons over a heap of what
the caption describes as "dead VC"—all lying face down on the
ground, *and with their hands tied behind their backs*. If, contrary
to the caption, the dead were not Viet-Cong but, instead, helpless
villagers shot by the Communists, I'd be only too happy if some
of my friends in Saigon corrected the record, or if the Pentagon
would issue a detailed denial of the event and a believable explanation of what actually happened.*

For the real problem of what such methods of warfare finally do,
to the men who practice them or who tolerate them in their sur-
roundings, will have to be faced up to by the United States, just as

---

* *The Pentagon subsequently issued a statement explaining that the caption
had been in error and that the picture showed live VC who had attempted to
escape.*

the problem of torture in Algeria finally had to be faced up to by the French: not just by their government but by every citizen, every educator, and every clergyman all the way up to the Cardinal Primate of Gaul. Even the French Army was split down the middle on the subject, with some Intelligence officers (just as some of their American counterparts in Viet-Nam now) protesting against torture on the practical grounds that it drove the enemy to a "no-surrender" attitude, while an even smaller minority protested on strictly moral grounds. The best-known case was that of Brigadier General de la Bollardière, a much-decorated combat veteran, who resigned from his command in Algeria because, in his words, he was a paratrooper and not a Gestapo torturer. The uproar in France compelled the Paris government to appoint a Commission of Safeguard to investigate the situation; and books by survivors of such tortures, such as Miss Djamila Boupacha and Henri Alleg, became known the world over.

Before I went on a napalm-bombing mission in Viet-Nam aboard a U.S. Air Force "Skyraider," I was given a full briefing on "E-and-E" (evasion and escape) procedures. I noted that among the items of the E-and-E kit there was a card with a copy of the Geneva Convention of 1929, informing the American pilot of his rights as a possible prisoner and of the obligations of the enemy toward him. It should not be impossible to provide every American serviceman in Viet-Nam (not just the pilots) with a handy résumé of *his* obligations under the existing laws and treaties toward the hapless civilian population as well as toward the enemy combatant.* And while we're at it, a half-million copies in Vietnamese could be printed up for the Arvins to read at their leisure.

There is one central factor in the Viet-Nam situation which becomes apparent in the field, although it is not yet recognized on the campuses in the United States and, to a certain extent, in Hanoi and Peking: the immense influx of American manpower and firepower, and the ruthless use of the latter, have made the South Viet-Nam war, in the *short run, militarily* "unlosable." The italicized qualifiers are of great importance—and I am sure that, as in *Newsweek* of September 27, I will be misquoted by their omission—but the core proposition is essentially correct.

* *Three weeks after this article appeared, the U.S. command in Saigon issued exactly such a card to all troops. A card for the ARVN was to be issued later.*

Early last spring, it was militarily almost feasible for the Viet-Cong to destroy, in a series of brutal frontal attacks, one or two Arvin divisions; cause the defection of thousands of dispirited South Vietnamese troops; and present the United States with the *fait accompli* of a nonexisting anti-Communist South Viet-Nam. Similar counterinsurgent nadirs have existed in other such wars: in Algeria and Cyprus, in Aden and Madagascar, in Palestine and Angola. The power of the insurgent is usually underestimated at the outset. Insurgency is at first left to the totally inadequate local police or security forces, and things go radically down-hill until the Queen's Own Fusiliers or *les Paras* appear on the scene in great numbers and are promptly backed up by jet fighters roaring overhead.

The fact that the British were soundly beaten at Khartoum by the Sudanese Mahdi and at Mafeking by the Boers of Paul Kruger did not stop them from stumbling on to victory. In the battles of Hoa-Binh and Cao-Bang in North Viet-Nam, the French lost more troops than at Dien Bien Phu two years later, but fought on. What broke at Dien Bien Phu was France's will to resist—not her ability. And there, it seems, lies the greatest difference between Viet-Nam in 1954 and Viet-Nam now; and there perhaps also lies the secret of what may yet become Peking's and Hanoi's greatest policy error with regard to Southeast Asia. In all likelihood both Asian Communist countries (and, for that matter, a great many Europeans, and notably Frenchmen) simply thought of the American effort as being, of course, somewhat larger and more modern than what the French were doing; but essentially of the same kind. Well, the truth is that the sheer magnitude of the American effort in Viet-Nam renders all such comparisons futile. The most striking example is of course the air war. Before Dien Bien Phu, the French Air Force had for *all* of Indochina (i.e., Cambodia, Laos, and North and South Viet-Nam) a total of 112 fighters and 68 bombers. On September 24, 1965, the United States flew 167 bombers against North Vietnamese targets alone, dropping 235 tons of bombs and *simultaneously* flew 317 bomber sorties "in-country," dropping 270 tons of bombs. In addition, a number of B-52's slammed a Viet-Cong stronghold north of Saigon, known as the "iron triangle." In that single day, *even without the B-52 raids*, the U.S. delivered more bomb tonnage than the French Air

Force did during the whole fifty-six days of the battle of Dien Bien Phu.

Confidence in total material superiority now pervades all of the governmental machinery dealing with Viet-Nam. The whole problem has in one sense become completely controllable; the build-up now can forgo crash programs and emergency troop lifts. In Viet-Nam itself, leases and construction contracts are being let for a three-year period. From a situation full of uncertainties, Viet-Nam has become a perfectly manageable situation, whose difficulties can seemingly be quantified. It takes a known number of B-52 raids to liquidate the VC redoubt of "Zone D"; it took a known number of weed-killer flights to eliminate 3,000 acres of rubber forest near Bencat; it will take some 300,000 tons of imported rice (South Viet-Nam used to export 1.5 million tons, but that was long ago, in 1939) to keep the country from starving this year.

The one unknown quantity is the Communists. Now that the fortunes of war have turned against them, they may find it to their long-range tactical advantage to let the war die rather than to openly admit defeat at the conference table. Or they may, as they did in 1951 against France's Marshal de Lattre de Tassigny, lick their wounds for a season and revert to small-scale warfare; and simply stay alive in the hope that a Stalinist coup in the Soviet Union might bring about an American-Soviet confrontation which might provide them with the sophisticated weapons they now need to stay in business. Or they may simply conclude, on the basis of America's new-found willingness to intervene almost anywhere with troops, that "liberation war" was just another tactic that failed (just as "counterinsurgency" has failed on our side) and revert to the nuts and bolts of political agitation.

William J. Pomeroy, who fought with the Huks against the Filipino government until he was captured, has recently published a small book, *Guerrilla and Counter-Guerrilla Warfare: Liberation and Suppression in the Present Period*,[1] in which he presents an interesting left-wing view of the causes of a Communist guerrilla failure. According to him, the Huks failed because "phases of legal struggle that were still possible and the creation of a broad united front of a nationalist character were neglected in favor of a rapid build-up of Huk armed forces."

[1] New York: International Publishers, 1964.

The same may have happened to the Viet-Cong in the face of the huge American military build-up, which has largely reduced the whole war to a slugging match between two military forces, the more so as the present Communist leadership in both Hanoi and the jungles of South Viet-Nam is so quagmired in the war and in its own rigid posture as to have no political leeway whatever. It is now Washington's turn to show whether it can come up with more statesmanship than Hanoi or the VC, or whether it will fall prey to the attractiveness of its own deployed firepower. In the latter case, a prostrate South Viet-Nam, plowed under by bombers and artillery and still in the hands of a politically irrelevant regime, may become the victim of aroused social and political forces for which no aircraft carrier or eight-jet bomber can provide a ready answer in the long run.

24. The Statistics of War

July, 1965

Not only has the war in Viet-Nam caused much confusion in the minds of the public as to whence it came and where it is going, but the simple physical dimensions of the conflict are often lost sight of—assuming that they were known to begin with. In fact, it can safely be asserted that population and area statistics are often wrong by as much as one third—depending upon who is doing the quoting. Needless to say, the "fog of war" becomes almost impenetrable as soon as the more sensitive parameters of "winning" or "losing" are touched upon.

The comparative areas of the two Viet-Nams are approximately 65,000 square miles for South Viet-Nam and 62,000 miles for North Viet-Nam, although some figures for North Viet-Nam go as low as 60,000 square miles. The population of the two zones has been the subject of some wild guesses, although North Viet-Nam took a fairly thorough (the statistics are readily available) population census in 1960. In South Viet-Nam the situation has never settled down enough to permit such a mundane activity, but partial censuses in key areas permit some educated guesses. Updated to early 1965, it can be stated that North Viet-Nam has a population of 18.4 million, rising at a net rate of about 3.2 per cent per year, and South Viet-Nam a population of about 14.8 million, rising at about 3 per cent a year.

The over-all cost of American operations in Indochina since the U.S. began to aid France in 1950, has given rise to a fantastic numbers game. Those who argue that every cent given to France for economic recovery, by freeing French funds for the Indochina War, contributed to the financing of the latter, throw in the whole French share of the Marshall Plan. They thus place the 1950–54

Reprinted, by permission, from "Viet-Nam: The Statistics of War," *Viet-Report*, An Emergency News Bulletin on Southeast Asian Affairs, July, 1965.

U.S. expenditures "for Indochina" at about $4 billion, which is plain nonsense. Others fail to see the important difference between "voted," "obligated," and *actually expended* funds. In the case of the French Indochina War, much of the $785 million voted in 1953 for the 1955 Navarre Plan never left the United States, for the good reason that the July, 1954, cease-fire immediately froze (until it was later violated) the importation of new war materials. In fact, Senator Long of Louisiana argued in August, 1954, against the allocation of funds "for a war that is no longer being fought," while about $450 million worth of equipment was still "at dockside" in the United States and another $600 million (that is *more* than had been voted for fiscal year 1953!) was "in the pipeline" and had to be hastily diverted to Thailand, Formosa, Japan, and Korea. Since 1954, actual expenditures have been juggled so often through overlapping budgets, the division of funds allocated to all of "Indochina" into separate Cambodian, Laotian, and South Vietnamese items, the evacuation from Viet-Nam of surplus equipment in the early years when the South Vietnamese Army actually decreased in size, etc., that it is by now totally impossible to tell even within the nearest hundred million what exactly has been spent, the more so as exact military expenditures are classified. But a 1954–64 figure of about $2 billion is a conservative educated guess.

It must, of course, be remembered that specifically *American* units in Viet-Nam, such as the Army Aviation companies, the Air Commando units, the Special Forces, the 3rd Marine Division, and the 173rd Airborne Brigade, are paid out of the U.S. Defense budget. Their cost, and such subsidiary items as the cost of their logistical support system or the pensions of the families of the men who are killed in action, all are part of the "price" of the Second Indochina War. A rough rule-of-thumb estimate is that a combat division costs over $1 billion a year in pay and equipment—and the farther it is from home the more expensive it gets.

But aside from the cold statistics of money, there are the blood-and-flesh statistics of the war itself. Here, not only are the statistics presented highly uncertain, but an element of deliberate falsification begins to creep in—not to speak of errors in the interpretation of what all those figures actually mean, or what comparisons they suggest.

Two comparisons readily come to mind: the Korean War and the French Indochina War. On March 16, 1965, Senator Birch Bayh, in a speech on Viet-Nam, gave precise figures on the Korean War, which lasted from June, 1950, until July, 1953: "U.S. forces reached a maximum strength of 328,000 troops. Other nations, including South Korea, committed forces totaling more than 300,000, [and] 1,789,000 American servicemen served in Korea at one time or another . . . [of whom] 33,629 were killed and 103,284 wounded. "In the same Senate speech, Senator Bayh listed French forces in Viet-Nam at "over 250,000" and their losses at 19,000 killed. Both figures are far below the mark. There were two different armies in Indochina: the French Union Forces (FUF), with a 1954 strength of 278,000 men, and the Vietnamese, Cambodian, and Lao national armies and their auxiliary forces with about 250,000 armed men, for a total of 528,000 men. The FUF in turn included, like the British forces in Malaya, colonial troops; and, vice versa, Vietnamese "national" units often included French officers and specialists. Hence it is statistically almost impossible to break down casualties by exact nationality, although it is possible to give them by army of origin.

During eight years of fighting between 1946 and 1954, the FUF lost 75,867 dead and the Indochina states armies lost 18,714; the FUF also had 65,125 wounded and the Indochina states had 13,002. A comparison of casualties between Indochina and Korea shows 140,000 French casualties as against 136,000 U.S. casualties (the term "casualty" represents a total figure of dead and wounded).

Figures on casualties for the Second Indochina War are not only harder to come by, but have been so deliberately "smudged" by all concerned as to be almost worthless. Let us start with the last fairly accurate figures on South Vietnamese forces given out by the Diem regime at a time when the situation was still relatively stable, early in 1963. There were then 225,000 ARVN regulars, 100,000 Civil Guards, 90,000 local and provincial police, and 85,000 village militiamen, for a total of 500,000 men. By December, 1964, an enormous reshuffling of military "categories" had taken place, with some of the men from other units transferred to ARVN and the rest transformed, like the Communist forces, into "regional" and "local" units, for a total of 610,000 men theoretically under arms. If that figure were correct (it is not, by probably 50,000 men), then South Viet-Nam today would be among the five major military powers of the Western world and have an army *twice* as large as the wartime Republic of Korea (ROK) force. In any case, its army already is larger than the force with which the French held much of *all Indochina* (300,000 square miles) for over eight years against a Communist force three times the size of the Viet-Cong. The latter was estimated in June, 1965, at 100,000 guerrillas, of whom only one half had weapons, 45,000 regulars, and 17,000 political cadres.

South Vietnamese combat losses are now often being used to "prove" that the ARVN is fighting well. The fact is that it indeed loses a great many men but experience and contacts with Western military observers in Viet-Nam seem to show that a great many are lost when under attack in static positions rather than while seeking out the enemy. In a speech on the Senate floor on February 23, 1965, Senator Thomas Dodd provided the public with many statistics which thus far have remained ignored. According to his figures the ARVN had lost in 1961–64 a total of 17,100 dead and 10,400 missing. In the previously cited speech by Senator Bayh, whose statistics are up to date through February, 1965, he speaks of a total of 26,000 ARVN "losses." Neither figure includes the wounded, which might run at least as high—and no one mentions the touchy subject of defectors or deserters; the difference between the terms being that a "defector" joins the other side while a "deserter" often simply goes home, if he can. In Viet-Nam, on the ARVN side, men desert rather than defect. Many of the above-mentioned "missing" fall into that category, except that their number is greatly understated. According to the very conservative and pro-American Australian journalist Denis Warner, a total of 34,000 ARVN troops deserted in 1964 alone.[1]

According to the equally conservative Senator Dodd, a total of 17,000 Viet-Cong defected to the ARVN side from February, 1963, to the end of 1964. Since, according to official South Vietnamese figures, a total of 12,067 Viet-Cong defected during the February, 1963–February, 1964, period,[2] that leaves a total of about 5,000 Viet-Cong defectors for 1964—or about six times less than

---

[1] *The Washington Post*, April 3, 1965.
[2] *Saigon Post*, February 26, 1964.

the ARVN seems to have suffered. As indicators of combat morale, those figures speak for themselves.

With the quickening of the tempo of the war in 1965, ARVN losses climbed astronomically. Total casualties stayed at over 3,000 a month (in fact, 4,140 in February and 3,855 in May) for what could well become a 50,000-men-per-year rate, or far above the French, American, or ROK rate in the Indochina or Korean wars.

On the Viet-Cong side, exact casualty figures are hard to estimate, since the Liberation Front forces make it a point to carry their dead and wounded from the battlefield as often as possible. Furthermore, the use of jet aircraft and of such area-destruction weapons as jellied gasoline (napalm) makes it difficult to tell whether the casualties caused are actually enemy combatants or hapless civilians. Officially, the U.S. Military Advisory Command— Viet-Nam claimed 23,500 "confirmed killed" (7,500 of whom by combat aircraft) in 1963 and 19,000 in 1964; but the Pentagon claimed a total "kill rate" of 75,000 for the 1961–64 period, updated to 85,000 by March (Senator Bayh) and 89,000 by April, 1965 (Secretary McNamara). As a rule of thumb it can be estimated that there were at least as many wounded as killed; and, in addition, the ARVN claims to have captured about 15,000 Viet-Cong in combat. Including the over 6,000 Viet-Cong casualties suffered in April and May, 1965, this brings the total number of "military" Viet-Cong casualties to about 190,000. There appears to be, on the surface, a contradiction between such huge casualty claims and the until recently very modest strength (even by official figures) of the Viet-Cong's military establishment. The inescapable conclusion seems to be that the "military" casualties claimed are either vastly inflated or must include a great number of innocent civilian bystanders. Both interpretations are equally true.

On July 30, 1962, long before the war reached its accute stage, Agence France-Presse in Saigon issued an extremely detailed statistical report on civilian and military casualties on both sides. According to the data provided by the Diem regime for the period from January, 1957, to June, 1962, total civilian and military losses on the government side had reached 35,000 and on the Viet-Cong side 79,000. Since then, civilian losses on the government side (including assassinated or kidnaped village chiefs, of whom there were 1,500 in 1964 and over 400 in January–April, 1965) have averaged over 5,000 a year. Hugh Campbell, a former Canadian member of the International Control Commission in Viet-Nam, estimated the total number of civilians killed in Viet-Nam between 1961 and 1964 at about 160,000.[3]

To all this must be added what is now a 60,000-man American force, whose own casualty list by mid-June, 1965, stood at over 425 killed in action and at about 2,200 wounded.

In all, then, what the Secretary of State has recently called a "dirty little war" may already have taken close to a half-million victims. That, if nothing else, would lift the South Viet-Nam situation out of the "little war" category.

A 1966 postscript: At the end of 1965, total Viet-Cong casualties, according to official U.S. sources, stood as follows for the just-ended year: 34,000 VC killed, 11,000 surrendered and captured. There were also an estimated 25,000–40,000 infiltrators from the North.

Officially, there had been 103,000 VC's inside South Viet-Nam on January 1, 1965, to which can be added the high infiltration figure of 40,000, for a total of 143,000 VC's on January 1, 1966— had they not suffered any casualties. Yet they did suffer at least 45,000 casualties in dead and prisoners; and by an accepted rule of thumb of warfare, they must also have suffered, at the very least, one permanently incapacitated wounded for every dead. Thus the cumulative total would be at least 79,000 casualties.

Hence, the theoretical combat strength of the Viet-Cong on January 1, 1966, should have been 143,000 minus 79,000—that is, 64,000. Yet, again according to official U.S. reports, total VC strength at that date was 237,000. In other words, the Viet-Cong in 1965 had recruited 173,000 (237,000 minus 64,000) inside South Viet-Nam. It has been stated that terror played a great role in recruiting that considerable force. How 64,000 men could force 173,000 to join them has never been explained; and it becomes even more interesting when one notes that on the Government of South Viet-Nam side, 600,000 troops were unable to prevent the desertion of 93,000 men during the same period.

[3] *Buffalo Evening News*, January 30, 1965.

25. The Year of the Hawks

December, 1965

According to the Chinese calendar, which is used also in Viet-Nam, 1965 was the Year of the Snake. But for all that was done to bring the Vietnamese problem nearer to a viable solution, it might as well have been called the Year of the Hawks. And it may well later become known as the Year of the Missed Opportunities.

On both sides political lines hardened as casualty lists lengthened and earlier predictions of rapid success proved false. What has happened in recent weeks between Pleime and Iadrang is as far from Secretary of Defense McNamara's view of October, 1963, that America's military tasks in Viet-Nam "can be completed by the end of 1965" as it is from Peking's view that the United States is a "paper tiger." The widening of the war also has brought out into the open an increasing polarization of viewpoints, with the moderates losing ground on both sides of the fence. The recently admitted failure on the part of Washington to follow up on certain North Vietnamese overtures for further discussions—they were not more than that and cannot by any stretch of the imagination be called "peace proposals"—offers an interesting example, and what is known about them should be once more clearly stated for the record.

By mid-1964, the situation in South Viet-Nam had clearly taken a turn for the worse. In April, Communist forces were estimated at forty-five regular battalions. An American helicopter carrier had been sunk by saboteurs in Saigon Harbor in May. On June 23, General Maxwell Taylor had taken over as Ambassador to attempt to stem the tide, but at the beginning of July three Special Forces camps had been severely attacked. South Vietnamese morale was low and the regime of General Nguyen Khanh was obviously unable to rally the Vietnamese people.

Reprinted, by permission, from *The New York Times Magazine*, December 12, 1965. © 1965 by The New York Times Company.

On the other hand, it became obvious that the United States was in the process of committing itself to a large-scale operation in Viet-Nam, as aircraft and troops began to stream into the little country. Then came a naval incident on August 2 whose true circumstances will have to await the judgment of a later-day historian—or one of those "leaks" on which the Washington press corps thrives. It seems that two United States Navy destroyers were at one point not far from two small North Vietnamese islands undergoing an attack by South Vietnamese naval craft, and were chased by North Vietnamese patrol torpedo boats. The United States craft repelled two attacks and sank at least two attackers. President Johnson ordered a series of severe reprisal raids against North Vietnamese shore installations, which left them aflame and smoking; and Congress voted, on August 7, a resolution which left no doubt in anyone's mind as to American intentions.

At about this time, Hanoi made its overtures for contact with the United States via Burma and U.N. Secretary General U Thant. It remains to be established (and U.N. sources have thus far kept a discreet silence on the subject) whether the move began before the American reprisal raids, or afterward. Either way, its timing is most interesting.

If it had begun prior to the reprisal raids and was not interrupted by them, then Hanoi seems to have been sufficiently interested in negotiations not to let American reprisals stand in the way. If, on the other hand, the initial contacts took place after the raids, then the North Vietnamese must have been willing to accept the risk of appearing intimidated. In other words, no matter when the actual contacts took place, Hanoi was certainly not at a clear advantage.

How extensive the possibilities for fruitful contacts were then can only be guessed at, but they receive an added dimension when it is remembered that at the very same time a high-powered North Vietnamese delegation arrived in Paris. It was, in fact, the highest-level mission since Ho Chi Minh himself had come to France in 1946 to negotiate independence within the French Union. Its head was one of Ho's most trusted associates, seventy-year-old Dr. Pham Ngoc Thach. A South Vietnamese with an M.D. from the University of Paris, Thach in 1945–54 had been one of the senior Viet-Minh leaders in South Viet-Nam; he had moved to the North after the 1954 cease-fire to become Minister of Public Health. Thach was accompanied in his mission by the rector of Hanoi University, Dr. Ho Dac Di.

Officially, both men attended a health congress, but they stayed far longer than was necessary. And they made contacts with French officials in a way that seemed to suggest they were waiting for a signal from elsewhere.

Remarkably enough, they also contacted in France South Vietnamese refugees who were known for their strong anti-Communist views, and sought to assure them that there would be a place for them in a postwar South Vietnamese state. As a token of their good faith, they promised that the refugees could return on French travel documents, assuring them a safe exit from Viet-Nam if they did not like what they found. But those commitments were subject to the success of the cease-fire negotiations to be held in the future. And the only signal the Pham Ngoc Thach mission ever got was apparently a telegram from Hanoi to come home.

All this was well known to observers and journalists in Europe. In the minds of many of them there was a clear correlation between the U Thant contact in Rangoon and the presence of the Hanoi mission in Paris. Had the initial contact in Rangoon proved profitable, the Thach mission would have been in an excellent position to pursue the matter at a higher level.

The argument was later raised that the middle of an American Presidential election campaign, in which policy in Viet-Nam was one of the principal issues, was perhaps not the best time to undertake delicate peace overtures. That suggestion, apparently, was conveyed by U Thant to North Viet-Nam.

But, to all appearances, Hanoi's offers lacked "sincerity"; they did not contain what Secretary of State Rusk on August 27, 1965, called "the key signal." It is not at this moment quite clear whether the key signal now would be (1) the withdrawal of North Vietnamese regulars from South Viet-Nam; (2) the acceptance of U.S. garrisons in South Viet-Nam for a given length of time; or (3) the yielding of Hanoi on one of its proposals, made in April, 1965, which included "negotiations on the basis of the program of the South Viet-Nam Liberation Front" (a catch-all that promises, among other things, a "liberal and democratic regime," "a foreign policy of peace and neutrality," preparations for "peaceful reunification of the country," and the active defense of "universal peace").

Nevertheless, when U Thant once more raised the possibility of contacts during the winter of 1964–65, after the American election, he again found Hanoi not unresponsive at first glance. But Washington still proved unconvinced. In retrospect, the explanation given on November 26, 1965, by Secretary Rusk for the repeated rejection of North Vietnamese offers of contact is not without merit: very few of the proposals made had much else in mind but saving the face of the United States—rather than saving South Viet-Nam.

An earlier,—and, for South Viet-Nam, perhaps more promising—opportunity for ending the war on acceptable terms had come immediately after the overthrow of the Diem regime. It was little understood abroad (though it was clearly reflected in the Liberation Front literature and radio of the time) how deeply the anti-Saigon cause had been wedded to the existence of an American-Diemist axis. When the United States openly turned against Diem, there was a clear air of bewilderment on the other side; and when Diem was overthrown and murdered on November 2, 1963, the Viet-Cong for a brief moment almost found itself to be a rebel without a real cause.

In some places fraternizing took place; four Hoa-Hao Buddhist battalions fighting against the Saigon regime in what had been in fact a three-cornered civil war (a fact carefully hushed up abroad) went over to the government side, where they still are. It looked for a very brief moment as if the elation at being rid of the hated Diem regime would infect the Viet-Cong just as much as the Saigonese who, freed of Madame Nhu's ban on dancing, were doing the twist all over town. But after a few timid attempts at making contact a policy of "Diemism without Diem" was evolved in Saigon. It has not changed to this day, and has thus deprived South Viet-Nam of any kind of initiative in finding an alternative to a last-ditch war.

There were two more attempts at an accommodation outside of total victory—one by the Soviet Union and another by North Viet-Nam. The Soviet intervention is noteworthy for two reasons: It was revealed by its ideological archenemy in Peking, and it came *after* the United States had further toughened its own stand by initiating around-the-clock bombing of North Viet-Nam on February 7, 1965, at the very moment when Soviet Premier Aleksei Kosygin was visiting there. According to the Chinese—and this was not denied in Moscow—on February 16, one day after his return home, Kosygin submitted to Peking and Hanoi a formal proposal to convene a new international conference on the whole Indochina question. As an extremely vicious article in Peking's *Red Flag* of November 11, put it, this "in fact was advocacy of 'unconditional negotiations' on the Viet-Nam question."

Three days later, a noted British journalist with excellent East European connections, Edward Crankshaw, reproduced in *The Observer* (London) long excerpts from a letter addressed by the Central Committee of the Chinese Communist Party to its Soviet counterpart, which further confirmed the view that the Soviet Union had attempted to bring about a settlement through yet another avenue of approach: "On February 23 [1965], disregarding the stand the [North] Vietnamese Government took against this proposal and without waiting for a reply from the Chinese Government [no doubt to Kosygin's February 16 note], you discussed with the French President [*sic*] the question of calling an international conference without prior conditions."

Ominously enough, the Chinese letter also cited some of the military steps the Russians had allegedly been willing to take in support of North Viet-Nam, and which Red China apparently aborted because of the political leverage they would have given Russia in any negotiations: "You wanted to send via China a regular army formation of 4,000 men to be stationed in Viet-Nam, without first obtaining her consent. Under the pretext of defending the territorial air of Viet-Nam you wanted to occupy and use one or two airfields in Southwestern China and to station a Soviet armed force of 500 men there."

Late in February, 1955, then, seems again to have been one of those "thresholds" on the road to the no-return point in the Viet-Nam war. It is now clear, from the record, that this was what the Secretary General of the U.N. had in mind when he told a press conference on February 24 that "the great American people, if only they knew the true facts and the background to the developments in South Viet-Nam," would view the conflict in a different light. There is also some evidence that a not totally unresponsive echo came forth from Hanoi on the following day. At the same time, however, the intensified bombardment of North Viet-Nam was beginning to pay real, if ephemeral, psychological dividends in South Viet-Nam and there was considerable pressure to give airpower its chance to bring the adversary to its knees.

This was done, concurrently with a temporary clarification of war aims, through President Johnson's Baltimore speech of April 7, followed in turn by a joint Soviet-North Vietnamese statement released on April 17 in Moscow, the gist of which was that both the North and South Vietnamese should be left to settle all outstanding problems by themselves, and that U.S. troops must leave Viet-Nam.

In view of Peking's constant drumfire of attacks against Moscow's "soft" line in the conflict, the issuance of the communiqué in Moscow constituted at least a temporary softening of Hanoi's attitude. Hanoi could not fail to realize that the American bombardment was destroying not only the whole formal communications network of the country but also many other targets which were not of a military nature. The often-voiced opinion that Hanoi does not "understand" the impact of American air-power takes either an overly dim view of North Vietnamese sophistication or, conversely, an overly modest view of American airpower. The French, thanks to their U.S.–donated air force, had destroyed every visible target in the Communist-held areas for eight long years. Hanoi knew full well that the United States could be counted upon to wreak far worse havoc than the French ever could.

There again is evidence that Hanoi not only toned down some extreme statements made in the spring by the now hard-pressed South Viet-Nam Liberation Front but that it was willing to water down its own four-point plan, particularly as far as the time limit of the departure of United States forces from Viet-Nam was concerned. (The points are [1] recognition of Vietnamese independence and immediate withdrawal of U.S. troops; [2] observance of the 1954 Geneva accords, forbidding the presence of foreign troops, pending reunification; [3] settlement of South Viet-Nam's internal affairs "in accordance" with the program of the Viet-Cong; and [4] reunification "without any foreign interference.")

In Washington, however, as this writer was personally told by one of the officials involved in the problem, the real "sticking point" of the North Vietnamese offer was that of negotiating on the basis of the Liberation Front program, and *not* the problem of American troops in Viet-Nam. Whether this was ever clearly conveyed to North Viet-Nam is not certain, but the point, in retrospect, looms large when the failure of the next North Vietnamese initiative is considered.

On May 13, the United States stopped bombing North Viet-Nam for approximately five days. As aircraft movements are classified information, it is not now possible to tell at what particular point in time the bombing ended and when it resumed—and, as will be seen, exact hours seem to have played an important role in the so-called bombing pause.

Much has been made of the bombing pause on both sides of the issue. It is argued on one hand that it would have been unthinkable for North Viet-Nam to make an overture after or during the pause because it would have been an implicit admission that the United States bombing of North Viet-Nam was indeed an effective means of driving that country to the conference table. On the other hand, there is a current of opinion which holds that the pause was simply too short for the North Vietnamese to make up their minds.

Lastly, some Administration members held the view that the North Vietnamese felt they were in the process of winning the war, bombing or not, and, therefore, would not respond to the pause. That seems to have been the conclusion which Secretary of State Rusk drew from his conversation about the subject with Soviet Foreign Minister Gromyko in Vienna, on May 15, when they met with their French and British counterparts to celebrate the tenth anniversary of the Austrian neutralization agreements. Gromyko is said to have told Rusk that day—i.e., two days after the beginning of the bombing pause—that Hanoi would not respond by one of the desired "key signals," which seems to have become the *sine qua non* condition under which unconditional discussions with North Viet-Nam would take place.

Two days later, on the last day of the bombing pause, a very senior French Foreign Office official had a rare visit from Mai Van Bo, the head of the North Vietnamese commercial mission in Paris. An urbane man in his early fifties, Mai Van Bo has become one of the main contacts between the outside world and Hanoi.

That day, he affirmed to his French counterpart that the departure of United States troops from Viet-Nam no longer was part of the preconditions to discussions. This was indeed important news, and to be quite sure that there was no misunderstanding the French official asked:

"Is this the view of your government, or is this your private position?"

The North Vietnamese diplomat's answer told more than he perhaps meant to convey:

"I have no private position."

What with the normal ponderousness of any diplomatic machine and the five-hour time difference between Paris and Washington, the news of that contact is said to have reached Washington just a few hours after the bombing pause had elapsed and United States aircraft were again pounding North Vietnamese targets.

But was the five-day pause long enough? The question is a tantalizing one. If, as Secretary Rusk was told in Vienna, the North Vietnamese simply were not interested in the pause, then five days were as good as five months, or none at all. But if the North Vietnamese *were* interested, it would appear that five days were not enough. If North Viet-Nam accepted the pause as a "signal," Hanoi, at the very least, would have had to consult Moscow, placate its own hawks, and persuade Peking to let it accept the proffered American feeler. In a far more clear-cut and vital situation— that of Soviet missiles in Cuba—involving merely the coordination of several government departments within one city, Washington took longer than that to make up its mind as to what to do next.

There is an interesting outside testimonial from a source who was unimpeachably pro-American throughout the whole period and who, in fact—as was revealed later—was the Administration's go-between with Hanoi. He is James Blair Seaborn, then the Canadian member of the three-power International Control Commission in Viet-Nam. In an interview recently published in the Canadian magazine *Maclean's*,[1] Seaborn told of his follow-up trip to Hanoi on May 31, 1965, in the course of which he saw both the North Vietnamese Foreign Minister and Pham Van Dong, the

[1] November 15, 1965.

Prime Minister. They were, in his words, "polite, courteous and tough." And Seaborn, who is still in active service as a Canadian diplomat, added that, in view of the proverbial patience of the North Vietnamese a five-day bombing pause was meaningless to them: "If it had been a five-month pause they might have attached more significance to it."

In the meantime, however, the deteriorating internal situation in South Viet-Nam led the United States to increase its commitments massively to prevent what was being widely advertised as a "Viet-Cong monsoon offensive" from overrunning large sectors of South Viet-Nam. From the American viewpoint, official statements notwithstanding, acceptance in 1964–65 of any cease-fire proposal would have surely ended in total disaster for Saigon. What kept South Viet-Nam afloat last spring—and what keeps it afloat now—is American power. No offer of "unconditional discussions" from Washington, or of concessions by Hanoi, is going to change that central fact.

Hence, while there understandably is a strong desire within the Administration for a clear show of "unity," the simple fact of the fluidity of the policy itself makes for a tremendous variety of "majority" positions. How ever-changing that majority is becomes clear if one remembers that many of the same people who now carry placards against bombing North Viet-Nam or committing American troops to the war worked hard for President Johnson's re-election last year—precisely because he had kept the lid on the Viet-Nam war.

Even within the small circle of those who are actively concerned with the Viet-Nam problem on an operating level, in Washington and in Saigon, there is by no means unity of view. Some hold that the war must retain its "Vietnamese" flavor, lest it become tagged among Afro-Asians as a "white-man's war." After all, it was barely a year ago that the State and Defense Departments jointly issued a question-and-answer pamphlet arguing that the introduction of United States combat troops in Viet-Nam "would provide ammunition for Communist propaganda."[2]

Others hold the view, expressed by Premier Nguyen Cao Ky on United States television, that "we need more American troops or allied troops, so thus to allow the Vietnamese troops and the Gov-

[2] *Viet-Nam: The Struggle for Freedom.*

ernment of Viet-Nam to reorganize the rear." That, whether General Ky knows it or not (he was a very young man, then), was the French Government's policy in Indochina in 1953–54: Use French Union troops to "break"—in Secretary of State Dulles's words—"the organized body of Communist aggression" while Vietnamese units mopped up the Viet-Minh guerrillas. How that policy fared is only too well known.

Among those who approve the central core of United States policy in Viet-Nam—that is, to "stay in"—opinions range from that of the retired Air Force Chief of Staff, General Curtis E. Le-May, who feels that the present bombing effort hits the wrong targets and comes "too little and too late," to that of the former Assistant Secretary of State for Far Eastern Affairs, Roger Hilsman, who recently testified that "the bombing of North Viet-Nam, for example, was a mistake" and that it is not Viet-Cong terrorism which drives hundreds of thousands of refugees from their homes, but "American and Vietnamese bombing and shelling."

In other words, although there is a statistically widespread approval of some sort of American action in support of some sort of a non-Communist South Viet-Nam, how much action and in support of what ultimate goal remains not too clearly defined. In fact, there is strong evidence that an evolution of some sort is right now under way, inasmuch as the sheer magnitude of the American commitment apparently permits some planners to envision a situation in which there will remain nothing to negotiate about because the Viet-Cong and its backers in Hanoi will have accepted the total implication of what is expected to be their military defeat.

It is that new set of premises that is now being described as leading to a policy of "unconditional triumph," "triumph by attrition," or a "total military solution." (These are the words of Senate majority leader Mike Mansfield, an Administration supporter.) According to some reliable observers, the will to achieve victory in the paddy fields and jungles rather than reach a compromise at the negotiating table is born out of two conclusions: that in a revolutionary war like Viet-Nam's a stalemate is harder to maintain than any other solution, and that Hanoi and Peking might rather see the Viet-Cong go down fighting, while conceding nothing, than once again diplomatically preside over the demise of a fellow-Communist movement.

Very few outsiders recall that Hanoi already has sold out the South Vietnamese Communists at least four times at the conference table: in March, 1946, when a French-Hanoi agreement recognized the existence of Ho Chi Minh's republic as a "Free State within the French Union," but left Cochinchina (South Viet-Nam proper) under French control; in September, 1946, when the modus vivendi signed by Ho in Paris again left the South Vietnamese question unsettled and the southern guerrillas to the tender mercies of the colonial power; in July, 1954, when the Viet-Minh accepted the "temporary" split of the country at the 17th parallel for two years; and in 1956, when both Hanoi and Russia (the latter as co-chairman of the 1954 Geneva conference) made hardly more than a perfunctory case for the slated reunification elections.

Hence, Hanoi—or so goes the "triumph-by-attrition" argument—might find it more palatable, both ideologically and from the standpoint of its own public opinion, to let the Viet-Cong face the music of American-Vietnamese "stability operations" rather than sell out the South Vietnamese Communists for a fifth time.

And that, surprisingly enough, may well be the opinion of Peking as well. In an 18,000-word article on September 2, 1965, Red China's Defense Minister, Marshal Lin Piao, made an extremely significant point that could hardly have been addressed to anyone else but Hanoi and the Liberation Front. In a section entitled "Adhere to the Policy of Self-Reliance," Lin Piao pointed out:

> To make a revolution and to fight a people's war and be victorious, it is imperative to adhere to the policy of self-reliance . . . and prepare to carry on the fight independently *even when all material aid from outside is cut off.* [Italics added.] If one does not operate by one's own efforts . . . but leans wholly on foreign aid—even though this be aid from Socialist countries which persist in revolution—no victory can be won, or be consolidated even if it is won.[3]

The fact that it was issued on September 2, the twentieth anniversary not only of the signature of the Japanese surrender but, in Hanoi, of the proclamation of the Democratic Republic of Viet-Nam, must have heightened the impact of the statement on the

[3] *Long Live the Victory of People's War!* (Peking: Foreign Languages Press, 1965), pp. 41–42.

North Vietnamese leadership. It also is in line with the hard-boiled policy adopted by the Communist bloc in the case of other Communist guerrilla movements which fell on hard times—in Greece, Azerbaijan, Indonesia, the Philippines, and Malaya. Reinforcing defeat, throwing good guerrilla cadres after losing ones, does not seem to be a major Sino-Soviet trait.

In that case, so goes the reasoning among some observers, a change of policy from one of "unconditional discussions" to openly "unconditional triumph" is in order, with the help of what one wit has called "a Rotterdam policy in the North and a Dominican policy in the South"—i.e., saturation bombardment of North Viet-Nam as the Luftwaffe did with Rotterdam in 1940, and saturation with ground troops in the South until the opposition simply is smothered.

On October 19, Senator Mansfield in a statement on the Senate floor strongly criticized what he called the "leaks" by "unnamed officials" who advocated what he viewed as a departure from official policy. The fact, however, is that precisely such views on the future of events in Viet-Nam have been openly entertained both by American and South Vietnamese officials ever since the rapid influx of American troops blunted the expected Viet-Cong "monsoon offensive" of last summer and the very size of the American commitment brought military victory within the realm of tactical feasibility.

In a September, 1965, television interview of great length, whose full text was distributed in Saigon by the USIS, and which received great attention in the Saigon press (but which in the United States was the object of only a brief film clipping in a newscast), Ambassador Henry Cabot Lodge described his view of how the war in Viet-Nam would end:

> I think that among the Vietnamese that I know there is a feeling that once the Viet-Cong and Hanoi have been convinced that their attempt at aggression is doomed to failure, that they will stop. They don't visualize that a Geneva-type meeting with a lot of people sitting around a table with little signs in front of them and paper coming out with seals and ribbons on it—that's not how they think it's going to happen . . . the thing is, there's going to be a silence, the way there was in the Philippines twelve years ago and the way there was in Malaya.

And that seems to be exactly the view of those who, in one form or another, have held power in South Viet-Nam since 1954. A program presented by the South Vietnamese Foreign Minister, Tran Van Do, on June 22, makes no concessions whatever as to what would happen to opposition elements inside South Viet-Nam. General Taylor, the previous American Ambassador to Saigon, stated on television in August, 1965, that the Vietnamese military "would never tolerate a [Vietnamese] Government that was caught surreptitiously or overtly negotiating with the Viet-Cong or Hanoi."

That this is indeed the view of the Vietnamese generals was made clear (again on television, which seems to have become a major policy medium) by General Ky in July, when he explained that "if Ho Chi Minh and the Communist leaders are smart enough, they will . . . stop fighting and continue in an underground fight. . . . That's why we never [will] accept a cease-fire, a so-called—you know—a peace, or this temporary peace."

In other words, the United States could conceivably find itself in the very same situation at a hypothetical conference table on Viet-Nam as the French and British did at Geneva in 1954, when South Viet-Nam refused to sign the cease-fire agreement, along with the United States. The difference, of course, would be that the United States would have a far greater leverage over South Viet-Nam than the defeated French had, and that probably no other major power would provide Saigon with much support for an intransigent position once the United States had made up its mind that the time for negotiations had come. But there cannot be any doubt that there is a growing consensus in Saigon, among both Americans and Vietnamese, that to cling to a policy of negotiation now is passé. There is solid expectation that, as on previous occasions, the alignment that will eventually take place will be in favor of the "harder" of the available policy choices.

As during the Korean War, the illusion comes to the fore that the war could be "shortened" (the word is actually being used) by all-out bombing, short of using nuclear weapons. As I have stated elsewhere, "underdevelopment carries its own kind of invulnerability," and thus the recently expressed threat that North Viet-Nam could be made to quit "or we're going to bomb them back into the Stone Age" does not carry the same weight in Hanoi that it would carry in Paris and Berlin. It suffices to read the U.S. Air Force's official history of the Korean War, when hundreds of bombers blasted a country one-third smaller than North Viet-Nam —and totally failed to stem a military transportation system which, deprived of its conventional bridges and railroads, simply returned to the "Stone Age" method of hordes of human coolies.

The same magic properties which were attached to the Manchurian "sanctuary" in the Korean War are now being attached to the Hanoi-Haiphong bomb-free zone, and by the same people. And President Johnson, with every mounting casualty list in South Viet-Nam, will be faced with increasing pressure to blast to rubble the North Vietnamese "sanctuary." If he yields—and North Viet-Nam does not—then the pressure will be for bombing the irrigation dikes, an act which might drown more than a million Vietnamese in low-lying areas; and, eventually, the United States will once more be face to face with the Red Chinese sanctuary. Whether done deliberately or under public pressure, that is "escalation."

Hanoi itself is, of course, desperately trying to zigzag through its own policy buzzsaw between the Viet-Cong—which it cannot afford to let down for a fifth time in twenty years without serious damage to its own stature and to its relations with Peking—and the thus-far moderating influence of the Soviet Union—which, however, offers no valid compensation or alternative for the sacrifices Hanoi already has made. For all Hanoi knows (and Washington piously hopes), Moscow might just write off the whole affair to serve as a lesson for the next aspiring "liberation war" leader who might decide to take counsel and support from Peking rather than from the Kremlin.

But that is by no means assured. It has now become clear from sources other than Crankshaw—the Polish anti-Chinese blast of December 2, for example—that the Russians did indeed consider the possibility of setting up bases inside Red China to help Viet-Nam. Had China accepted, the hawks today would have to advocate, as they did in Korean War days, the bombing of the Chinese sanctuary.

It is possible, of course, that Russia may yet move to set up bases in China near the North Vietnamese border. Should she lose more missile crews in North Viet-Nam than she likes, or find the eventual razing of the Hanoi-Haiphong sanctuary unacceptable, all bets are off.

In the meantime, the moderates are losing ground on both sides —and they may well include the Johnson Administration, for a vocal segment of highly influential persons now openly advocates the temptingly easy course of "victory through airpower." On both sides the hawks have beaten not only the doves but even those who merely question their infallibility, into vocal ineffectualness. And matching the unconditional triumphalism of the South Vietnamese generals, the Viet-Cong recently addressed an open letter to the American people in which it warned that "there can exist no contact and no political solution with the United States imperialists . . . as long as the South Vietnamese [Viet-Cong] armed forces and people have not yet vanquished the United States aggressors completely."

This leaves the chances of some sort of accommodation—on a basis of other than five years of all-out war and ten years of "pacification"—on shaky ground. And it offers grounds for the contentions of the out-and-out hawks that, basically, there is nothing to negotiate on either side. After all, such straightforward, no-quarter wars have been waged as recently as the 1940's. The question is simply whether the Viet-Nam conflict is that kind of war, and whether that kind of war is still possible in the nuclear age.

On both sides, however, most responsible leaders, including President Johnson and Premier Kosygin, agree that the Viet-Nam problem is, as such, negotiable. In that case, several approaches become possible:

1) Let us do away with the nonsense that there is such an animal as "unconditional discussions," let alone "unconditional negotiations." Both sides have some pretty good ideas about the shape of future contacts. The United States does not want to sit down with a co-equal Viet-Cong delegation and does not accept the Liberation Front program as the sole basis for discussion of the Viet-Nam problem. The Viet-Cong does not want to preside over its own total extermination and Hanoi does not like to negotiate to a background noise of collapsing North Vietnamese cities.

2) The kind of messy revolutionary war prevailing in Viet-Nam lends itself ideally to "multilayered" negotiations. Several recent experiences clearly show how well this approach can succeed. In

Algeria, the French negotiated with the nationalists in their own jails, such as Ben Bella, the Liberation Front in Tunis, and the guerrillas in the field. In such a situation there are excellent chances of developing splits among the opposition and obtaining better terms. Fearful of being "negotiated out," one major guerrilla leader inside Algeria surrendered to the French; tensions developed between the leaders in Tunisia and those in jail in France, etc. The fact that three years after Algeria's independence the French Army still launches missiles and satellites from the Sahara and holds the Mers-el-Kebir naval base clearly shows that the negotiation was a great deal less than a "surrender."

In Cyprus, the British negotiated simultaneously with Archbishop Makarios, tucked away in a British prison in the Seychelles Islands, the EOKA guerrillas on Cyprus, and their foreign backers in Athens, and the Turks. I am not saying that the Cyprus outcome was a howling success: I am merely noting that, though militarily stalemated with a force of 40,000 troops against fewer than 400 Greek Cypriotes, Britain achieved a political settlement in which she obtained all the essentials she desired—and subsequent troubles were adequately handled by the U.N.

Similarly, Yemen is worthy of study. The republican regime propped up by President Nasser's Soviet tanks and jets and 50,000 Egyptian troops totally failed in its "counterinsurgency" operation against Prince Al-Badr's royalist troops, modestly supported by Saudi Arabia. With the fighting still going on, and with the help of a U.N. mission, the foreign backers got together on one level and the internal combatants on another. The negotiated outcome seems acceptable to all concerned.

In all three cases, the outside power was not compelled to withdraw prior to negotiation, or to move out rapidly thereafter and abandon its associates.

3) The United Nations, aside from Secretary General U Thant's personal attempts at mediation, has not been given a chance to play its appointed role in Viet-Nam. In response to a question from a Congressman, Assistant Secretary of State Douglas MacArthur II replied that U.N. action in Viet-Nam "would not receive necessary support among members of the Security Council or the General Assembly in the absence of agreement from the Communist side." The answer to that point is that one

would never know until one tried, and that overwhelming pressure for a Viet-Nam settlement, even if vetoed or even if only the object of a General Assembly recommendation, might well break the deadlock.

There are some timid souls (or, conversely, some ultra-Machiavellians) who feel that the U.N. might be "fatally harmed" by having to tackle the Viet-Nam problem. The U.N. and the whole world might be harmed even more grievously if the problem is allowed to fester on uncontrolledly; and, thus far, the non–U.N. attempts at settling the Viet-Nam problem have not exactly been shining examples of success. In fact, if there is one reproach to be made to the Secretary General as well as to some of the other intermediaries in the Viet-Nam situation, it is their excessive timidity. If, Clemenceau observed, war is too important a matter to be left to the generals, then perhaps peace is too important a matter to be left to the diplomats.

4) Within Viet-Nam itself, it is about time that the rules of war, whose respect by U.S. troops there was recently reinforced by a strict order from General Westmoreland, also be applied by the South Vietnamese forces. The International Red Cross should immediately be given the visitation rights and inspection powers to which it is fully entitled by treaties signed and ratified by the United States and both Vietnamese regimes.

The Red Cross has played an admirable role in the past in Indochina and in Algeria, mitigating the fate of prisoners on both sides. Recognition of the Viet-Cong Red Cross and inspection of South Vietnamese camps by the IRC would serve to improve the lot of more than 50,000 prisoners held by both sides—including almost 100 Americans now missing in both South and North Viet-Nam. Prisoners can and should be exchanged, and a protecting power duly named. Such measures would serve to bring about a psychological climate in which the adversary could again be considered as a rational human being rather than the embodiment of all evil, to be exterminated at all costs.

5) All military actions in North Viet-Nam not essential to the security of American and South Vietnamese troops should be de-escalated. Even former Vice President Nixon, an ardent advocate of the use of American military power in Viet-Nam since 1953, has specifically denied that he would extend this to include nuclear

weapons. But nonnuclear air action has already—in the Korean War and in the French Indochina War—proved singularly ineffective, particularly when faced with a high density of light anti-aircraft guns. Hence, little would be lost militarily, and North Viet-Nam would have a chance to cast about for an alternate stance to the present murderous cul-de-sac in which it finds itself.

6) Inside South Viet-Nam, a solid dose of sober thinking is more than necessary. To arrive at a situation where the range of permissible political thinking is allowed to go only from a fight to the last ditch inside South Viet-Nam (the "moderates") to an all-out war with Red China (the "militants") is hardly conducive to carrying out President Johnson's discussion policies. In a sense, the Sino-Soviet split gives North Viet-Nam a far wider range of permissible thinking, since the Moscow line envisages an accommodation like that between the two Germany's while only pro-Chinese extremists would advocate in all seriousness an all-out war with the United States. Even they must be tempered by the brutal fact that Peking, while shouting a great deal, religiously abstains from getting embroiled in the war.

7) It would be ridiculous to prescribe an exact course of negotiations at this point. Determining that is precisely the purpose of the "unconditional discussions" which the President has been consistently advocating since April. The strength of the United States is so overwhelming, in Viet-Nam as everywhere else, that the United States will never be thought of as having negotiated from fear, simply because she did not fear to negotiate.

In the Sino-Vietnamese calendar, the passing year was not only the Year of the Snake but also the Year of Fire—a combination which is not propitious to new initiatives. The new year will be that of the Horse and of Water, a good combination in which the water sometimes succeeds in extinguishing the fire. It may perhaps also dampen somewhat the cries of the hawks.

26. Old War, New War

March, 1966

If one reckons America's military involvement in Viet-Nam from December 14, 1961, the day the late President Kennedy sent Viet-Nam's late President Diem a letter promising "to help the Republic of Viet-Nam to protect its people and preserve its independence," then the United States has been at war in Viet-Nam longer than it was in Korea or during World War II.

The question often arises, as in other campaigns, whether the war being fought now is more difficult than preceding ones. "You know, getting Charley [the Viet-Cong] out of those caves was harder than fighting the Japs at Saipan," a Marine officer said to me after the battle of Chulai. But he would be one of the few in the field still able to make such a comparison. And even junior officers or sergeants who were on the line in Korea are often hard to come by in Viet-Nam today.

In this respect, one fact has remained true for both the French and American commitments in Viet-Nam. The French lost 2,005 officers in Indochina (of whom 1,140 were lieutenants—the essential infantry platoon commanders and advisers), along with about 70,000 dead of other ranks. Their officer deaths finally amounted to five graduating classes of the St. Cyr military academy and represented 2.7 per cent of the total.

In 1965, 205 U.S. officers lost their lives in Viet-Nam as against 873 enlisted men, an officer death rate of 19 per cent. As early as November, 1964, long before the huge American troop build-up, General Creighton W. Abrams, Jr., the Vice Chief of Staff of the U.S. Army, indicated that Viet-Nam had absorbed "the equivalent of 4.8 divisions' worth of majors and captains, about 3.5 divisions'

Excerpted, by permission, from "And Still the Little Men of the Vietcong Keep Coming," *The New York Times Magazine*, March 6, 1966. © 1966 by The New York Times Company.

worth of lieutenants, and about three divisions' worth of master sergeants." The present cadre drain may well reflect a figure twice that indicated by General Abrams and in fact may absorb up to half of the cadres of the U.S. Army. That is exactly what the earlier war did to the French.

American involvement in Viet-Nam often prompts other questions: How did the French do in the First Indochina War? Did they experience the same frustrations—large-scale operation after large-scale operation netting only a handful of suspects, miles of nearly indestructible tunnels and mounds of rice? Did they have to pay the same price in blood for every stretch of road reopened, for every village so temporarily secured, for every enemy weapon taken? Were they plagued by unknown strains of mosquitoes, stubborn dysentery, and festering wounds? Basically, these peripheral questions, so often addressed to the "old Indochina hand," hide one question no one wants to ask: "All these things happened to the French, of course, and they lost the war, finally. Can it happen to us?"

The old Indochina hand looks at the news photographs or, in the streets of Saigon, at the young, lean, sun-tanned Americans. And suddenly he remembers, barely a decade earlier, the young, lean, sun-tanned French paratroopers with their jaunty berets, the muscular Foreign Legionnaires, the bearded North Africans. To think that, in sheer physical terms alone, such men could be defeated by pint-sized Asians seemed preposterous. Then it happened: the paratroopers and Legionnaires were defeated. Not only at Dien Bien Phu but everywhere—in the Red River Delta, in the South Vietnamese mountain plateau, on the Central Vietnamese coast. French bases were infiltrated; French airplanes were shot out of the sky by small-arms fire.

Yet, like most of the Americans, those troops were "professionals" (the American press preferred the term "mercenaries"). Their American equipment was fairly plentiful. There were airplanes, World War II vintage but sturdy; amphibious vehicles and tanks; artillery; even aircraft carriers. There were few helicopters (no one used them for combat then), but there were plenty of parachute battalions—far more than in 1966 and far more often used. Yet they lost. And the old Indochina hand, particularly if he is French, will look at the lean, young Americans and ask himself: "Can it happen to *them?*" In fact, many of the old hands go to Viet-Nam today for no other reason than to find an answer to that question.

Such was the case of the French writer Jean Lartéguy, who recently published a book on his experiences with the American troops in South Viet-Nam; its French title answers the question beautifully: *Un million de dollars le Viet* (*A Million Dollars for Every Viet-Cong*). That figure, of course, is hyperbole, but when President Johnson received the additional $12.3 billion authorization for the current fiscal year to prosecute the war in Viet-Nam, making a total of $15.8 billion for the year, the per capita expenditure for every captured or killed Viet-Cong in 1965 came to a substantial $351,111. And if one remembers that 45,000 *known* Viet-Cong dead or captured no doubt include a hefty percentage of bystanders caught in the crossfire but counted anyway, then a figure of a half-million dollars per Viet-Cong becomes plausible.

Such a dollar-and-cents approach to the cost of war may be inhuman and, by and large, misleading, but it conveys to some extent the immediate impression of enormous and irresistible power that the whole American effort in Viet-Nam makes upon the returning old-timers. . . .

It all begins when the civilian airliner from Bangkok or Hong Kong attempts a landing approach to Saigon's Tan Son Hut airport and finds itself stacked up for an hour because, below, several dozen military aircraft are in the process of landing or taking off on priority missions. The landing itself, between neat wing-to-wing rows of new combat or transport aircraft, is an eye-opener to the old hand: Each Hercules transport can carry as much payload as a small squadron of the French-copied German Junkers-52's (1931 vintage), which were a large component of the French transport fleet in Indochina until 1952; a flight of American "Huey" helicopters can airlift a whole unit into combat, with all its heavy gear following in wide-mouthed Chinook choppers; liaison helicopters are as available now as jeeps were in Europe in 1944.

As the old hand travels, he finds that Tan Son Hut is just a somewhat disorderly version (disorderly because of the civilian traffic) of the bigger and better airfields everywhere in South Viet-Nam. And that means *everywhere*—up north at Danang and Phubai, down south in the Mekong Delta at Soctrang, and inland at

Pleiku or at Ankhe, where the First Airmobile Division spreads its 453 airplanes and helicopters over a base area one-third the size of Manhattan.

By comparison, even the busiest French airfields during 1946–54 had only a couple of dozen World War II–type planes. At the height of the battle of Dien Bien Phu, in the spring of 1954, the French, who were fighting for their lives, possessed a total of 136 transport aircraft, 112 fighters, 58 bombers, 5 helicopters, and a few dozen observation planes. Of the transports, only 24 American-loaned Flying Boxcars could carry payloads of more than 2.5 tons or 20 paratroopers; of the bombers, only 8 French Navy Privateers could carry a 3-ton payload as far as the Chinese border to bomb the unending stream of Chinese and Russian supplies reaching Ho Chi Minh and his forces in their jungle hideouts. Not one French aircraft was a jet, and the French High Command lived in constant fear that a single raid by China's then-powerful force of MIG-15 jets would destroy all French airfields within its reach (many of which were, since the war was being fought in the North), and put the whole French Far Eastern Air Force out of business.

If the French High Command wanted to parachute two full battalions (1,800 men) in a given operation, it took 90 C-47 Dakotas to do the job, which meant that almost all of Indochina had to make do without air transport for the better part of a week. Usually the French also commandeered all the civilian transport planes they could find, and the resulting disruption of civilian air traffic was an excellent tip to the enemy of an impending major operation.

For example, Dien Bien Phu required 200 tons *per day* of airborne supplies to stay alive, and an overland rescue column from Laos had to be stopped simply because there were not enough planes to feed it and Dien Bien Phu simultaneously. Once the battle had been joined, the French Bomber Command had to make an agonizing decision: Would it continue to bomb the Communist supply lines in the jungle or use its meager resources to give the embattled ground troops the close-in support they were clamoring for? The answer was obvious, and an estimated 4,500 tons of supplies per month reached the enemy via the jungle trails with little hindrance.

By contrast, and within the limits of the censored figures made available, an estimated 3,000 American planes operate in the general Indochina area in 1966; of them about 1,200 are helicopters, 800 transports, and 1,000 combat craft. Again, while *all* French aircraft operated from bases inside Indochina (with the exception of one small escort carrier in the Gulf of Tongking), the United States now uses bases in Thailand, the Philippines, Okinawa, and Guam. Aircraft belonging to neutral Laos fly bombing operations along the Ho Chi Minh trail; the Seventh Fleet, with its three or four huge carriers, including the nuclear-powered "Enterprise," has by itself more combat planes than the French could muster throughout all of Indochina.

Planes in such numbers change the "quality" of the whole event. This came through clearly in a series of articles published in *Le Figaro* in August, 1965, after a visit in South Viet-Nam by General Beaufre, a former senior NATO commander who now heads the Institute of Strategic Studies in Paris. Despite his friendliness toward the United States, Beaufre spoke of the "failure" of the American air escalation because "air power, when armed with conventional bombs, does not have the force attributed to it by far too many theoreticians." He conceded that such conventional air power had proved effective in the past, but "only when thousands of planes are being committed." However, by December, the authoritative *Revue de Défense Nationale*, which often echoes high French political or military views, stated that the "Viet-Cong . . . had failed," and that the "military situation is completely reversed."

In ground warfare, it is less easy to make comparisons, as the vast panoply of American firepower unfolds from its enormously effective heavy artillery and ubiquitous armor to individual rifles firing 750 rounds a minute if necessary. With so much superlightweight communications equipment, a total loss of contact between a forward unit and its headquarters becomes almost impossible; during the French Indochina war, on the other hand, effective control of a forward unit almost ceased by the time it had left its bivouac. Today an attacked unit or post is soon under the surveillance of a reconnaissance aircraft; at night, a "flare ship" illuminates the countryside with artificial daylight.

While on patrol last summer with American or Vietnamese units in the forlorn jungles north of Kontum, I observed that at no time was our totally unimportant outfit, on a totally unimportant mission, left without the services of a "bird-dogging" surveillance aircraft and a "credit" of fighter-bomber missions available on a few minutes' notice. Artillery was zeroed in on our path of advance and withdrawal (it almost hit us, too); armor was not far behind on standby; and more infantry was on call if needed. As I trudged on with my host unit, I met a veteran of the French Indochina War, a journalist from Agence France-Presse who had attached himself that day to a U.S. cavalry troop—cavalry with tanks, needless to say.

"Just look at them," he said, admiringly. "Now *that's* the way to fight a war. Ah, ces Américains!"

A few figures can also tell a story. In 1954, the French fought a ground war over the 310,000 square miles of all four states of Indochina: the two Viet-Nams, Cambodia, and Laos. For this they had (including an 11,000-man air force and a 7,000-man navy) a total so-called French Union Force of 240,000 troops. Among these were about 80,000 indigenous soldiers serving directly in the French Army as Gurkhas serve to this day in the British Army. The rest were divided into about 90,000 mainland Frenchmen, 50,000 North and Central Africans, and 20,000 Foreign Legionnaires. . . .

In addition, there existed after 1950 progressively expanding Cambodian, Laotian, and Vietnamese national armies; in 1954 these numbered 247,000 men, of whom about 200,000 were Vietnamese. The national armies comprised regulars, auxiliaries, and poorly armed militia elements; in many cases French officers and soldiers served as cadres with them because an insufficient number of indigenous officers and specialists had been trained by the French in the past. The "friendly" forces, therefore, totaled 447,000 men. On the other side, the Viet-Minh fielded six infantry divisions and one artillery division with a total of 80,000 Main Force regulars, plus 60,000 semiregular provincial forces and 200,000 local militiamen, a total of 340,000 troops.

It has become an accepted rule of thumb that—with the requirements for protecting fixed positions, bridges, and towns (as well as the fact that Western forces use a great deal of noncombatant logistical support)—there must be 8 to 15 counterinsurgents for every guerrilla put into the field if one wishes to go from a not-losing situation to one that will produce victory by attrition.

There are many variables to the rule, depending on the amount of outside support available to both sides, the terrain and the popularity of the local regime or the competing revolutionary leaders. But as the figures clearly show, the French operated for eight years with a ridiculously low 1.5-to-1 troop ratio. And since they were fighting not only in South Viet-Nam—not one point of which is more than 130 air miles from the shore—but all over North Viet-Nam, Laos, and Cambodia as well, they also scored low in troop ratios per square mile: on the average, there were only 3 soldiers for every 2 square miles.

The picture in South Viet-Nam is entirely different now. There are, according to the recent report of Senate Majority Leader Mike Mansfield, 635,000 troops in the South Vietnamese Army. Of those, 120,000 are in the semiregular Regional Forces and 140,000 in the village Popular Forces. Another 25,000 serve with the Special Forces in what is called the Civilian Irregular Defense Groups and 50,000 in the National Police. In addition, there are in Viet-Nam more than 205,000 United States troops (not to speak of the 60,000 men with the Seventh Fleet), 21,000 South Korean troops, and, finally, 1,200 Australians and about 200 New Zealanders.

To round out the picture of troops involved in Viet-Nam, one must also include the Strategic Air Command units flying B-52's out of Guam and the U.S. Air Force planes operating out of Thailand, for which no exact figures are available. Even so, there is thus a present on-the-spot commitment of more than 900,000 friendly troops in South Viet-Nam *alone*, as against a half-million French and allied troops throughout all of Indochina in the earlier war.

The enemy, on the other hand, is far weaker than he used to be. According to Senator Mansfield, there are 230,000 Viet-Cong troops inside South Viet-Nam, of whom 73,000 are Main Force regulars (including 14,000 North Vietnamese People's Army men), and another 100,000 are local militia forces. There are also 17,000 support troops along the Ho Chi Minh trail and "approximately 40,000 political cadres" whose use as combatants is, to me at least, somewhat dubious. Be that as it may, the above figures give the

West a somewhat low tie-down ratio of about 3.7 to 1, but an impressive saturation ratio of 12 Western soldiers to the square mile.

In the training of manpower, the advantage also lies with the American forces now and their South Vietnamese allies. The French had dragged their feet in training the indigenous forces; when they transferred these responsibilities to the United States in 1955–56, there were only a handful of senior Vietnamese officers who had commanded more than a battalion in combat. Since 1955, however, hundreds of thousands of South Vietnamese have gone through American-advised training cycles and courses. . . .

By 1963, the conversion of the Vietnamese military to American methods was deemed so successful that Major General Charles J. Timmes, then in command of the Military Assistance Advisory Group, stated confidently: "The Vietnamese armed forces are as professional as you can get . . . under ideal conditions, if all this equipment is used properly and barring any political upheavals, I feel we could wrap this thing up by the end of the next dry season." Even in the event of "setbacks," he added, "we will have driven the Viet-Cong sufficiently underground by the end of next year that they will no longer be a national threat."[1]

Yet, on January 10, 1947, only twenty-two days after the French Indochina War had broken out, Vice Admiral Georges Thierry d'Argenlieu, then French High Commissioner in Indochina, had also been hopeful of early victory. "It is untrue to speak of war in Indochina," he had said. "The truth is that operations with a view of re-establishing order are being undertaken."

In Paris, Paul Coste-Floret, then Minister of Defense, had declared on May 13 that "there no longer is a military problem in Indochina" and on October 15 that "present operations" were "merely a police action." So it went for seven years. . . .

In 1966, more foreign troops than ever are engaged in the attempt to turn over the Viet-Nam "guerrilla problem" to local troops.

Tactically speaking, the present situation in Viet-Nam closely resembles that of the French in, say, 1951. By then, an influx of well-trained French troops and plentiful American equipment had saved the French from being thrown into the sea. A series of

[1] The Pacific Stars and Stripes (Tokyo), November 1, 1963.

more or less well-fortified perimeters surrounded by hundreds of forts (917 in the Red River Delta, manned by 100,000 troops) were being built around heavily populated areas in the lowlands. This dismayed American observers, who felt that the French were falling victim to yet another bout of "Maginot Line" psychosis. Yet, without the population on one's side, it seems impossible to keep installations from being blown up by raiders or saboteurs, as the Americans are now finding out.

Fernand Gigon, a Swiss observer in Viet-Nam for almost twenty years, wrote recently: "After the reign of cement imposed by the French, there now begins the reign of barbed wire imposed by the Americans. . . . Between those two worlds of foreign origin, the Viet-Cong imposes his own—that of bamboo."

With both the Americans and the French, the so-called "static positions" were meant to be a temporary expedient until more aggressive operations could be undertaken beyond the perimeters. After 1952, for example, the French undertook wide-ranging paratroop operations (transport helicopters not being available). At least four offensives, with airborne and armored "pincers," and supplemented by navy landing craft, involved more than 20,000 troops. (The largest offensive thus far undertaken by U.S. forces in Viet-Nam involved a total of 12,000 troops.) Yet in every case the enemy refused to fight except on his own terms. The French armored pincers would close on a melee of frightened peasants or the infantry would finally find a few bodies, usually stripped of all weapons and equipment. Larger and larger French units would be offered as "bait" in the hope of making the enemy stand and fight, but to little avail.

Americans have encountered similar frustration. During the past year there were more than 20,000 small-unit operations per week. Less than half of 1 per cent made enemy contact. More than 60 battalion-size operations took place, involving days of marching, fighting insects, stepping into traps, getting sniped at, drinking lukewarm water, and sleeping in wet clothes. The result: a few corpses, a few weapons, a handful of suspects. Twenty-five thousand air sorties are flown a week in Viet-Nam, often with 200 planes in a single raid. And still, as they did 12 or 15 years ago, the little men keep coming, with their awkward, sauntering gait, the mark of a lifetime of transporting heavy loads on carrying poles.

In the past four years, American or ARVN units have fallen into traps at precisely the same places French units did in 1954—traps often laid by the same Communist units, which succeed far more often than they should. The very superabundance of fire-power and air-borne transportation makes operations in many cases little more than a jumble of careless moves, with trucks bunching up at unexpected stops or with units coming to a halt even under light sniper fire because it is now habitual to call for artillery or fighter-bombers to steamroller all opposition. Airpower and fire-power may have stopped the Viet-Cong from winning the war in the summer of 1965, but they have yet to break its morale.

Here again official figures tell a story: On January 1, 1965, the Viet-Cong was estimated at 103,000 men and was known to suffer an estimated 15 per cent casualties each year. On January 1, 1966, the Viet-Cong was estimated to have lost 34,000 dead and 11,000 captured. Yet its combat strength was then estimated at 230,000. In spite of losses, the enemy had more than doubled its strength from within. It was the realization of this fact that led Senator Mansfield's study group to conclude that Communist forces escalated right along with the American troop increase during 1965.

To be sure, the United States is capable of staying in that kind of race almost indefinitely—something the French could not do. By an act of the French Parliament in 1950, the French Army could not send draftees to fight in an undeclared war, which limited the French effort to the military professionals. The financial burden of the war was also heavy. By the time the United States, in 1953, began to pay most of France's Far Eastern bills, the war had cost France over $8 billion—about twice what she had received under Marshall Plan aid at home. In the United States, even a yearly $10 billion expenditure in the Far East, though painful to the Great Society programs, is but a tiny drop in a $700 billion economy.

One last comparison—the influence of events at home on the war. Many Americans, concerned over teach-ins and other forms of opposition to U.S. official policies, point to the "collapse" of French home-front morale as a major cause of the loss of the Indo-china war. But to allege this, as General Maxwell D. Taylor did during the recent hearings before the Senate Foreign Relations Committee, is, to say the least, an oversimplification of the facts.

On the contrary, all French political parties, with the exception of the Communists, more or less went along with the government's Indochina policy until far too late. It was not civilian morale at home that placed 16,000 troops at Dien Bien Phu and allowed them to be defeated there. Noisy students on U.S. college campuses cannot be held responsible because 96,000 South Vietnamese troops left their units at one time or another this past year, and more than student demonstrators in Paris must be blamed because, in the spring of 1954, only 7,000 out of 100,000 Vietnamese draftees reported for induction (the present induction rate is just a little better). Being professionals—or mercenaries—the French regulars, the Moroccan *tirailleurs*, or the Foreign Legionnaires were as much affected by morale in France as by the weather in Paris. But when *they* were defeated on the battlefield, the French government and people lost their taste for Asian adventures, not vice versa.

If anything, the American commitment in Viet-Nam is moving toward the kind of military "unlosability" that characterized the British operations on Cyprus and the French operations in Algeria —or the American presence at Guantánamo. Once the position has been made impregnable, its transformation from a militarily acceptable liability into a political asset is a matter of governmental decision and judgment and may take a long time. Meantime, the conflict may go on unchecked, and escalate even further, as it did in the earlier Indochina war. . . .

In the present stage, it is difficult to tell where the resemblance with the French Indochina war will stop and where a distinct American pattern is likely to emerge. The technological differences, for all their magnitude and importance, are thus far more superficial than is often realized.

What has apparently remained the same is the political environment of the conflict. The French, for narrow colonial interests they were as yet unwilling to relinquish, felt that the time was not ripe for political freedom which could also turn against them. At the same time, anything less than complete freedom was resented as a sham by the majority of the population and thus lost its political effectiveness.

Twelve years later, the United States, for far broader strategic interests—the credibility of American defense of a small state, the belief in the "stoppability" of wars of national liberation—also feels that the struggle for freedom would be self-defeating if it included the right to vote freely for tyranny. The resulting compromises contribute to making Viet-Nam the incredible quagmire it really is. In the long run, the population is likely to follow the side that offers it the most freedom—so the argument goes. But if we offer it that kind of freedom *now*, the Communists are the only group sufficiently organized to take full advantage of it. And the purpose of the whole war is, precisely, to keep them out.

Here again, perhaps, the new pacification plans of the 1966 Honolulu Declaration echo an old French dilemma: how to promote real reforms while prosecuting a war and without making the government one supports look like a "puppet." The United States has staked her reputation and South Viet-Nam's survival on succeeding where the French failed. . . .

General James Gavin has recently indicated that the United States probably could afford to take up a defensive stance around secure base areas and "outwait" the Viet-Cong or Hanoi. Surely, such a tactic would be less expensive in manpower than offensive operations. But here again, the example of the French "Marshal de Lattre Line" in Tongking is worth pondering.

The French had decided to deny to Ho Chi Minh the "useful" lowland parts of North Viet-Nam in the hopes of preventing the enemy from getting supplies and replacements. In fact, the De Lattre Line of concrete bunkers, artillery batteries, airfields, and all was an extremely leaky sieve. The same can be said, in all charity, of the various American defensive perimeters in Viet-Nam today; all are easily penetrable even by Viet-Cong units carrying cumbersome 120-millimeter mortars.

Both sides in South Viet-Nam today, in a certain sense, refight an old war: the Viet-Cong and Hanoi, who do not wish again to be deprived of the spoils of war by an international conference (as they feel they were in 1954); and the United States and South Viet-Nam, to whom any new conference seems but another step toward an eventual total loss of the Indochina peninsula to Communism. . . .

Epilogue

As the Second Indochina War continues to escalate, and there is expectation of the commitment of an additional 400,000 American troops, the task of the detached observer seems to become simpler again. One by one, compromise solutions become less likely as the very size of the human and material sacrifices made on both sides becomes so great that only "victory" can justify them retroactively.

Inside Viet-Nam, the accumulated hatreds born of the hundreds of thousands of casualties—it was a senior South Vietnamese official who, in an interview with a Swiss journalist, called them *"le poids des âmes mortes"* ("the weight of the dead souls")—must also bear heavily on those who have thus far hoped that at least one narrow path to a solution of the Viet-Nam problem still lay within the reach of the South Vietnamese themselves, on both sides of the fence.

For this is still very much (at least until heavy American reinforcements have been committed) a *South* Vietnamese war. Even the most inflated American official statistics* concede that at the end of 1965 North Vietnamese components of the Viet-Cong amount to less than 10 per cent of the total enemy force, and that as of March, 1966, the Viet-Cong was still recruiting 3,500 men a month inside South Viet-Nam. And, as in the French Indochina war, the heavily armed foreign regulars fight largely the enemy's Main Force components in fairly empty jungle country, while the Vietnamese government troops must face the day-to-day deadly grind of flushing out local guerrillas from among a largely uncommitted, if not outright hostile, rural population. At that level, the high-flying arguments of "containment" or "deterrence of foreign aggression" become largely meaningless as the realities of revolutionary warfare take over, with their nonmilitary criteria of

* See Chapter 24.

343

population support and low-level socio-economic performance; here, victory goes to the side that "outadministers" the other, not to the one that outfights or outguns the other.

It is there, in the rice paddies where 80 per cent of the South Vietnamese live, that a viable South Vietnamese solution—not an American, Chinese, French, or even *Realpolitik* solution—to the problem can, and must, be found. Just as the proverbial bumblebees, defying every tenet of aerodynamics, fly (despite the smallness of their wingspan in relation to body weight and muscle-power), so viable solutions for the survival of small countries on the Sino-Soviet rim, from Finland and Austria to Nepal and Burma, have been found. And while the existence of a strong Communist Party is never a major contribution to internal comfort, the record shows that the presence of large Communist electorates in France and Italy, and of large Communist parties in Indonesia and Algeria, did not, *of itself*, guarantee a Communist takeover, even when the opposition parties—as in the cases of France and Italy—were divided among themselves, as would surely be the case in South Viet-Nam.

In the United States, where a certain enamorment with slogans sometimes tends to obscure the facts, the presence of a large Communist voting potential has automatically been equated with "coalition government," and a coalition with an equally automatic Communist takeover. As Chapter 2 has shown in graphic detail, France's weak and divided Fourth Republic eliminated all Communists from a *real* coalition regime in 1947, when there was no more of an American commitment to save France from Communism than there was to save Czechoslovakia a year later. From then on, as in Italy to this day, the Communists have retained their voting strength, but have *never* become members of the government—i.e., they have remained outside the coalition. Such coalitions in both France and Italy generally have been directed by the non-Communist parties *against* the Communists. In fact, Secretary Dean Rusk is perfectly right in saying that countries do not vote themselves into Communism voluntarily. What it takes is the *uncontested presence* of Communist armed force. That, of course, is not the case in South Viet-Nam today, where even the non-foreign anti-Communist troops outnumber their enemy by better than 3 to 1.

Furthermore, large segments of the South Vietnamese population, hitherto ignored by the kind of self-delusion whose record has been amply documented here, have a certain stake in a non-Communist state of South Viet-Nam that would, in contrast to its predecessors, maintain viable relations with its northern brother. Among these are the Hoa-Hao Buddhists (whose leader was murdered by the Communists*), who disliked the Diem regime but have no quarrel with Saigon now; the Cao-Dai Buddhists, who are in the same position; the Catholics, many of whom are refugees from North Viet-Nam; the *montagnards*, who like no lowland Vietnamese of any kind but will support a Vietnamese regime that provides them with meaningful autonomy (they might be compared with, say, the South Tyroleans in Italy or the French Canadians in Quebec); the nearly 1 million "Vietnamized" Chinese, who—if not totally alienated by economic purification measures that could be construed as being directed mainly against them—do not look kindly upon a Communist takeover. Even a superficial canvassing of these groups would provide a non-Communist Saigon coalition with a comfortable margin in any kind of fair electoral test, provided the groups were not hell-bent on their own destruction—which, it must be admitted, they have always been in the past.

But the taste for political hara-kiri and self-destructive infighting among the Vietnamese non-Communists—games in which they have unhappily been engaged for half a century and which their acquaintance with similarly bent French politics has honed to a fine edge—cannot be blamed on the Viet-Cong, on Hanoi, or on Peking any more than the instability of Latin American politics over the past century can be blamed on Fidel Castro. In other words, the *real* permanent problem in South Viet-Nam—and one that cannot and will not be solved by the presence of even a million American troops—is the reconstruction of the non-Communist Vietnamese body politic.

That this assertion is fully correct can best be confirmed by what happened in the neighboring Indochinese states of Cambodia and Laos. In Cambodia, where the traditional monarchic leader, King (later Prince) Norodom Sihanouk, led the struggle for independence from the French, the 1955 national elections super-

* See Chapter 11.

vised by the International Control Commission gave the Communists a vote of exactly 3 per cent! In neighboring Laos—where the accumulation of American errors up to 1961 roughly equals those committed in Viet-Nam*—the left-wing Pathet-Lao movement garnered in 1958 in what was universally viewed as a fair election a total of thirteen seats in a parliament of fifty-nine, and two minor cabinet posts (foreign aid and religion). The fact that this outcome was considered unacceptable (and was sabotaged) by an earlier version of today's "Hawks" still does not detract from the fact that, when faced with the choice between a broadly acceptable but uncommitted government on one side and Communism on the other, the people of the Indochinese peninsula are likely to vote for the former. But there is, of course, a vital difference to be noted in what has happened in South Viet-Nam. There, one Saigon regime after another has been allowed for more than a decade to demonstrate in full view of all its people its inability to govern with popular consent, even when not challenged by guerrillas; its unwillingness to implement reforms or make concessions of any kind except under the threat of military catastrophe; and the apparent failure of its foreign advisers to push their protégés firmly in the right direction, though proclaiming all the while that this has been done and has yielded impressive results. Communist North Viet-Nam, for all its obvious faults—and they are perhaps better known to the average Vietnamese than is believed—at least can point to its nationalist record of having defeated the colonial power. It is difficult to argue with Dien Bien Phu.

Still, the National Liberation Front of South Viet-Nam is a fact—for all its outside Communist support, technical advice, and even direction. Here also, only after a total "demythologizing" of the Viet-Cong problem† can we hope to develop more effective policies to deal with it. It would, for example, be helpful to remember that European resistance movements in World War II were not created out of whole cloth by the British Special Operations Executive in London, but were the result of *internal* pressures in the Nazi-occupied areas: the worse the pressure, the more vigorous the movement. Once the movement was under way,

* See Arthur Dommen, *Conflict in Laos* (New York: Frederick A. Praeger, 1964).
† See Lacouture, *op. cit.*

however, "foreign" support (British, American, or by exiles) certainly did not vitiate its "national" character. To cite an example from the author's own past, the fact that the French Resistance fought with British Sten guns and American explosives against fully French-equipped and French-led units of Marshal Pétain's Vichy regime did *not* detract from the popular image of the men and women of the Resistance as native "insurgents," even though Vichy proclaimed to its dying day that we were "Anglo-Saxon agents." And the Vichy French, who in all truth fought most of the time without German direction and most certainly without German equipment (let alone troop leadership), could never wash away the stain of "collaborationism" with the German occupier. The unfairness of the double standard may be deplored, but it is a hard fact.

The same goes for the truly obscure status of the NLF's leadership—a point this writer raised in *The Two Viet-Nams* in 1963. Here again, the record of the European Resistance is eloquent: *Not one* movement was led *inside* the occupied area by a well-known personality, and almost none of the leaders (Marshal Tito of Yugoslavia is the lone exception) are well known today. The first over-all leader in France, Jean Moulin—he died under Gestapo torture in 1943—was a prefect of some obscure French *département* in 1939. His successor, Georges Bidault, was an English teacher in a *lycée*. All the "nice people," the respectable pillars of society, were with Field Marshal Pétain and Vichy. And the Free French in exile were led by an obscure colonel, temporarily commissioned a brigadier general, whose unorthodox ideas about warfare would surely otherwise have led him to an early retirement—Charles de Gaulle.

Indeed, the sole valid case that one could make for the total subservience of the NLF to Hanoi must rest on the former's unswerving adherence to the latter's policies. And here the record is singularly unconvincing as one views the NLF's leadership's *three* changes of secretary generals—from a pro-Peking man to men less sympathetic to the Chinese; as one examines how statements made by the NLF get changed in transmission by Hanoi; and when one realizes that Hanoi—and Washington, apparently—stand for the strict application of the Geneva agreements of 1954, while the

Viet-Cong openly does not (in fact, the ten-point manifesto of the NLF fails even to mention them).

But even if all this could be dismissed simply as eyewash—as a temporarily successful attempt to make the outside world believe that a South Vietnamese guerrilla movement, though sentimentally committed to reunification (aren't *all* the divided states committed to it?), is nothing but an emanation from Hanoi (just as Archbishop Makarios' Cypriot EOKA movement was an emanation from Athens and was committed to reunification with Greece)—still, it would be worth while, and for the most practical reasons of political-military expediency, to deal with the Viet-Cong as an existing *South* Vietnamese reality. Comparisons are always shaky, for situations are never quite identical, but it is an established fact that the Algerian problem came nearer to a settlement when the French ceased to look for its solution in Cairo (by bombing Port Said or invading the Suez Canal zone) or in Tunisia (by strafing its border towns) and began to consider it as the specifically Algerian problem it was, no matter what its overtones of outside support were.

A more realistic appraisal of the Viet-Cong in the light of what has happened in South Viet-Nam over the past decade, and the recognition of what even Secretary Rusk, in the Fulbright hearings of February, 1966, conceded to be the "elements of civil war in this situation," would finally permit the United States to regain a measure of the political initiative which seems to have passed almost entirely into the hands of Saigon. At the very least, it would increase the division of views between Hanoi and the NLF and would permit the emergence in Saigon of those elements which still command a measure of popularity and countrywide respect. Such elements still exist, but they can do little good if the penalty for even speaking of a compromise settlement along the lines of present American policy earns them an expulsion across the 17th parallel into North Viet-Nam—if not worse.

As these pages have shown, the highly explosive tinder that eventually ignited the Second Indochina War was present long before the Communist leaders in Hanoi intervened. Hence even a total military crushing of the Viet-Cong and the wholesale destruction of North Viet-Nam are not very likely to change the basic vulnerabilities of South Vietnamese society and the lack of true popular roots of whoever (or whatever) is in power in Saigon. Stability and political conformity of sorts might be achieved, and perhaps even a modicum of physical well-being for the survivors— but the end result might well be comparable to the stability and relative economic success of the East German regime, permanently propped up by foreign occupation troops.

As has been the case in the past, the temptation is great for the concerned observer to throw in his lot with those who have always viewed Viet-Nam in the simple terms of power politics, grand strategy, or Chinese aggressiveness; or, on the other side of the ideological fence, in such equally simple terms as the American "lust for power." But both those high roads of error may well find a major war, if not a world war, at their end.

That is why it is more important than ever not to succumb to the temptation of the easy way out, no matter how difficult the trail of the truth and how heavy the burden of the record.

B. B. F.

March, 1966

Selected Bibliography of Related Writings by the Author

BOOKS

Le Viet-Minh: La République democratique du Viet-Nam. Paris: A. Colin, 1960.

Street Without Joy: Insurgency in Indochina 1946–1963. Harrisburg, Pa.: Stackpole, 1961; 4th rev. ed., 1964.

The Two Viet-Nams: A Political and Military Analysis. New York: Frederick A. Praeger, 1963; rev. ed., 1964; 2d rev. ed., 1966.

The Viet-Nam Reader: Articles and Documents on American Foreign Policy and the Viet-Nam Crisis. (Co-editor, with Marcus Raskin.) New York: Random House, 1965.

Hell in a Very Small Place: The Siege of Dien Bien Phu. New York and Philadelphia: J. B. Lippincott, 1966.

CONTRIBUTIONS TO BOOKS

"The Refugee Problem" and "The Tribesmen," in Richard W. Lindholm (ed.). *Viet-Nam: The First Five Years. An International Symposium.* East Lansing, Mich.: Michigan State University Press, 1959.

"Theory and Structure of Government" and "Foreign Relations," in David J. Steinberg *et al. Cambodia: Its People, Its Society, Its Culture.* Rev. ed.; New Haven, Conn.: Human Relations Area File Press, 1959.

"Foreign Relations," in Frank M. LeBar (ed.). *Laos: Its People, Its Society, Its Culture.* New Haven, Conn.: Human Relations Area File Press, 1960.

Note: This bibliography does not include book reviews or articles reprinted in this volume.

" 'Straight Zigzag': The Road to Socialism in North Vietnam," in A. Doak Barnett (ed.). *Communist Strategies in Asia: A Comparative Analysis of Governments and Parties.* New York: Frederick A. Praeger, 1963.

Introduction and notes, in Truong Chinh. *Primer for Revolt: The Communist Takeover in Vietnam.* New York: Frederick A. Praeger, 1963.

Profile of General Giap, in General Vo Nguyen Giap. *People's War, People's Army: The Viet Cong Insurrection Manual for Underdeveloped Countries.* New York: Frederick A. Praeger, 1963.

Introduction, in Roger Trinquier. *Modern Warfare: A French View of Counterinsurgency.* New York: Frederick A. Praeger, 1964.

"The Pathet-Lao," in Robert Scalapino (ed.). *Communist Revolution in Asia.* Englewood Cliffs, N.J.: Prentice-Hall, 1965.

RESEARCH MONOGRAPH

The Viet-Minh Regime: Government and Administration in the Democratic Republic. Ithaca, N.Y.: Department of Far Eastern Studies, Cornell University, 1954; 2d rev. ed., New York: Institute of Pacific Relations, 1956.

ARTICLES

"Indochina—The 7 Year Dilemma," *Military Review,* October, 1953.

"Indochina," *Wehr-Wissenschaftliche Rundschau* (Darmstadt), August, 1954.

"Ho Chi-Minhs Bodenreform," *Ost-Probleme* (Bonn), November 19, 1954.

"Formosa," *Wehr-Wissenschaftliche Rundschau,* December, 1954.

"Indochina Since Geneva," *Pacific Affairs,* March, 1955.

"Thailand in militärpolitischer Sicht," *Wehr-Wissenschaftliche Rundschau,* June, 1955.

"Rückblick auf Französisch-Indochina," *Atlantis* (Zurich), June, 1955.

"La Politique américaine au Viet-Nam," *Politique Etrangère* (Paris), June-July, 1955.

"Indochinas Christen," *Geopolitik* (Stuttgart), August, 1955.

"Recent Publications on Indochina," *Pacific Affairs*, March, 1956.

"Corée et Indochine: Deux programmes d'aide américaine," *Politique Etrangère*, April, 1956.

"The Labor Movement in the Communist Zone of Viet-Nam," *Monthly Labor Review*, May, 1956.

"The International Relations of Laos," *Pacific Affairs*, March, 1957.

"Vietnam's Chinese Problem," *Far Eastern Survey*, May, 1958.

"Die Rechtslage in der Demokratischen Republik Vietnam," *Osteuropa Recht* (Stuttgart), July, 1958.

"La Situation internationale du Sud-Vietnam," *Revue Française de Science Politique* (Paris), September, 1958.

"Deux ouvrages américains d'inégale importance sur le Viet-Nam et le Cambodge," *France-Asie* (Saigon-Tokyo), September, 1958.

"Communist POW Treatment in Indochina," *Military Review*, December, 1958.

"North Viet-Nam's Draft Constitution," *Pacific Affairs*, June, 1959.

"De certains problèmes des pays sous-développés," *France-Asie*, November-December, 1959.

"Die Neue Verfassung der Demokratischen Republik Vietnam," *Osteuropa Recht*, May, 1960.

"Constitution-Writing in a Communist State—The New Constitution of North Vietnam," *Howard Law Journal*, June, 1960.

"North Viet-Nam's Constitution and Government," *Pacific Affairs*, September, 1960.

"Das Ende der Kampfgruppe 100," *Wehr-Wissenschaftliche Rundschau*, November, 1960.

"Cambodia's International Position," *Current History*, March, 1961.

"The Laos Tangle," *International Journal*, Spring, 1961.

"Reappraisal in Laos," *Current History*, January, 1962.

"South-East Asia's Problems," *India Quarterly* (New Delhi), January-March, 1962.

"Power and Pressure Groups in North Vietnam," *The China Quarterly*, January-March, 1962.

"Problèmes politiques des Etats poly-ethniques en Indochine," *France-Asie*, March-April, 1962.

"Laos—Who Broke the Ceasefire?," *The New Republic*, June 18, 1962.

"Laos—Will Neutralism Work?," *The New Republic*, July 2, 1962.

"Red China's Aims in South Asia," *Current History*, September, 1962.

"Pourquoi Dien Bien Phu?," *Aux Carrefours de L'Histoire* (Paris), November, 1962.

"Vo Nguyen Giap—Man and Myth," *Marine Corps Gazette*, August, 1963.

"Guerre au Bouddha!," *Les Nouvelles Littéraires* (Paris), August 29, 1963.

"Peking Strikes South," *Current History*, September, 1963.

"North Vietnam Eating Cake of Another's War," *The Washington Post*, September 29, 1963.

"A Talk with Ho Chi Minh," *The New Republic*, October 12, 1963.

"What de Gaulle Actually Said About Viet-Nam," *The Reporter*, October 24, 1963.

"Vietnam: New Faces, More Chaos," *The Nation*, December 7, 1963.

"Our Options in Vietnam," *The Reporter*, March 12, 1964.

"Dien Bien Phu: Battle to Remember," *The New York Times Magazine*, May 3, 1964.

"The Adversary in Vietnam," *War/Peace Report*, May, 1964.

"Voici dix ans, c'était Dien Bien Phu!," *France-Amérique* (New York), May 31, 1964.

"A Grain of Rice is Worth a Drop of Blood," *The New York Times Magazine*, July 12, 1964.

"Why the French Mistrust Us," *The New York Times Magazine*, September 6, 1964.

"The John A. Lejeune Forum: Southeast Asia: A Recapitulation," *Marine Corps Gazette*, October, 1964.

"How Democracy Returned to Viet-Nam," *The Nation*, April 5, 1965.

"Theory and Practice of Counterinsurgency," *Naval War College Review*, April 8, 1965.

"How the French Got Out of Vietnam," *The New York Times Magazine*, May 2, 1965.

"The Mess: Three Views," *The Nation*, May 17, 1965.

"Vietnam—Mosaic of Peoples," *Washington Post,* May 23, 1965.
"Vietnam: European Views," *The New Republic,* August 24, 1965.
"This Isn't Munich, This Is Spain," *Ramparts,* December, 1965.
"Viet-Nam: The New Korea," *Current History,* February, 1966.

INTERVIEW

"The Truth About the War the U.S. Is Losing," *U.S. News and World Report,* September 28, 1964.

Index

Abderrhaman, Bensalem, 244–45
Abrams, Creighton W., Jr. (General), 331–32
"Agreement on the Cessation of Hostilities in Viet-Nam," 72–75, 79; see also Geneva agreements of 1954
Algeria, 8, 77, 233, 241, 244, 245, 253, 284, 291, 302, 304, 328, 341, 344, 348
Alsop, Stewart, 265
American Friends of Viet-Nam, 178
Army of the Republic of Viet-Nam (ARVN), 197, 199, 200–201, 278, 284, 297, 309–11, 337, 340; see also Vietnamese National Army

Ba Cut, 153, 154, 156, 157, 159
Bandung conference of 1955, 170
Bao-Dai (Emperor), 15–16, 20, 41, 42–43, 46 n., 47–50, 52–55, 57, 63, 65, 66–67, 74, 76–77, 145, 147, 148, 153, 155, 157, 159, 170, 182, 212, 218, 221, 258, 269
Barrows, Leland, 163
Bayh, Birch, 245, 309, 311
Beaufre, André (General), 335
Bidault, Georges, 55–56, 70, 270, 347
Binh-Xuyen sect, 63, 142, 155–58, 235; see also Buddhist sects
Blum, Léon, 22
Bonnet, Gabriel, 265
Borodin, Mikhail, 117
Buddhist sects, 7, 138, 141–59, 184, 185, 207, 217, 235; see also Binh Xuyen sect, Cao-Dai sect, Hoa-Hao sect
Buddhists, 182, 197, 198–201, 208, 209, 240, 273, 284, 286–87, 290; see also Buddhist sects
Bundy, McGeorge, 82

Burma, 17, 63, 190, 229, 231, 262, 288, 314, 315, 333, 344
Buu-Loc (Prince), 50, 51, 53–54, 56–58, 148

Cambodia, 17, 31, 34 n., 37, 41, 53, 62, 63, 64, 71, 72, 74, 122, 123, 159, 167, 229, 235, 243, 247, 258, 259–62, 263, 267, 272, 276, 304, 308, 309, 336, 337, 345
Campbell, Hugh, 312
Can-Lao Party, 286
Canada, 73, 80, 105, 214, 216 n., 276, 345
Cao-Dai sect, 70, 137, 142–48, 152, 153, 156, 157–58, 235, 241, 345; see also Buddhist sects
Carrington, Lord, 270
Catholics, 50, 57, 59, 60, 62, 76, 101, 102, 142, 153, 156, 182, 199, 200, 207, 208–9, 216, 241, 249, 273, 287–88, 345
Catholics for National Salvation, 122
Central Intelligence Agency (CIA), 195
Chaffard, Georges, 204
Chassaigne (Bishop of Saigon), 198
Chassin, Lucien-Max, 39–40, 227, 253
Cheverny, Julien, 285, 286, 290
Chiang Kai-shek, 15, 117, 233, 285
Chin Peng, 262 n.
China, 117, 118, 119, 133, 146, 190, 208, 229, 248, 262
China, Communist, 4, 7, 15, 16, 19, 20, 21, 29 n., 34, 35, 55, 61, 65, 66, 68, 70, 71, 74, 81, 82, 83, 85, 99, 104, 106, 107, 108, 114, 115, 116, 119, 122, 124, 128, 129, 130, 132–35, 137, 166, 203, 204, 214,

357

China, Communist (*Cont.*)
233, 242, 243, 246, 247, 251, 252, 254, 270, 276, 292, 293, 303, 304, 316–19, 320, 322, 323, 324, 326, 330, 334, 344, 345, 347, 349
China, Nationalist, 7, 15, 120, 123, 126, 189, 203, 233, 292
Chinese Communist Party (CCP), 117, 119, 120, 317
Chinese People's Liberation Army, 247
Chou En-lai, 55, 71, 99, 130, 133
Chu Ba The, 225
Chu Van Tan (General), 248
Churchill, Sir Winston, 69, 256, 274
Civil Irregular Defense Groups (CIDG), 195, 337
Cogny, René (General), 34
Collins, Lawton (General), 158
Cominform, 17
Comintern, 111, 117–19
Communist Party of the Soviet Union (CPSU), 124, 126, 130, 317
Confucianism, 208, 287
Cook, H. C. B., 279
Coste-Floret, Paul, 338
Coty, René, 54
Couve de Murville, Maurice, 270, 274
Crankshaw, Edward, 326
Cuba, 4, 110, 133, 200, 241, 341, 345
Cyprus, 81, 219, 253, 274, 279, 284, 291, 304, 328, 341

D'Argenlieu, Georges Thierry, 338
De la Bollardière (General), 303
De Lattre de Tassigny, Jean (Marshal), 30, 31, 305, 342
Delteil, Henri (General), 62, 72, 275
Devillers, Philippe, 8, 75, 131 n., 237
Dien Bien Phu, 6, 7, 9, 14, 30, 34–36, 38, 39, 50, 51, 55, 58, 70, 119, 148, 168, 171, 185, 218, 225, 231, 232, 233, 244, 247, 251, 253, 255, 257, 269, 279, 284, 302, 304, 305, 332, 334, 341, 346
Dodd, Thomas, 310
Dong Duong Cong San Dang, *see* Indochinese Communist Party
Donovan, William J., 17
Duclos, Jacques, 26
Dulles, John Foster, 6, 16, 31, 55–56, 71, 81, 322

Duong Van Duc, 141
Duong Van Minh (General), 198, 207, 209, 213, 289
Durbrow, Elbridge, 186 n.

Eden, Sir Anthony, 61, 71, 74, 270, 274
Eisenhower, Dwight D., 6, 9, 53 n., 69, 71, 76, 158, 236
Ely, Paul (General), 30, 39, 58
Elysée agreements of 1949, 145

Fatherland Front, 216
Fishel, Wesley, 281
Foreign Legion, 37, 332, 336, 341
France, 5–9, 11, 13–40, 43, 47, 50, 51–55, 58–59, 60–61, 63, 65, 66, 67–68, 69, 70, 74, 77, 85, 87, 89, 101, 105, 106, 108, 110, 112, 116, 118, 119, 120, 121, 123, 125, 132, 133, 134, 141, 144–47, 149, 150, 152, 153, 156, 157, 158, 159, 161, 162, 166, 168, 170–71, 174, 176, 177, 180, 185, 191, 192, 193, 194, 199, 200, 204, 206, 207, 212, 213, 214–15, 217–18, 219, 220, 223, 228, 230, 231–33, 236, 240, 243, 244, 245, 247, 249, 250, 254, 255–56, 257–58, 260, 264, 265, 269, 270, 274, 278, 279, 284, 287, 288, 289, 296, 301, 303, 304, 307, 310, 311, 314, 315, 318, 319–20, 323, 325, 326, 328, 331–45, 347–48
French Army, 13–14, 15–19, 25, 30–40, 51, 58, 70–71, 72, 76, 77, 93, 120, 144, 146, 162, 173, 225, 227, 229, 253, 259, 273, 275, 276, 278, 281, 284, 291, 303, 304, 309, 322, 328, 332, 334, 336, 340
French Communist Party (PCF), 13, 22–29, 111, 116, 120
French Expeditionary Corps (Force), *see* French Army
French Socialist Party, 25, 111, 116
French Union, 7, 16, 23, 52, 53, 54, 61, 62, 92, 94 n., 95, 147 n., 225, 232, 233, 314
French Union Forces, *see* French Army

Gaulle, Charles de, 247, 256, 261, 274, 317, 347

Gavin, James M. (General), 39, 342

Geneva agreements of 1954, 14, 16, 19, 20, 30, 39, 41, 50, 51–58, 60–62, 65, 69–83, 85, 120, 123, 124, 135, 148, 156, 169, 204, 215, 236, 237, 239, 241, 248, 251, 257–58, 269, 275–77, 300, 318, 323, 325, 347

Geneva Convention on War Victims, 301, 303

Germany, 16, 25, 69, 82, 111, 139, 206, 214, 220, 234, 241, 276, 326, 330, 333; East, 108, 215, 219, 252, 277, 349; West, 123, 178, 219, 221, 277

Gigon, Fernand, 339

Gourou, Pierre, 87

Great Britain, 8, 25, 56, 61, 71, 74, 78, 80, 111, 118, 151, 214, 219, 221, 256, 262 n., 263, 264, 270, 272, 273, 274, 279, 288, 290, 291, 304, 309, 319, 325, 328, 336, 341, 346–47

Great Viet-Nam Party (Dai-Viet), 41–42

Greece, 29, 234, 238, 324, 328, 348

Gromyko, Andrei A., 319

Guam, 335, 337

Guillain, Robert, 169

Gulf of Tongking incidents, 252, 289, 292

Haiphong, 19, 42, 44, 59, 79, 89, 102, 232, 327

Hanoi, 7, 15, 42, 44, 45, 59, 89, 97, 98, 99, 103, 105–14, 127, 133, 151, 194, 217, 232, 252, 327

Hickey, Gerald C., 192–93

Hilsman, Roger, 264 n., 322

Ho Chi Minh, 5, 7, 13, 15, 16, 19, 20, 23–24, 29, 44, 57, 60, 64, 69, 70, 71, 74, 76, 77, 81, 82, 85, 87, 97, 98, 99, 101, 105, 109, 111–13, 114, 116–20, 123, 126, 130, 135, 147, 148, 210–11, 212, 223, 236, 239, 248, 249, 257, 267, 277, 314, 323, 325, 334, 342

Ho Dac Di, 315

Ho Hue Ba, Josef-Marie, 241

Ho Phap, *see* Pham Cong Tac

Ho Viet Thang, 96, 98

Hoa-Hao sect, 70, 137, 142, 146,

Hoa-Hao sect (*Cont.*) 148–54, 157–59, 235, 316, 345; *see also* Buddhist sects

Hoang Co Binh, 44

Hoang Minh Thao (General), 248

Hoang Quynh, 48, 287

Holyoake, Keith J., 270

Honey, P. J., 281

Hong Kong, 117, 118, 214, 333

Honolulu conference of February, 1966, 137, 255, 256, 342

Hungary, 96, 97, 103, 104, 111, 134, 166

Huynh Phu So (the Mad Bonze), 149–53, 155

Huynh Tan Phat, 240, 241

India, 73, 80, 105, 107, 170, 263, 276

Indochinese Communist Party (ICP), 24, 92, 118–20, 122, 248

Indonesia, 5, 63, 75, 229, 238, 241, 324, 344

International Commission for Supervision and Control (ICSC), or International Control Commission (ICC), 73, 75, 77–81, 102, 105, 131, 216 n., 239, 276–77, 312, 320, 346; Joint Commissions (JC) of, 73, 77

International Cooperation Administration (ICA), 161, 165, 174, 177, 178

International Red Cross, 300, 302, 329

Italy, 344, 345

Jacquet, Marc, 59

Japan, 63, 87, 119, 123, 134 n., 139, 144, 150, 151, 175, 178, 190, 203, 214 n., 218, 262, 308, 323, 331

Johnson, Harold K. (General), 242

Johnson, Lyndon B., 7, 81, 269, 314, 318, 321, 326, 327, 330, 333

Johnston, Clement, 163

Kennan, George F., 6, 8, 255

Kennedy, John F., 81, 138, 239, 265–66, 267–68, 283, 331

Khmer (Cambodian) National Liberation Army, 123, 276

Khmer Resistance Government, 242

Khrushchev, Nikita S., 110, 111, 124,
    200
Koenig, Pierre (General), 35
Korea, 15, 16, 17, 19, 30, 31, 70, 81,
    82, 120, 139, 215, 233, 277, 278,
    285, 308, 310, 311; North, 20,
    29 n., 65, 134; South, 64, 65, 174,
    337
Korean War, 5, 13, 14, 19, 35, 40,
    69, 70, 71, 133, 203, 251, 257,
    276, 309, 311, 325-26, 330, 331
Kosygin, Alexei, 133, 317, 327
Kuomintang, 17, 247

La Chambre, Guy, 67
Lacouture, Jean, 8, 75, 131 n., 237,
    255
Ladejinsky, Wolf, 281
Lai Huu Tai, 155
Lam Thanh Nguyen, 153, 154, 159
Laniel, Joseph, 47, 53, 54, 56, 69
Lansdale, Edward (General), 256,
    289
Lao-Dong, or Dang Lao-Dong (Viet-
    Nam Worker's Party), 92, 96-99,
    103, 104, 110, 122, 124, 125, 131,
    211-12, 227, 238, 266
Laos, 17, 19, 31, 34, 36, 37, 38, 39,
    41, 53, 54, 62, 63, 64, 71, 72, 74,
    81, 106, 122, 123, 135, 151, 190,
    195, 201, 203, 204, 225, 231, 243,
    245, 247, 249, 257, 258 n., 259-60,
    262, 263, 269, 272, 304, 308, 309,
    334, 336, 337, 345, 346
Lartéguy, Jean, 333
Le Duan, 134, 212, 238
Le Hong Phong, 118-19
Le Huu Tu (Monsignor), 48, 59
Le Kan Kim (General), 191
Le Quang Ba (General), 194, 248
Le Thanh Nghi, 129 n.
Le Van Hoach, 145
Le Van Luong, 98
Le Van Vien (Bay-Vien), 62, 66,
    155, 156, 157, 159
League for the National Union of
    Viet-Nam, 122
League for Revolution and Inde-
    pendence, see Viet-Minh
Leclerc, Philippe de H. (Marshal),
    24
LeMay, Curtis E. (General), 322

Lenin, V. I., 88
Lien-Viet (League for the National
    Union of Viet-Nam), 92, 122
Lin Piao (Marshal), 323
Lippmann, Walter, 204
Lodge, Henry Cabot, 324
Long, Russell B., 308

MacArthur, Douglas, II, 328
McNamara, Robert, 269, 274, 284,
    311, 313
Magsaysay, Ramón, 170, 259
Mai Van Bo, 319
Makarios (Archbishop), 328, 348
Malaya, 234, 238, 253, 258, 262, 263,
    272, 273, 279, 283, 290-91, 309,
    324
Malaysia, 274
Mansfield, Mike, 286, 322, 324, 334,
    340
Mao Tse-tung, 116, 223, 251, 253,
    265, 266, 283, 297
Marshall Plan, 29, 307, 340
Marxist Studies Association, 120, 122
Mazet (Monsignor), 59
Mecklin, John, 9-10 n., 11
Mekong Delta, 36, 70, 149, 159, 185,
    186 n., 195, 199, 238, 240, 259,
    298, 333
Mendès-France, Pierre, 56, 58, 61, 63,
    215
Messmer, Pierre, 248-49
Minorities School (Hanoi), 194
Molotov, V. M., 61, 71, 72, 258
Molotov-Ribbentrop pact, 119, 248
Montagnards, 10, 190-96, 200, 248,
    249, 288, 345
Moulin, Jean, 347
Movement for National Union and
    Peace, 56, 62
Mowrer, Edgar Ansel, 277
Mus, Paul, 8, 24, 87 n.

Nam-Bo Resistance Veterans Organ-
    ization, 238
National Liberation Front (NLF) 10,
    138, 194, 199, 204, 216, 217, 236,
    237, 238-43, 292, 293, 296-97,
    311, 315, 316, 318-19, 323, 327,
    346-47, 348; see also Viet-Cong
National United Front, 152

Navarre, Henri (General), 17, 30–40
Navarre Plan, 9, 14, 30–40, 58, 233, 308
Netherlands, 75
Ngo Dinh Can, 286
Ngo Dinh Diem, 5, 10, 50, 52, 57–58, 59, 60, 62, 65, 66–68, 74, 76–77, 79, 80, 81, 102, 105, 112, 131, 138, 148, 156–59, 160–61, 166, 169–71, 175–76, 184, 186, 187–89, 191, 193, 197, 198–201, 207–9, 213, 216, 217–18, 219, 220, 221, 235–37, 238, 264, 270–71, 275–77, 278, 281–83, 285–86, 288–89, 290, 309, 311, 316, 331, 345
Ngo Dinh Luyen, 60
Ngo Dinh Nhu, 5, 52, 60, 177, 198, 201, 209, 236, 273
Ngo Dinh Nhu, Mme., 5, 198, 201, 208, 316
Ngo Khai Minh, 146
Nguyen Binh, 144, 152 n., 155
Nguyen Cao Ky (General), 208 n., 321–22, 325
Nguyen Chi Thanh, 247, 248
Nguyen Duy Trinh, 134
Nguyen Giac Ngo, 153, 154
Nguyen Huu Tho, 76, 236–37, 240
Nguyen Huu Tri, 48
Nguyen Khanh (General), 191, 198, 207, 209, 213, 218, 270, 287, 289, 313
Nguyen Ngoc Tho, 213
Nguyen Quoc Dinh, 55, 56, 57, 68
Nguyen Thanh Phuong (General), 147–148, 157
Nguyen Trung Vinh, 54
Nguyen Van Hieu, 241
Nguyen Van Hinh (General), 67, 148, 159
Nguyen Van Hung, 48
Nguyen Van Long (General), 17
Nguyen Van Tam, 42, 43, 47, 146, 179
Nguyen Van Vy (General), 159
Nhiek, Tioulong, 276
Nixon, Richard M., 53 n., 269, 329
Nolting, Frederick E., 138, 200
Norodom Sihanouk (Prince), 258, 260, 261, 345
Nu, U, 170

Pathet-Lao, 81, 122, 123, 201, 276, 346
Peasant International (Krestintern), 116
People's Armed Security Forces, 246
People's Army of Viet-Nam (PAVN), 79
People's Revolutionary Party (PRP), 240–41
People's Self-Defense Forces, 239
Pétain, Henri (Marshal), 347
Pham Cong Tac (the Ho Phap), 142 n., 144–48, 157
Pham Huu Chuong, 60
Pham Kiet (General), 246
Pham Ngoc Chi, 59
Pham Ngoc Thach, 204, 314–15
Pham Van Dong, 43, 96, 99, 111, 112, 113–14, 117 n., 212, 267, 320–21
Pham Van Ngoi, 48
Phan Ke Toai, 212
Phan Khac Suu, 290
Phan-Khoi, 127, 128
Phan Quang Dan, 183
Phan Van Giao, 48
Phan Van Hy, 48
Phan Xuan Thai, 66
Philippines, 167, 186, 234, 253, 258, 259, 270, 290–91, 305, 324, 335
Phoumi Nosavan (General), 262
Phung Van Cong, 240
Pineau, Christian, 170
Poland, 73, 79, 80, 96, 97, 103, 105, 234, 241, 260, 261, 262, 276, 326
Pomeroy, William J., 305
Prapas Charusathien (General), 263

Radical Socialist Party, 240
Radio Hanoi, 98, 102, 134 n.
Ramadier, Paul, 25, 26
Red River Delta, 19, 31, 34, 36, 37, 38, 39, 46, 51, 59, 60, 63, 64, 105, 232, 249, 332, 339
Rhee, Syngman, 60
Robertson, Walter S., 78
Rostow, W. W., 264 n., 266 n., 267
Rusk, Dean, 300, 312, 315, 316, 319–20, 344, 348

Saigon, 45, 51, 57, 59, 66, 70, 74, 76, 77, 78, 79, 102, 120, 146, 151,

Saigon (*Cont.*)
154, 155, 158, 160, 163, 170, 171, 185, 187, 188, 193, 200, 238, 255, 259, 272, 284, 300, 302, 304, 313, 316, 331
Sarit Thanarat (Field Marshal), 285
Schlesinger, Arthur, Jr., 3
Scigliano, Robert, 283
Seaborn, James Blair, 320
Senate Foreign Relations Committee, hearings of 1966, 340, 348
Siam, 259–60; *see also* Thailand
Sieu Heng, 122
Smith, Walter Bedell, 55, 74
Son Vong, 199, 240
Souphanouvong (Prince), 122, 258
Southeast Asia Treaty Organization (SEATO), 258, 270, 274, 278
Soviet bloc, 17, 20
Soviet Union, 20, 21, 23 n., 24, 25, 27, 28, 29, 51, 55, 61, 62, 65, 69, 71, 74, 78, 80, 81, 82, 83, 85, 88, 89, 104, 107, 108, 114–20, 123, 124, 129, 130, 132–35, 200, 219, 242, 246, 247, 251, 252, 253, 254, 261, 262, 263, 292, 305, 316–18, 320, 323–24, 326, 328, 330, 334, 344
Stalin, Joseph, 116, 117, 223
"Strategic Hamlet" program, or "New Life Hamlets" program, 197, 213, 271, 279
Strategic Problems of China's Revolutionary War, 265, 266
Stump, Felix B. (Admiral), 186 n.
Sun Yat-sen, 117

Ta Quang Buu (General), 72, 123, 248, 275
Taiwan (Formosa), 63, 163, 308
Tam Chau, 198
Tay Nguyen (*Montagnard*) Autonomy Movement, 240
Taylor, Maxwell D. (General), 11, 138, 270, 295, 313, 325, 340
Tep Phan, 62
Thailand, 17, 19, 36, 63, 111, 190, 229, 231, 261–63, 272, 275, 308, 335, 337
Thant, U, 314–16, 317, 328–29
Thien, 183
Thompson, R. K. G., 272

Thorez, Maurice, 22, 23, 25, 26, 27
Timmes, Charles J. (General), 338
Tito (Marshal), 7, 120, 347
Ton Duc Thang, 90 n., 122, 126
Tran Huu Duc, 129
Tran Nam Trung, 241
Tran Quang Vinh, 144
Tran Van Chuong, 60
Tran Van Do, 58, 60, 61, 62, 74, 325
Tran Van Giau, 152 n.
Tran Van Huong, 290
Tran Van Huu, 145
Tran Van Soai, 151, 153, 154, 156, 157, 159
Tri Quang, 198
Trinh Minh The, 145, 157, 158
Truman, Harry, 29
Trung-Gia military truce talks, 60, 67
Truong Chinh, 96, 98, 99, 119, 120, 122, 124, 211, 212, 253, 266
Truong Kim Cu, 235

Ubernia (Monsignor), 59
United Front of National Forces, 157
United Nations, 31, 68, 71, 74, 102, 104, 168, 173, 178, 214, 257, 267, 276, 278, 314, 328–29
United States, 3, 4, 5, 8, 10, 11, 13, 15, 17, 21, 25, 28, 40, 43, 50, 51, 52, 60, 61, 63, 67, 70, 77, 78, 79, 81, 85, 105, 110, 111, 112, 131 n., 132, 133, 134, 135, 157, 158, 161–68, 169, 170, 171, 172, 173–81, 186 n., 190, 193, 195, 198, 200, 203, 205, 217, 218, 219, 221, 223, 230, 234, 235, 239, 241, 242, 243, 247, 252, 255, 256, 259, 260, 262, 264, 265, 267, 273, 276, 285, 286, 287, 288–89, 290, 291, 292, 295, 297–306, 307–8, 313–30; economic aid, 156, 161, 173–74, 176, 177, 187, 189, 192, 193; military aid, 10, 12, 15, 30, 31, 39, 68, 70, 71, 79–80, 113, 114, 201, 204, 224, 238, 245, 246, 251, 258, 271, 273, 278–79, 283, 284, 290, 293, 294, 298–306, 308, 321, 331–35, 337–42, 343–44, 347–49
U.S. Agency for International Development (AID), 284

U.S. Information Service (USIS), 45, 162, 190, 324
U.S. Military Advisory Command, 197 n., 239, 291, 311
U.S. Military Assistance Advisory Group (MAAG), 71, 162, 163, 338
U.S. Military Assistance Command, 79
U.S. Operations Mission (USOM), 161, 162, 163, 173, 180, 201 n.
U.S. Seventh Fleet, 335, 337
U.S. Special Forces, 190, 195, 196, 263, 266, 288, 308, 313, 337

Viet-Cong (VC), 76, 82, 83, 133, 137, 195, 198, 199, 201, 209, 218, 223, 224, 234–43, 244, 246, 249, 250, 251, 254, 266, 273, 283, 285, 286, 291, 295, 295–306, 310, 311, 316, 318, 321, 322, 323, 324, 325, 326, 327, 329, 331, 333, 335, 337, 338, 339, 340, 342, 343, 345, 346, 348; *see also* National Liberation Front
Viet-Minh, 9, 13, 15, 19, 20, 23, 37, 42–43, 45–47, 50, 51, 52, 53, 55, 56, 59–60, 62, 63, 64–66, 67, 69, 70, 71, 72, 76, 82, 87–95, 96, 101, 121–22, 134, 141, 144, 145, 146, 151–52, 153, 155, 159, 164, 175, 184, 185, 193, 215, 216, 218, 233, 237, 238, 244, 249, 253, 257, 258 n., 266, 283, 287, 302, 322, 323, 336

Viet-Nam People's Army (VPA), 30–31, 33–37, 39, 70, 82, 98–99, 104, 108, 110, 129, 152, 212, 223, 224, 225–29, 232–33, 234, 244–54, 275–76, 292, 337
Viet-Nam Social Democratic Party (Dan Xa), 152, 153
Vietnamese Democratic Party, 240
Vietnamese National Army, 31, 62, 67, 70, 148, 156, 159, 160, 162, 170, 173, 188, 195, 240, 249, 271, 274, 308; *see also* Army of the Republic of Viet-Nam
Vo Chi Cong, 240
Vo Nguyen Giap (General), 33–38, 70, 82, 99, 101, 104, 110, 119, 134, 226, 228–29, 245, 247, 248–49, 253–54, 264 n.
Vo Quang Anh, 109
Vu Van Mau, 277
Vuong Thua Vu (General), 248

Warner, Denis, 240, 278, 310
Westmoreland, William C. (General), 329
Whampoa Military Academy, 117, 212
Wickert, Frederic, 193
Women for National Salvation, 122
World War II, 119, 141, 144, 175, 190, 207, 231, 253, 331, 332, 334, 346

Ybih Aleo, 240
Yugoslavia, 20, 115, 122